Ad fontes Lutheri: Toward the Recovery of the Real Luther: Essays in Honor of Kenneth Hagen's Sixty-Fifth Birthday

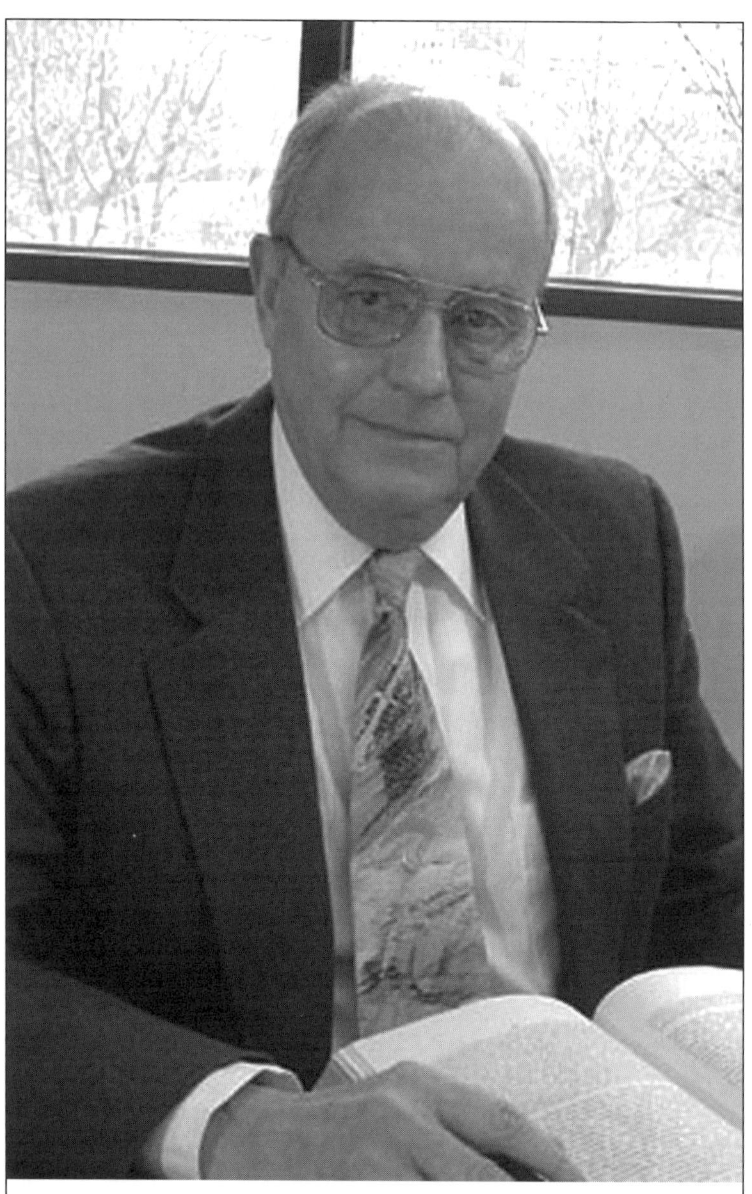

Professor Kenneth Hagen
in his Marquette University office,
April 2000

Ad fontes Lutheri: Toward the Recovery of the Real Luther: Essays in Honor of Kenneth Hagen's Sixty-Fifth Birthday

Edited by
Timothy Maschke, Franz Posset,
and Joan Skocir

2001

MARQUETTE STUDIES IN THEOLOGY No. 28
Andrew Tallon, Series Editor

Library of Congress Cataloguing in Publication Data

Ad fontes Lutheri : toward the recovery of the real Luther : essays in honor of Kenneth Hagen's sixty-fifth birthday / edited by Timothy Maschke, Franz Posset, and Joan Skocir.
p. cm. — (Marquette studies in theology ; no. 28)
Includes bibliographical references and index.
ISBN 0-87462-677-3 (pbk. : alk. paper)
1. Luther, Martin, 1483-1546. I. Hagen, Kenneth. II. Maschke, Timothy, 1947- III. Posset, Franz. IV. Skocir, Joan. V. Marquette studies in theology ; #28.
BR333.3 .A3 2001
284.1'092—dc21

2001001056

Member, THE ASSOCIATION OF AMERICAN UNIVERSITY PRESSES

MARQUETTE UNIVERSITY PRESS
MILWAUKEE

The Association of Jesuit University Presses

2001

CONTENTS

Graphics Credits

Cover design: Joan Skocir, with titlepage border from Luther's 1519 *Commentary on Galatians* by permission of Houghton Library, Harvard University.
ii: Digital photograph, Joan Skocir.
4: Dover Publications
23: Photograph courtesy of Aldemar Hagen
41: *The Works of Orestes S. Brownson*, Milwaukee: Marquette University Press, 1998-.
50: Digital photograph, Joan Skocir.
81: Houghton Library, Harvard University.
94: Arttoday.
117: *The Postilla of Nicholas of Lyra on the Song of Songs*, Sean Donnelly, cover. Milwaukee:Marquette University Press, 1998.
168: By permission of *Evangelische Stadtkirche*, Wittenberg.
190: Concordia Historical Institute, St. Louis, Missouri.
248: (Vadiana) St. Gallen, Switzerland, *Kantonsbibliothek.*
260: Houghton Library, Harvard University.
284: Dover Publications.

The balance of images are in public domain.

PREFACE

Almost a decade ago, Kenneth Hagen described his professional and scholarly activities most succinctly in the following way:

> Luther, Scripture, and medieval commentaries have occupied my research and writing for over 25 years. Having been influenced by German, American, Norwegian, and Swedish methods of Luther research, I have learned much from their basically nineteenth-century methods. My research, however, forced me to return to the "original" Luther ... .[1]

This collection of essays in honor of Dr. Hagen's sixty-fifth birthday reflects his studies and interests in returning to the historical Luther and to the sources of Luther, as the title for this volume indicates and as Dr. Hagen's own bibliography illustrates. The essays in this book cover a wide range of topics on Luther and Lutheranism from the perspective of American and European scholarship.

The idea for a *Festschrift*, a book of celebration, to honor Dr. Hagen was proposed by Franz Posset who provided continuing encouragement to pursue its production. Over several years the details of a plan were developed by the three undersigned who set the wheels in motion for the present volume. Posset's suggestion to search for a comprising title for this *Festschrift* resulted in the loaded catch-word *Ad fontes Lutheri* which tries to summarize the essentials of Dr. Hagen's Luther-study program.

Initially our invitations went to those graduate students of Dr. Hagen who had worked on Luther. We expanded our invitations to include colleagues and teachers who are still active in Luther studies. Some were unable to offer a contribution to this *Festschrift* because of time constraints or scholarly commitments in other areas. However, all expressed a sincere desire that such a work be presented to Dr. Hagen for his life's commitment and scholarly contributions in the area of Luther studies.

The editors wish to express their deep appreciation to all the people who have contributed to this work, including the translators of contributions that were offered originally in a foreign language. We also wish to thank our often-silent and certainly unseen colleagues who have worked behind the scenes for almost a decade in produc-

[1] Kenneth Hagen, *Luther's Approach to Scripture as seen in his "Commentaries" on Galatians 1519-1538* (Tübingen: J.C.B. Mohr [Paul Siebeck], 1993), vii.

ing the annual collection of Luther studies in *Luther Digest*, edited by Dr. Hagen; they were a constant source of support in this enterprise. Luther Academy (U.S.A.), the "mother" of *Luther Digest*, provided funding for some aspects of our project. The founder of the Luther Academy, Dr. Robert Preus (+1995), was a respectful friend of Dr. Hagen and would have been pleased to offer a contribution to this work. His son, Dr. Daniel Preus, has taken up his leadership of the Academy, giving his personal support in several areas.

Marquette University Press has provided the funding for the production and publication of this book. Particularly, we wish to acknowledge our singular indebtedness to Dr. Andrew Tallon, Director of the Press, for his cooperative spirit and confidence in our endeavors. Mention of Aldemar Hagen, Ken's helpmate in innumerable ways, cannot be omitted from a list of persons who contributed so much to the scholarly production of any of his work. We thank her for her behind-the-scenes help with personal contacts and insights for this project.

Finally, we wish to express our individual thanks to each other for the various and diverse contributions made on this book. Joan Skocir, more than anyone else in this project, has served as the uniting force in editing, formatting, preparing, and producing the final product. She is most appreciated by us for her indefatigable efforts, indomitable strength and artistic creativity. Timothy Maschke helped make the initial contacts with potential authors and letters of invitation along with some editing, proofreading, and indexing. Together we have worked on the cover design, final copy of the text, and index, and so we also take mutual responsibility for any errors which may have inadvertently crept into the final text. Overall, we needed each other throughout the year and together we have produced something which embodies our admiration and respect for the abilities and guidance that Dr. Hagen has provided us for so many years. We cannot think of a more appropriate conclusion to this preface than the words of Martin Luther himself: "We can spare everything except the Word."[2] Dr. Kenneth Hagen has provided each of us with a sure witness to that Word who truly sets us free. Thank you, Ken.

On the anniversary of Luther's death, 18 February 1546
Timothy Maschke - Franz Posset - Joan Skocir

[2] Martin Luther, "Concerning the Order of Public Worship," *Luther's Works* 53 (Philadelphia: Fortress Press, 1965), 14; see WA 12:37.

INTRODUCTION

John Patrick Donnelly, S.J.

Kenneth Hagen has long been an established expert in Luther studies and has long merited a *Festschrift.* Recently several of his past and current doctoral students conspired together to organize a *Festschrift* which would be presented to him as a surprise on a proper occasion. The key conspirators were Timothy Maschke, Franz Posset and Joan Skocir, all of whom have contributed essays as well as direction to this project. They asked me to write this Introduction, largely because I work in Reformation studies and have been at Marquette University nearly as long as Ken Hagen. I have co-operated with Ken on several projects over the years: for instance, presentations commemorating the 500th anniversary of Luther's birth and hosting an annual meeting of the Sixteenth Century Studies Conference at Marquette. I have also served on several dissertation committees which he directed and published two volumes of *Reformation Texts with Translations (1350-1650),* which Hagen edits.

If one were to design an education for an American Luther scholar, it would be hard to better that of Hagen. He did his undergraduate work at Augsburg College in Minneapolis, a Lutheran college in America's most Lutheran metropolis. He then did a bachelor's degree in Sacred Theology at the Harvard Divinity School (1961), crowned by a doctorate in Divinity at Harvard University (1967). Most recipients of those degrees would have sought ordination; Hagen remained a lay scholar. While doing his dissertation research he spent a year at the University of Bonn. Can one be a Luther scholar without working in Germany? His dissertation, "Luther's Lectures on Hebrews in Light of Medieval Commentaries on Hebrews," did much to shape the long range direction of his scholarship. His dissertation director at Harvard was Heiko Oberman, who has done more than any scholar to trace the importance of medieval roots of Luther's intellectual development. Hagen's first teaching experience was as a teaching Fellow at Harvard. From 1965 to 1967 he taught religion at Concordia College in Moorhead, Minnesota.

In 1967 two people took a chance with long range consequences. Vatican II had just ended. American Catholic universities wanted to broaden their intellectual horizons. Most Catholic theological faculties had been restricted to Catholics. Most Protestant faculties were similar. Bernard Cooke, chair of the Theology Department at Marquette University, began looking for a Lutheran to teach Luther studies. The Department was expanding and becoming more professional. For decades most theology courses at Marquette had been taught by Jesuits who were professors in other departments. Now the Theology Department was to offer a doctorate and needed a larger, more professional, and more ecumenical staff of professors. Hagen applied for the position in Luther studies and was hired without even an on-campus interview. He has been a pillar of that Department ever since, aside from a semester of 1980 as a Fullbright Professor at the University of Oslo; the semester gave him an opportunity to renew his Norwegian ethnic roots and observe how Lutheranism has developed in a country outside of the United States and Germany.

Since one of the essays in this volume deals with Luther's family life, it is appropriate to note that during his years in the Milwaukee area Professor Hagen has enjoyed the unwavering love and support of his wife Aldy and has been blessed with their daughters Susan and Carolyn, their son Erik, and four grandchildren.

Most of Hagen's teaching at Marquette has focused on the subjects he loves: junior/senior courses on the theology of the Reformation era and on Martin Luther, and six regular graduate courses: Christian Thought in the Later Middle Ages and the Reformation, Interpretation of the Bible in the Renaissance and Reformation, Erasmus, Luther, Calvin, and the Council of Trent. While at Marquette Hagen has directed twenty dissertations, with more still in the pipeline. Of the twenty, ten dealt with Luther, four with exegesis, and six with other topics, largely other Reformation theologians. The essays of Burnell Eckhardt, Gordon Isaac, and James Kiecker in this volume build upon and carry forward their dissertation research under Professor Hagen.

Hagen has also published a steady stream of books and articles. Since there is a bibliography of his publications at the end of this volume, here we highlight the major directions his writings have taken. As is quite usual, his first book was a revision of the dissertation he wrote under Professor Heiko Oberman: *A Theology of Testament in the Young Luther: The Lectures on Hebrews,* published in 1974. He broadened his coverage of commentaries on Hebrews in his 1981 *Hebrews Commenting from Erasmus to Bèze, 1516-1598.* In 1993 Hagen returned to Luther's exegetical method in *Luther's Approach to Scripture as seen in his "Commentaries" on Galatians, 1519-1538.* More popular in tone and broader in coverage was *The Bible in the Churches: How Different Christians Interpret the Scriptures* (first edition, 1985; second, 1994; third, 1998).

Less esteemed in the academy than monographs but arguably more helpful are editions of texts and bibliographies. Here with the help of his graduate students Hagen has edited three Luther bibliographies: *Annotated Bibliography of Luther Studies, 1967-1976,* (1977); *Annotated Bibliography of Luther Studies, 1977-1983,* (1985); *Annotated Bibliography of Luther Studies, 1984-1989,* (1991). Following these three volumes Hagen edited eight annual abridgments of Luther studies, the *Luther Digest*, from 1993 to 2000 and counting.

Finally Hagen has edited two *Festschriften* presented to distinguished scholars. The first was for his mentor at Harvard, Heiko Oberman, esteemed by many as the greatest living Reformation scholar: *Augustine, the Harvest, and Theology (1300-1650): Essays Dedicated to Heiko Oberman in Honor of his Sixtieth Birthday* (1990). The second was for George Tavard, the distinguished French ecumenist, who in the early 1990s held the Presidential Chair in Theology at Marquette: *The Quadrilog: Tradition and the Future of Ecumenism: Essays in Honor of George H. Tavard* (1994). Appropriately, both Professors Oberman and Tavard have contributed essays to this book in honor of Professor Hagen. Like Tavard, Hagen has contributed much to ecumenical dialogue between the Lutheran and Roman Catholic traditions and drew great satisfaction when, on the anniversary of Luther's Ninety-five Theses, representatives of the Lutheran and Catholic Churches were able to sign a joint declaration on justification at Augsburg in 1999.

Many *Festschriften* share a weakness: the essays they contain often lack unity. Some seem to be kept together only "by Scotch tape and bailing wire." Often, editors simply send out invitations to established scholars to contribute an essay covering a topic as broad as the Renaissance or Reformation. Such volumes usually give reviewers nightmares. For some years, *The American Historical Review* has merely listed them at the back of the journal along with their contributors and the titles of the essays.

In contrast, this volume has a double unity. All the contributors have a real link to Professor Hagen, and the essays have a common focus. Five contributors wrote dissertations under Hagen: Drs. Burnell Eckhardt, Gordon Isaac, James Kiecker, Timothy Maschke, and Franz Posset. Joan Skocir is currently writing hers. In addition Posset worked with Hagen on the annotated Luther bibliographies; Maschke, Posset, Kiecker, Eckhardt, and Skocir are on the staff of the *Luther Digest.*

Kiecker, Donnelly, and Skocir have contributed volumes or translations to the series published by Marquette University Press, *Reformation Texts with Translation* (1350-1650), of which Hagen is the editor-in-chief. As noted above, Hagen honored Professors Oberman and Tavard by editing their *Festschriften*. Here they honor him. Patrick Carey and George Tavard were his colleagues in Marquette's Theology Department. Hagen and David Steinmetz studied together at Harvard under Heiko Oberman. Nils Bloch-Hoell became Hagen's friend during his semester teaching at Oslo. Helmar Junghans serves as editor of the *Lutherjahrbuch*. Ulrich Asendorf was the Director of the Luther Akademie, Ratzeburg, Germany, for many years, publishing Luther studies each year in a similar way to Hagen's *Luther Digest*. Gottfried Krodel recently retired as the American editor of *Archiv für Reformationsgeschichte* (*Archive for Reformation History*); its annual *Literaturbericht* is the best guide to recent publications in Reformation history. Despite these common links to Professor Hagen, the contributors to this volume come from many nations. Four were born in Germany, one each in France, Norway, and the Netherlands, and there are eight Americans. They thereby reflect the international scope of Luther studies. More important, the three editors of this volume have achieved a unity of subject matter unusual in *Festschriften*: twelve of the essays deal directly with Luther's life and teaching. One deals with Catholic attitudes toward Luther in the twentieth century, another with Norwegian Lutheranism. The precise aspects of Luther studies that most interest Hagen are Luther's biblical approach, its medieval background, and its continuing relevance today. The essays of Asendorf, Isaac, Kiecker, Posset, Skocir, and Tavard deal with Luther's biblical approach. Those of Eckhardt, Kiecker, Posset, and Steinmetz take up Luther's relationship to older theologians. The contributions of Krodel, Steinmetz, Oberman, Posset, and Tavard closely examine short texts from Luther. The essays of Skocir, Maschke and Asendorf show how Luther's exegetical methods and theological insights are still valuable today and transcend mere historical interest.

Just when this volume was nearly complete Professor Hagen announced his retirement from teaching, effective in May, 2000; he will continue to mentor his doctoral students and will now have more leisure for his writing and research. All of us involved in this book thank him for all he has taught us in the past and pray that his work as a scholar will continue. *Ad multos annos!*

HOLY SCRIPTURE AND HOLY SPIRIT

ULRICH ASENDORF

Since dialectical theology, the Word of God has been one of the most discussed themes of theology, particularly as kerygma since Rudolf Bultmann—that is, as preached Word before all else, connected more extensively with subsequent reflections on Heidegger. Not by chance, the same track is found in Luther research, especially as manifested in the work of Gerhard Ebeling under keywords such as "word happening" and "language event" (*Wortgeschehen* and *Sprachereignis*).[1]

Here, the work of Kenneth Hagen marks a noteworthy and possibly crucial turning point, with Holy Scripture as programmatic entry—yes, as the overall basis for theology and proclamation.[2] Luther is situated there in the tradition of monastic theology and its centering in the sacred page (*sacra pagina*) that was *the* quintessential theology prior to scholasticism, a situation immanently important today for ecumenical theology.

The separation of Scripture and Word of God[3] in the Enlightenment is also implicitly subjected to a fundamental criticism. Furthermore, the return to Scripture carried out by Kenneth Hagen is more significant in the present-day context because it recovers a principal hermeneutical output from the written Word that corresponds to the French linguists' (Ricoeur, Derrida, Levinas) new linguistic exercise.[4] Therefore the hermeneutical axis is turned back and oriented to Scripture in an unambiguous way against that which ruled German theology almost exclusively from Schleiermacher-inspired

[1] Gerhard Ebeling, *Luther. Einführung in sein Denken* (Tübingen: Mohr, 1964), 1ff, 18ff, 37ff.

[2] Kenneth Hagen, *Luther's Approach to Scripture as seen in his "Commentaries" on Galatians, 1519-1538* (Tübingen: Mohr, 1993).

[3] Johann S. Semler, "*Heilige Schrift und Wort Gottes ist gar sehr zu unterscheiden,*" *Abhandlung von freier Untersuchung des Canon I, 75"* (1771), cited in Udo Schnelle, *Einleitung in das Neue Testament* (Göttingen: Vandenhoeck & Ruprecht, 1994), 17.

[4] Ulrich Asendorf, *Lectura in Biblia. Luthers Genesisvorlesung 1535-1545*, Forschungen zur systematischen und ökumensischen Theologie 87, (Göttingen: Vandenhoeck & Ruprecht, 1998), 56-64; K. Huizing, *Homo legens. Vom Ursprung der Theologie im Lesen,* Theologische Bibliothek Töpelmann 75 (Berlin-New York: Walter de Gruyter, 1996); Ulrich H. J. Körtner, *Der inspirierte Leser. Zentrale Aspekte biblischer Hermeneutik* (Göttingen: Vandenhoeck & Ruprecht, 1994).

hermeneutics. The new understanding of Luther includes fundamental sequences. This new way attempts to mark the sequential considerations.

Luther's departure rests on Scripture, initially followed from that by the preached Word from the trinitarian self-opening of God, and, following from that, in the understanding of the Word laid out so exemplarily in the Johannine prologue. This opens itself anew in a double dimension, from the incarnation and from the Holy Spirit. But the Holy Spirit and creation are also newly related to each other. According to John 1:1 in view of creation, the Holy Spirit has a double function—to maintain and preserve all life (*omnia vivificat tenens et conservans*) according to God's eternal will or good pleasure (*aeterna voluntas seu beneplacitum*).[5]

Luther's trinitarian-based scriptural theology also unites the following components—Word of God, Trinity, sacraments—in a reciprocal, perichoretical, penetrating relationship. This differentiation in the Holy Spirit will be broadened in the following. It happens for a double reason. Luther's theology of the Word experiences a decisive definition and expansion through his theology of the Spirit, especially as it is recognized not only in his papers but also in the exegesis of 1527 that attains a key role here.[6]

Namely, the relationship of Scripture and Spirit is newly discussed here in an extensive way as it draws from hermeneutical considerations in Luther's early period, which represents the initial stage for the pneumatological wealth of the *Catechisms* of 1529.[7] The theological leap that this represents has generally only recently become evident in Luther research, if at all and then only in passing.

Through its pneumatological wealth compared to the general deficiency in the west in matters of the third article of the Creed, Luther's special position establishes itself in western theology as well as in tradition.[8] Inasmuch as it uses the theme of the Holy Spirit in

[5] WA 24: 30, 1-3. Ulrich Asendorf, "*Die Trinitätslehre als integrales Problem der Theologie Martin Luthers,*" in *Luther und die trinitarische Tradition. Ökumenische und historische Perspektiven* (Veröffentlichungen der Luther-Akademie Ratzeburg 23, Erlangen, 1994), 113-130.

[6] *Wider die himmlischen Propheten*; *Der Prophet Sacharja ausgelegt*; *Predigten über das 1.Buch Mose*; *Daß diese Worte Christi noch feststehen*.

[7] Eilert Herms, *Luthers Auslegung des Dritten Artikels* (Tübingen: Mohr, 1987).

[8] Christian Schütz, *Einführung in die Pneumatologie,* (Darmstadt: Wissenschaftliche Buchgesellschaft, 1985), 1f, 5, 71, 90, 113-118; similarly, Wolf-Dieter Hauschild, TRE 12, 196-217. The ground-laying work of Regin Prenter: *Spiritus Creator. Studien zu Luthers Theologie* (München: C. Kaiser, 1954) originates from the year 1944 and needs penetrating expansion.

an especially forceful way, Luther's trinitarian-based theology of the Word updates his Scripture theology in a way hardly heeded until now. Provided that this is interconnected with Reformation spirituality in a sublime way, it creates the crucial prerequisites for an extensive criticism of modern hermeneutics. The Holy Spirit, indeed as the concrete Spirit effective in the incarnation of the Logos, also reveals the latent spiritualism of modern theology, perhaps stemming from its sacramental indifference, and therein it is separated through worlds from Luther. This is uniquely shown in texts from "*Daß diese Worte Christi noch feststehen.*"

Moreover, Luther's thinking does not occupy itself with obtuse theories. Rather, through God's grace the Word of God comes to light as it has happened in his eschatological breakthrough in which this Word succeeds at the last day by virtue of the divine Spirit when it is exposed to attacks by its satanic opponent.[9] That is the distinctive historical-theological implication in Luther's confession of the Word of God.

In a characteristic way, this is precisely exemplified further in "*Wider die himmlischen Propheten,*" in which Luther's opposing remarks appear with significantly increased dignity. His text is truth about the whole, not about a confrontation with an individual opponent on a limited basis. The context first opens the thought that "the *Schwärmer* (enthusiasts) strangle for me Christ my Lord and God the Father in his Word, besides my mother Christendom who gathers my brothers."[10] This characteristic accent on the Church as mother should not be overlooked.

The *Schwämer* therefore follow a doubly satanic inspiration that does not focus on parts of the biblical God image but on the Trinity and with it on the totality of belief in general. Thus the sin against the Holy Spirit is meant, as in the previous passages.

What is perceived here is the vehemence with which Luther fights for the Trinity in which the divine Word is thoroughly supported. Therefore, today's current general Word-God-theology, similar in whatever form and without trinitarian reference, completely misses the dignity of the divine Word and the divine revelation connected with it. That is the consequence of the *schwärmerische* minimalization of God's Word. Namely, the *Schwärmer* prove that none of the godless can highly esteem God's Word, that compared to their own dreams

[9] Ulrich Asendorf, *Eschatologie bei Luther* (Göttingen: Vandenhoeck & Ruprecht, 1967), 207f, 214ff, 221ff.

[10] WA 23: 82, 3-5.

They knew him in the breaking of the bread. Christ at Emmaus. (Albrecht Dürer, "The Small Passion," 1511.)

they hold Christ's Word and work as chatter so that love and unity should yield to their cheaper way. "But a true Christian illuminates and points out that God's Word involves God's honor, Spirit, Christ, grace, eternal life, death, sin, and all things."[11]

All in all, the *schwärmerische* attack on the dignity of God's Word is not only aimed at the Trinity but equally against Christendom as the mother of all Christians and against all Christian brothers with it. Therefore Luther uses totally different connotations for the divine Word than does modern hermeneutics in which one looks in vain for the complete fulfillment of the Trinity as well as for the catholicity of the Church.

Accordingly, the radius of the thus-understood divine Word is widely composed. God's Word stands synonymously for God's honor,

[11] WA 23: 82, 23-29.

his Spirit, for Christ and therefore also for grace and eternal life, death, sin, and all things—that is, for an understanding of the world and the human being that is oriented to God's Word. This comparatively short passage therefore shows in all clarity the general foreignness of a modern Word-God-theology to Luther's meaning.

The shibboleth lies in the "*gantzen Gott*" (the whole God) who does not let himself be separated.[12] Therefore, according to Ephesians 4:5, Christian unity consists in the Spirit. The following lines read as a timely warning for a hasty ecumenism: "we want universal unity with each other, that is, to keep physical, temporal peace, but spiritually we shun, damn, and fight."[13] The context goes together with real presence as proof of what God's Word is and means. The starting point is that when Christ gives us his body to eat he also extends the bread.[14] The meaning of the meal is also professed with the words of institution, but the mystery of real presence escapes explanation. However, seeing and hearing direct us to the way to the mystery of the presence of Christ in the Sacrament of the Altar. Oecolampadius assumes "body" in the sense of sign of the body. Similarly, Zwingli and Karlstadt torture the words "*mein leib*" (my body).[15]

The opponents' different attempts at interpretation lead to a strained principle (*petitio principii*), namely, uncertainty proved through uncertainty (*incertum per incertum probare*), upon which Luther drastically comments with the sentence, "Oh, how the devil's pants stink here!"[16] They also confuse their own dreams with the Holy Spirit,[17] which leads to more human darkness and unbelief, since God's Word should validify and ground our faith.[18]

Meanwhile, what Luther means is far from a legislated fundamentalism; for the words of institution in their invariable form and resistance against every self-empowering interpretation go back to the incarnated Word of John 1:4. There one cannot separate the presence of the body of Christ from the Word. On the other hand, according to the words of the *Schwärmer*, the body of Christ is devoid of Word in the bread, which is not possible if one does not want to move from the frying pan into the fire. Namely, if the body of Christ is without the external Word, "it cannot be there without the inner

[12] WA 23: 85, 2-4.
[13] WA 23: 85, 31-34.
[14] WA 23: 86, 29-35; similarly, WA 23: 87, 28-35.
[15] WA 23: 107, 2-27.
[16] WA 23: 99, 3-22.
[17] WA 23: 113, 28.
[18] WA 23: 121, 32f.

eternal Word" that is God himself, according to John 1:1. Thus, the sacramental real presence reflects upon the God who is the Word and who as the eternal inner Word of God is at the same time his incarnated Word. Only then were healings of the sick possible or could Christ, with physical voice, call Lazarus from the grave. Moreover, thus did he touch lepers as well as go to the sea and reach out his hand to the sinking Peter.[19]

This passage is of great principal importance. It shows the essential connection of the Word with the incarnated Christ as the Word that existed in the beginning. In this understanding of the Word, the pre-existence and the incarnation of Christ are joined in an insoluble unity, without which God's Word is not what it is. A general Word happening is not recognized in contrast to what the speech is. It also becomes clear from the prologue that Luther is totally divorced from a fundamentalist as well as a positivist understanding of the Word.

Against that, the opponents think "that the divine Word should carry forth vain spiritual things and deal with no external bodily things." This is the spawn of Müntzer's and Karlstadt's spirit "that would also suffer nothing externally until they are entirely and wholly drowned in the flesh. But God turns that around and gives us no Word nor commandment that he has not framed and delivered for us as a physical external thing."

This framework of the divine Word is made apparent in various biblical examples, such as in the promise of Isaac to Abraham, or that Saul should kill the Amalekite, or as the rainbow in Noah's time. Precisely so, the body of the crucified is fastened to the Word. In the same way, Isaac must come forth bodily and become Abraham's son and the rainbow after the deluge "must be there physically as the Word professes."[20]

Two accents are set here. First, the opponents are paradoxically drowned with their spirits in the flesh because they do not comprehend at all what occurs in the real presence in the sacrament. The absence of all spirits in the biblical sense leaves behind only the flesh and earthly banalities that as such have also lost every sense. On the other hand, before the background of the Johannine prologue in the extensive context of the divine Word, the Lord's Supper Word stands above all as the framing Word that withdraws from every spiritual vaporization. These elementary spiritual contexts have again exposed a new theology of the Spirit in Luther.

[19] WA 23: 257, 15-31.
[20] WA 23: 261, 5-24.

There is still a need to comment critically regarding the current research position that until now has lagged far behind Luther. Different attempts at a Word-God-theology have been carried forward in its framework which have an altogether negative characteristic—the absence of the Holy Spirit. That absence addresses two things: a deficient pneumatology that at the same time makes startlingly clear how little strength the entire New Protestant tradition had in its principal trinitarian thinking—with the exception of Karl Barth.

It will therefore be the task of future Luther research to make this pneumatological accent fruitful for the new opening of God's Word in the framework of a trinitarian theology. This is not only a simple recollection. It belongs together with a discussion of a revision regarding the topic of the Holy Spirit and the criticism regarding a too-narrowly-composed hermeneutic in succession from Schleiermacher—more specifically, that which ignores Anders Nygren's incredibly neglected "logical analysis of presuppositions."[21] Analytic philosophy cannot be renounced if the claim of a modern hermeneutic truly expects to become respected. Precisely here a clear remnant of German research connected with the influence of Heidegger, which is too seldom critically questioned, is not to be overlooked. In other words, Luther's newly-grasped theology of the Word in the framework of a new theology of the Holy Spirit belongs in a more extensive and larger horizon than current theology possesses. Like hardly any other, Luther's theology is appropriate to open new perspectives and to strike breaches into old walls.

In the process, these intentions will show more and more clearly that Luther's theological origins are other than that of the scholastic system of nature and grace. In the meanwhile, however, a firm intermediate result of Luther's positive theology of the Holy Spirit will be studied in the light of the critique on *schwärmerische* understanding of the Spirit.

Once again, this is from the other perspective of the more external dimension of God's Word that has already been indicated with the glimpse at the rainbow after the deluge and Isaac's birth. Both are "external physical things," "but because they are grasped in the Word, Abraham must attach his faith to the promised Isaac, who was composed in God's Word. The devil, who with his *Schwärmer* will first separate the Word from external things, is thus the enemy of the Word. But God will reconnect and adhere one to the other." The *Schwärmer*, however, maintain that external things are useless. The

[21] Anders Nygren, *Meaning and Method. Prolegomena to a Scientific Philosophy of Religion and a Scientific Theology* (Philadelphia: Fortress Press, 1972), 127ff, 187ff, 209ff, 227ff, 265ff.

sentence, "An external thing is not needed," is therefore something like the *Schwärmer's* creed.

But the *Schwärmer* will not be emptied of the Münsterist spirit until they have prepared the same misfortune that it did, for the fruits correspond to the tree. "Because from such a spirit it must follow that temporal authority is not necessary as an external thing, for one will neither hear nor see that it is written in God's Word nor believe that it is God's command. (Rom. 13:1ff)." Consequently, this *schwärmerische* spirit must remain mutinous and deadly.

Luther's conclusion is this: "Temporal order is an external thing; it is not connected to faith yet is also an article of faith because of the Word to which it is attached." He then argumentatively turns the same thought around as follows: The *Schwärmer* believe that a God exists and that God's Son has become human. The same is applied to all articles of faith "which are never in any reasoning dropped." Luther would also like to know whether they have learned all of this from the Spirit before they heard or read of it physically and externally. If they must deny that, "then they have it through the physical, external Word and Scripture." If this Word should be unnecessary, through what does the Holy Spirit bestow with all his gifts? Consequently, it is a blind arrogance—along with spiritualistic usurpation—"that they have locked Christ in a chamber to the right of God and do not believe that he is present in his Word and in external things of which his Word speaks."[22]

Indisputably, the whole context has the standing of a key position for Luther's understanding of the Spirit and the Word. It shows they are virtually synonymous. As already noted, examples are the rainbow after the deluge and Isaac's birth, which for Abraham is bound to the Word and is not separable from it. But the *Schwärmer*, driven by the devil, tear this divinely-willed unity asunder. Their abstract understanding of the Word has nothing to do with the divine Word.

That invariably bears its fruits in disorder and destruction of all terrestrial order. This key precisely shows paradoxically how far removed Luther is from all prevalent thoughts of order in the twentieth century. Terrestrial order is not per se sacrosanct and therefore it has nothing to do with faith. But because of the Word that authors this order, it will be an article of faith. Thus it follows that it lies beyond all theocratic experiments of a false visibility and analogy, as Karl Barth's example only too clearly shows. This false visibility is directly contrary to the mystery of the divine will, hidden and revealed in the Word of God.

[22] WA 23: 263, 4-36.

From these points, Luther also derives his subsequent logical attack. The articles of faith, such as the existence of God and the divine Sonship of Christ that the *Schwärmer* also admit, they have from Scripture, not from reason nor the Spirit. This double standard only betrays the short-circuited logic of the *Schwärmer*. It is, however, only an argumentative side issue compared to the central message—that the Christ seated at the right of God is hidden in his Word and in external sacramental signs and objects.

The position of the *Schwärmer* leads to a direction contrary to Scripture, the narrow-minded self-blockade of the Spirit. On the other hand, Luther's own position has an unambiguous foundation of Scripture as prerequisite. Said differently, only from the prerequisite of Scripture is the whole passage conclusive. An abstract kerygmatization of the Word proves to be confining. In plain words, Luther's scripturally-grounded theology is incompatible with the mainstream of modern theology, which falsifies itself because the premises in each case are different. As long as a broadly-meshed concept of kerygma, as always understood, is operative, a hermeneutic of quite diverse variability is possible, not opposed, when Scripture is the unalterable starting point or the sole basis. In stark contrast to Luther, the words of institution of the holy meal that have no recognizable meaning for modern hermeneutics are shibboleth. In the meantime, however, modern theology holds a firm grip on interpretation-orientated hermeneutics and also on Luther research. This only underscores the urgency of a renewed theology of holy Scripture.

Altogether, however, the polemic against the *Schwärmer* is only the negative foil of a deeper development—what the Holy Spirit is for Luther. It will show how foreign every Christomonism is for Luther. If God is Spirit and only can be recognized as Spirit, then here lies the crucial faulty position of New Protestant theology in general and its understanding of Luther in particular.

As the following citations show, Luther begins his argument: "I can very certainly be in another," as it were, the first prerequisite for Christ's real presence under bread and wine. "I can be in the air, in clothing or house, as well as gold in a purse and wine in barrel and tankard." Then comes the turning point:

> But here, there is not body but Spirit, yes, who knows what it is that God is called? He is above body, above Spirit, above everything that one can express, hear, and think; how can such a one be wholly and at all present in a particular body, creature, and nature everywhere at the same time and, on the other hand, must not be everywhere, but external and above all creatures and natures as

> our faith and Scripture both show of God? Here, reason must strictly conclude. Yes, that is certainly nothing and must be nothing. Has it discovered the way that his own divine nature can wholly and fully be in all creatures and especially in particular, more deeply, more inner, more present than the creature himself is; and yet on the other hand not anywhere and in no one. And can it grasp that he is wholly within and without all things, but nothing is within him? Should it not also comprehend some wisdom such as his body was in many places fully and equally and yet the same was nothing that he is. Oh, we poor human children who from our arrogance and opinion point at God and his works as if he were a shoemaker or day laborer."[23]

Here the Spirit comes in transcendent simplicity above all human and creaturely in-being, for precisely thereby is he active in sacrament, namely, because of the *right* presence of God in the Spirit. In-being and external-and-above-all-creatures-being flow together. Precisely this joining together of the extremes, as the divine manner of being revealed in Scripture as divine presence, is the content of Scripture *and* faith that attests both are from God.

Admittedly, this lies beyond all speculation regarding the mystery of the divine Word itself, namely, that the Word may be deeper and more present in the creature than is the created-being in relationship to itself. On the other hand, this is connected in the closest way with the total contrast that God envelops all things but nothing envelops him. Because it is true that God is in all creatures and above all creatures *at the same time*, then human comprehension fails in wanting to grasp the creative presence of God in, outside, and over all creatures according to the image of human occupation or activity. A reality in the Holy Spirit is meant. However, this is not tangible for theoretical subjectivity as the *Schwärmer* think—and Idealist philosophy after them and their model. The mystery of the universal presence of God in and above all creatures is the Spirit who reveals himself in Scripture and whose presence is not otherwise accessible to us. Therefore, Spirit and incarnation belong together. This doubling is generally separated from spiritualism—the old as well as the new.

Two things follow that become even clearer in the section that follows this: ubiquity is no support-construction for sacramental theology but is connected much more with the nature of the revealed Word in Scripture. Here the Spirit is also concealed in the letters. Because that is so, the divine ubiquity of being in and outside of all creatures is not to be separated from his presence in Spirit. It is much

[23] WA 23: 137, 20-139, 3.

more inalienably characteristic of his Spirit and therefore of divine revelation itself. The *schwärmerische* error is not that they speak so intensively of the Spirit but that their dreams are the basis rather than Scripture.

Luther also argues virtually anti-biblicistically when he speaks of the Spirit, namely, of that Spirit who since creation is in the divine Logos and who has spoken through the prophets. On the one hand, the *Schwärmer* do not truly need Scripture. On the other hand, Luther speaks under the presupposition of reading and hearing in sacramental context. The sacramental component of the Word shows how far he is distant from an abstract biblicism—and equally how far from a kerygma in which the written Word is lost.

Again, the words of institution are the key to Luther's understanding of the Word. Here in the invitation to take and eat belongs the physical essence of the body of Christ: "Now the Word can indeed pursue no one through the throat into the stomach, but it must grasp through the ears into the heart." As soon as it is considered only a spiritual meal, then "there is not only no use but also harm to whoever eats the sacrament without such a Word or without such a spiritual meal" (1 Cor. 11:27).[24]

Accordingly, the further context in which this hearing belongs now appears along with the kerygma *in the framework* of the sacramental event. Luther's intentions are already clear from his words, yet not in a narrow sense of a scriptural proof. Scripture here has the sense to note unequivocally the other side of sacramental reception next to the bodily food and drink. The thrust of the argument is thus directed against *schwärmerische* spiritualism in which the flesh is of no use. In their spirits, the *Schwärmer* do not comprehend that they not only withdraw the divine foundation of the sacramental presence but of reality altogether. Therefore, if they put aside the Word in the Lord's Supper that refers to the bodily reception of Christ's real presence, in truth they say much more, to the extent that without the Word "there is neither God nor creature."

Therefore, all faith statements are not based on the facticity of dogma in itself. Rather, they are first disclosed through the accompanying opened and mediated Word, through which they reach the heart, the faith center of human beings. First, the Word makes the world of objects and the facts or elements communicable so that the physical does not become spiritually cursed but comes to its spiritual dignity with the help of the Word alone.

[24] WA 23: 179, 25-34.

The spiritualism of the *Schwärmer* also misses the concrete Spirit because only in this sense do Spirit and Word belong together. Consequently, in Luther's understanding the Word has a double function. It establishes and provides everything that is connected with human salvation, *extra nos*. That it should be used for our salvation is, so to speak, the second function of the divine Word, which is not removable from the first. Therefore, spiritualism totally destroys the divine Word, in *re* as well as in *fide*. On the contrary, only this concretely mediated Word is the key to the reality of God in this world in the comprehensive and total sense.

It is this Word that has created heaven and earth. Therefore it has the power to give the full presence of God spiritually. Consequently—and therein the *Schwärmer* also err—the sacramental presence of Christ under the bread and wine is by virtue of the Word. Their faithful reception is not a special topic but it adjudicates over the successful or abortive contact of the human being with the reality of God in the world.

Luther's words intensify in an exemplary way in two biblical figures, Mary and Simeon. The example of Mary clarifies the paradoxical reality of the flesh of Christ in sacramental real presence. This flesh in spiritual or physical nature, visibly or invisibly, is always "true, natural, bodily flesh that one can grasp, feel, see, and hear, born of a woman, died on the cross; but there it is called 'spiritual' because it comes from Spirit, and it will and must be united to us in a spiritual way. The object is not always spiritual (*objectum non est semper spirituale*), but the use gives the meal spirituality (*sed usus debet esse spiritualis*)."[25]

Physically and spiritually, as contrary as they are, can fully exist next to one another and in one another, yes, *must* exist next to and in one another. The coincidence of opposites (*coincidentia oppositorum*) comes about through two conditions that work together, namely, through the hearing and the heart. In Mary's believing heart both physicality and spirituality join together for spiritual and physical birth. Mary thus embodies the sense and nature of the spiritual in their unity with the physical and incarnate, and that has consequences. She is the quintessential anti-spiritualistic paradigm. Not only is she the human being in whom the spiritual and temporal, true deity and true humanity, are joined through the Word, but she precisely represents what brings heaven and earth together —that is, the Holy Spirit.

That is further clarified in two additional biblical paradigms. The shepherds and Simeon see the child physically, "but seeing does not help where a spiritual sight is not there, too. Who gave them the

[25] WA 23: 185, 1-6.

spiritual sight? Undoubtedly, not the look of the child but the Word of the angel who pointed them toward Bethlehem to see the Savior. And the answer of the Holy Spirit, who had come over Simeon, that he should see Christ the Lord before he died."[26]

The physical/spiritual relation therefore comes about through the Word and that happens in faith. Luther speaks of fourfold, inclusive, double relations—of physical/spiritual, of Word and faith. All four exist in a reciprocal relationship that altogether determines the nature of the Holy Spirit. When the *Schwärmer* carry forward the axiom "the flesh is not needed," they precisely lack this fourfold entwined enfolding. Instead of true spirituality, the result is a spiritualism that loses every foundation and is indebted only to its dreams and, in the final instance, to subjectivity.

The Spirit will then be one of human-founded principle that has no more commonality with biblical reality. That principle is undoubtedly exemplary in love of neighbor. But again there is the axiom: the Spirit is in the use, not in the object (*in usu, non in obiecto spiritus est*). The body that does not know what it does allows itself to be driven like an animal, but the heart knows well what the body does, not from neighbors but from God's Word that commands love of neighbors.[27]

God gives us both his work and his Word. "The body should do that work. The Word should grasp the soul," because work without the Word is not useful. If God had let Christ come from Mary without the Word, her work would not have been needed, yes, she would not even know of it. "If he had let Christ die and rise from the dead, and let such work remain hidden and not proclaim it through the Word, why was it needed?" God also shares his gifts "measured according to both kinds and gives the Word for the soul and work for the body, from which they both become blessed and the same grace enjoyed under two ways."[28]

With that, the circle completes itself. The universality of divine salvation from the virgin birth up to the cross and to resurrection is all set in the physical connected to the Word. Thus God's hidden work is proclaimed through the Word. In this way, total salvation in Christ is implied in real presence. Whoever separates everything spiritual from everything physical exits at the same time from the foundation of biblical reality. In this sense the Lord's Supper is "part for the whole" (*pars pro toto*) of the entire biblical reality as a happening in the Spirit. In physically-composed Word, Word and Spirit are one.

[26] WA 23: 185, 30-36.
[27] WA 23: 189, 13-22.
[28] WA 23: 189, 23-37.

Mary, the shepherds, and Simeon have summarized the train of thought that represents the Word as bridge to spiritual understanding. It is truly natural flesh, born from a woman and died on the cross, that one can grasp, feel, and hear. But it is called spiritual because it "comes from the Spirit and will and must be eaten by us in a spiritual manner: the object is not always spiritual but the use gives the meal spirituality" (*obiectum non est semper spirituale, sed usus debet esse spiritualis*). Thereby, the biblical example flows out.[29]

The error of the *Schwärmer* therefore lies in that they do not grasp the physically-connected sense of the biblical tradition. The history of the Lord in its physical, earthly reality is an event in the Holy Spirit, yes, the manifestation of the Spirit itself. First, in this context everything from its sense-unlocking Word is received in its particular sense. Precisely, this physical context is clearly lost in the modern kerygmatization of the Word and precisely here lies the hermeneutical key. Inasmuch as it is exemplified in respect to Luther, the thoroughgoing lack in modern hermeneutics lies in that the boundary to spiritualism remains blurred.

For Luther, the appearance of the *Schwärmer* means that the heretics of the ancient world have returned. In this sense, his understanding of the Holy Spirit is precisely concerned as the whole foundation of the Gospel: "What comes from the Holy Spirit, what the whole thing of Spirit, spiritual, and spirits is and is called, is as physical, external, and visible as it always may be. Furthermore, flesh and fleshly is always what comes without the Spirit from natural strength of the flesh. It is as inner and invisible as it always is.[30]

"Spiritually" is also the keyword of a transformation process and qualification process that leave behind the contrast of external and internal so that the Spirit's coming can be fleshly or bodily or vice versa. That is the background of John 6, from which the ancient church prepared the keyword for the exact definition according to the manner of understanding the Lord's Supper, namely, transformation through the spiritual food because it transforms those who eat it. That is the Word from heaven that gives life to the world.[31] Thus, Luther formulates the general consensus of the early Church: "therein he will be in us naturally (said Hilarius) both in the soul and the body according to the Word of John 6, 'who eats me remains in me and I in him.' If one eats him spiritually through the Word, so he remains spiritually in us in the soul. If one eats him physically, so he

[29] WA 23: 184, 1-6.
[30] WA 23: 202, 3-11.
[31] WA 23: 202, 23-30.

remains physically in us and we in him. Because he is not digested nor transformed, but transforms us without omission, the soul in righteousness, the body in immortality. Thus have the Fathers spoken about the bodily meal."[32]

At this point, the text of Luther's total concept focuses under the keywords "Holy Scripture and Holy Spirit," and that occurs under four sequences of the argument that are intertwined in one another. First, the Word of God, established and created from the absolute priority of Holy Scripture, crystallizes itself in the words of institution of the Sacrament of the Altar. These are therefore something like key- and foundation-words for the understanding of the Word of God on the basis of Scripture, which as such is the testimony of Christ.

Second, the thus-grounded sacramental celebration—in the sense of the presentation of the spiritual meal—completes the unity of the contrasts of physical and spiritual, of the earthly and the heavenly, and precisely implies the unity of divinity and humanity in Christ as the Pantocrator who overcomes space and time, including both heaven and earth, the visible and invisible world. Thus is manifested the reality of Christ who sits at the right of the Father in his ubiquity for the faith community in the Sacrament of the Altar. This mediation occurs in the Holy Spirit under bread and wine. The Spirit-filled Word is at the same time the Word of the sacramental presence of Christ as heavenly meal.

Third, the reality of the Holy Spirit created in Word and sacrament causes a double transformation process in which the soul is transformed in righteousness and the body in immortality. Fourth, justification has its place here, contained within the new creation of the whole person. It has its place in the eschatological framework of the new creation of all things as it is appropriately paraphrased with the formula, "justification or regeneration" (*justificatio seu regeneratio*).[33]

The dispute over the Lord's Supper that Luther has fought here is the battle for the one catholic Church of all times. The pre-determined framework includes the dogmatic history of the ancient Church from the christological dogma at Nicea (325) to the confession of

[32] WA 23: 255, 21-29. See also Ulrich Asendorf, "Das Wort Gottes bei Luther im sakramentalen Zusammenhang patristischer Theologie. Systematische and ökumenische Überlegungen zu Luthers Schrift "Daß diese Worte Christi" (1527), *Kerygma und Dogma* 39 (1993): 31-47.

[33] *Apologie* IV: 72. *Die Bekenntisschriften der evangelisch-lutherischen Kirche* [2] (Göttingen: Vandenhoeck &Ruprecht, 1952), 174: 21-44. Gunther Wenz, *Theologie der Bekenntnisschriften der evangelisch-lutherischen Kirche* II (Berlin-New York: Walter de Gruyter, 1998), 127; 161, 603.

the divinity of the Holy Spirit at Constantinople (381).[34] Luther's understanding of the Word follows this grounding. With it, he renews the confession of Christ as God's Son born from the virgin Mary. God's greatest miracle is Christ's conception through the Holy Spirit. The deity who lives in Christ on earth and yet in eternity, and also sits to the right of the Father, is not in front of the eyes.[35]

In their false antithesis of spiritual and physical, the *Schwärmer* do not want to see this miracle of God mediated through the Spirit. In that way the virgin birth is the true paradigm of the Holy Spirit. Luther's meaning leads to one enormous synthesis:

> We know that God's power, arm, hand, nature, countenance, Spirit, wisdom, etc., are all one thing. Outside of the creature is none other than Godhead itself. And also undoubtedly have been God's power and hand, God's reality before creation of the creature; so after the creation of the creature, would he become something other? He makes nothing except through his Word (Gen. 1, John 1), which is his power. And his Word is not a hatchet, axe, saws, or files through which he works, but he himself. His power and Spirit is now everywhere and in all things, in all the most inner and external, thoroughly present; if he then must exist, so must his divine right hand, nature, and majesty also be everywhere. He must truly exist thereby if he should cause and maintain that.[36]

All of that has a double biblical prerequisite, namely, Col. 2:9, where the whole fullness of Deity resides in Christ incarnate, and John 14:9f, according to the Word directed to Philip that whoever sees Christ sees the Father.

In Luther's embracing systematics, particularly in this impressive section containing his comprehensive theology of the Word of God, at the same time in the sense of a biblical summary, he draws in the great patristic tradition. Luther's theology of justification also represents itself as such, for it holds within itself the sum of Holy Scripture and of the divine Word grounded in the Trinity. In this respect, the material presents a unique meaning in the total context of ecumenical efforts for the conquest of old fronts and the opening of new horizons.

Translated from the German by Joan Skocir

[34] Wolfgang A. Bienert, *Dogmengeschichte, Grundkurs Theologie* 5, 1 (Stuttgart: W. Kohlhammer, 1997), 163ff, 185ff, 188ff, especially 188.

[35] WA 23: 165, 1-16.

[36] WA 23: 139, 4-30.

GERMAN INFLUENCE ON LUTHERAN NORWAY

NILS E. BLOCH-HOELL

This tribute to Luther and German Lutheran influences in Norway is written as a warm token of friendship for Kenneth Hagen and in memory of the inspiration given to me by the Churches in the USA. Dr. Hagen has correctly said: "To understand nineteenth century Norwegian Confessionalism, one needs to know the background to Lutheran identity and Norwegian nationalism."[1] This essay recalls that broader background for Luther and Lutheran scholarship in Norway today.

PRELIMINARY OBSERVATIONS

The idea of the Christianization of Norway as a result of the brutal and superficial activity of the three "mission" kings—Haakom Adalstainsfostre (d.961), Olav Tryggvasson (d. 1000), and Olav Haraldsson (St. Olav; d. 1030)—has been revised after extensive research. The one-sided opinions of the German scholar Konrad Maurer, which lasted for more than a century and were supported by the Norwegian Marxist historian, Edvard Bull, Sr., are finally and fully discredited.[2]

The sea was always Norway's link with the world outside, especially with western Europe. Norway is a mountainous country with a coastline of 2650 km. and a shoreline of 33,795 km., mostly westward.[3] Norwegians were sailors long before the Vikings, who began with the Lindisfarne raid in A.D. 793 and ended about A.D. 1030 with the battle of Stiklestad. Thus, the mission time of Norway actually lasted for nearly three hundred years. The mission kings mentioned above brought missionaries, priests, and bishops to Norway.

[1] Kenneth Hagen, *Luther's Approach to Scripture as seen in his "Commmentaries" on Galatians 1519-1538* (Tübingen: J.C.B. Mohr [Paul Siebeck], 1993), 39f.

[2] Konrad Maurer, *Die Bekehrung des Norwegisches Stammes zum Christentum* (München: C. Kaiser, 1855-1856); Edv. Bull, *Folk og kirke i middelalderen Kristiania* (Kristiana: Gyldendal, 1912).

[3] Aschenhoug/Gyldendal Store, *Norske Leks.* Vol. 8, 659.

Their efforts to renew the legislation according to Christian thinking and to offer basic Christian education were invaluable.[4]

Christian influence on Norwegians came from nonprofessional, unknown women and men who had been introduced to the Gospel on merchant tours in Ireland, England, and Scotland and through their relations with Scandinavian settlements in these countries. Postwar excavations made in Dublin, York (Jorvik), and several places in Norway, demonstrate Christian settlements in Norway from the eighth century onward. Fredrik Paasche's book on Norwegian/Icelandic saga-literature and poetry (1914) indicated important, high-quality Christian elements in post-Viking poetry. It goes without saying that this transition period was to some extent also syncretistic.[5] In my book on *Catholic Christians and We Other Ones*, I have reinterpreted some of the legends of Norwegian saints, pointing out clear elements of Christian anthropology.[6] There I also note the remarkable literature on archeological material proving early Christian settlements in Norway.[7]

In the Middle Ages, the Germanic influence on Norway was limited. We have some vague information regarding German/Danish mission efforts during that time. Professor Carl Fr. Wisløff wrote in his Church history text book in 1966:

> One single mission enterprise has come from the south. Anskar's effort in the first half of the 9th century had no great results, and the mission did not come to Norway, as far as we know. In 831, however, the archbishopric of Hamburg-Bremen was established, and from 848 the North German bishopric city had the Nordic countries as part of its area of responsibility.[8]

[4] Rudolf Keyser and Oluf Kolsrud, *Den Norske Kirkes Historie under Katholicismen* I-I, Christiania 1856-1858 (Oslo: Noregs kyrkjesogel, 1958 (1943)).

[5] *Nord. Teol. Uppslagsbok* III (Lund:København, 1957), 256 f.

[6] Nils E. Bloch-Hoell, *Katolske Kristine og vi andre* (Oslo:Land og Kirke. Gyldendal Norsk Forlag, 1986); Nils E. Bloch-Hoell, "Kirkejubileet et krisningsjubileum," *Vårt Land* 15. Juni 1994; "1000 år siden Norge ble kristnet?" *Aftenposten* January 22, 1995.

[7] Fridtjov Birkeli, *Norske steinkors i tidlig middelalder* (Oslo:Universitetforlaget, 1973); Charlotte Blindheim, *Kaupang by the viksfjord in Vestfold. Vikinger pirater eller handelsmann? Excavations and Research* (Oslo: Universitetsforlaget, 1975); Charlotte Blindheim, "Vikinger, pirater eller handelsmann?" *Det Norske Videnskaps-Akademi* (Oslo: Universitetsforlaget, 1978); Brit Solli, *Narra of Veøy* (Oslo: Universitetsforlaget, 1996); Oskar Skarsaune, "Nytt lys over kristningen av Norge?" *Tidsskrift for Teologi og Kirke* (1996): 49-52.

[8] Carl Fr. Wisløff, *Norsk kirkehistorie* 1 (Oslo: Luther Stiftelsen, 1966), 52; Absalon Taranger, *Den angelsachsiske kirkes Indflydelse paa den norske* (Christiania: Grøndahl & Sons bogtrykkeri, 1890); Jan Inger Hansen and Knut G. Bjerva, *Fra*

The German impact on the church of Norway was not significant during the fifty years when all the Nordic countries were under the jurisdiction of Hamburg-Bremen (1053–1103).

Bergen, Norway's largest city in the Middle Ages, was an open gate for German influence. For more than three hundred years until the Hanseatic office closed in 1650, Bergen was a center for contact between Norway and Germany. The Hanseatic League rented houses for its offices and docks for its mercantile activity of importing and exporting. Using the Roman Church, Mariakirken, it had its own priests with monthly German masses well into the 18th century.[9]

The Hanseates did not limit their activity to the import of food articles and export of fish. They also brought altarpieces, especially from Lübeck, for instance, for the beautiful Mariakirken in Bergen. Altarpieces for the stone church in Harstad in northern Norway also were contributed by the Hanseates. The famous Bernt Notke of Lübeck constructed these pieces.[10] The effect of the import of church art seems to be limited in its influence on the Norwegian conception of Christianity; for example, the Mary-cult came relatively late to this country.

The Lutheran Reformation in Norway

The Lutheran Reformation came quietly to Norway. The decision was made in Denmark, where the Reformation first appeared. In 1536, the king of Denmark and Norway, Christian III, imprisoned the Danish Catholic bishops. This signaled a final break with the Roman Catholic Church. Based on German and Danish concepts, a new Lutheran Church Ordinance was signed by the king on September 9, 1537. At the same time, one Norwegian and seven Danish superintendents were ordained in Copenhagen by Dr. Johann Bugenhagen, pastor to Martin Luther and organizer of a number of Lutheran churches in German dukedoms.[11] The Church Ordinance for Denmark was printed in Latin in 1539. A Norwegian Church Ordinance for Norway was edited in 1604 and authorized in 1607.

hammer til kors. 1000 år med kristendom (Oslo: Schibsted, 1994), 234ff.; *Viking og Hvideskrist: Norden og Europa 800-1200: den 22.Europarådsudstilliug* (Copenhagen: Nordisk Ministerråd; samarbejde med Europarådet, 1992), 398ff.

[9] Sverre Steen, *Bergen: Byen mellom fjellene* (Bergen: Eide, 1970), 55ff.; A.E. Herteig, *Bryggen i Bergen* (Bergen: Private, 1960/1969); Knut Helle, *Bergen bys historie* I (Bergen: Universitetsforlaget, 1979/1985), 731 ff.

[10] Eivind S. Engelstad, *Senmiddelalderens kunst* (Oslo: Universitets Oldsaksamling, 1936),12 and 21; Povel Simensen, *Trondenes kirke* (Harstad: Grefiek Forum, 1980), 26.

[11] Wisløff, 381-451.

The Reformation in Norway was a long educational process. It started with a royal decree and slowly developed through the education of Lutheran ministers and, after two generations, a reeducation of the lay people. The catechization of the laity took place in the church after a thirty-minute sermon. Very few lay people could read or write in those days; therefore, Luther's *Small Catechism* was used to instruct the people in the basics of the faith.

No revival had introduced the Reformation to Norway. As a matter of fact, in spite of the royal decrees, the Church of Norway for many years lived almost unchanged. This was by no means against the will of King Christian III. In a letter from the summer of 1537 to the feudal lord of Bergenshus Castle, the king instructed him that "everything should remain the same until one could gently find means to bring the people to a better understanding of the word of God."[12]

With merely one exception, all the priests in Norway remained in their offices. This meant that the Reformation was not felt as a revolution or a complete break with the past. The Roman Catholic bishops, however, were removed or arrested, with the exception of the archbishop of Nidaros (Trondheim) Olav Engelbrektsson, who left the country and died in exile in Holland. In addition, the worship of saints was stopped and only one altar was kept in each church.

Politically the Reformation was a disaster for Norway.[13] The king confiscated the enormous properties of the Church, and degraded Norway to a province of Denmark. The Reformation had been more political than spiritual.

Even so, Norway had a genuine Lutheran Church. The *sola scriptura* principle was a matter of course and Luther's *Small Catechism* and the *Augustana invariata* were accepted as the sole confessional rules. Conservative Orthodoxy ruled until Pietism conquered it in the first part of the 18th century. To a certain degree, Pietism can be thought of as a German version of a British congregationalist understanding and practice of Christianity—not a form of Calvinism but more in accordance with Methodism.[14]

The conservative Norwegian dogmatist Dr. Knud Krogh-Tonning, who became a Roman Catholic some years later, published

[12] Ingun Montgomery, in *Reformationens konsolidering i de norduska länderna 1540-1610*, Ingmar Brohed, ed. (Oslo: Universitetsforlaget, 1990).

[13] Helge Faehn, in Brohed, 279ff.

[14] Einar Molland, "Norway, Lutheranism" in *The Encyclopedia of the Lutheran Church*, III, col. 984; E.M. *Nordick teol. Uppslagsbok* III, col. 984.

a book called *Die Gnadenlehre und die stille Reformation* (The Teaching of Grace and the Quiet Reformation).[15] Those words could be used as a headline for what was going on in the Church of Norway during the process of the Reformation. It was quiet and its message was about grace. This is also visible in the church art, as Dr. Sigrid Christie has demonstrated in her dissertation on the Lutheran iconography in Norway until 1800.[16] Church art through the centuries has been a great preacher, especially for those who could not read. The first printing press in Norway was established in 1643. Before that time, all books came from Denmark or Germany.[17] The general practice in Norway in liturgical matters was to use Danish and German models. Professor Fæhn has investigated this in detail and is able to prove that Norwegian liturgy, including the liturgy of baptism and the High Mass (morning service) depended upon German material, often via Denmark. Luther himself is often mentioned.[18]

Ecclesiastical legislation against Roman Catholicism was extremely harsh. In the time of Orthodoxy, according to King Christian VII's Law of April 15, 1687, monks, Jesuits, and other Roman Catholic priests were not admitted to Denmark/Norway. Transgression meant the death penalty. This death penalty principle was enjoined in later legislation in this country until Norway adopted its liberal Dissenter Law in 1845.[19] It is interesting to observe that the first non-Lutheran congregation in Norway after that time was Roman Catholic. The permission was given by a royal decree, supported by the French-born king of Sweden and Norway.[20] The first post-Reformation priest in Norway was a German, Father Gottfried Montz. In the next 150 years, he was followed by 64 priests, all from Germany.[21]

In the Middle Ages only a few select priests from Norway went abroad for advanced studies at universities in Oxford, Paris (Sorbonne), Orleans, and Bologna, later also to German universities

[15] K. Krogh-Tonning, *Die Gnadenlehre und die stille Reformation* (Christiana: In commission bei Jakob Dybwad, 1894).

[16] S. Christie, *Den lutherske ikonografi i Norge inntil 1800* (Oslo: Land og Kirke, 1973).

[17] Helge Fæhn, *Gudstjenestelivet i Den norske kirke fra reformasjonen til våre dager* (Oslo: Universitetsforlaget, 1993), 42.

[18] Fæhn, 42, 26, 36, 65, 109f., 137ff., 163, 189, 394f., 410ff., 426, 443.

[19] Nils E. Bloch-Hoell. "Forholdet meelom Den norske kirke og den romersk-katolske kirke i Norge i tiden 1843-1892," *Norsk Teologisk Tidsskrift* (1958): 91.

[20] Ibid.

[21] John Willem Gran, ed., *Den katolske kirke i Norge* (Oslo: Aschenhoug, 1993), 413ff.

such as Greifswald and Rostock.[22] The favorite university for Norwegians was Rostock. In this city Norwegians even had their own residence, *Regentia Sancti Olavi*. My ancestor, Haagen Mogenssøn from Jemtland of the Swedish/Norwegian family Gyllenax (Gyllenaar), was matriculated in Rostock in 1585.[23]

Two Norwegian ministers in the 18th century were well acquainted with German university life and mediated some German influence in Norway. The Danish-born Jacob Nicolai Wilse (1735–1801) became an ardent Norwegian patriot. He was a vicar in Spydeberg and later in Eidsberg in southeast Norway. Wilse was more interested in topography than in theology, but he obtained his master's degree in Copenhagen in 1767. Despite being a rationalist, he became an honorary professor of theology in Copenhagen in 1784. He had traveled in Hamburg and Berlin and became a member of the *Königliche Gesellschaft der Wissenschaften* in Göttingen in 1781.[24]

The second German-influenced theologian to be mentioned here is Peter Olivarius Bugge (1769–1849). He was brought up in a Moravian family. His father was a vicar. As a youngster, Bugge joined a Moravian uncle in Herrnhut, the birthplace of Moravianism, and remained a pious Moravian all his life. He wrote a collection of sermons in the Moravian spirit, published in Copenhagen in 1790 and translated into German and Finnish. Strange to say, he was at the same time a rationalist theologian. This is more evident in his doctoral dissertation, *De perversitate humana morali* (Göttingen, 1796). Bugge was Bishop of Nidaros (Trondheim) (1803–1843) and was an eloquent preacher who gathered great assemblies.[25]

Whereas Denmark had two prominent and trend-setting theologians, the hymnwriter N. F. S. Grundtvig and the philosopher Søren Kierkegaard, Norway had its famous lay preacher, Hans Nielsen Hauge (1771–1824). None of these influential churchmen were sectarians, but the Norwegian lay preacher wanted *explicitly* to remain Lutheran. He strongly admonished his followers, the Haugians, to remain faithful to the Church of Norway and to use its sacraments.[26]

In 1814 Norway was a small country at the outskirts of Europe with 900,000 inhabitants. Germany seemed to be the Holy Land for Norwegian ministers of the Church. The talented preacher, ortho-

[22] Nils E. Bloch-Hoell, *Katolske*, 43.

[23] Oluf Kolsrud, *Presteutdanningi i Noreg* (Oslo: Universitetsforlaget, 1962), 41.

[24] *Kirke-Leks. for Norden* 4, 868; *Norsk Biograf. Leks.* 19, 235.

[25] *Norsk Biograf. Leks.* 2, 415.

[26] Andreas Aarflot, *Hans Neilsen Hauge: liv og budskap* (Oslo: Universitetsforlaget, 1971).

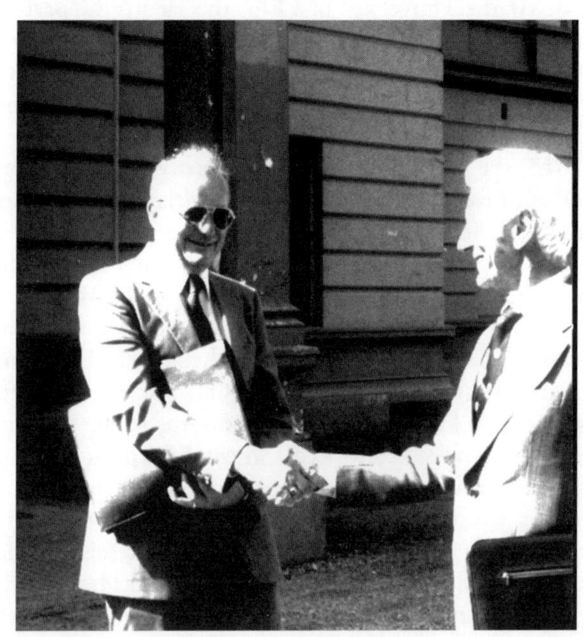

Kenneth Hagen and Nils Bloch-Hoell in Norway, after "Bowing to the King," May 1986.

dox polemicist, and later bishop, Johann Christian Heuch (1838–1904), wrote that "according to the way of thinking in those days [1845], the world of theology did not go beyond the borders of Germany."[27] Our nation had a sense of inferiority versus the old-culture nations with long university traditions. We listened eagerly to what foreigners said about our country, such as the British salmon lords who praised this land of fjords and mountains and the German tourists who commented about the fantastic scenery. The loud-speaking German emperor Wilhelm II was a great admirer of Norway and came back to this country on his summer vacations every year. Two memorials witness to this admiration: the oversized Fridtjov Viking statue in the Sognefjord and the medieval stave church which he bought and brought to Germany.

Sweden established its first university in Uppsala in 1477 and Denmark followed two years later with the University of Copenhagen. Norway founded its first university in 1811. Since 1938, the University of Oslo (*Universitas Oslonensis*) was named the Royal Frederiks's

[27] Einar Molland, *Norges kirkehistorie* 1(Oslo: Luther Stiftelsen, 1948), 192.

University. At the University of Oslo, the faculty (department) of theology ranks number one, as is still evident in academic processions. In the first hundred years of its history, the theology faculty was completely dominated by German theology. Then, in the spirit of the Enlightenment (*die Aufklärung*) Danish theology also became popular.

In 1813, the young Norwegian university started its work very modestly, with five full professors, one associate professor, and seventeen students. Some students preceded their studies in Copenhagen. The first theology professor was a teacher at the *Metropolitanskolen* in Copenhagen, Svend Borchmenn Hersleb (1784–1836). He had graduated in 1807 from Copenhagen with excellent marks and was called upon as the principal professor in theology in 1813 and as full professor in 1814. He taught dogmatics, Old Testament, and for some years also Hebrew. Hersleb was a follower of the young anti-rationalist Grundtvig and he was a convinced and committed Lutheran. He also initiated the foundation of the Norwegian Bible Society in 1816.

Hersleb's younger colleague Stener Johannes Stenersen(1789–1835) had a more extroverted personality and exercised a more distinct Lutheran influence on the faculty than did Hersleb, although they are both characterized as "moderate conservatives." Stenersen also graduated with excellent marks, *laudabilis et quidem egregie*[28] and was appointed associate professor in 1814 and full professor in 1818. He was an extraordinarily diligent teacher and writer of theological textbooks, lecturing twelve hours weekly and writing close to four thousand pages of theology. Like Hersleb, he was influenced by the young biblical scholar, Grundtvig. As a young professor Stenersen was a supporter of "the newest German philosophy," which meant the "nature philosophy" of the young Fr. von Schelling. Two years later he again wrote to Grundtvig that, after studying the Bible and after reading Luther and Francke, he had arrived at an answer to his struggle for an assurance of faith. From this time onward, a Lutheran conception of Christianity served as the governing idea in his writings.[29] Stenersen taught New Testament and Church history, and considered the discipline of biblical studies as the most important. He was certainly not haughty. Stenersen stated that he did not write for the scholars but to give his students the necessary textbooks. And so he did, producing four commentaries on the most important

[28] Andreas Brandrud, in *Det Kongelige Fredriks Universitet 1811-1911* (Kristiana: A. Aschenhoug, 1911), 3-15; Nils E. Bloch-Hoell, "Stener Johannes Stenersen," "Stener Johannes Stenersen: Den førstelærer i kirkehistorie ved Det Kongelige Frederiks Universitet," *Tidsskrift for Teologi og Kirke* (1960): 218-236.

[29] Nils E. Bloch-Hoell, "Stenersen," 223.

epistles of Paul and altogether publishing 1441 pages in Latin, plus preparing one commentary in Danish on the Catholic epistles.[30] Stenersen admitted frankly that his New Testament commentaries were not original. He acknowledged that he depended upon German scholars, especially Pott.

Stenersen's most original contribution is his 1827 book on Hans Nielsen Hauge—his life, activity, teaching, and publications. He is not polemical against the lay preacher, except on one point—Hauge did not have a *rite vocatus;* that is, the Church had not called him and Hauge was not ordained. Stenersen argues as a strict Lutheran but not as a legalist.

He also said that the following New Testament epistles could not be used as sources for the Christian faith, because their authenticity cannot be proven: Hebrews, James, 2 Jude, 2 Peter, 1 and 2 John.[31] In a "brief" Bible history textbook of 284 pages, he discloses his biblical Lutheranism and its emphasis upon *sola Scriptura, sola fide*, and the necessity of the sacraments.[32] In a textbook on general Church history for students, he relies much on the enormous work of Johann Mathias Schröck (1733–1808), *Christliche Kirchengeschichte*, which appeared in 35 volumes! He used Schröck in spite of Schröck's supranaturalism. After all, Schröck was a Lutheran.

The strongest Luther influence in Stenersen's contributions is found in his voluminous survey of the Lutheran Reformation, based on open lectures which he gave twice a week in the Reformation anniversary year of 1817. His lectures were extremely popular, with 300–400 listeners. He modestly claims to have taken all his information from the German scholar Schröck, but this is not the case. He also consulted other German historians, such as L. von Seckendorf and Ph. K. Marheinecke, the last mentioned forty times in Stenersen's footnotes.[33] In the first volume of his Reformation history, Stenersen has 114 references to the Bible, and in his introductory chapters hardly any modern scholars are used. It is, however, true that in volume II, Stenersen has many, in fact 239, references to Schröck. But, according to my own observations, he has as many as 690 references and quotations from the works of Luther.

In the Reformation jubilee festival on November 3, 1817, Stenersen played a prominent role. The festival was arranged by the

[30] Ibid., 243f.
[31] Ibid., 232.
[32] Ibid., 231f.
[33] Nils E. Bloch-Hoell, "Stenersen," 226.

University and Stenersen wrote a cantata that was solemnly performed in honour of "that Giant, Dr. Martin Luther."

In 1819 Stenersen was so overworked that he was granted several months leave, which he spent in Denmark and Germany, particularly in the cities of Copenhagen, Kiel, Duisberg, Dresden, Herrnhut, and Magdeburg. Stenersen died young, in 1835. But he and Hersleb left a generation of well-educated and qualified ministers who exercised their ministry in warm appreciation of their hard working Evangelical Lutheran professors.[34]

Thus, the young Norwegian university had a relatively rapid growth. In 1823 its staff included sixteen full professors, one associate professor and 630 students. Two hundred of them were students of theology.[35] What did foreigners, above all German professors, think of our University? In 1824, the theology professor from Greifswald Fr. Wilhelm von Schubert published a description of his journeys in Scandinavia in 1817, 1818, and 1820. He visited Christiania in October 1817 and wrote favorably about the new university. "Schon in 1817 fand ich die Friedrichsuniversität im schönsten Aufblühen; eine frische jugendliche Tätigkeit herrschte überall."[36] Even more interesting are comments by the famous theologian and philosopher Friedrich Schleiermacher (1758–1834), who wrote from Christiania to his wife in September, 1833: "Freilich sehr in miniature angelegt, aber sie hat einige bedeuteende, eigentümliche Vorzüge welche ich sie beneide."[37] It is a pity that Schleiermacher did not explain what the distinctive, significant advantages were that he envied in the Norwegian university. Schleier-macher was one of the most influential German theologians of his time, affecting both Norwegian theology and Church life. As the Danish theologian E. C. Krarup wrote: "However the Protestant theology will develop, one thing is for sure: the development will not come excluding S., only through him."[38]

The Hersleb-Stenersen period lasted until about 1850 and was succeeded by the Gisle Johnson-Caspari period. In the year between the death of Stenersen in 1835 and Hersleb in 1836, the training of ministers was taken care of by the brightest disciples without any real

[34] Erik Nicolai Saxild, *Bidrag til Professor Stener Johannes Stenersens Biographie ved hans mangeaarige Ven* (Christiania: Grøndahl, 1835); *Stener Johannes Stenersen Mindenkrands fra hans søregende Disciple* (Christiania: Grøndahl, 1835).

[35] Brandrud II, 9.

[36] *Det Kongelige Fredriks* I, 59.

[37] Ibid., II, 85.

[38] *Kirke-Leks.* II IV, 85.

reward or recognition. They all had their obligatory study journeys to German universities. Some of these professors wrote valuable things, without any signs of German influence, as far as I can see.

The young and talented *candidatus theologiae* Gisle Johnson (1822–1894) traveled from university to university in 1846–47: Berlin, Leipzig, Tübingen, Erlangen, and Heidelberg. In Germany, Johnson met the learned Jew, Carl Paul Caspari (1814–1892), who had been baptized in 1838 under the influence of Franz Delitsch the Old Testament scholar and Karl Graul the strong and polemical Lutheran dogmatist. Johnson made a real achievement when he persuaded Caspari to come to Norway and accept an appointment as associate professor in 1847 and ten years later as full professor in Old Testament theology. Caspari was a high-level scholar who mastered Hebrew, Arabic, Latin, Greek, and, of course, German. He had published an Arabic/Latin grammar and the three-volume *Geschichte des Taufsymbols und der Glaubenregel,* 1866–1875. Together with Johnson in 1866, he translated the Lutheran confessional book, *The Book of Concord,* into Norwegian. Caspari also wrote the preface to a Norwegian (Danish) edition of a book by the strong Lutheran confessionalist and mission leader, Dr. Karl Graul (1814–1864), that came to its second Norwegian edition in 1864 in Christiana. The German original, *Die Unterscheidungslehren der verschiedenen christliche Bekenntnisse,* was published in at least six editions.[39] In Caspari, Johnson had the perfect coworker for training future ministers on a high level as well as a committed coworker in his struggle to make the Church of Norway a genuine Lutheran stronghold.

To this end, Gisle Johnson found it necessary to fight Danish Grundtvigianism as it had developed after the change in the movement in 1825.[40] He wanted to protect conservative Lutheranism in the spirit of the *Erlangentheologie* or *Erfahrungstheologie*, a Lutheran experimental theology, emphasizing infant baptism but warning against unworthy participation in holy communion, an attitude which is more Pietistic than actually Lutheran. Gisle Johnson taught dogmatics from 1849–1875 and Church history from 1875–1894. He

[39] The Norwegian edition was published in 1864; the 6th German edition was entitled, *Die Unterscheidungslehren der verschiedenen christlichen Bekentnisse.* See *Weltkirchen Lex.*, 644; *Kirke-Leks. II*, 251.

[40] Einar Molland, *Norges kirkehistorie i det 19.århundre* I (Oslo: Gyldendal, 1979), 266 ff.; Anders Skrondal, *Grundtvig og Noreg* (Bergen: A/S Lünde & Co., 1929).

became the instrument of a great revival, starting with students and ministers in the 1850s and covering the entire country by the 1860s.[41]

The revivals by Hauge and Johnson are probably the main reason why more than ninety percent of the Norwegian people remain Lutheran. Within the category of active churchgoers, conservative Lutherans are in the majority. In 1950, Godvin Ousland published his doctoral dissertation on Gisle Johnson. One section in his book has the headline, "Gisle Johnson a German epigon?" The answer is a reluctant, "yes."[42]

A few words must be said about the Moravians, *Die Brüdergemeine*. The Moravians were never numerous in Norway and they never separated themselves from the Church. When the Norwegian Missionary Society was founded in 1842, the leaders were Haugians and Moravians.[43] The most important representative for the Moravians in Norway was the Dane, Niels Johannes Holm. He worked in Christiania from 1820 to 1834 and had considerable influence on students and ministers. Holm was a prolific and pious hymn writer and missionary initiator.

In Norwegian churches, many German hymns in Norwegian translation have been and continue to be sung. In *Landstads Salmebog* from 1868, we find 160 out of 791 hymns which are directly translated from German and about 20 hymns which were originally Latin and came from Germany. Thus, approximately every fifth hymn in this hymnbook is translated from German.

There are also influences on Norwegian Lutheranism less often recognized. For example, Norwegian Lutherans pastored a small Norwegian congregation in Berlin. Among them were the theology professor Hans Ording and the Bishop Arne Fjellbu. In addition, Bishop Eivind Berggrav visited German during World War I and wrote about his impressions.[44] In 1909, a German congregation, *Die Deutsche Evangelische Gemeinde: Evangelische Gemeinde Deutscher Sprache*, was founded in Christiania (Oslo). Of the pastors who served there during World War II, I mention V. H. Günther and after the

[41] Molland, 189ff.

[42] Godvin Ousland, *Gisle Johnson som teolog og kirkemann* (Oslo: Lutherstiftelsens Forlag, 1950), 57.

[43] Torstein Jorgensen, *I tro og tjeneste. Det Norske Misjonsselskap 1842-1992* I (Stavanger: Misjonshøgskolen, 1992), 15ff.

[44] Arne Fjellbu, *En biskop ser tilbake* (Oslo: Gyldendal Norske Forlag, 1953), 127 f.; Gunnar Heiene, *Eivind Berggrav. En biografi* (Oslo: Universitetsforlaget, 1984), 127ff.; Nils E. Bloch-Hoell, *Eivind Berggravs teologiske profil.*, 25ff., in Per Voksø, *Eivind Berggrav: Brobygger og kirkeleder* (Oslo: Gyldendal Norske Forlag, 1953).

war, Friedrich Graf zu Lynar, a prudent and modest minister of the church. Two others I met are S. Riemenschneider and Gerhard Heilmann, who later became a secondary school teacher. For about a year, I also served this parish in Norway as leader of the communion services.[45] Neither the German congregation in Oslo nor the Norwegian congregation in Berlin had a profound impact on world Lutheranism, but both had an effect which I value as positive for the surrounding communities.

In 1907, the Free Faculty of Theology was founded and started its work one year later. The leading dogmatist, inner mission leader, and famous preacher, Ole Hallesby, obtained his doctorate in Erlangen in 1909. Together with Bishop Berggrav, he was a resistance leader in the Norwegian struggle against the Nazi system and practices. The establishment of the Free Faculty of Theology can also be looked upon as a traditional Lutheran protest against the new Ritschlian professor of dogmatics Dr. Johannes Ording, who denied any sacramental effect in infant baptism. After five years, the Free Faculty was granted the right to educate *candidati theologiae*, men qualified to be ordained as ministers in the Church of Norway. After just one decade, this faculty educated more ministers than the university faculty. The strong Lutheran character was heavily strengthened by the appointment to the faculty of two brothers, Leiv Aalen (1906–1980) and Sverre Aalen (1909–1980), respectively professors of dogmatics and New Testament theology. Their most important contributions in German were Leiv Aalen's *Die Theologie des jungen Zinzendorf* (Berlin, 1969) and Sverre Aalen's *Die Begriffe Licht und Finsternis im A.T., Spätjudentum und im Rabbinismus* (1951).[46] These two strong Lutherans had a profound impact upon a generation of pastors and professors of theology. In addition, Dr. Olaf Moe served as associate professor in the university for ten years and full professor at the Free Faculty of Theology, the *Menighetsfakuletet*, from 1916–1953. He published his dissertation in German.[47]

However, the first Norwegian to publish in German or to have a contribution translated into German was Frederik Wilhelm Klumpp

[45] *Deutsche Evangelische Gemeinde 75 Jahre* (Oslo: Gemeindebüro, 1984).

[46] Ole Hallesby, *En hovding i Guds rike* (Oslo, 1962); Ole Hallesby, *Korsets ord og troens tale. Festskrift* (Oslo: Lutherstiftelsen, 1949); Leiv Aalen, *Die Theologie des jungen Zinzendorf* (Berlin: Lutherstiftelsen, 1969); Sverre Aalen, *Die Begriffe Licht und Finsternis im A.T., im Spätjudentum und im Rabbinismus* (Oslo: J. Dybwad, 1951).

[47] Olaf Moe, *Levet og lært* (Oslo: Lutherstiftelsen, 1956); John Nome, *Brytningstid. Menighetsfakultetet i norsk kirkeliv* (Oslo: Lutherstiftelsen, 1958).

Bugge, who taught New Testament theology at the university in Christiania (Oslo) for 26 years, 23 years as full professor, until 1894 when he was appointed Bishop of Oslo. His popular commentary on the Gospel according to John came in Norwegian editions and was published in Germany as *Das Johannes-Evangelium* in 1894. Another pioneer in this line was the great preacher, polemicist, and bishop, Johann Christian Heuch (1838–1904). His book on pastoral care for the sick came from Leipzig in 1883[48] and as a new edition from Gotha in 1887 as *Die Praxis der Krankenseelsorge*. The following year, his book on the nature of unbelief was published in German translation as *Das Wesen des Unglaubens*. A passage from this book was quoted in the German *Reichstag*.[49]

It should be mentioned that Norwegian theology has profited from many well-known scholars who have given lectures and taken part in discussions in our country. I mention those whom I remember having heard—E. Sommerlath, Leonhard Goppelt, Hans Freiherr von Campenhausen, Hans Küng, Gerhard Ebeling, Jürgen Moltmann, Gert Haendler, and Ernst Käsemann. Ebeling's book *Luther: Einführung in sein Denken*, with a warm dedication, and Haendler's (Günther Wartenberg) *Lutherbriefe* are on my bookshelf, too.

The Church of Norway has received so much knowledge and insight from German and particularly Luther scholarship that we feel it is unable to be repaid. Yet sincere attempts have been made to demonstrate our gratitude by producing international Luther scholarship, by honoring German scholars, and by serving in the Lutheran World Federation.

Norwegians have served the Lutheran World Federation in different capacities over the past several decades. Dr. Sigurd Aske was associate director of the Department of Mission, 1958–1960 and 1968–1969. Bishop Dr. Fridtjof Birkeli, director of the same department from 1954–1957, was a man of vision who arranged the first all-African Lutheran conference in 1955 and also was member of the Lutheran World Federation executive committee (1957–1972). Dr. Gunnar Ostenstad served with the Department of Stewardship and Evangelism (1958–1960) and Bishop Dr. Andreas Aarflot, Bishop of Oslo, was a forceful church leader and member of the executive committee (1973–1990). Last but not least is Dr. Gunnar Stalsett, Bishop of Oslo, who served as General Secretary of the Lutheran World Federation from 1985–1990 and who mastered English, German and

[48] J.C. Heuch, *Die Praxix der Krankenseelsorge* (Leipzig: J. Naumann, 1883).
[49] Wisløff, 18.

French. At the General Assembly in Evian (1970), he was proposed as president because he was "the perfect conference leader," alert and able to grasp the point and summarize the essence.

All the three schools (faculties) of theology in Norway are Lutheran according to constitution and in practice. The last of these institutions is the Mission High School of Theology in Stavanger. It started as a mission school in 1859, was reorganized in 1977 and was recognized by the government in 1979 with the right to educate *candidati theologiae* to become ordained ministers.

At least two Norwegian professors have had academic assignments in Germany, Dr. Ernst Baasland, New Testament Professor and now Bishop of Stavanger, and Dr. Tarald Rasmussen, Church History Professor at the University of Oslo. With his dissertation in 1985 (German edition in 1989), *Inimici ecclesiae. Das ekklesiologische Feindbild in Luthers Dictata super Psalterium (1513–1515) im Horizont der theologischen Tradition*, Rasmussen is recognized as an established Luther scholar.

Once again two brothers must be noticed, the distinguished Per Lønning (1928–) and Inge Lønning (1938–). They both have an enormous number of publications and positions. Here I only mention Bishop Per Lønning's profound exposition, *Das begreiflich unergreifbare-Sein Gottes und modern-theologische Denkstukturen*, 1986, and Inge Lønning's *"Kanon im Kanon." Zum Grundlagenproblem des neutestamentlichen Kanons*, (1972). For many years, Inge Lønning was also the *Rektor* (president) of the University of Oslo. Of international interest is the dissertation by Dr. Kjetil Hafstad, *Wort und Geschichte, Das Geschichtsverständnis Karl Barths* (München, 1985).

As we have seen, Norwegians have contributed significantly to Luther research. Four more scholars are worthy of mention. Bishop Dr. Sigurd Normann (1879–1939) wrote a significant and challenging dissertation on the difficult topic of the freedom of the will and predestination in the Lutheran Reformation until 1525. The conservative church historian Carl Fr. Wissløff's 1957 dissertation appeared in Germany in 1969 under the title *Abendmahl und Messe*. He also wrote a book on Luther's theology in 1983. Dr. Ivar Asheim, who for some years also served the Lutheran World Federation as director of its Division of Theology, wrote his dissertation on *Glaube und Erziehung bei Luther* (Heidelberg, 1961). His colleague, Dr. Ole Modalsli, wrote his dissertation on *Das Gericht nach den Werken. Ein Beitrag zur Lehre vom Gesetz* (Heidelberg) in 1963.

A more popular but also more widespread interest in Luther is seen in books on Luther before and after World War II. Here I mention just the better known of them. Sigurd Normann edited *Var Lutherske Arv* (our Lutheran heritage) and "Martin Luther," in the three-volume *Hovedverker av den kristne litteratur* (Oslo, 1931). Ivar Welle wrote *Luthers liv og Luthers tro* (Bergen, 1946). Other Luther books have been translated, such as Roland Bainton's *Here I Stand* to Swedish and Frederic Nohl's *Luther* (Stavanger, 1963).

The Church of Norway has not only maintained, but it has strengthened its Luther interest after the war. One of the latest publications relevant here comes from a missionary to Japan, Knut Alfsvåg, who wrote *The Identity of Theology: An Investigation of the Relation between Exegesis and Doctrine in Luther's De Servo Arbitrio* (Luther Theological Seminary, Bangalore, 1995). The last to be mentioned here is Oddvar Jensen's *Kristi person: Til betydningen av læren om Kristi person i Martin Luthers teologi 1520–1546* (Bergen 1997).

Without a doubt, Luther and his understanding of the Gospel have had the strongest influence in Norway in its post-Reformation history. It was not my task to trace German influence in literature, philosophy and art.[50] Twenty years after the adoption of the liberal Dissenter Law, the country was still all-Lutheran. In 1875 only four *pro mille* of the population were not members of the Lutheran state Church. By 1946 the number had increased to nearly four percent. The statistics demonstrate three facts: (1) the all-Lutheran character of Norway is no longer absolute; (2) this is one step in the general secularization; (3) the two most rapidly growing denominations are the Roman Catholic Church and the Pentecostal movement. The significance of the American denominations is also becoming more evident.[51] Similarly, secularization continues. The daily family devotion and the editions of devotional books have nearly been discontinued. The Bishop of Christiania (Oslo) from 1720–1737, Peder Hersleb, delivered long sermons; nevertheless, he was a very popular preacher, and twelve volumes of his sermons were translated into German and published.[52] A similar event would have been unthinkable in our time. With reverence I look at magnificent copies of heavy and well used Luther editions on my own bookshelves—Dr. Martin Luther's *Prædikener over alle Sön-og Festdages Evangelier og Epistler*

[50] Aschehoug/Gyldendal Store, *Norske Leks.* vol. 11, 420.

[51] Nils E. Bloch-Hoell, "Dissentersamfunnene i framgang," *Afternosten* 11 Jan.1951; Nils E. Bloch-Hoell, "Norwegian Ideas of American Christianity" in *Americana Norwegica* IV, 69-88; "The Impact in Norway of American Religious Dissent," in A.N.J. den Hollander, *Contagious Conflict* (Leyden: E. J. Brill,1973), 214-243.

[52] Eivind Berggrav, *Oslo bispegalleri i Domkirken* (Oslo: Universitetsforlaget, Booklet based on articles in Morgenposten, 1954), 16.

samt Lidelses-Historiens første Deel, Nyt Oplag, (Bergen, 1858) and *Dr. Martin Luthers fuldstændige Kirke-Postille* (1862) of nearly 900 pages.

I return, after this brief excursus, to my presentation on Norwegian contributions to international theology using the German language. Perhaps the most influential Norwegian New Testament scholar is Dr. Nils Alstrup Dahl (1911–). Dahl has divided his service as theology professor between the University of Oslo and Yale University, USA. He published his dissertation *Das Volk Gottes* in 1941 (new edition 1963). It is trend-setting in New Testament ecclesiology. In the Roman Catholic standard dictionary, *Lexikon für Theologie und Kirche* (second edition), his book is listed as number one in the literature on the phrase, "Volk Gottes." This book has without doubt also influenced the Roman Catholic understanding of the nature of the church as this is formulated in Vatican II documents, especially in the Constitution on the Church, *De Ecclesia*.

From the list of outstanding Norwegian scholars in biblical disciplines, I mention only one more man, Sigmund Mowinckel (1884–1965) who was offered flattering professorships in Germany but stayed in Oslo. His six-volume *Psalmen Studien* (1921–1924) is his best known work. He interpreted the Old Testament psalms as poetry in the service of the temple cult. Mowinckel's research is characterized by his great creativity and his original viewpoints with strong and penetrating force and a vivid way of expressing his message.[53]

Can we find possible Norwegian theological influence in Germany? Besides the impact made by N. A. Dahl and Sigmund Mowinckel, it is a fact that at least three theology professors in Oslo have been called upon to join the editorial board of German periodicals. Inge Lønning is a member of the editorial board of *Kerygma und Dogma* and of *Neue Zeitschrift für systematische Theologie*. Our Swedish-born Church historian and expert on Reformation history in Scandinavia and Germany, Dr. Ingun Montgomery, is a member of the editorial board of *Zeitschrift für kirchliche Zeitgeschichte*. And finally Dr. Magne Sæbø is a coeditor for *Zeitschrift für Alttestamentlische Wissenschaft* and of *Jahrbuch für biblische Theologie*. His doctoral dissertation was *Sacharia 9–14 von Text und Form* (1945).[54]

The Nazi regime under Adolf Hitler, 1933–1944, is sometimes labeled as a culture break, *eine Kultur-Pause*. Even so the heroic

[53] Magne Sæbø, "Mowinckel, Sigmund," *Theologische Realenc.* XXIV, 357; Sigurd Hjelde, "Mowinckels Lehrjahre in Deutschland," *Z.A.W.* (1997): 597ff.

[54] Ludwig Schübeler, *Kirkekampen slik jeg så den* (Oslo: Lutherstiftelsen, 1945), 350 ff.; Nils E. Bloch-Hoell, "Den norske kirke under okkupasjonen. Kirkekamp, infornasjonstjeneste og litt Mf-historie," *Tidsskrift for Teol. og kirke* (1995): 5-26.

Dietrich Bonhoeffer (1906–1945) has also inspired a generation of pastors and scholars in Norway. Two of his well-known books are in many libraries in Norway.[55] When Dr. Hallesby was a prisoner in the Grini concentration camp, he was called to the camp commander for a discussion. Hallesby mentioned the culture break and maintained that this affected all academic disciplines. It was the ambition of the Nazi occupation power to "nazify" the entire population, starting with children and young people. During the five years of harsh Nazi occupation, there could be no positive German influence in Norway. On the contrary, the occupation released an intense resistance movement in Norway. Therefore, Norway suffered less than other countries in Europe.

The war and occupation did not mean that the confessional identity of the Church of Norway was forgotten. When all the bishops and the vast majority of the ministers had resigned their offices on Easter day, 1942, the Church of Norway was no longer a state Church. The clergy lost their state income and forfeited their right to perform wedding ceremonies. Yet, all their other pastoral activities proceeded. On this famous Easter day in Norway, the bishops had written a statement called *Foundation of the Church: A Statement and a Confession*. It was read from the pulpits all over the country. It begins: "From our heart we are convinced that the Evangelical Lutheran Confession is the true and right guidance in the matter of faith."[56]

In opposition to the occupation powers' violation of national and international law, Bishop Berggrav asked Dr. Andr. Seierstad and the Rev. Amund Bentzen to collect an arsenal of Luther quotations. Some of these were used in the so-called illegal information paper of the Church, *Kirken i Dag*. The editor of this monthly paper (1944–1945) was Dr. Seierstad, assisted by Hans Höivik, a well-known leader of the Christian Student Movement, and by the author of this essay. I was also the producer and distributor of the paper. When all the judges of the Supreme Court of Norway on December 21, 1940, resigned their offices in protest against the Nazi regime, this gave the forthcoming resistance movement a strong moral support. The occupation power had no moral right to demand obedience.[57]

[55] Dietrich Bonhoeffer, *Nachfolge* (Munich: Christian Kaiser, 1937), Norwegian translation, 1956; Dietrich Bonhoeffer, *Widerstand und Ergebung* (Munich, 1955), Norwegian translation, 1959.

[56] H. C. Christie, *Den norske kirke i kamp* (Oslo: Land og Kirke, 1945), 165.

[57] Nils E. Bloch-Hoell, *Dennorske kirke*, 20 ff.; *Norsk Restidende* (1990):132.

The Nazi occupation of Norway did not squeeze Luther out of the Norwegian Church. The well known Norwegian Dominican Father Finn Thorn published his book *Luther i mitt liv som katlikk* in 1983. For this ecumenical priest, Luther was a mentor for his Christian life. *Levende Luther* is the title of a book written by Dr. Inge Lønning in 1967; "Luther is still alive" in Norway. From 1979 to 1983, together with Sigurd Hjelde and Tarald Rasmussen, Lønning published six volumes of selected Luther works. Last but not least is the American Luther scholar Dr. Kenneth Hagen of Norwegian ancestry. Dr. Hagen was invited to give guest lectures at the University of Oslo. In recognition and as a token of Norway's appreciation of Dr. Hagen's Luther study in Norway, Dr. Hagen was elected to membership in the Norwegian Academy of Science and Letters, *Det Norske Videnskaps-Akademi*, founded in 1857. Within the past 50 years, no country outside Scandinavia has honored more foreign members of the Academy.[58]

At the centennial of the University of Oslo in 1911, five out of nine new honorary doctors of theology were Germans.[59] On the other hand, a number of Norwegians have been awarded honorary doctorates or membership in German academies. Several Norwegian theologians have been subject to German academic honors. Bishop Dr. Eivind Berggrav received the Goethe Prize from the hand of the Rector of *Universität Hamburg* on May 18, 1953, because he had "rendered invaluable aid in forming the contemporary ethics, being at the same a recognized leader in the ecumenical movement, as well as for building brotherly understanding between the nations."[60] Similarly, the internationally renowned missiologist Dr. O.G. Myklebust was honored. At the 75th anniversary of the *Deutsche Gesellschaft für Missionswissenschaft*, the editor of the book, Dr. Hans-Werner Gensichen, dedicated the publication to "Olav Guttorm Myklebust den Freund und Weggenossen."[61]

German influence in Lutheran Norway comprises many facts, stretching back to the Middle Ages. This recollection of the past only highlights the significance and continuing need for Luther and all Lutheran scholarship in Norway and beyond.

[58] Nils E. Bloch-Hoell, "Det Norske Videnskaps-Academi. En fellesskapets kraftkilde," *Tidsskrift for Teologi og Kirke* (1992): 339-349.

[59] *Universitetet i Oslo 1991-1961* (Oslo: Universitetsforlaget, 1961), 326ff.

[60] Gunnar Heiene, *Eivind Berggrav*, 421.

[61] Hans-Werner Gensichen, *Invitatio ad Fraternitetem* (1918, 1993, Munster/ Hamburg: LIT Verlag, 1993).

LUTHER IN AN AMERICAN CATHOLIC CONTEXT

Patrick W. Carey

In 1967 Kenneth Hagen came to Marquette University to begin a thirty-three year career as a historical theologian whose research and teaching focused upon Martin Luther and late medieval theology. In the course of those years he taught hundreds of Catholic, Lutheran, and other Christian graduate and undergraduate students about Luther's theology in its Catholic and Reformation contexts. Hagen was one of the first Lutheran theologians to be hired as a full time professor by a Catholic university, and he has most certainly been the one with the longest tenure.[1] The *Milwaukee Journal*, the Marquette student newspaper*The Marquette Tribune*, and a host of other local and national newspapers noticed the event.[2]

Hagen was hired in the immediate aftermath of the Second Vatican Council (1962–65) when the ecumenical atmosphere in the United States was in high gear. The Council had fostered a new Catholic approach to other Christian Churches and world religions, calling for Catholics to emphasize the unity that already existed with other Christian communions. The new atmosphere replaced the previous prevailing attitude of mutual suspicion and polemics and promoted a desire for fuller Christian unity through dialogue. The Council

[1] At the time Hagen was hired, seven other Lutheran theologians were hired for either full time or part time positions in Catholic colleges and universities. For an account of these appointments, see *The Lutheran Forum* (February, 1968): 24. Of the seven, only Hagen has remained at a Catholic university from 1967 to the 1999–2000 school year. On the phenomenon of Catholics hiring Lutherans, see also Ronald B. Bagnall, "Lutherans on R. C. campuses are teachers, not missionaries," *The Lutheran Forum* (September, 1968):8-9.

[2] On this, see, for example, "Lutheran Picked to Teach His Theology at Marquette," *Milwaukee Journal* (April 8, 1967); "Lutheran Will Teach Theo," *The Marquette Tribune* (April 12, 1967): 3. For a sampling of the numerous other newspaper accounts of Hagen's hiring, see also, *The Catholic Standard and Times* (Philadelphia, May 12, 1967); *Telegram* (San Bernardino, California, April 28, 1967); *Press Gazette* (Green Bay, Wisconsin, April 9, 1967); *The Times Record* (Troy, New York, May 19, 1967); *Gazette* (Taunton, Massachusetts, June 13, 1967); *Houston Chronicle* (May 5, 1967); *The Minneapolis Star* (April 1, 1967); *The Lutheran Standard* (Spring, 1967).

also called for Catholic theologians and theological schools to do theology within an ecumenical context, studying the original sources of theological division and discovering ways to heal the divisions.

In the upper Midwest the new ecumenical atmosphere was manifested in a variety of ways, especially between Catholics and Lutherans, the dominant religious communions in the areas of Wisconsin, Minnesota, and the Dakotas. Ecumenical prayer services took place in various small towns and larger cities, ecumenical television and radio shows featured Protestant and Catholic ministers discussing religious and doctrinal issues, and Protestant and Catholic laity gathered together in their homes to engage in what were then called "living room dialogues" on issues of faith and doctrine. The Council had sparked a new flame, and it produced some immediate results in stimulating warm sensibilities among Catholics and Lutherans in the upper Midwest. The hiring of Hagen was part of this era of good feeling but it also acknowledged that the divisions between Catholics and Lutherans were not going to go away only with those new feelings of openness. It was going to take rigorous study, and Catholic universities had to make a long term commitment to a serious historical and theological study of the issues that separated Catholics from Lutherans. Hiring Hagen was a first step in that direction because he could provide Catholic students and faculty with insights into the tradition of Luther. Having a Lutheran theologian on a faculty of Catholic theology, it was hoped, would engage Catholic and Lutheran theologians in frank discussion about issues that united and divided them.

To study Luther with a Lutheran was something new in the context of American Catholicism. For the previous hundred and fifty years the American Catholic attitude towards Luther was primarily polemical, manifesting a Counter Reformation mentality that was characteristic of Catholicism throughout the Western world.

The remainder of this essay focuses upon the portrait and uses of Luther in the writings of some representative American Catholic religious leaders, demonstrating in the concrete what the changed atmosphere in the 1960s represented. The current state of scholarship tells us much more about American Protestant attitudes toward and movements against Catholicism than it does about Catholic attitudes toward Protestants in general and Luther or Lutherans in particular. Much more research needs to be done on this phenomenon in order to understand how Catholics of the past were shaped in their attitudes and understanding of Protestantism. This essay is only an outline that needs to be tested by much more detailed historical investigations of the sources.

From the time of John Carroll (1736–1815), the first Catholic bishop in the United States, until Gustave Weigel, S.J. (1906–64), the first well-known American Catholic ecumenical theologian and a *peritus* at the Second Vatican Council, the American Catholic view of Luther exhibited the intense religious hostility between Catholics and Protestants in the United States and fundamental theological disagreements over issues of sin, justification, and grace. The perceived disagreements were exaggerated because they were based upon inadequate, distorted or false information about Luther's actual positions, but they reflected the knowledge that most Catholics had about Luther and a Catholic emotional disposition that distanced Catholics from Lutherans.

Research for this essay suggests that throughout the period prior to the Second Vatican Council the view of Luther was, with an exception here and there, primarily negative. In the nineteenth century, however, that view was neither as negative as that of John Cochlaeus (1479–1552) in the sixteenth century nor as that of Heinrich Denifle (1844–1905) or Hartmann Grisar (1845–1932) in the twentieth century. Nineteenth-century American Catholics viewed Luther as the leader of the "Protestant Revolt," but his personal character and motives were not assaulted as they were in the works of Denifle and Grisar. No American Catholic until the 1950s, moreover, had an understanding of Luther that was based upon a personal or systematic study of Luther's sources; most of the information on Luther derived from secondary sources, primarily foreign (French and German). Only after World War II, furthermore, did Catholic attitudes towards Luther began to shift and show some respect for his life and thought, but that shift took place among only a few individual theologians. The shift was important, however, because it helped to shape a younger generation of scholars and was part of a larger movement that led to the Second Vatican Council and that anticipated the Church's future within the ecumenical movement. The Second Vatican Council brought about an epochal change that had surprising effects even on the preconciliar Catholic ecumenists who could not have anticipated the glacial transformation in the relations between Catholics and Protestants during and after the Council. Hagen was a part of this change.

American Catholic apologetical literature of the late eighteenth and early nineteenth centuries has only a few references to Luther but none of them assail his character or motives. This literature suggests that Catholics, while disagreeing with Luther, used him to support their own Catholic doctrines. Such a view was evident in the writings of John Carroll and John England (1786–1842), the first bishop of Charleston, South Carolina.

In 1784, John Carroll employed Luther to defend Catholic doctrines against what Carroll perceived to be the more radical Protestant departures from the Catholic understandings of the Scriptures and the Eucharist. In an apologetical tract Carroll quotes Luther as an authority that his opponent would surely accept on the insufficiency and obscurity of the Scripture. Luther acknowledged in the preface to his commentary on the Psalms, Carroll wrote, that, "It is a most audacious presumption in any one to say, that he understands every part even of one book of scripture."[3] Even Luther, Carroll implied, did not hold to a narrow view of the perspicuity of Scripture that some of his Protestant successors held. For Luther the Scripture was not entirely clear even to those who made it their life's study, but some things were eminently clear, as was the case in the biblical passages on the Eucharist. Carroll agreed with Luther that Christ's words "this is my body" at the Last Supper were not to be interpreted figuratively, as had been done by Ulrich Zwingli and others. Luther's view of the Eucharist was much closer to Catholic tradition on the real presence than was that of those in the Zwinglian tradition.

Like Carroll, other Catholic clergy in the early nineteenth century used Luther against their Protestant opponents, but they also could harangue Luther and Lutherans from the pulpit, as was the case in 1834 when Peter Henry Lemcke, O.S.B., pastor of the German Catholic parish of Holy Trinity in Philadelphia, verbally assaulted Luther and Lutherans in a Reformation Day Sunday sermon. After the sermon the German lay trustees went to the priest and told him, "as we wish to live in peace with our Protestant neighbors, we have come to tell you that you must not preach any more sermons like that in this Church."[4] Considering the reprimand an infringement

[3] "Scio esse impudentissimae temeritatis eum, qui audeat profiteri unum scripturae librum a se in omnibus partibus intellectum." Luth. Praef. In Psal. Ap. Bell. De R.P. 1.3.c 21. In *The John Carroll Papers*, ed. Thomas O'Brien Hanley, 3 vols. (Notre Dame, Ind.: University of Notre Dame Press, 1976), 1:139, see also, 129. Hereafter JCP. Carroll quoted from Robert Bellarmine's "De Verbi Dei Interpretatione," book 3, ch. 1, in *De Controversiis Christianae Fidei Adversus Huius Temporis Haereticos*, 4 vols. in 2 (Cologne: Bernard Gualtheri, 1619), 1:134. The quotation comes from Luther's preface to his *Operationes in Psalmos*, 1519–1521. See WA 5:23. Carroll followed Luther in the punctuation, but Bellarmine in the word order (reversing Luther's *scripturae librum*). I would like to thank Kenneth Hagen for locating the Luther quotation for me.

[4] On this, see Francis J. Hertkorn, *1789–1914. Retrospect of Holy Trinity Parish as a Souvenir of the One Hundred Twenty-Fifth Anniversary of the Foundation of the Church* (Philadelphia, 1914), 94.

of his evangelical freedom as a Catholic priest, Lemcke resigned from the parish, never to return. The German lay trustees, like most Catholic trustees of the period, wanted to live in harmony with their Protestant compatriots and considered verbal battery upon their religious feelings as violations of common civility.

John England took a more irenic approach to Luther and like Carroll used Luther against some American Lutherans on the doctrine of the Eucharist, but also made it clear that Luther was no apostle of religious liberty as some Lutherans and many in the American Protestant community had repeatedly asserted. In 1838, England became involved in the first public American Catholic-Lutheran theological debate. John Bachman, the Lutheran pastor in Charleston, South Carolina, and president of the General Synod of the Evangelical Lutheran Church in the United States, had preached a sermon before the General Synod in November of 1837, attempting, among other things, to separate the Lutheran understanding of the Eucharist from the Catholic understanding of transubstantiation.[5] England argued *á la* Jacques Bossuet (1627–1704) that the variety of opinions on the Eucharist among Protestants was itself an indication of their falsity, but then went on to assert that Luther's understanding of the Eucharist was much closer to the Catholic doctrine than to the Zwinglian because of Luther's adamant insistence upon the real, substantial, and corporeal presence of Christ in the Eucharist. The biblical evidence for the doctrine of the real presence was so overwhelming, England quoted Luther as saying, that Luther could not deny it even if he wanted to.[6] No matter how much pain it might bring to Bachman, Luther's position was much closer to Catholicism than to Zwinglianism. England argued, moreover, that many American Lutherans had a Zwinglian understanding of the Eucharist and had thus abandoned Luther's doctrine of the real presence.[7] Luther, it was true, denied transubstantiation (or that understanding of the mode of the real presence) but unlike Zwingli he had not denied the real presence. In fact, even a Catholic could subscribe to the tenth article of the *Augsburg Confession,* and especially Philipp Melanchthon's explanation of it, England maintained.[8]

[5] For accounts of the sermon and John England's response, see England's "Letters on the Catholic Doctrine of Transubstantiation," *The Works of the Right Rev. John England*, ed. Ignatius Aloysius Reynolds, 5 vols. (Baltimore: John Murphy, 1849): 1:347-474.

[6] Ibid., 362.

[7] Ibid., 365.

[8] Ibid., 364.

Although the doctrine of the Eucharist was the primary focus of the exchange between Bachman and England, another issue was central to England's concerns. Bachman charged that Catholics were in principle intolerant and asserted that Luther and Lutherans had supported religious liberty during the Protestant Reformation. Catholics, England countered, had no monopoly on intolerance. Luther had manifested the spirit of intolerance when he called the pope the antichrist, a "wolf," and one "possessed of an evil spirit." Luther also used the power of the state during the Peasants' War in 1525 to put down the rebellion and did not fail to use the power of the state to enforce reforms upon the Churches.[9]

The mixed American Catholic reviews and uses of Luther—to affirm Luther's positions in opposition to more radical Puritan or Reformed positions and to criticize him when Catholic identity was threatened—were most clearly evident in Orestes A. Brownson (1803–76), a convert from Unitarianism who became the most prolific of the antebellum Catholic apologists. An analysis of his complicated understanding of Luther in the thirty or more volumes of his writings between 1826 and 1876 cannot be undertaken here. Even a cursory review, however, reveals what some might call a very ambiguous view of Luther and his role in the history of Christianity.

Orestes A. Brownson.

Brownson stressed the negative side of Luther and the Protestant Reformation between 1844, the date of his conversion to Catholicism, and 1855—a period when Catholicism was under constant attack from American Nativists. The Catholic Church, he believed, needed a strong and clear assertion of its identity and a sharp separation from its enemies. During this period of his life, when he was

[9] Ibid., 439-40.

also trying to separate himself intellectually from his immediate Unitarian and Transcendentalist past, he viewed Luther as a revolutionary who had no justifiable reasons for reforming the life and doctrine of the Catholic Church. As a religious propagandist, moreover, Luther would not subject his novel doctrines to the judgment of the professional theologians of the schools, but instead solicited the support of the people. Luther knew, Brownson asserted, that his "novelties" would be rejected by the schools and therefore petitioned an unprofessional jury, the people, appealing "from science to ignorance." According to Brownson, the people, "if made arbiters, will always decide that what transcends their understanding is unintelligible, and that what is unintelligible is false, non-existent."[10] In 1855, furthermore, when reviewing Jean Marie Vincent Audin's (1793–1851) life of Luther, Brownson argued that Luther's central doctrine of justification by faith alone was a virtual rejection of dogmatic theology because for him faith was "simply a sentiment of the heart." Luther, too, did not create or introduce Protestantism; Protestantism was a heretical idea that manifested itself periodically in different forms throughout Christian history. Thus Protestantism was a movement in continuity with all previous heresies in the Christian Church.[11]

By contrast, from the mid-1850s to the end of the Civil War, a period when Brownson believed that the fundamental problem in American society was civil and social upheaval and that all members of society needed to band together to overcome the threat to the nation's unity and integrity, he emphasized the positive side of Luther and the Reformation. He could see that there was something more to Luther than he had presented in his earlier polemical pieces. Those Catholic historians and theologians[12] who simply assailed Luther or assigned some petty reason for the rise of Luther and the Protestant Reformation had simply missed the point that great effects stem from substantial causes. It was superficial to view the Reformation as a symptom of the pride, vanity, ambition, jealousies, rivalries, and sanctity of the monk Luther. Luther was "a man terribly in earnest, a genuine man, and no sham, as Carlyle would say."[13] Luther's trip to

[10] *The Works of Orestes A. Brownson*, ed. Henry F. Brownson, 20 vols. (Detroit: Thorndike Nourse, 1882–87), 19:272, see also 6:288. Hereafter *Works*.

[11] Ibid., 10:467.

[12] Brownson may have been thinking of John Cochlaeus and those who followed his lead in presenting scurrilous attacks upon Luther's character and in assigning petty motives of monkish envy and jealousy for the rise of Luther's reform. On Cochlaeus's views of Luther, see James Atkinson, *Martin Luther: Prophet to the Church Catholic* (Grand Rapids, Mich.: William B. Eerdmans, 1983), 7-9.

[13] *Works*, 9:219-20.

Rome, Brownson claimed in 1862, was the first occasion of his doubts about Catholic practices and doctrines and in fact that trip "quickened in him the spirit of the reformer" because of his "honest disgust of the abuses he everywhere encountered." Thus, in the beginning of the reform movement Luther was "moved by a sincere Christian spirit, an earnest love of truth, and an honest desire to advance the real interests of religion." Furthermore, he would not have resorted to separation from the Catholic Church had he been properly appreciated by the Roman court and the leaders in the Church. The fault for the separation was not all his. For at least a century before Luther other members of the Catholic Church had acknowledged the need for a reform in head and members, but the officials of the Church paid no attention to the appeals and complaints.[14] The Church's unwise resistance to reform ultimately drove the reformers into heresy and schism. Knowing how such assertions might jar American Catholic sensibilities, Brownson was quick to say that one could be a pious Catholic and still recognize that there was a "good motive and a Catholic thought" in the Reform movement and that it was, in fact, a Catholic movement for reform.[15] At the beginning of the reform Luther was a pious monk, an exemplary priest, and a learned theologian who had no "schismatic or heretical thought or intention." He intended to bring out prominently "certain elements of catholic truth not sufficiently insisted upon by contemporary Catholics."[16]

After the Civil War and the publication of Pius IX's *Syllabus of Errors* (1864) Brownson reverted back to his earlier negative view of Luther. The civil unity of the country was no longer threatened as it had been during the height of the abolitionist crusades and the Civil War. Pius IX's ultramontane papacy, moreover, was emphasizing with absolute clarity the differences between Catholic and Protestant understandings of the tradition. Within this historical context Brownson returned to a fiercely negative view of Luther and his importance within Christianity.

Although Brownson's perspectives on Luther appear on first reading to be contradictory, they are two sides of Luther that could not be denied in his eclectic philosophy.[17] Brownson never fully rejected

[14] Ibid., 12:538.

[15] Ibid., 12:565.

[16] Ibid., 12:581.

[17] The French eclectic Victor Cousin was the source of Brownson's philosophical eclecticism (that is, his understanding that truth can and must be found even in exaggerations of the truth, and that those who err have some fundamental truth that they are trying to protect).

either view. If he focused his attention on the early Luther he emphasized the Catholic nature of his movement; when he focused on the later Luther, the Luther particularly after 1530, he stressed the negative and "unconstitutional" nature of the reforms he carried out.[18] Rarely, however, does one find among American Catholics of the nineteenth century the kind of positive understanding of Luther that Brownson showed immediately prior to the Civil War. His negative views are more typical of the apologetical literature of the century.

During the nineteenth century American Catholics generally identified Luther as a religious revolutionary, but I know of nothing in American Catholic literature of the nineteenth century to match the passionate and unsubstantiated attacks on Luther's immorality or mental sickness that are found in the twentieth century works of the Dominican Church historian and Vatican archivist Heinrich Denifle and the Jesuit professor of Church history at Innsbruck Hartmann Grisar.[19] Both authors were given great attention in the early twentieth century because of their scholarly reputations. Many early twentieth-century American Catholic scholars tended to rely upon Denifle's acknowledged scholarship and followed his judgments on Luther's moral turpitude, and/or followed Grisar on Luther's psychological weaknesses.[20]

In the twentieth century the negative views of Denifle were evident in the Catholic diocesan priest Henry George Ganss's (1855–1912) article on Luther for the *Catholic Encyclopedia* (1910),[21] the most significant manifestation of American Catholic scholarship in the first half of the twentieth century. American Catholic readers of the *Encyclopedia* took their understanding of Luther from this source.

[18] On the unconstitutional and illegal reforms, see *Works*, 14: 456-59.

[19] On Denifle and Grisar, see Richard Stauffer, *Luther As Seen By Catholics* (London: Lutterworth Press, 1967), 13-19. Stauffer asserted, p. 16, n. 2, that Denifle's German work, *Luther und Luthertum* (1904), was not translated into English. On the contrary, see *Luther and Lutherdom from Original Sources*, trans. by Raymond Volz (Somerset, Ohio: Torch, 1917). Grisar's work—*Luther*, 3 vols. (Freiburg-im-Breisgau, 1911–12)—was translated as *Luther*, trans. by E. M. Lamond, 6 vols. (London: K. Paul, Trench, Trubner, 1913–16). The relatively early translation of these works indicates something of their perceived value within the apologetical tradition of American Catholicism. It would be interesting to trace out how they were used in the periodical literature produced by American Catholics.

[20] In the early twentieth century German Lutherans created a renaissance of historical scholarship on Luther in response to Denifle's supposedly objective historical interpretation of Luther—an interpretation that was based upon an abundant use of primary sources that gave his interpretation a degree of immediate credibility for Catholics who were not themselves students of the sources.

[21] *Catholic Encyclopedia* (1910), s.v. "Luther, Martin."

To give the article a sense of scholarly objectivity, Ganss informed his readers that he had relied primarily upon German Protestant authors as his authorities, and when he cited Catholic authorities he put an asterisk beside the authors' names. The lengthy article quoted selectively from the Protestant sources and from a few of Luther's own texts to verify the negative assessments of Luther found in the Catholic historian Denifle. Throughout the article, the early Luther is presented as a deeply disturbed personality, one with a brooding melancholy, scrupulosity, and morbidity that was susceptible to spiritual depression. Luther, Ganss asserted, would later attribute his own personal religious anxiety to the Church's teachings on good works. Thus the central doctrine of the Reformation was, in Ganss's view, the product of a "hypochondriac asceticism." Ganss failed to examine in any detail the substance of Luther's teachings and presented Luther as an isolated figure in the history of Christianity, neglecting to place Luther in the context of the late Middle Ages, except to agree with Denifle's judgment that Luther's "historical inaccuracies have been proved so flagrant, his conception of monasticism such a caricature, his knowledge of Scholasticism so superficial, his misrepresentation of medieval theology so unblushing, his interpretation of mysticism so erroneous, ... as to cast the shadow of doubt on the whole fabric of Reformation history."[22]

Luther's Reformation ideas were successful, however, primarily because he pleaded with the masses in the language of the populace when he could not win his scholarly battles in the academy through the regular process of disputation. His appeal, moreover, was to the "latent slumbering national aspirations" of the German princes and people. And by such solicitations the reformer became "the revolutionary." His physical ailments and his "congenital heritage of inflammable irascibility and uncontrollable rage" isolated him during the days of his decline and he ended his life in a "deluge of vituperation" against the Jews and the papacy.[23] From Ganss's perspective Luther was a tortured and unhappy soul whose own self-delusion operated as a driving force behind the Reformation. It was a moral and psychological analysis that isolated the individual from the wider historical currents of thought and culture, and that gave no insight into the theological discoveries Luther had made.

It is difficult to know in the present state of scholarship how widespread Ganss's view of Luther had become in early twentieth century American Catholicism. Similar negative views of Luther were

[22] Ibid., 448.
[23] Ibid., 456.

evident in Father Patrick F. O'Hare's (1848–1926) *The Facts About Luther* (1916), a popularized account of Luther's character and motives reminiscent of Denifle and Grisar. Luther, in O'Hare's view, was no religious reformer but "a deformer."[24]

By the mid- and late-1920s American Catholic scholarship turned in the direction of Neo-Scholastic or Neo-Thomist philosophy and theology.[25] Among other things the retrieval of the thought of Thomas Aquinas was perceived as a perfect antidote to the individualism and subjectivism of a modern world that had its origins in Luther and the Protestant Reformation. To some extent such a view was nothing new in American Catholicism. Throughout the nineteenth century, American Catholics had identified Protestantism in general with individualism and subjectivism. What was new in the early twentieth century was a significantly organized and institutionalized Neo-Scholastic offensive upon Luther that was propagated through philosophy departments in Catholic colleges and universities across the country, new Catholic scholarly organizations, and new periodicals of an emerging Neo-Scholasticism. Between the World Wars, American Catholic scholarship feasted on works like Jacques Maritain's *Trois Reformateurs: Luther-Descartes-Rousseau* (1925), which was quickly translated into English.[26] The three reformers, Maritain argued, advanced the modern movements of individualism and subjectivism in religion, philosophy, and morality. The Catholic Neo-Scholastic countermovement promoted the cause of the Church as the mystical body of Christ and the revival of a communal sense of the liturgy, the role of reason in philosophy and theology, and the status of objective moral norms (norms of the natural law) in morality. Supposedly Luther had started a domino deterioration that American Catholics in the twentieth century were in a position to counter with the help of a revived scholasticism. Such a view of Luther may well have been widespread in seminary education as well as in other institutions of higher education in the years between the wars, but much more evidence needs to be gathered before such a claim can be made with any assurance. Most American Catholic clergy educated during this

[24] (New York: Frederick Pustet, 1916), 330.

[25] On this revival, see Patrick W. Carey, ed., *American Catholic Religious Thought* (New York: Paulist Press, 1987), 46-62; William M. Halsey, *The Survival of American Innocence: Catholicism in the Era of Disillusionment, 1920–1940* (Notre Dame, Ind.: University of Notre Dame Press, 1980); and Arnold Sparr, *To Promote, Defend, and Redeem: The Catholic Literary Revival and the Cultural Transformation of American Catholicism, 1920–1960* (New York: Greenwood Press, 1990).

[26] *Three Reformers: Luther-Descartes-Rousseau* (New York: Charles Scribner's Sons, 1929).

period, it could be argued, were probably unaware of the Neo-Scholastic sources of their understanding of Luther and the Protestant Reformation.

The portrait of Luther that had developed between the World Wars continued after World War II, but an explicit American Catholic interest in the ecumenical movement began to emerge in the postwar years. Edward F. Hanahoe, S.A. (1913–), Gustave Weigel, S.J., and George Tavard, A.A. (1922–), represented three different approaches to a postwar Catholic ecumenical movement, each reflecting different assessments of and attitudes toward Luther. Hanahoe represented perhaps the dominant tradition in American Catholicism at the time. He was a priest of the Atonement (that is, a religious order that promoted since 1908 a prayer crusade for the reunion of Christians, the Chair of Unity Octave) and one of four North American theologians to receive a Vatican appointment as consultant to the Roman Secretariat for Promoting Christian Unity, established in 1960 prior to the Second Vatican Council.[27] Hanahoe had studied at the Catholic University of America under Francis J. Connell, C.SS.R., and Joseph Clifford Fenton, Neo-Scholastic theologians of the Roman School—a school whose theology was based primarily upon papal documents and the retrieval of scholastic sources through the sixteenth century scholastic commentators on Thomas Aquinas. Hanahoe's interest in the ecumenical movement emerged first in his dissertation, *Catholic Ecumenism: The Reunion of Christendom in Contemporary Papal Pronouncements*,[28] directed by Fenton. Hanahoe viewed Christian unity or ecumenism as did the papal documents he studied, namely as a return to Rome. He pointed to the futility of prior attempts at corporate ecclesial reunions and emphasized the role of individual and corporate conversions to Catholicism as the means of Christian unity. He also discerned in the Protestant ecumenical movement of the twentieth century the workings of divine Providence, revealing as it did the necessity of reunion. In 1959, he edited a book to commemorate the golden jubilee of the Chair of Unity Octave.[29] One of his own essays in that book, "*Vestigia Ecclesiae*: Their Meaning and Value,"[30] cited Grisar's *Luther* to support the idea that Luther himself upheld the idea of the necessity of a Church that was a concrete,

[27] The other appointees were Weigel, Tavard, and Gregory Baum, O.S.A., of Toronto.

[28] (Washington, D.C.: Catholic University of America Press, 1953).

[29] See *One Fold*, ed. Edward F. Hanahoe and Titus F. Cranny (Graymoor, Garrison, New York: Chair of Unity Apostolate, 1959).

[30] Ibid., 272-383.

historical reality, and not just an invisible body of believers.[31] In his arguments with the Anabaptists in 1522, moreover, Hanahoe claimed, Luther made it clear that he understood the necessity of the Church's divine mission even though his judgment was "a trifle blurred in its application."[32] Like some others in the past he cited the Luther who supported the Catholic side of the tradition.

Return to Rome, although the dominant motif in the postwar Catholic ecumenical movement, was not the only Catholic approach to ecumenism. A few American Catholic voices spoke out in the postwar period calling for a fresh approach to Protestantism and a renewed understanding of Luther and his reform movement. The war had demonstrated to some that the fundamental threat to world order was Communism and secularism, not other religious traditions. Even before the war an unprecedented Catholic understanding of Luther and the Reformation was being fostered in Germany particularly through the scholarship of Joseph Lortz (1887–1975), a Church historian at Münster (1935–47). In 1939 and 1940 he published his magisterial two-volume history of *Die Reformation in Deutschland.* That book reversed the picture of Luther created by Denifle and Grisar and presented him as *homo religiosus*. Lortz's scholarship was not widely available in the United States during the war but after the war his approach had some impact here and there upon a few Catholic scholars.[33] One of them was Gustave Weigel, S.J., a professor of ecclesiology at the Jesuit theologate in Woodstock, Maryland.[34] Weigel became perhaps the best known among the American Catholic preconciliar ecumenists. He spent much of his teaching and publishing career trying to understand American Protestants, entered into dialogue with them on numerous occasions, and manifested a spirit of openness that many Protestants had not experienced from Catholic theologians in the past. In 1953, Weigel was on a tour of Europe for the State Department. In Germany he met Lortz and

[31] Ibid., 310 n. 55.

[32] Ibid., 329 n. 81.

[33] The book was not translated into English until after the Second Vatican Council. *The Reformation in Germany*, 2 vols. (New York: Herder and Herder, 1968). A book and two articles by Lortz, however, were published in English in the late 1930s and 1940s: *History of the Church*, trans. Edwin G. Kaiser (Milwaukee: Bruce Publishing, 1938, and subsequent editions); "Reformation theses put forward as a friendly approach for oecumenical conversations," *Eastern Churches Quarterly* 7 (1947): 76-91; and "The Catholic Attitude Towards the Reformation," *Oratre Fratres* 23 (1948–49): 455-61.

[34] On Weigel, see Patrick W. Collins, *Gustave Weigel: A Pioneer of Reform* (Collegeville, Minn.: The Liturgical Press, 1992).

informed him about the ecumenical situation in the United States. Lortz told him that it was a "disgrace and a sin" that Catholics and others were not working for Christian unity in the United States. He asked Weigel, "Why don't you do something?"[35]

Weigel spent the remainder of his life promoting a mutual understanding of Protestants and Catholics in the United States, but he remained pessimistic about the prospects for unity because of the great diversity of religious traditions in the United States and because of the wide gap that separated them doctrinally and theologically. Still, he felt that the task at hand was to change attitudes and to promote understanding; if unity was to come it would come through God's grace and in God's own time. His own focus was primarily on the Reformed tradition because he saw that tradition as the dominant religious tradition in the United States. Warren Quanbeck, a Lutheran theologian from Luther Seminary in St. Paul, Minnesota, considered Weigel an open person but one whose ideas were fairly fixed in the scholastic mode of thought, making it difficult for him to understand and truly appreciate other religious perspectives. In particular, Quanbeck believed that Weigel's knowledge of Luther and of the Lutheran tradition was "'old hat' and filled with clichés." To Quanbeck Weigel seemed "emotionally negative" toward Luther.[36] That may well have been the case, and given the kind of education that Catholic clergy received in the seminary there is little reason to believe that he could have had anything other than the negative emotions that Quanbeck thought he saw in Weigel. Nonetheless, Weigel was not closed to Lutheran scholarship and in fact studied current trends among Lutheran theologians, but he did not have much specific first-hand knowledge of Luther's works and thought. He was aware of the Luther Renaissance of the early twentieth century and was particularly fond of the Lundensian theology of Gustav Aulén and Anders Nygren, judging that their thought revealed that "There is a strong tendency to interpret the Lutheran message in the light of the total Christian reality, and therefore there is a serious meditation [*sic*] of Catholic substance in Lutheranism."[37]

Weigel helped to change attitudes of Catholics toward other religious traditions. His published works had that effect on me in the

[35] Ibid., 174.

[36] Ibid., 190.

[37] "A Survey of Protestant Theology in Our Day," in Catholic Theological Society of America, *Proceedings* 6-8 (1951–53), *Proceedings of the Eighth Annual Convention of the Catholic Theological Society of America* (Baltimore, June 22–24, 1953), 68.

late 1950s and early 1960s when I first read some of his works and then became part of a theological dialogue between students of St. John's Seminary in Collegeville, Minnesota, and students at Luther Seminary in St. Paul. Many others of my generation would have been similarly affected prior to and during the Second Vatican Council.

George Tavard, A.A., an émigré French theologian who taught at Assumption College in Worcester, Massachusetts, in the mid 1950s and from 1959 to 1966 at Mount Mercy College (now Carlow College) in Pittsburgh, Pennsylvania, was another of the preconciliar ecumenists whose knowledge and appreciation of Luther transcended that of those in the American tradition who were educated in the Neo-Scholastic tradition.[38] Educated at Lyons, France, and taught, among others, by Henri de Lubac in the 1940s, Tavard had been influenced by the historical more than the scholastic method of theology. Like others in the *nouvelle théologie* tradition, he was interested in renewing theology by retrieving what was valuable and forgotten or covered over by the scholastic tradition of theology. His method for doing theology differed considerably from theologians like Weigel who used the deductive methods of scholastic theology. Like the Germans of the Lortz school of research, Tavard tried to rehabilitate Luther in Catholic circles after decades of polemics upon his character and motives.

George H. Tavard, A.A.

[38] On Tavard, see Marc R. Alexander, *Church and Ministry in the Works of G. H. Tavard* (Leuven: University Press, 1994), and Kenneth Hagen, ed., *The Quadrilog: Tradition and the Future of Ecumenism: Essays in Honor of George H. Tavard* (Collegeville, Minn.: The Liturgical Press, 1994).

According to Richard Stauffer and other scholars who have followed his lead, Tavard opened up to the English speaking world the new research on Luther in his *The Catholic Approach to Protestantism* (1954).[39] Although Tavard presents Luther as one who lacked moderation, he also indicates that the issues Luther was trying to raise for the whole Church were legitimate issues that the Church's leadership failed to acknowledge. Luther was not an isolated phenomenon in the sixteenth century and had the Church responded to him more effectively Luther's lack of moderation might have been curtailed by the faith of the universal Church. In 1959, Tavard published *Holy Writ or Holy Church: The Crisis of the Protestant Reformation*,[40] a work that focused upon the *sola scriptura* issue within the Church. Tavard hoped that his research on this issue would advance the ecumenical movement. He put the issue of Scripture and tradition, as understood during the Protestant Reformation and at Trent, into a historical context, arguing in effect that Luther's *sola scriptura* position was inconsistent with the Church's traditional understanding of the organic and synthetic relationship between Scripture, tradition and the Church. "In the person of Martin Luther the cleavage between Scripture and tradition became irreconcilable."[41]

Although critical of Luther's lack of a "sense of proportion" in his understanding of the relationship of Scripture and Church, Tavard maintained that one could understand his case with sympathy because he suffered the "tragic fate" of living in a period of theological confusion and in a Church that needed reform. Tavard argued that Luther's understanding of the relationship of Scripture and tradition was incompatible with the Catholic understanding, but in *Protestantism* (1959) he acknowledged that there was no incompatibility between Luther's doctrine of justification and the Catholic tradition. Luther's doctrine was justifiably opposed to a rampant semi-Pelagianism in the sixteenth century Catholic Church.[42] In subsequent years, Tavard developed a much more appreciative attitude toward Luther than was manifested in his 1959 works. He declared in 1983, for example, that Luther was "right" on the doctrine of justification, a doctrine which in *Holy Writ* Tavard consid-

[39] *Luther As Seen by Catholics*, 63. Tavard's French original of that work was entitled *A la rencontre du Protestantisme* (Paris: Le Centurion, 1954).

[40] (New York: Harper and Brothers, 1959). Chapter six was entitled, "The Glad Tidings of Dr. Luther," 80-98.

[41] Ibid., 80.

[42] See (New York: Hawthorn Books, 1959), 30. *Protestantism* was a translation of *Le Protestantisme* (Paris: Librairie Arthème Fayard, 1958).

ered dangerously narrow when used as an exclusive interpretive principle of the Bible. Luther's understanding of that doctrine was a legitimate interpretation of the Catholic tradition and a key to the ecumenical movement.[43]

Unlike Weigel and perhaps many others involved in the incipient Catholic ecumenical movement during the 1950s, Tavard had a first-hand acquaintance with Luther's texts and quoted from them consistently to argue his points, interpreting them within the larger historical framework of a developing theological tradition. In this, Tavard was a very rare phenomenon in American Catholicism. His attitudes toward Luther and the Protestant Reformation, moreover, do not appear to have been shaped in his early education by the works of Denifle and Grisar. He inherited a French post-World War openness to Protestantism that was not always appreciated by his fellow American Catholics, especially by those like Hanahoe with some claim to interest in the Catholic ecumenical movement of the 1950s.

By the time Kenneth Hagen was hired at Marquette, much had changed on the ecumenical scene and the inchoate ecumenical stirrings among American Catholics of the 1950s seemed like cold polemics when compared to the new attitudes produced by the Second Vatican Council, the new attention of Catholic scholars to the sources of the Protestant Reformation, and the willingness of Catholics to study with Protestant scholars to learn the Protestant tradition from those whose scholarship was shaped by that tradition. One manifestation of the new circumstances was the publication of the article on Martin Luther for the *New Catholic Encyclopedia* in 1967,[44] an implicit disavowal of the earlier article on Luther in the 1910 *Catholic Encyclopedia.* That article—written by a Catholic Reformation scholar, John P. Dolan, professor of history at the University of Notre Dame and author of an irenic *History of the Reformation: A Conciliatory Assessment of Opposite Views*[45]—argued, for example, that no evidence existed for prior Catholic assertions that Luther's family's poverty "created an abnormal atmosphere" for his early development. It was absolutely absurd, moreover, to contend that Luther was a "crass ignoramus," and it was no longer tenable to hold, as Denifle did, that Luther was an "ossified Ockhamite." To question Luther's religious motives for entering the monastery, furthermore, did Luther

[43] *Justification: An Ecumenical Study* (New York: Paulist, 1983), 107-8, 110.
[44] *New Catholic Encyclopedia* (1967), s.v. "Luther, Martin," 1085-91.
[45] (New York: Desclee Co., 1965).

a fundamental injustice. Dolan instead focused upon Luther's religious and theological discoveries and admitted the scandalous and immoral simoniacal acts associated with the sale of indulgences. Dolan's article recognizes precisely what religious and doctrinal issues were at stake in the Reformation, a view that was not evident in the earlier twentieth or nineteenth century views of Luther.

Luther and the Protestant Reformation have received a sympathetic reading in the American Catholic scholarly community since the Second Vatican Council. Kenneth Hagen's published scholarship and teaching have contributed much to that new reading. As a member of the Lutheran-Catholic bilateral conversations in the United States for over a decade, moreover, Hagen has helped to advance the cause of mutual understanding between Catholics and Lutherans in this country. Among the major accomplishments of that dialogue was a document hammered out over a number of years on the doctrine of justification. On 31 October 1999, Reformation Sunday, representatives of the Vatican and the Lutheran World Federation signed a mutually agreed-upon statement on justification that was the culmination of thirty years of discussion between Catholics and Lutherans throughout the world. That historic agreement will serve Catholics and Lutherans for generations to come as they enter ever more deeply into the unity that Christ intends for his Church. Hagen has been a significant part of these events of the last thirty years, and we at Marquette hope to carry on his legacy by emphasizing the mutually agreed-upon doctrine that we are justified by faith in the grace of Christ.

LUTHER AND ANSELM: SAME ATONEMENT, DIFFERENT APPROACH

BURNELL F. ECKARDT, JR.

Among many twentieth century scholars who wish to regard the thought of Martin Luther as being in some sense akin to their own, there has been a clear tendency to pass negative criticism on St. Anselm of Canterbury (1033-1109) for his presentation of the atonement as vicarious satisfaction. Largely for this reason Anselm has been caricatured as a legalist emphasizing justice over love. John McIntyre once lamented that "no major Christian thinker has suffered quite so much as St. Anselm from the hit-and-run tactics of historians of theism and soteriology."[1] At the same time, particularly those Luther scholars rejecting the "Anselmic" vicarious satisfaction have shown a tendency to portray Luther as one whose views were likewise irreconcilable with those of Anselm. Ever since the nineteenth century, certain influential scholars could always be found who have wrenched Luther and the vicarious satisfaction apart, condemning Anselm, whom they call the father of the vicarious satisfaction, while praising Luther as their own father. Having examined both Anselm and Luther from the standpoint in particular of their grammar, I do not believe the lines have been drawn on the right canvas, however. The purpose of this essay is to demonstrate that in his christological thought Luther is quite Anselmic, but that it is their different manners of expression which are irreconcilable. The credit for my own understanding of what I consider to be this most important factor in the history of Christian thought belongs to Doctor Kenneth Hagen, my own teacher, colleague, and friend, for whose *Festschrift* I am pleased to offer this token.

ANSELM, LUTHER, AND THE ATONEMENT QUESTION

The debate over Anselm and Luther began in the nineteenth century, when Johann Christian Konrad von Hofmann (1810-1877) declared his opposition to what he referred to as the "orthodox doctrine of vicarious satisfaction," calling it biblicism and offering his

[1] John McIntyre, *St. Anselm and His Critics* (Edinburgh: Oliver & Boyd, 1954), 2.

own alternative, a *heilsgeschichtliche* theology.[2] Hofmann declared that "the saving truth which the Scripture proclaims authoritatively to the Church does not consist in a series of doctrinal propositions," by which he meant doctrinal formulations having to do with the vicarious satisfaction, "but rather in the fact that Jesus has mediated a connection between God and mankind."[3] For Hofmann, the Bible is not "a textbook teaching conceptual truths but rather a document of a historical process," that is, *Heilsgeschichte*.[4] The return volley came from Theodosius Harnack (1817-1889) who, on behalf of his "orthodox" Lutheran colleagues, rejected Hofmann's views and in so doing attempted to show Luther's adherence to the vicarious satisfaction.[5] Hofmann responded by working to demonstrate that Luther cannot be associated unambiguously with the doctrine of vicarious satisfaction.[6] Hofmann quoted Luther at great length, in an attempt to embarrass the orthodox.[7] He was supported by Albrecht Ritschl (1822-1889), who took the matter yet a step further, not only challenging Harnack over Luther,[8] but also now attacking St. Anselm of Canterbury (1033-1109), who was (and is) rather universally regarded as the first to lay out in systematic terms the idea of atonement as vicarious satisfaction.[9] Ritschl claimed that in Anselm the glory of God and the justice of God are incompatible, since the glory of God puts him above man while the justice of God makes him man's equal; but satisfaction holds only for equals.[10] Therefore, said Ritschl, either Anselm should adhere to the notion of the glory of God and insist that God punish all sinners and allow no satisfaction, or lay emphasis only upon the possibility of satisfaction, thus forcing Anselm's famous disjunction *aut poena aut satisfactio* upon the author himself.[11]

[2] See Gerhard Forde, *The Law-Gospel Debate: An Interpretation of Its Historical Development* (Minneapolis: Augsburg, 1969), 3.

[3] Johann Christian Konrad von Hofmann, *Interpreting the Bible*, translated from the German by Christian Preus (Minneapolis: Augsburg, 1959), 76.

[4] Ibid., 204.

[5] Theodosius Harnack, *Luthers Theologie mit besonderer Beziehung auf seine Versöhnungs - und Erlösungslehre* (first edition, Erlangen: Andreas Deichert, 1886, reprint edition, Amsterdam: Rodop. 1969), 339-350.

[6] Forde (1969), 57f.

[7] Forde (1969), 63, quotes Hofmann.

[8] Ibid., 81.

[9] Albrecht Ritschl, *The Christian Doctrine of Justification and Reconciliation*, translated and edited by H. R. Mackintosh and A. B. Macaulay (Clifton, New Jersey: Reference Book Publishers. Ritschl, 1966), 4-7.

[10] Ibid., 263f.

[11] McIntyre, 90.

In the twentieth century the debate was revived when *Christus Victor*, the monograph by the Swedish Lutheran Gustaf Aulén, was published in English, in 1931. Aulén's division of the Christian views on the atonement according to their imagery in interpretation of it has gained considerable renown, enough to suggest that his work may be considered a twentieth-century classic.[12] At one end of Aulén's spectrum is what he called the "Latin" view, characterized especially by Anselm, and at the other end is the so-called "classical" view, for which Aulén claimed the support of Irenaeus and Martin Luther.[13] The division of atonement theories along these lines labels the Anselmic, or Latin, view as the "legal satisfaction" view.

> The Latin idea of penance provides the sufficient explanations of the Latin doctrine of the Atonement. Its root idea is that man must make an offering or payment to satisfy God's justice; this is the idea that is used to explain the work of Christ.[14]

Like Hofmann and Ritschl before him, Aulén contrasted this against his understanding of what he now labeled the classical view, which interprets the atonement in terms of a cosmic battle in which the forces of good win victory over the forces of evil.[15] Thus was the debate revived and with it once again the idea of a fundamental theological separation of Luther from Anselm.

In the early 1970's Jürgen Moltmann rejected traditional christological formulations altogether in favor of his radical kenotic Christology.[16] Moltmann too made bold to contend for the support

[12] Gustaf Aulén, *Christus Victor: an Historical Study of the Three Main Types of the Idea of the Atonement*, translated by A. G. Hebert, with forward by Jaroslav Pelikan (New York: Macmillan. 1969). In his introduction, Jaroslav Pelikan makes reference to the work as "a modern classic" (xi).

[13] Without debating whether Aulén has overstated his case, it is nonetheless clear that the making of distinctions in atonement theories along the lines he has put forward is certainly a valid exercise, even if one does not wish to make these distinctions in as sharp and mutually exclusive terms as he has.

[14] Aulén, 82.

[15] "The Word of God, who is God Himself, has entered in under the conditions of sin and death, to take up the conflict with the powers of evil and carry it through to decisive victory. This has brought to pass a new relation between God and the world; atonement has been made. The mercy of God has delivered men from the doom which rested upon them" (Aulén, 32).

[16] See David P Scaer, "Theology of Hope," in *Tensions in Contemporary Theology*, ed., Stanley N. Gundry and Alan F. Johnson (Chicago: Moody, 1976, 197-236), 213. See also my "Luther and Moltmann: The Theology of the Cross" in *Concordia Theological Quarterly* 49 (1985): 22-25.

of Luther,[17] while dismissing Anselm's terms as radical.[18] Indeed some of Moltmann's favorite terms—crucified God, theology of the cross—have been borrowed from Luther. Although Moltmann is not entirely uncritical of the Reformer,[19] it is nonetheless clear that he wished to be seen as one whose own thought was begotten by Luther's.

F. W. Dillistone's 1968 study on the atonement (republished in 1984) likewise cast aspersions on Anselm's view while praising Luther. Echoing the earlier contentions of Sir Richard Southern, Dillistone saw the *Cur Deus homo* as the product of a medieval culture characterized by feudalism and monasticism, giving Anselm no credit for the ability to take from his images without being subject to them. The *Cur Deus homo* is only impressive, he claimed, "if set in the midst of medieval feudalistic conceptions of authority, of sanctions and of reparation."[20] And although Martin Luther is likewise seen as a child of his times, he is likened nonetheless to none other than St. Paul himself.[21] Luther's struggles are praised as a reaffirmation of his identity "within the pattern of the Cross."[22] In 1985 Joseph Burgess also claimed that the "satisfaction" theory of atonement, though not originating with Anselm, is nonetheless not compatible with justification by faith.[23] Likewise Gerhard Forde in the dogmatics text now in use in seminaries of the Evangelical Lutheran Church in America clearly shows his own bias, taking great pains to demonstrate Anselm's great deficiency when compared to Luther. Forde asserts that Anselm erred in pitting justice against mercy, a complaint coming near to Ritschl's contention.[24]

So the debate has transpired for well over a century, yet without much consideration at all of a difference between Anselm and Luther at a level beneath the level of theological substance, a difference which contributes largely to the perception of differences in theology where

[17] Jürgen Moltmann, *The Crucified God: the Cross of Christ as the Foundation and Criticism of Christian Theology*, translated by R. A. Wilson and John Bowden (New York: Harper & Row, 1974), 70f et passim.

[18] Ibid., 260, 261.

[19] Ibid., 72f.

[20] F. W. Dillistone, *The Christian Understanding of Atonement* (London: SCM, 1984), 193.

[21] Ibid., 370-76.

[22] Ibid., 376.

[23] Joseph Burgess, "Rewards, but in a Very Different Sense" in *Justification by Faith: Lutherans and Catholics in Dialogue VII*, ed., H. George Anderson, T. Austin Murphy and Joseph A. Burgess (Minneapolis: Augsburg, 1985), 98.

[24] Gerhard Forde, "The Work of Christ" in *Christian Dogmatics*, vol. 2, ed. Carl E. Braaten and Robert W. Jenson (Philadelphia: Fortress, 1984), 23.

they do not exist. The remainder of this essay is devoted to demonstrating first the fundamental theological agreements of Anselm and Luther, and second to a consideration of their differences in approach to the theological task, differences whose significance ought not be underestimated, but which appear to have been ignored in the heat of battle over the vicarious satisfaction.

Theology in Anselm and Luther: Not the Heart of the Difference

The Anselmic Luther

In the first place, we will do well to heed the caution that Anselm's grammar is separated from Luther's by over four centuries. Such a span, coming before the invention of the printing press, should not be underestimated. Differences of expression would have to be significant even among those whose common scholarly tongue is Latin, to say nothing of the differences in native tongue. A chief proponent of this caution is Kenneth Hagen. In my estimation, Hagen's careful and painstaking insistence on the reading of primary manuscripts without trusting the presuppositions of the editors of those manuscripts, is a critical lesson which scholars would do well to heed.[25]

Secondly, the presuppositions of critics need also to be taken into account, another salient feature of Hagen's approach. While it is true that no historian can be fully objective, and thus no history without its biases, it is also true that objectivity in historical writing and evaluation is a feature which ought to be sought after. Some historians seek to arrest their own presuppositions when approaching the task; others do not. Without passing judgment on any, it may be said that a simple acknowledgment of this truth is key to the gaining of trustworthy insight.

It is evident to me that the scholars who opt for a serious christological chasm between Luther and Anselm seriously misread them both on some crucial points. McIntyre's lament of hit-and-run tactics rings true especially for two critical points: first, that regarding the substantial meaning of the vicarious satisfaction, Luther is Anselmic, and second, regarding Christology, Anselm is, *avant le mot*, Lutheran.

[25] This was a consistent thread in the lectures of Kenneth Hagen at Marquette University, during the years I was privileged to be his graduate student, 1988-1991.

It is patently incorrect to say that Luther's theology does not deal with the Anselmian theme of vicarious satisfaction. His manner of discourse certainly differs from that of St. Anselm, a fact which has thrown some researchers off the trail while abetting the preconceptions of others, but the substance of his thought is as bound to the theme of substitution as is that of the latter. For Luther, justification by faith is the *Hauptartikel* of the Christian faith[26] and can be expressed in an abundance of images, all of which are generally quite compatible with Anselm's thought. Luther's discourse on justification most frequently speaks in terms of the *fröhlicher Wechsel*—the happy exchange—between Christ and the sinner. The bride/bridegroom metaphor was a favorite image of Luther's,[27] being for him a most fitting vehicle for his explanation of this happy exchange between Christ and the Christian. As bride and bridegroom share all things in common, so also do the Church and her Christ. "We are in Him, and He is in us. This Bridegroom, Christ, must be alone with His bride in His private chamber." [28] The Church as a bride is "a lily among thorns."[29] In the exchange, the bride receives all good, and the Bridegroom all evil; she receives from Christ grace, life, and salvation; that is, all that which Christ has earned by his atonement; as Christ receives in exchange her sin, death, and damnation in his passion.

> The believing soul can boast of and glory in whatever Christ has as though it were its own, and whatever the soul has Christ claims as his own. Let us compare these and we shall see inestimable benefits. Christ is full of grace, life, and salvation. The soul is full of sins, death, and damnation. Now let faith come between them and sins, death, and damnation will be Christ's, while grace, life, and salvation will be the soul's; for if Christ is a bridegroom, he must take upon himself the things which are his bride's and bestow upon her the things that are his.[30]

Some have misunderstood the *fröhlicher Wechsel* as immature Luther, with the mistaken premise that it occurs through the mystical presence of Christ, *propter Christum in nobis*, which would create

[26] WA 40¹: 441; LW 26: 282.

[27] Other references, in addition to the quotation below, for Luther's use of this metaphor can be found in WA 22:339,9-20; WA 22:337,29-34; WA 57³:224,13-15 (LW 29:226); WA 7:597,13ff (LW 21:351).

[28] WA 40¹:241,13-14; LW 26:137. Galatians commentary (1535).

[29] WA 2, 604:36; LW 27:391. Galatians commentary (1519).

[30] WA 7:54,36-55,4; LW 31:351.

a tension with forensic justification.[31] That is, if the exchange is mystical, then it becomes in effect akin to the scholastic *gratia infusa*, according to which the righteousness by which the Christian stands before God has been made inherent in the Christian's nature. But Luther's preference for the *fröhlicher Wechsel* cannot be called supportive of this position; rather, for him the exchange is actually quite forensic. Christ need be no more mystically present with the soul for the exchange of righteousness to occur than the soul need be mystically present with the crucified Christ for the exchange of sin to occur. In his 1535 Galatians commentary, Luther declares that sin is not imputed to the Christian, because "His righteousness is yours; your sin is His."[32] Christ is wrapped up in our sins,[33] and sin was imposed upon him.[34] Luther goes as far as to say that Christ clothed himself in our person, laid our sin upon his shoulders, and said, I have committed the sins which all men have committed.[35] Thus Christ became guilty of all laws, curses, sins, etc., because he "stepped in between."[36] Thus all doubts may be laid to rest in the knowledge that "if I am a sinner and err, He is righteous and cannot err."[37] Luther's sermons are also full of this exchange. The conscience may rejoice "if you ... recognize the Lamb of God carrying your sin."[38] Christ is the Savior come from heaven, who has "taken upon himself our sins and made himself a sacrifice to the everlasting wrath of God which we had merited by our sins."[39] For Luther, the *fröhlicher Wechsel* occurs only by imputation; indeed, what Anselm calls vicarious satisfaction Luther calls *fröhlicher Wechsel.*

[31]This has contributed largely, in my estimation, to some misunderstandings which have in turn produced the Joint Declaration on the Doctrine of Justification signed by the Roman Catholic Church and the Churches of the Lutheran World Federation in 1999.

[32]WA 40[1]:369,25; LW 26:233.

[33]WA 40[1]:434,26-28; LW 26:278

[34]WA 40[1],436:18; LW 26:279.

[35]WA 40[1]:442,31-443,14; LW 26:283f.

[36]WA 40[1]:452,14; LW 26:290.

[37]WA 40[1]:578,30-31; LW 26:379.

[38]AP 1:133; StL 11:117.

[39]AP 3:448; StL 11:1188.

Anselm of Canterbury.

The Lutheran Anselm

There can be little question about the high Christology of Luther among those who have studied his thought. Jesus Christ is God, emphatically. He is the full incarnation and revelation of God, and since he is the full incarnation of God, God can be found nowhere else, and there is "no other God than this Man Jesus Christ."[40] So consistently does Luther aver this that we may consider it as being as important to Luther as justification by faith, and a hallmark of Luther.[41] Luther's stress on the full divinity and honor of the man Jesus is consistent throughout his life, and unexcelled. Not only does Luther follow the Chalcedonian tradition of calling Mary *mater Dei*;[42] he unpacks this: God is laid in a manger, Mary makes broth for God, God suffers, and God dies. Luther follows completely Augustine's declaration that "the Father, in sending the Son, sent his other self."[43] Siggins sees the strongest stress in Luther's doctrine of Christ to be the unity of Christ's person.[44] He quotes Luther's assertion that Christ's being in the Father is "the chiefest article and cardinal point" of Christian faith, to support this contention.[45] Luther gives us a sense that the facts of the atonement are not as necessary to stress as that which makes it the wonderful work it is, namely, the truth that God himself is the one who does this work. It is in this truth that the significance of the atonement lies for Luther, who prefers continually to emphasize the incarnation when dealing with soteriology. This is likely to be a major contributing factor to the erroneous conclusion many have drawn

[40]LW 26:29; WA 40:78. See also WA 20:727:6; 30[3]:132,23; 35:456,14; 31[1]:63; 40[2]:256,20; 45:550,13; 45:589,1; 46:763,2.

[41]So Ian Siggins, *Martin Luther's Doctrine of Christ* (New Haven, Connecticut: Yale University Press: 1970), 79.

[42]For example, StL 11: 436; AP 2: 25.

[43]Augustine, *Tract. in ev. Ioh.*, XIV, 11; quoted in Siggins, 81.

[44]Siggins, 227,232.

[45]Ibid., 85; WA 45:589,25.

that Luther does not accept the vicarious satisfaction. Luther's points of stress are always those generally considered more germane to Christology proper than to the redemptive work of Christ. The impression derived from this is that Luther cannot bring himself to do analysis on the work in abstract because he is too impressed with the reality of the incarnation in it. What makes the work of Christ truly wondrous is the fact that this Man Christ is fully and bodily God, making the work that of God himself and no one less. In calling Christ Victor over sin, death, and damnation, Luther means to say concurrently that this Christ is God by nature.[46] Discussions of the source and cause of our salvation tend to end with Christ himself, rather than with the Father: "Christ Himself is our Reconciliation, Righteousness, Peace, Life, and Salvation."[47] For Luther, Christ is the "quintessence" of God's relation to man.[48] Luther is so consistent in his expressions of the divinity of Christ as to lead his readers to the understanding that even when he does not say so explicitly, he wants it understood.

A basic christological agreement between Anselm and Luther is to be expected in view of the appreciation both had for their Western tradition, particularly for Augustine. That Anselm's Christology was as Chalcedonian as Luther's is beyond legitimate dispute, although Aulén contended that for Anselm, the work of Christ is not God's from start to finish. Rather, he insisted, because Anselm places so much emphasis on the necessity that the satisfaction be made by man, there is no real need in his thought for the incarnation at all, but only that God provide that Man who would be able to make sufficient satisfaction.[49] But Aulén has misread Anselm. What Aulén tried to show is that Anselm is guilty of failing to answer his own question: *cur Deus homo?* The satisfaction must be made by man, says Anselm, because it is man who has sinned; but there is really no corollary requirement here, in terms of the claims of justice, that the satisfaction be made by God; at least that is what Aulén's contention assumes. Therefore, he concludes, the necessity for the atonement is in effect removed. God must provide the sacrifice, but not necessarily *be* the sacrificial victim—so Aulén charges that Anselm has not proven the necessity for the incarnation. But Aulén's suggestion that for Anselm the work of Christ is not God's work from start to finish

[46]WA 40[1]:441,31-33; LW 26: 283.

[47]WA 40[1]:261,26-27; LW 26:151.

[48]WA 46:637,31; LW 22:17, cf. n90; WA 33:19,27; LW 23:16. Siggins (85) contends that quintessence is a better translation of *ausbund*, a rare term, than "exemplar" as rendered by LW 22:117, cf. n90, and LW 23:16.

[49]Aulén, 86f.

can claim only the support of Aulén's own mistaken inferences. The primary difference is simply that Anselm prefers to speak "from above;" that is, when dealing with the Person of Christ, he starts with his divinity and moves to his humanity. Luther, on the other hand, proceeds from Christ's humanity to his divinity. This is a reflection of their respective perceptions of the theological task, which are discussed below. Suffice it to say regarding Christology that Anselm's speaking "from above" appears to me to resonate perfectly with his being first among the scholastics, and Luther's speaking "from below" appears to resonate perfectly with his consistent attention to the divinity of the Man Jesus Christ.

Anselm declares, "the Lord Jesus Christ, we say, is true God and true man, one person in two natures, and two natures in one person."[50] In Anselm's explanations and defense of the Trinity, it is easy to see his affirmation of full divinity of the Second Person. In the *Monologion*, the full divinity of the Son is emphasized repeatedly. The Son is the essence of the Father, the strength of the Father, the wisdom of the Father,[51] the understanding, wisdom, knowledge, and cognition of the Father.[52] Indeed, "the Father and the Son and their Spirit exist equally in one another,"[53] and therefore "the Son considered by himself ... is the Supreme Being."[54] The *De Incarnatione Verbi* is Anselm's most polemical work, having been written to defend the doctrine of the Trinity against Roscelin of Compigne, and in it Anselm is just as clear, in just the same sort of terms: the Son, he says repeatedly, is God, and this same Son, "through unity of person, is man."[55] The Son is Jesus; that is, "both God and man, Son of God and Son of the Virgin."[56] Anselm nowhere denies this; as we have seen, Aulén bases his claims exclusively on Anselm's stress on the humanity of the Christ, but nowhere does Anselm indicate that he means thereby to deny Christ's divinity. Anselm is as little vulnerable to a charge of Arianism as Aulén would be to a charge of docetism,

[50]CDH I:8; S II, 59:20-22. The following are abbreviations used in this essay for Anselm's works: CDH, *Cur Deus homo* (Why God Became Man); DIV, *Epistola de Incarnatione Verbi* (The Incarnation of the Word); M, *Monologion* (A Soliloquy); P, *Proslogion* (An Address); S, *Sancti Anselmi Opera Omnia*. Schmitt edition (Edinburgh, 1946).

[51]M 45; S I, 61:26-7.

[52]M 46; S I, 62:20-1,23.

[53]M 59; S I, 70:2.

[54]M 77; S I, 84:7-8.

[55]DIV 10; S II, 26:14.

[56]DIV 11; S II, 29:10.

and perhaps the latter charge is more appropriate than the former. Any charge that stressing the humanity of Christ in itself amounts to a denial of his divinity is tantamount to a denial of the possibility of the incarnation altogether.

METHOD IN ANSELM AND LUTHER: WHY THEY APPEAR SO DIFFERENT

Aulén's contrast of Luther against Anselm was really made at altogether the wrong level. The most prominent points of contrast between Luther and Anselm are found in the realm of prolegomena and specifically in the areas of method, approach, and intention. In areas where it is really misleading to say they disagree, the reason Anselm and Luther appear to some to bear contrasting views is their respective differences in approach. Their methods do not differ simply because of something as insignificant as personality, culture, or milieu. Luther's approach, or the structure of his thought, is generally quite different from that of Anselm, whose *sola ratione* (by reason alone) principle lay at the root of his well known *fides quaerens intellectum*—faith seeking understanding. This method is not seen in Luther, who was not so optimistic about the results of the inquiry of reason, due to his different understanding of sin's essence.

Anselm's method intentionally included a robust exercise of reason as an apologetic for the Christian faith. The primary characteristic of this method was a chain-of-reasoning progression of thought, according to which a point is built on a previous point, ascending a ladder of logical reasoning leading finally to the conclusion which Anselm had set out to prove. Anselm generally determines to lay out his argument *sola ratione*, known in the *Cur Deus homo* by the term *remoto Christo* (Christ being removed), to wit, that what is already known of Christ or of his work from Scripture or ecclesiastical tradition is not used at all in the discourse. Anselm then resorts, quite deliberately, to his remaining raw material, namely reason. Using reason alone, then, he constructs his case by using one conclusion to lead to another, in a chain-of-arguments form of reasoning. In the course of this method's employment, Anselm poses certain questions to which his own answers are radically different from the answers of many of the later scholastics;[57] yet in the introduction of the method

[57] In particular, Duns Scotus, Jean Gerson, and Gabriel Biel are seen by Luther to be opposed to what he considers "catholic." See his "Disputation against Scholastic Theology" (1517), LW 31:9-16.

by which these questions were raised and addressed, he was himself partly responsible for their positions so diametrically opposed to his own.[58] Anselm can in this way be seen as the first of the scholastics, because his method in itself suggested the extent to which dialectics may be taken and indeed was taken not only by his irascible adversary Roscelin, but also by the later scholastics. Anselm's *sola ratione* approach was not born of any desire on his part to discredit the authority of Scripture, as anyone at all familiar with Anselm can testify.[59] Yet Anselm's approach does appear to belie a lack of the confidence Luther would later manifest in the power and purpose of the Word of God. Thus it may be said that what seem to be differences between Anselm and Luther on the question of the atonement and its necessity can be understood more clearly as differences of method and intentions.

Unlike Anselm, Luther was never wont to embark on topics of abstract thought. This difference is easy to consider insignificant, until one appreciates the intentions with which Luther undertakes the theological task. Luther confessed to being compelled to speak and write, even against his will, as one driven by the exigency of his vocation. One does not get this impression upon reading Anselm. This striking contrast suggests something more significant than stylistic preference. Anselm introduced to the theological world a method of inquiry from reason alone into theological truths, and this method of probing theological questions was employed for centuries after him. It was a method by which scholasticism itself can be marked, and from which the schoolmen were not to depart throughout the medieval period. Seen from Luther's perspective, which was ever suspicious of reason, this exercise is bound to produce spoiled fruits, whether at once or upon centuries of growth. For Luther, reason cannot be expected to provide the understanding faith seeks, regardless of whether one can successfully harmonize the answers of reason with the articles of faith. The *summae* of the medieval period may

[58]Gillian Evans is right, however, in setting Anselm apart from the later scholastics on this score: "Although he loved the unraveling of puzzles, not all of which seem as urgent or central today as they did to his contemporaries, he is never guilty of the trivialization of which Luther and others complained in the work of later mediaeval scholasticism. There is always an issue of perennial concern at the heart of any matter he considers," *Anselm*, in *Outstanding Christian Thinkers Series*, ed. Brian Davies (London: Geoffrey Chapman, and Wilton, Connecticut: Morehouse-Barlow, 1989), x.

[59]For example, Richard W. Southern, "Anselm at Canterbury" in *Anselm Studies: an Occasional Journal*, I, edited by Marjorie Chibnall, Gillian Evans, et al. (Millwood, New York: Kraus International Publications, 1983), 7-22.

claim Anselm as their father, but certainly not Luther as their heir. That Christ is our salvation is for Luther "the thing over which all reason and wisdom stumbles."[60] For Luther, the Sacred Page must itself provide what Anselm expected reason to provide, namely *intellectum*. For Anselm, although *fides quaerens intellectum* certainly meant that faith is indeed the root of understanding, his attempt to understand *remoto Christo* belies what Luther would have to regard as a failure to see the Sacred Page as not only the source and root of understanding, but also of its deepening.

[60]WA DB 7, 83; LW 35, 380.

THE CHANGING IMAGE OF LUTHER AS BIBLICAL EXPOSITOR

Gordon L. Isaac

No single view of Martin Luther is universally accepted and affirmed. A character of the stature and importance of Luther invites a number of interpretations and evaluations. Even during the lifetime of the Reformer the assessment of him ranged widely. From the seven-headed Luther, who threatened the stability of the Church, to the heroic image of the German Hercules, who single-handedly seemed to clear away the deadwood of scholastic excess, the Reformer of Wittenberg has been viewed in starkly contrasting ways. In the age of Protestant Orthodoxy, and in each successive era, the image of Luther has gone through its various mutations. It comes as no surprise, then, that when we turn to the issue of Luther's image as biblical expositor the same panorama of overlapping and contradictory views should present themselves.

In current discussions, the collision of various competing and complementary ways of viewing the data are jostling with one another for pride of place. Certainly in our century, which has been quite occupied with issues relating to hermeneutics, the question of how Luther's approach to the Bible compares to that of the medieval context has been key. On this axis there are those who see Luther's hermeneutic as the precursor to the modern critical approach to Scripture and on the opposite end are those who would describe Luther's approach to the Bible as following an ancient tradition which has very few contacts with modern techniques. Another axis centers on Luther's view of language. Some maintain that Luther eschews allegory in his search for the clarity of Scripture while others claim that it is precisely by the use of allegory and metaphor that Luther intends to bring the hearer into the world of scriptural truth. And yet another axis of thought relates to the much-studied reformational breakthrough and its place in ongoing Luther research. Some would argue that a hermeneutical shift corresponds to the breakthrough and others are less willing to allow the 1545 reflection on the "tower experience" to carry the freight that Luther research has sometimes asked of it.

The Luther Renaissance

At the turn of the century, Ernst Troeltsch emphasized the medieval element in Luther's theology and the cultural effects of the Reformation.[1] This was particularly striking in an atmosphere which was used to viewing Luther as the hero of German culture and known more for the break with Rome than for any antecedents he might have had in the tradition. To hear that Luther may have had much in common with the medieval Church was cause to return to the sources again.

This was the task that Karl Holl and some of his students took up. Holl expressed his opposition to Troeltsch in a number of areas. The tension produced more pointed questions regarding Luther's relationship with his medieval surroundings and the explicit ways in which he broke with tradition. Holl emphasized the "new" elements in Luther's theology and the positive effects of the Reformation on culture.[2] Focus turned to the *initia Lutheri,* the young Luther and the events in his life during the year 1517 and before.

At least part of the impulse for the interest in the *initia Lutheri* was due to the rediscovery of three major unpublished Luther manuscripts. The first lectures on the Psalms, 1513–15,[3] the lectures on Romans, 1515–16,[4] and the lectures on Hebrews, 1517–18,[5] had all newly come to light. These new pieces fueled the interest surrounding the new Luther research and stimulated work in the field. Taken individually, any one find would have created quite a stir, but all three coming to light in a short span of time was nothing less than explosive. These manuscripts had particular importance for the whole question of Luther's approach to Scripture because in these texts Luther still adheres to the medieval exegetical practice, which in-

[1] A. G. Dickens and John M. Tonkin with Kenneth Powell, *The Reformation in Historical Thought* (Cambridge, Massachusetts: Harvard University Press, 1985), 187-88.

[2] Ibid, 202-3. Karl Holl, "Luthers Bedeutung für den Fortschritt der Auslegungskunst," in *Gesammelte Aufsätze zur Kirchengeschichte*, Band I, *Luther*, 7th ed. (Tübingen: J. C. B. Mohr [Paul Siebeck], 1948), 544-82.

[3] Two of Luther's manuscripts of these lectures were found in the late nineteenth century and were published in the Weimar edition as volumes 3 and 4 in 1885. A new edition was deemed necessary and was completed with the publication of WA 55.

[4] Johannes Ficker, paleographer and Church historian, plays prominently in the fascinating story of how this Luther manuscript was discovered. In 1908 a provisional edition was published with the Weimar edition following in 1938. For a full account see his introduction in WA 56.

[5] A student notebook of this lecture series came to light only in 1877. It was published in 1916 with the Weimar edition (WA 57) following in 1939.

cluded gloss and scholia. Here were texts that offered researchers a window into Luther's move away from the medieval exposition of Scripture.

LUTHER AND HERMENEUTICS

It was into this heady atmosphere of new discovery and the inevitable emergence of a renewed vision of Luther's original contributions that Ebeling brought forth his "Erstlingsbuch." According to his own comment, *Evangelische Evangelienauslegung: Eine Untersuchung zu Luthers Hermeneutik* (Munich, 1942) has continuity with the rest of his scholarly work.[6] In view of this fact, the book could be called a fundamental work in that many of the themes originally set forward appear and are reshaped in Ebeling's many later essays.

Ebeling adduces the research of Karl Holl, K. A. Meisinger, H. Schuster, and Reinhold Seeberg to the effect that Luther's importance in the history of exegesis is the fact of his break with the allegorical interpretation of Scripture, even more than the particulars of his biblical interpretation. Ebeling points out that previous research maintains that Luther abandoned the fourfold sense of Scripture by 1517.[7] But when one looks specifically at the Gospel texts which are at the heart of Ebeling's research, it is not possible to say that Luther abandoned allegorical exposition as such. Ebeling admits that at the same time Luther rejects the fourfold sense, he continues to interpret Scripture in allegorical fashion. Ebeling reviews the exposition of Gospel texts used by Luther from the year 1522 and following. The findings seem to indicate that the years 1524 and 1529 are turning points in Luther's work. Ebeling informs us that the surrender of allegory is not basic until the end of that time period.[8]

Even though there is a fair amount of ambivalence with respect to the basic data of his thesis, Ebeling sets it forward in his dissertation and in subsequent essays on Luther. In dealing with the early lectures on the Psalms, Ebeling notes certain adjustments that move Luther from the fourfold method of biblical interpretation to his

[6] Gerhard Ebeling, *Evangelische Evangelienauslegung: Eine Untersuchung zu Luthers Hermeneutik*, Forschungen zur Geschichte und Lehre des Protestantismus, 10. Reihe, Band I; (München: Kaiser, 1942; reprint Darmstadt: Wissenschaftliche Buchgesellschaft, 1962; reprint Tübingen: Mohr-Siebeck, 1993). To this effect, see the newly attached "Nachwort" of the 1993 edition.

[7] The literal, the allegorical, the moral or tropological, and the anagogical senses correspond to what happened, what you must believe, what you must do, and what you may hope for.

[8] *Evangelische Evangelienauslegung*, 44-85.

reformational understanding of Scripture. This includes an understanding of 2 Corinthians 3:6 that overturned the traditional platonizing interpretation which served to affirm an allegorizing approach to Scripture. In place of Origen's allegorizing tendency, Luther understands the critical passage more in line with Augustine, who in *Letter and the Spirit* recognized that in 2 Corinthians 3:6 *littera* and *spiritus* were not general exegetical terms but referred to the distinction between law and grace. So, Luther began to use the distinction between letter and spirit in new, more comprehensive way. Luther is no longer satisfied to make a distinction which identifies letter with the literal sense and life-giving Spirit with allegorical or spiritual interpretation. Rather, he sees that the whole text is either the letter that kills or the whole text is life-giving Spirit. This allows Luther to make significant strides toward the hermeneutical shift which will make itself felt so profoundly in Luther's later theology.[9]

Ebeling's work on Luther's hermeneutic is arguably the most influential in this past century. This is true in part because of Ebeling's longevity and productivity of detailed Luther studies. These advances came roughly at the same time as the more general increase in importance of hermeneutical discussions in the theological sciences. Ebeling's prominence as an ecumenist and his efforts in the now-spent theological movement known as the "New Hermeneutic" has certainly made Luther's importance in the tradition of biblical interpretation more than just a matter of interest for a handful of Luther scholars.

Certainly the image of Luther as biblical expositor that emerges out of Ebeling's work is impressive. His groundbreaking work has helped to show the relationship of Luther's scriptural exegesis to that of his medieval background. His detailed studies have ranged widely in topics from Luther's lectures on Psalms to his understanding of political ethics. In all these ways Ebeling has raised significant questions and has given them, at the very least, provisional answers. But questions do remain.

Karl Froehlich suggests that work in medieval and Reformation texts must be done in humility, expecting that some of our original theories about the matters we are studying may have to be scrapped and new ones minted.[10] If this sentiment is correct, as indeed I believe it is, what is it about the work of Ebeling that will remain, and

[9] Gerhard Ebeling, *Luther: An Introduction to His Thought* (Philadelphia: Fortress Press, 1970), 93-109.

[10] Karl Froehlich, "The Significance of Medieval Biblical Interpretation," *Lutheran Quarterly* 10 (Summer 1995): 139-150.

what will be amended? It may be too soon to tell, but certain faultlines are becoming evident.

As profoundly influential as Ebeling's work has been in the recent past, the sure convictions motivating the Luther Renaissance which first gave this work impetus no longer sustain unquestioned allegiance. In the area of language it has been pointed out that the definition of allegory used in his doctoral study is not one derived from Luther but comes from Adolf Jülicher.[11] This is significant in that Jülicher has a negative appraisal of allegory as being an inauthentic manner of expression.[12] Even later in his career, when Ebeling is more amenable toward metaphorical language, the question remains as to how much a commitment to an existential understanding of faith and the spoken word effects the ability of one to understand Luther on his own terms.[13]

Ebeling's attempts to balance the great weight of the Reformation breakthrough on a corresponding hermeneutical shift has also come under fire. It is increasingly difficult to see how the rough-hewn tension between Troeltsch and Holl, which played off the stark contrasts of medieval/modern or Catholic/Lutheran, could produce anything other than false alternatives. Trying to find evidence of an abrupt reversal in Luther that corresponds to a "Catholic" or a "Lutheran" position forces Luther research into an artificial reductionism that must find the "key" to his mature theology.[14] Great effort has been expended in this endeavor but the lasting results have been meager. More recent descriptions of Luther have abandoned the focus on the so-called tower experience altogether.[15]

[11] *Evangelische Evangelienauslegung*, 46-47.

[12] Jan Lindhardt, *Martin Luther: Knowledge and Mediation in the Renaissance*, Texts and Studies in Religion; vol. 29 (Lewiston, New York: The Edwin Mellon Press, 1986), 184-91.

[13] Ebeling speaks of the word-event in human language as being the most suitable form of God's communication with man in "The New Hermeneutics and the Early Luther," *Theology Today* 21 (1964): 34-46. Compare this to Helmar Junghans who insists that by applying the modern categories of "existentialism" we have imposed a needlessly psychological overtone to our discussion of Luther. Helmar Junghans, "Das Wort Gottes bei Luther während seiner ersten Psalmenvorlesung," *Theologische Literaturzeitung* 100 (1975): 161-74.

[14] It should be noted that various different accounts attempting to explain Luther's conversion experience have been proposed. Ebeling's suggestion that it is a hermeneutical shift is simply one among many attempts to find the "key" to the young Luther. For others, see Kenneth Hagen, "Changes in the Understanding of Luther: The Development of the Young Luther," *Theological Studies* 29 (1968): 472-96.

[15] Ibid., 492.

Another question that is emerging has to do with how Luther should be depicted with respect to the competing approaches to biblical interpretation of his day. Ebeling views Luther in terms of what is new in his approach. While antecedents are acknowledged, Luther is not associated with any existing approach to Scripture.[16] Jan Lindhardt gives a view of Luther who is an adherent of sixteenth-century rhetoric and its view of language as the conveyor of truth. He thus seeks to place Luther in his historical context, identifying Luther with biblical humanism.[17] Franz Posset, on the other hand, claims that Luther's concerns, when it comes to biblical exposition, are those of monasticism with its emphasis on the vocabulary of Scripture.[18]

One interesting window into the current discussions which deal with the hermeneutical issue touches on the interpretation of one of Luther's comments at the beginning of the *Operationes in Psalmos* of 1519 in which he says, "Our first concern will be for the grammatical meaning, for this is the truly theological meaning."[19] Are we to understand this text as Ebeling does, that the grammatical sense equals the literal sense? Or are we to understand this as Lindhardt does, that Luther's reading of Scripture is dominated by the rhetorical concern for "scopus," or the intention of the text? Or are we to understand the grammatical sense as one which is synonymous with the simple sense of monastic origin as Posset asserts?[20]

A further question that will no doubt be explored over time with respect to the work of Gerhard Ebeling has to do with the matter of

[16] Ebeling views Luther as standing at the beginning of a line of biblical exegesis that leads directly through to the historical-critical method of the nineteenth century. See his "Significance of the Critical Historical Method," in *Word and Faith* (London: SCM, 1963), 35ff.

[17] *Martin Luther: Knowledge and Mediation in the Renaissance*, especially 156ff.

[18] The phrase, Bible reading "with closed eyes," is identified by Posset as a monastic-mystical way of medieval interpretation, or exegetical meditation. Paradoxically, by closing one's eyes, one sees farther. By urging that one adhere to the Word against all of one's own feeling and thought, Luther is commending the idea that Scripture interprets Scripture. Rules for interpreting Scripture are unnecessary and actually inhibit the work of Scripture in the reader's life. Franz Posset, "Bible Reading 'With Closed Eyes' In The Monastic Tradition: An Overlooked Aspect of Martin Luther's Hermeneutics," *The American Benedictine Review* 38:3 (1987): 293-306.

[19] WA 5:27,8.

[20] Gerhard Ebeling, whose work highlights Luther's uniqueness over against the medieval background, is convinced that Luther's early hermeneutical principles inevitably implied the abandonment of the fourfold meaning of Scripture. The changes once set in place cause Luther to return to the *sensus literalis* as the genuine meaning of the text. According to Ebeling, this indicates that for Luther there is only one meaning of Scripture. This is the literal sense, which as such is spiritual because of the content of Scripture (Christ). *Luther: An Introduction to his Thought*, 107.

his presuppositions. Graham White has taken Ebeling to task for his work in medieval logic, more specifically his commentary on Luther's disputation *De homine*.[21] White asserts that Ebeling describes logic in the way that German Idealists do, which makes a negative ap-

Jan Lindhardt, who comes to a study of Luther from a more or less strict rhetorical approach without recourse to any monastic reference, tells us that this view of Ebeling is not helpful. To speak of Luther as an adherent of the literal sense involves us in modern ideas and sensibilities of history which do not apply to sixteenth-century ways of reading the text. Modern sensibilities think of that which is "literal" or "historical" as having to do with verifiable facts. Those in the twentieth century find it difficult to allow that typological interpretation, for example, might be able to tell us anything important about "reality." But for Luther this was no problem.

Lindhardt claims that Luther's reading of Scripture is dominated by the *scopus* of the text. For his part, Luther maintains that the *scopus* of Scripture is Christ. A reading of the text will account for the varying modes of composition, genre, and stylistic devices, even if that includes such things as allegorical or typological references which do not fit nicely into modern categories of historical verifiability.

Thus, to say that Luther returns to a literal sense of the text is misleading, because our idea of literal is much more restrictive than Luther's. Additionally, to use the terminology of "literal sense" only makes sense within the framework of the fourfold approach to Scripture. What in fact occurred is that Luther did away with not only the three allegorical senses of Scripture but also with the whole *quadriga*. In its place Luther had only a single concept of Scripture which permitted typologies, metaphors, allegories, and so forth. But he insisted that the text was not amenable to multiple meanings so that faith would have something certain to cling to. *Martin Luther: Knowledge and Mediation in the Renaissance*, esp. 212-217.

Franz Posset, who recognizes both the rhetorical and the monastic matrix out of which Luther comes, sees the importance of the second lectures on the Psalms in yet another manner. Rather than speaking of the hermeneutical principles, as does Ebeling, or a literary reading as does Lindhardt, Posset cites the fact that Luther disliked any rules applied to Scriptures because rules imprison the Word of God which teaches all freedom (WA 7:9, 27-31). While Posset seems to agree with Ebeling that Luther operates with the fourfold method of scriptural interpretation in the first lectures on the Psalms, he maintains that Luther turned to the "simple sense" by 1520 in his second lectures. At that time he took up a threefold, "orational" approach which highlights prayer, meditation, and experience/temptation (*tentatio*). "Bible Reading 'With Closed Eyes,'" 294.

A review of these positions makes it quite clear that where one places Luther in the conflicts between the various intellectual camps of his day has a profound significance on how one reads the data. Of course, the issue of identifying Luther's approach to Scripture is much larger than the interpretation of this particular quotation. But this one isolated Luther utterance, if nothing else, is an enlightening window on current Luther scholarship.

[21] Graham White, "Theology and Logic: The Case of Ebeling," *Modern Theology* 4 (October 1987): 17-34. By the same author see, *Luther as Nominalist: A Study of the Logical Methods Used in Martin Luther's Disputations in the Light of Their Medieval Background* (Helsinki: Luther-Agricola Society, 1994).

praisal of logic inevitable. In contrast, White maintains that Luther used logic as a linguistic tool, in order to attack the metaphysics of the time. Miika Ruokanen has analyzed the hermeneutical methodology of Ebeling. His findings show that Ebeling's interpretation of the Reformation is highly dependent upon the method of transcendental anthropology expressed by the Neo-Kantian theologians. Ebeling is convinced that Luther parts company with an ontology of substance, preferring to speak of the nature of being in terms of the relational.[22] This line of interpretation is one which the Finnish interpretation of Luther is presently seeking to revise.[23]

LUTHER AND RHETORIC

Tracing Luther's relationship to sixteenth-century rhetoric is a growing field of inquiry.[24] Jan Lindhardt, a Danish professor of rhetoric, is one who thinks that rhetoric may well provide a new way of understanding Luther's use of the Bible. Lindhardt maintains that Ebeling, along with a great deal of modern Luther scholarship, suf-

[22] Miika Ruokanen, *Hermeneutics as an Ecumenical Method in the Theology of Gerhard Ebeling*, Publications of Luther-Agricola Society vol. 13 (Helsinki: Luther-Agricola Society, 1982), esp. 52-71.

[23] Carl Braaten and Robert W. Jenson, eds. *Union With Christ: The New Finnish Interpretation of Luther* (Grand Rapids: Eerdmans Publishing Co., 1998).

[24] Swedish Germanist Birgit Stolt has shown that far from being casual in linguistic formalities, Luther was well aware of the discipline of rhetoric, making use of it in both German and Latin texts. See "Studien zu Luthers Freiheitstraktat mit besonderer Rücksicht auf das Verhältnis der lateinischen und der deutschen Fassung zu einander und die Stilmittel der Rhetorik," *Stockholmer germanistische Forschungen* 6 (Stockholm: Almquist & Wiksell, 1969). From the same author see, "*Docere*, *delectare*, und *movere* bei Luther. Analysiert anhand der 'Predigt, dass man Kinder zur Schulen halten solle,'" *Deutsche Vierteljahrschrift* XLIV (1970): 433-74. Marjorie O'Rourke Boyle has analyzed the debate between Erasmus and Luther from the perspective of the discipline of rhetoric. Boyle argues that their controversy was grounded not only in the substantive issues surrounding the will but also on the formal and rhetorical issue of whether the question should be argued on the basis of deliberative or juridical rhetoric in *Rhetoric and Reform: Erasmus' Civil Dispute with Luther* (Cambridge: Harvard University Press, 1983). Ulrich Nembach maintains that Luther's study of Quintilian played a particularly important role in Luther's practice of rhetoric in *Predigt des Evangeliums: Luther als Prediger, Pädagoge und Rhetor* (Neukirchen: Neukirchener Verlag, 1972). Klaus Dockhorn makes the case that Luther's concept of faith is determined by affective states transferred and mediated in ways prescribed by Quintilian in "Luthers Glaubensbegriff und die Rhetorik," *Linguistica Biblica* 21/22, (1973): 19-39. Knut Alfsvåg uses rhetorical analysis as a means for getting at the content of Luther's theologizing in "Language and Reality. Luther's relation to classical rhetoric in *Rationis Latomianae*," *Studia Theologica*, 41 (1987): 85-126.

fers under a common misconception in which symbol and allegory are confused. According to Lindhardt, Luther rejected the symbolic fourfold interpretation of Scripture but never rejected allegory. Thus, Luther was always able to find allegories, metaphors, suggestive etymologies and other kinds of pictorial language, although he did so without resorting to the fourfold interpretation. In short, Luther said "No" to the *quadriga* and "Yes" to allegory.

Modern scholarship has thought it impossible that Luther should be an allegorist. This is in spite of the allegorical tracks that can be found throughout his work, early and late. When it appears from the evidence that Luther must be a practitioner of rhetoric with its embrace of allegories, we are simply told that Luther's surrender of allegorical interpretation is mainly tacit, or that he was unable to make good on all his Reformation insights.

This situation in which the evidence leads in one direction but the consensus of scholarship indicates another is fascinating. Lindhardt muses over this instance of scholarship so dominated by prejudices that the outcome of the research is skewed. The content of the materials demands that Luther's attitude toward allegory be more than merely acknowledged. But instead, scholarship has been content to make some extraordinarily contradictory statements or merely give excuses of one sort or another.

Why is this? Lindhardt offers two comments. First, he claims that modern study of Luther's approach to Scripture is really located in a different place than it thinks itself to be.[25] With regard to terminology, modern scholarship has failed to see that the entire textual theory of the Middle Ages presupposes symbolic interpretation. When the authors of the Middle Ages termed their understanding "allegorical," this was taken at face value. The terminology that would more accurately fit our modern usage is "symbolic." Luther did not break with the use of allegory but with the symbolic interpretation of Scripture. He objected to the polysemeity of the fourfold interpretive schema in use at the time. With regard to the contents of the problem it is clear that modern scholarship lauds Luther for his break with the medieval method of interpretation and the surrendering of allegory. This show of solidarity with Luther would mean a great deal more if indeed allegory had been abandoned!

Second, Lindhardt suggests that it is usually on the basis of false preconceptions that the modern reader understands and agrees with Luther's break with the allegorical method. Lindhardt makes the as-

[25] *Martin Luther: Knowledge and Mediation in the Renaissance*, 192.

tonishing assertion that the modern reader is closer to the symbolism of the Middle Ages than to the rhetorical use of metaphor and allegory used during the Renaissance. To use Lindhardt's own words,

> Being symbolists ourselves, we make a symbolist of Luther too, (or else he would not be a reasonable man), just as we also assume that he broke with the allegorical method (which he did not). We further assume that Luther understood the understanding of language and text enjoyed by modern scholars (which he certainly did not).[26]

Lindhardt's point is that when modern scholarship approvingly cites Luther's break with medieval interpretive method as being a rejection of allegory in favor of a symbolist view of language and (of course) the insistence on the literal meaning as the sole sense of Scripture, then scholarship has ironically sided with a view opposed to that of Luther!

Lindhardt is not alone in offering reassessments of conventional wisdom or commonplaces of Luther research. Helmar Junghans carries out his work in self-conscious tension with the approach that has characterized much of the Luther Renaissance up until the present time. Researchers have scrutinized the Reformation breakthrough with an almost unflagging zeal since the turn of the century. The fundamental questions surrounding this event are of timing and nature. When did this event take place? Was it before the first lectures on the Psalms (ca. 1513), or during Luther's preparations for the second lectures on the Psalms, or was it later?

Junghans is convinced that a one-sided attention to the so-called reformational discovery distorts a full presentation of Luther's theology. The attempt to locate a single explanation or starting point for the complex theology of the Reformer is bound to distort.

> To me the quest for a point of departure appears to be too strongly tied to the mechanistic worldview of the nineteenth century, according to which everything follows according to a set of principles from a single cause (that is, the point of departure) which consequently can then be logically deduced.[27]

Instead of the single-moment theory of Luther's break with the late Middle Ages, Junghans portrays the development as the outcome of

[26] Ibid.

[27] Helmar Junghans, "The Center of the Theology of Martin Luther," in *Martin Luther in Two Centuries: The Sixteenth and the Twentieth* (St. Paul, Minn.: Lutheran Brotherhood Foundation Reformation Research Library at Luther Northwestern Theological Seminary, 1992), 32.

the application of the expectations, philological advances, and academic methods of biblical humanism. This was a process over time which may have contained many "breakthroughs" of thought and application.

Viewing Luther as a biblical humanist provides a more simple solution to the question of Luther's development into a Reformer than previous proposals. It obviates the need to seek and find a certain teaching such as justification by faith, or a particular event such as a hermeneutical breakthrough, to describe the unfolding character of his thought. According to Junghans, when one sees the significance of biblical humanism for Luther's development, it is no longer useful to distinguish between a pre-reformational and reformational Luther. Instead, one comes to see that Luther entered a process in which he held a critical view of the tradition on the basis of the criterion given to him through his biblical humanistic studies.

The work of Helmar Junghans has the force of moving the emphasis away from a preoccupation with the so-called reformational insight, an approach that is too heavily influenced by nineteenth-century notions of cause and effect. It takes too seriously the idea of a single starting point for Luther's theology, thus necessitating the great rush to identify, with absolute certainty, the moment of Luther's discovery. Junghans bypasses the developmental or the systematic ways of depicting Luther's theology, opting instead for a view of Luther as biblical humanist. Junghans is convinced that the methods, expectations, and approach to the text that biblical humanism taught Luther are vitally connected with the manner in which the Scriptures were read anew and became the basis for Luther's theology.[28]

The work of Lindhardt and Junghans and others who have pointed out the importance of sixteenth-century rhetoric for understanding Luther have done us a great service. While Luther has long been appreciated as an innovator in his creative use of speech, it is of tremendous value to have detailed studies which demonstrate specific aspects of his use of rhetoric. One area of promise that may come out of future studies in this area is developing a greater understanding of Luther's view of language. The fact that for Luther Law

[28] Helmar Junghans, "Luther als Bibelhumanist," *Lutherjahrbuch* 53 (1982): 1-9. *Der Junge Luther und die Humanisten* (Göttingen: Vandenhoeck & Ruprecht, 1985) and "Luther's Development from Biblical Humanist to Reformer," in *Martin Luther in Two Centuries: the Sixteenth and the Twentieth* (St. Paul, Minn.: Lutheran Brotherhood Foundation Reformation Research Library at Luther Northwestern Theological Seminary, 1992), 1-14.

and Gospel are voices that speak to the conscience may well be a fruitful avenue of inquiry with respect to the discipline of rhetoric.

Serious questions remain, however, regarding this image of Luther as biblical expositor. Luther's adherence to humanism is seen as the reason he is critical of scholasticism. But it should be pointed out that monasticism also was critical of the same movement. In addition, when Luther's use of rhetoric is given as proof of Luther's ties to the humanist constellation, it needs to be pointed out that monasticism also had ties to the rhetorical tradition. Luther's own appropriation of Latin does not seem to be consistently driven by the most refined form of humanism. He was aware that he did not write in elegant Ciceronian Latin and later commented, "But I do have the content."[29] We cannot assume uncritically that Luther adheres to the principle of humanistic rhetoric as though rhetoric were an undifferentiated subject. We only need to recall the opening lines of *De servo arbitrio* to be reminded that there were differing measures for eloquence. There Luther claims that he does not have the eloquence (the aim of rhetoric) of Erasmus. Luther does not appeal to the learned language of the classical authors but to the words of Paul who did not come with eloquence or worldly wisdom, but with the testimony about God. It may well be that Luther's rhetoric has more connections with monastic theology and its focus on the vocabulary of Scripture than with the humanist rhetorical ideal based on Ciceronian imitation. We will have to wait to see.

LUTHER AS CATHOLIC THEOLOGIAN

Kenneth Hagen holds in common with Junghans the desire to overcome the developmental bias of much of Luther scholarship. But rather than seeing Luther as a biblical humanist, Hagen describes Luther in his medieval context as a trinitarian creedal theologian.[30] Hagen's presentation brings out certain characteristics of Luther's theologizing that have elemental connections with monasticism.[31] This

[29] WA TR4, No. 4967.

[30] *Luther's Approach to Scripture as seen in his "Commentaries" on Galatians* 1519–1538 (Tübingen: J.C.B. Mohr [Paul Siebeck] Tübingen, 1993).

[31] There is a growing body of literature pointing to the monastic legacy in Luther's theology. For example, Ernst Schering, "Martin Luther und das Erbe der monastischen Theologie," *Lutherjahrbuch* 59 (1985): 22-27; Hedwig Bach, "Bernhard von Clairvaux und Martin Luther," *Erbe und Auftrag* 46 (1970): 347-51; 453-59 and 47 (1971): 36-43; 121-25; 193-96; Erich Kleineidam, "Ursprung und Gegenstand der Theologie bei Bernhard von Clairvaux und Martin Luther," *Dienst der Vermittlung*. Festschrift zum 25 jährigen Bestehen des philosophisch-

represents a 180 degree shift from those that tend to present Luther as the first modern exegete, or first practitioner of biblical criticism.

As Hagen sees it, the sixteenth century was a time in which at least three distinct approaches to scriptural interpretation existed side by side.[32] These differences of form among sixteenth-century biblical interpreters can be traced to the differences among the competing ways of theologizing represented by monasticism, scholasticism, and humanism. Each has different ways of going about its work and each has slightly different goals. Scholasticism is concerned to derive sacred doctrine from the Bible. Humanism is concerned to revive the study of letters and to establish the philosophy of Christ in such a manner that would lead to piety, morality, and justice. Hagen asserts that Luther should be understood as following an ancient tradition of Bible interpretation that extends through monasticism which is centered in the vocabulary of Scripture. Rather than a focus on doctrine, or on programs of renewal within the Church and society, the sole work of theology, according to Luther, is to promote God against the Devil.

Luther's work as biblical theologian takes the form of *enarratio* or "comments" on Scripture. Just as Paul freely quotes from the Psalms, Isaiah, and the prophets, Luther's comments on Scripture take the form of Scripture interpreting Scripture. In addition, we find that Luther's comments on the text display no sense of historical gap that needs to be overcome. That is a characteristic of later methods which begin to emerge at this time. *Enarratio*, as Luther practices it, has in view the grammar of theology versus the grammar of philosophy. Luther also practices commentary by concordance, where one word in a passage may recall that same word in another passage. The comments thus lead from one text to another in an unbroken chain as Scripture interprets Scripture.

theologischen Studiums im Priesterseminar Erfurt, ed. Wilhelm Ernst et al. (Leipzig: St. Benno Verlag, 1977), 221-47; Reinhard Schwarz, "Luther's Inalienable Inheritance of Monastic Theology," *The American Benedictine Review* 39:4 (1988): 430-50; and especially Franz Posset, *Pater Bernhardus: Martin Luther and Bernard of Clairvaux* (Kalamazoo: Cistercian Publications, 1999), 91-161, who elaborates on Luther in the tradition of monastic theology.

[32] Hagen's description of the three major approaches to Scripture can be found in "The History of Scripture in the Church," in Kenneth Hagen, Daniel J. Harrington S.J., Grant R. Osborne, and Joseph A. Burgess, eds., *The Bible and the Churches* (New York: Paulist Press, 1985), 3-34. "What did the term *Commentarius* mean to sixteenth-century theologians?," in Irena Backus and Francis Higman eds., *Thèorie et pratique de l'exégèse*, Actes du troisième colloque international sur l'histoire de l'exégèse biblique au XVIe siècle (Genève, 31 août-2 septembre 1988) Etudes de Philologie et d'Histoire, Vol. 43 (Geneva: Libraire Droz, 1990), 13-38.

What Hagen shows in his work on Luther's "commentaries" on Galatians is that Luther has been edited as a nineteenth-century exegete. The editorial practices of the prodigious WA (*Weimarer Ausgabe*) have not been faithful to Luther's medieval context. They have chosen, rather, to see him through the eyes of nineteenth-century concerns and presuppositions. The editors of the WA saw fit to exclude the original identification found in the 1519 prints of Luther as a friar and an Augustinian. These designations of Luther's medieval and Catholic context were not in harmony with nineteenth-century Protestant concerns. The religious identity of Paul as Divine or Saint in the original is also excluded.

More importantly, the WA includes a header on each page which reads *commentarius* which is not the case in the original. This is apparently done without any recognition of the differences between commentaries in Luther's day as compared with commentaries of the nineteenth and twentieth centuries. Luther himself did not consider his work to be a commentary. Instead we find Luther claiming that his work "is not so much a commentary as a testimony of my faith in Christ."[33] He was not concerned to create a commentary with "originality" as its goal. The work that Luther undertakes goes under the term *enarratio,* or "comments" on Scripture. The point of Luther's work is to tell the story, to promote the theology of Paul, to go public with the "Faith of Christ." This is no academic exercise, this is the battle of life against death.

Hagen's proposal is a device for differentiating Luther's approach to Scripture. By placing the discussion in the context of the various approaches to interpretation and the methodological debates of the time, a greater degree of historical sensitivity can be brought to bear on the question. It recognizes the milieu in which Luther is operating and provides the context in which the antecedents of Luther's thought can be acknowledged. It releases the researcher from captivity to a Luther who single-handedly overcame the medieval approach to the Bible and started the modern methods.

When compared with the presentation of Ebeling, Hagen shows once again his independence. The matter of allegory, which is so important to Ebeling's initial work on Luther, is hardly mentioned in Hagen's. Rather matter of factly, Hagen points out that allegory is a rhetorical device that Paul used and, because Paul used it, Luther did too. Luther never gave up using allegory. There is no warrant in Scripture for him to have done so. The idea that the abandonment of

[33] *Luther's Approach to Scripture,* 2.

AD GALATAS FOLIO .I.

Argumentum Epiſtolæ Pauli ad Galatas.

Alatæ primum ab Apoſtolo ſanam fidem, id eſt, in ſolum Ieſum Chriſtum, non in ſuas, aut legis iuſticias, fidere docti: poſt, per pſeudoapoſtolos, rurſum deturbati ſunt, in fiduciam operum legalis iuſticiæ. decepti videlicet ꝙ facillime, magnorum & verorum Apoſtolorum falſe cõmendato, & nomie, & exemplo. Neq; enim in omni vita mortalium, quicq; fallacius eſt ſuperſtitione. hoc eſt, falſa & infœlice imitatione ſanctorum. Quorum cum opera ſola, nõ etiam cor, ſpectaris: in procliui eſt, vt ſimia fias, & Leuiathan. id eſt, additamentum addas. quo ex vera religione, ſuperſtitionem, vel impietatem facias. Nam: vt exemplo præſente monſtrem: Apoſtoli per eccleſias Iudeas, nonnullas legum ceremonias ſeruabant. Sicut de Marco, Philonem ſcripſiſſe, Hiero, teſtatur. Hoc auem ſtulti illi, qua ratione id facerent, ignorantes, mox de ſuo addiderunt, neceſſaria eſſe ad ſalutem, quæ a tantis Apoſtolis obſeruari viderant. nec vni9 Pauli: qui Chriſtum, ne.ꝑ vidiſſet, neq; audiſſet in terra, habendam rationem. At Apoſtoli: vt manifeſtiſſime Act, xv. Petrus definierat: non vt neceſſaria, ſed vt quæ licerent, & nihil obeſſent ijs, qui non in ipſa, ſed in Ieſum Chriſtum ſalutis fiduciam ponunt, ſeruabant. Nam in Chriſtum credentibus, omnia munda, indifferentia, licita ſunt: quæcunq;, vel præcipiuntur, vel prohibentur externis ceremonijs, corporalibuſq; iuſticijs: niſi quantum ſua ſponte, aut pro charitate, ſeſe eis ſubijcere velint. Ad quam intelligentiam PAVLVS, tanto æſtu laborat Galatas reuocare, vt & PETRI, & omniũ Apoſtolorum, prorſus nullam rationem habeat, quantũ ad perſonam, conditionem, id eſt, dignitatem (& quod dicunt) qualitatem, attinet. Deniq;, ſe ab eiſdem nihil accepiſſe, quin cõmendatum ab eis fuiſſe, gloriatur ſanctiſſima quadam ſuperbia. nihil cedens Apoſtolorum quoq; opinioni: qua euangelicæ veritati videbat calumniam ſtrui apud rudiores longeq; melius ducens, inglorios eſſe, ſeipſum & Apoſtolos ipſos, ꝙ Chriſti euangelium euacuari.

Galatæ ab Apl̃o pri9 docti, nõ cõfidere ĩ legis iuſticiã, poſtea in fiduciã legalis iuſticiæ reciderũt.

Lapſus ĩ ſuperſtitionem facillimus.

Fieri ſimiã & Leuiathan.

Nõnullæ legũ ceremoniæ ab Apoſtolis ſeruatæ.

Ceremoniæ licitæ, non neceſſariæ.

In Chriſtũ credentib9 oĩa cooperãt in bonum.

Paul9 ĩ Apoſtolis perſonã nõ reſpexit.

Paulus ſanctiſſima ſuperbia gloriatur.

Epiſtolæ Pauli ad Galatas, caput Primũ.

AVLVS APOSTOLVS. Quãdo iam græcatur totus orbis Chriſtianus: & ERASMI Theologiciſſimi annotationes omnium manibus teruntur, non eſt neceſſe indicare, quid Apoſtol9 græce ſignificet, niſi ijs, q̃bus non ERASMVS, ſed ego ſcribo. Apoſtolus enim idem, quod miſſus ſignificat. Et doctore. d. Hiero, hæbreorum vocabulum eſt, quod ſilas apud eos ſonat, cui a mittẽdo, nomen miſſo impoſitũ eſt. Ita apud Ioã. ix. Vade, laua in natatoria Silohe, quod interp̃tatur miſſus. Cuius

B

Eraſmus Theologiciſſim9.

Apoſtolus. Silas

Locus apud Io-

Original print: Luther (1519) on Paul's Letter to the Galatians, upon which Hagen based much of his *Luther's Approach to Scripture as seen in his "Commentaries" on Galatians, 1519-1538.*
See also page 260 for another page from this folio.

allegory would aid one's reading of Scripture comes from the Enlightenment and not the sixteenth century.

Hagen also parts company with Ebeling when he asserts that Luther never changed his mind on the *quadriga*. This is a singularly shocking statement when viewed in contrast to the standard position in Luther studies. Hagen asserts that because the term *quadriga* is not found in Scripture, it does not have the authority of Scripture behind it. As a Doctor of the Bible, motivated as he was by the vocabulary of Scripture, Luther was not too concerned about it.

But what is perhaps the most important aspect of Hagen's proposal is the attention that he gives to the original prints. This move in itself, which bypasses the WA with its editorial presuppositions, already sets a tone and a course which is bound to yield its own set of rewards. One such reward is the knowledge that will be gained by a better understanding of early editorial and printing practices. Attention to these matters may yield important insights into how Luther was read and received in his own time. This kind of historically conscious move calls for greater care in the kind of terminology applied to Luther's work. The anachronism of applying modern terminology to Luther's work, such as "hermeneutics," "exegesis," "commentary," etc., will have to be critically reviewed. With this action, the very first steps of disengaging Luther from the modern philosophy of development is undertaken.

A further advantage to Hagen's proposal is the fact that it presents a positive image of Luther as a Catholic theologian. Luther is viewed in continuity with his medieval heritage while retaining the objectivity of including the great break with Rome. The matter of Luther's continuity with the tradition is of great importance, particularly when so many accounts of Luther have keyed on his innovations, or his apparent departures.

This is an important step toward allowing Luther to speak for himself. The contemporary theological task, difficult as it is, needs all the tools at its disposal. That is why a recovery of a more accurate view of Luther's approach to Scripture is invaluable. It is not merely a matter of setting the record straight, as important as that may be. The significance lies in setting loose a new statement of Luther's mode of speaking and his manner of theologizing. This has consequences for the current theological scene and clears the way for Luther's possible significance for contemporary theology.[34]

[34] Ulrich Asendorf, "How Luther Opened the Scripture," translated by Oliver Olson, *Lutheran Quarterly* 9 (Summer 1995): 177-199.

It is precisely this significance of Luther for contemporary theology that is being addressed by Oswald Bayer. At the beginning of his new systematic theology, Bayer takes the time to point out a critical juncture in the development of theology as a science. He claims that the collision between the scholastic and the monastic theologies can best be understood in the tension between faith and understanding, affective and intellective states, in short, between heart and head. Scholasticism concentrated on disputation, monasticism proceeded with meditation. In this competition of approaches, Bayer asserts that Luther stands squarely in the monastic tradition.[35] It is with the threefold commitment to prayer, meditation and experience/temptation, *oratio*, *meditatio*, and *tentatio* that Luther approaches the work of theology.[36]

The work of Bayer, while it may begin with integrating Luther in the tradition, does not remain there. He goes on to struggle with the past interpretations of Luther in this century so that a new contemporary understanding might emerge. Interacting with the work of Kant, Hegel, Schleiermacher, Tillich, Barth and Bultmann, Bayer goes to work to uncover the thought-forms and presuppositions that would block theology from winning through to a statement that could speak to a new circumstance that many are describing as "postmodern." Bayer's course takes him in direct opposition with existential philosophy and theory of personalism that describes the act of faith as something wholly unrelated to one's objective life in the world. Instead, Bayer sets forward the object of theology as consisting in the interplay of God, the world, and the self. This understanding proceeds with the conviction that the wisdom of the biblical texts need not be set asunder from the First Commandment, as it is in the modern philosophies.[37]

The theological outlook of Luther, which holds together wisdom and experience is foundational for Bayer. It allows him to proceed with a scientific theological program that is willing to ask difficult questions while simultaneously taking seriously the authority of Scripture and its application to life. For Luther, theology is the expo-

[35] *Handbuch Systematischer Theologie* I (Gütersloh: Gütersloher Verlaghaus, 1994), 27-31.

[36] WA 50:659, 3f. See also Oswald Bayer, "*Oratio, Meditatio, Tentatio*. Eine Besinnung auf Luthers Theologieverständnis," *Lutherjahrbuch* 55 (1988): 7-59.

[37] As Bayer puts it, "Ohne die Weisheit der Weltwahrnehmung wäre das Erste Gebot leer; ohne das Erste Gebot wäre jene Weisheit blind." *Handbuch Systematischer Theologie*, 432.

sition of Scripture.[38] Incorporated into this manner of pursuing theological science is the word of promise as authorized by the text.

CONCLUSION

It is clear from the foregoing that the image of Luther as biblical expositor continues to go through its changes. At present, Luther is seen as the first hermeneutician, as biblical humanist, or as Catholic (one could read this, monastic) theologian. Underneath these views certain trends become apparent.

First, studies on Luther, on the whole, are moving away from a one-sided concentration on the *initia Lutheri* of the Luther Renaissance. The idea that in the study of the origins of Luther's theology one deals with the roots of the difference between Rome and Reformation has faded. Instead there is concern to place Luther in his historical context with greater certainty. This has been attempted in a number of directions. Some see Luther's approach to Scripture as aligning most completely with biblical humanism. Others are certain that Luther's is a monastic way of dealing with Scripture. What we are seeing is a trend that favors studies which do not attempt to interpret Luther in light of a single key to his development. Search for the real Luther is most lively and interesting in quarters where a serious attempt is being made to look again at historical context.

Second, one of the driving forces of the changing image of Luther as biblical expositor is the question regarding his view of language. What is Luther's relationship to sixteenth-century rhetoric? Does he or doesn't he eschew allegory? Current research has made the case that we cannot uncritically assume that Luther had the same view of language that we have. The emerging view of Luther will be determined by how well some of the issues surrounding this matter can be sharpened in our thinking.

The issue of Luther's view of language is something that is taken up by each of the competing views. In various ways, each gives some answer to this question. Even those who are interested in Luther for his contemporary significance for theology have found the Reformer's understanding of language to be of critical importance. Oswald Bayer counts Luther's use of performative language in the forgiveness of sins to be one of his most important discoveries.[39]

[38] Ibid., 55-66.
[39] Ibid., 443 ff.

Third, given the ongoing character of the contextualizing of Luther's work, it is inevitable that the question of how Luther's approach to Scripture can be understood with respect to our own. The older explanation that Luther stands as the creator of a new Protestant hermeneutic is being challenged in a number of ways. The current hermeneutical principles, built as they are on methodologies of textual and literary criticism, do not seem to correspond to the impulse driving Luther. At the very least this portrayal of Luther links Luther with a specific movement within the history of the development of scriptural interpretation and the field of hermenueutics which first emerged in its present form in the nineteenth century. This casts Luther into an unfamiliar world which does not reflect his own concerns.

The emerging image of Luther as biblical expositor is attempting to articulate his approach to Scripture within the context of his entire work as a theologian. There are an increasing number of interpreters who view Luther's inheritance from monasticism as being of critical importance to getting it right with respect to Luther as biblical expositor. Luther's publishing of his threefold understanding of theology (*oratio*, *tentatio*, *meditatio*) sets the framework in which his work as Catholic theologian is carried out. This also means, however, that in order to explicate this world one must carefully enter a world which is unlike our own. The questions of what is Lutheran and what is Catholic are unwelcome here. One must recognize that at the end of the high Middle Ages, before the Council of Trent, there is no monolithic Catholic theology, there are only various Catholic theologies. Here anachronisms of all kinds need to be reviewed and questioned.

In this new century of research, the image of Luther as biblical expositor will undoubtedly go through even more change. Whether consensus will light upon one of the images being presented here or whether a new amalgam will be formed in the collision of ideas already circulating remains to be seen.

KATHARINA LUTHER IN THE LIGHT AND IN THE SHADOW OF THE REFORMATION

Helmar Junghans

"Kete von Bora is the morning star of Wittenberg,"[1] Luther stated in 1532 as an example of a metaphor. He explained to his table companions that a metaphor indicates something that can be understood differently, but he did not explain what he meant by Katharina being a "morning star." Did he intend to present his wife as the Venus among the women of Wittenberg or declare that she began her daily work earlier than anybody else? In any case, for us she also continues to be a morning star: on the one hand, she emits a bright light until this very day; on the other hand, much remains hidden in the fog of vague tradition. Her life proceeds in three clear sections: her youth, her marriage, and her years of widowhood. In conclusion we have to consider how to remember her.

I. The Early Years: 1499 to 1525

Katharina von Bora experienced this period of time as a child, as a nun, and as a refugee.

1. Her Childhood

There is little to report about Katharina's childhood. She was probably born on January 29, 1499, at the estate of Lippendorf near Neukieritzsch. Her parents belonged to the Saxon nobility. Her father's name was Hans von Bora; her mother's, Katharina von Haugwitz. Besides that she had three brothers and at least one sister. Growing up in the security of a family was denied her. Her mother died early. When her father remarried in 1505, Katharina was already living at the boarding school of the nunnery at Brehna. Her father apparently realized that she would get a better education there than in a motherless household.

[1] WA TR 2: 649.14 (2772 a), 28 September to 23 November 1532.

2. A Nun at Nimbschen

Four years later, in 1509, the ten-year-old could be found as a candidate for the novitiate at the Marienthron cloister at Nimbschen. Here she shared the same fate with other daughters of noble Saxon families who could not supply their daughters with an adequate marriage dowry. For all that, she did not have to do entirely without the companionship of relatives since the Abbess Margarete von Haubitz was probably her mother's sister and the nun Magdalena von Bora her father's sister.

The Cistercian nunnery at Nimbschen was a substantial establishment. It owned the parish church as Wessnig, the churches at Torgau and Altbelgern—with 23 branch churches—as well as the village of Polbitz with a lake, besides the parish church at Grimma with the Grossbardau and Greten branches. From 1277 onward it received one-tenth of the metal contained in the slagheaps of the mines. A mill proved to be profitable. The cloister was largely exempt from taxes. That way it had at its disposal sufficient means to buy nine villages around Nimbschen. The nunnery also owned a large farm that employed forty persons and where cattle, horses, hogs, and geese were kept. In these ways, more than 40 nuns and several lay sisters could be adequately provided for.[2]

In 1514 Katharina entered the novitiate; on October 8, 1515, she made the vows of obedience, of poverty, and of chastity. Her father forwarded thirty Groschen for the consecration. As far as he was concerned, his daughter was now taken care of for good.[3] The Rule of the order determined the course of each day for her, including six daily prayer times in the cloister church, fasting, and a frugal nourishment. It is not reported how strictly these rules were kept nor if they were grossly neglected. Katharina knew how to read and write and knew Latin so she could participate in the horary prayers. She became acquainted with a large household that had its own housekeeping and care of the sick. We do not know if she entered the vocation of a nun grudgingly, from an inner desire, or if she simply accepted her fate. At any rate, she could live in the understanding of the late Middle Ages that she was walking on the more certain road to life eternal because, with an ascetic life, she chose the meritorious, better Christian existence.

But scarcely two years after Katherina took her vows, Luther challenged the piety that surrounded her. In October 1517 he began

[2] Schlesinger 2, 274 f.

[3] Martin Treu, *Katharina von Bora* (Wittenberg: Drei Kastanien Verlag, 1995), 12.

his critique against the indulgences, which raised doubt as to the efficaciousness of the 367 relics in the cloister church at Nimbschen. According to the conviction of the Reformers, the Christians who listened to the proclaimed Word of God and received the Lord's Supper belonged to the worshipping congregation. Then memorial masses for the dead lost their meaning and most of the twelve altars of the cloister church their importance.

In 1522 Luther shook the foundations of monasticism directly. After monks began leaving their cloisters as a result of the message of the Reformation, Luther showed in his pamphlet "Judgment on Monastic Vows" (*De votis monasticis iudicium*) that the vocation of monks and nuns could not be meritorious because, in the first place, nobody can earn the grace of God. He described how lifelong monastic vows were in contradiction to the biblical message and therefore were no longer binding. With his writing, "The Estate of Marriage," he reinforced in the same year not only his conviction that clerics, monks, and nuns ought to marry, but simultaneously paid tribute to marriage as an estate ordained by God himself. He encouraged matrimony because what is done and suffered in it becomes holy, divine and precious.[4] He did not consider the estate of monks and nuns as more holy but, on the contrary, that marriage is the more excellent estate. For being a Christian, the ascetic life had lost its meaning, yes, it now appeared as a haughtiness toward God's creation, because what was being praised here was a life that was inconsistent with the divinely-created nature.

This message did not go unheard. As early as 1522 Wolfgang von Zeschau left the Augustinian monastery at Grimma. He had two nieces who were nuns at Nimbschen. In whatever way it may have happened, Luther's thought about nuns and marriage, and the ensuing withdrawals from the cloisters, did not remain unknown at the Nimbschen convent. Some of the nuns realized that they were wrong to trust in their ascetic achievements. They asked their families to help them leave the nunnery. But their families either would not risk it or did not want to provide for their daughters. The Torgau wholesaler, Leonard Koppe, who supplied the Nimbschen cloister, came to their aid. Twelve nuns escaped from the nunnery during Easter night between the 5th and the 6th of April, 1523.[5] Koppe transported them away between empty herring barrels on his horse-drawn vehicle. Three of the twelve nuns were able to return directly to their families. The other

[4] WA 10^2:297.16-19.

[5] In reference to the number of the escaped nuns, compare WA Br 3:3.54 Anm. 6 (599), according to which Nikolaus von Amsdorf informed Georg von Spalatin on April 11, 1523, that not just nine but twelve nuns had left.

nine accompanied the Torgau pastor, Gabriel Zwilling, to Wittenberg, where they arrived on April 10, not without attracting attention.

3. Refugees at Wittenberg

On the very same day, Luther approved of their flight from the nunnery by sending to the printer the pamphlet, "Reason and Answer, that Virgins May Leave Cloisters in a Godly Way." Thereby he wanted to avoid the impression that their flight was something scandalous. At the same time he wanted to encourage aristocrats and burghers to get their daughters "who had been pushed into the cloister as young, inexperienced womenfolk"[6] out of the nunneries where the Word of God was wanting. Luther knew from 1 Corinthians 7:7 that there is God's gift of celibacy—that means complete sexual abstinence—so that a person can serve God without caring for a family. But nobody could boast about a gift from God. As a rule "a woman must be a woman, must bear fruit, for which God has created her, and not make herself any better than God has made her."[7] Luther assured Koppe that he acted correctly when he led "these poor souls out of the prison of human tyranny."[8] For Luther it was irrefutable that it was Christ himself who brought his Gospel back to light and thereby destroyed the domain of the Antichrist.[9] Part of this was to rescue the consciences and the souls of these nuns.[10] The light of the Reformation had penetrated Nimbschen and guided Katharina to Wittenberg, from where this light came.

The young Katharina
by Lucas Cranach.

[6] WA 11:396.29f.
[7] WA 11:398.10-12.
[8] WA 11:395.1f.
[9] WA 11:395.11f.
[10] WA 11:396.16f.

Katharina found accommodation with a Wittenberg family, presumably with the painter Lucas Cranach. He maintained the largest household in Wittenberg, which included journeymen painters as well as guests. Here Katharina could learn a great deal, not only about a large household but also about the contents of the Reformation message, which Cranach and his workshop turned into pictures. At the same time Luther and his friends endeavored to provide permanently for the refugee nuns, which largely meant to get them married off. Katharina fell in love with the son of a Nuremberg patrician, Hieronymus Baumgartner, but his parents refused to give their consent to a marriage with an impecunious, runaway nun. When Luther's friend, the professor of theology Nikolaus von Amsdorf, suggested to Katharina, at the request of Luther, that she marry Kaspar Glatz, pastor of Orlamünde, she declined and declared self-assuredly that she would marry only Amsdorf or Luther. Luther commented resignedly: "If she does not want him, she may just as well wait yet awhile for someone else."[11]

II. THE YEARS OF MATRIMONY: 1525 TO 1546

Katharina found in her marriage a broad field of activity that we want to bring to mind under the perspectives of wife, hostess, mother, and also lady of the house.

1. The Wife

When in May of 1525 the Peasants' Revolt assumed alarming proportions, Luther decided to get married. With the marriage contract, he wanted to put his teaching into practice and substantiate it. He wished to please his father, whom he had bitterly disappointed twenty years before by his entry into the monastery and who disclosed to Martin at the end of April that he wanted very much to see him as husband and father. Luther, however, aimed to outwit Satan before the world came to an end. We do not hear anything about his love for Katharina; indeed, later he even declared that he did not love her and thought her to be haughty.[12] Neither do we know what kind of feelings Katharina's clear-cut declaration gradually evoked in

[11] Martin Brecht, *Martin Luther*, Volume 2: *Ordnung und Abgrenzung der Reformation* 1521–1532 (Stuttgart: Calwer, 1986), 194f.

[12] WA TR 4:503.20f (4786).

him. But one thing was evident to the forty-one-year-old bridegroom: the twenty-six-year-old Katharina von Bora would not turn him down. So the one now willing to get married decided in her favor. His horrified friends shouted: "Not her, but another one." She obviously was not regarded as a lovely bride. The Wittenberg jurist Hieronymus Schurf commented: "If this friar marries, then the whole world and the devil will laugh and he himself will again destroy what he has created."[13] But Luther would not let himself be stopped by such talk; rather it hurried him along. On June 13, 1525, Katharina and Martin got married in the Black Cloister. Fourteen days later the newlyweds publicly processed from the Cloister to the church and the wedding celebration followed.

Luther was not the only friar who married a nun. This marriage received special attention but did not meet unanimous approval. Three years later the Leipzig magister Joachim von der Heyden directed an open letter to Katharina as the "poor seduced woman." He accused her of having left the nunnery and proceeded to the University of Wittenberg in order to find herself a *Katschenknecht*—someone to kiss (*schmatzen*). This proved to be a nasty defamation for which he reproached her. He charged Luther with having enticed her out of the cloister under a false pretext into the alleged Christian freedom and accused her of having brought many poor innocent children out of the convent into misery by her example. In view of the eternal punishment of hell for the breaking of her vow, he called upon her to "desist in the future from this devilish life ... to leave this black, horrible friar" and to return to the cloister.[14] Luther, who received a similar letter from another Leipzig magister, made short work of both with satires. Nevertheless, one has to keep in mind that Katharina contracted her marriage in opposition to public opinion as far as this was still formed by late medieval ideas. The marriage of theologians still had to struggle for public recognition.

Out of the marriage that was contracted for sensible reasons grew a tender relationship. Luther's salutation in a letter has often been quoted: "My friendly dear Master Katharina Lutherin." Thus she appeared as the lady of the house, perhaps also as domineering sometimes. But these greetings parodied salutations that were common at that time, for example, in letters to the Elector. What is more, in these salutations an intimate teasing between husband and wife becomes apparent whereby Luther pictures himself as the subservient

[13] Heinrich Boehmer, "Luthers Ehe" in *Lutherjahrbuch* 7 (1925): 65.

[14] WA Br 4:527-31 (1305 enclosure).

one. Moreover, this salutation was reported in 1529 and 1530 only. It is more informative that Luther used the attributes "friendly," "dear" and "darling" more frequently in salutations and greetings. In his letters from 1534 on, Luther called himself "Your Truelove" or "Your Sweetheart." Neither was he afraid to talk about the most intimate relations, as when he wrote sixteen days before his death: "So that you can be assured that I would love you with pleasure, if I could, as you know. ..." One senses from Luther's letters to his wife how much Katharina worried about him during his travels and how Luther made an effort—often in a jocular tone—to dispel her worries.

The relationship between the couple was not limited to the private sphere. Katharina kept in close touch with the Reformation. She urged Luther to respond to the challenge of Erasmus of Rotterdam, which Luther resolutely did with his *De servo arbitrio*. She read in Holy Scripture and in the Catechism. She participated in theological conversations during Luther's table talks. In 1529 Luther informed her about negotiations during the religious Colloquy at Marburg. We can infer from this that the couple talked about theological questions at other times as well. A letter regarding the filling of a vacancy in a parish gives reason to suppose that Luther discussed many questions about personnel. Luther obviously respected his wife as an empathizing conversation partner even in matters of the Reformation.

The Swedish Germanist, Birgit Stolt, who has examined Luther's letters to his wife, came to this conclusion: "from these texts follows ... unequivocally, that this marriage between two mature personalities developed into a warm, harmonic relationship, a loving marriage that did not decrease in tenderness over the years but, on the contrary, intensified."[15]

2. The Hostess

The newlyweds had no time to devote themselves to each other undisturbed by others and to become acquainted. Barely had the last wedding guests departed from the Black Cloister late in the evening of June 27, 1525, when a shadow of the Reformation began to fall upon the house: Andreas Bodenstein from Karlstadt asked for a hiding place.[16] As a professor of theology at Wittenberg, he had origi-

[15] Birgit Stolt, "Luthers Sprache in seinen Briefen an Kaethe," *in Katharina von Bora, die Lutherin: Aufsaetze anlaesslich ihres 500. Geburtstages*, edited by Martin Treu by commission of the Foundation for Luther Studies in Sachsen-Anhalt (Wittenberg: Stiftung Luthergedenkstätlan in Sachsen-Anhalt, 1999), 24.

[16] Boehmer, 67.

nally supported the theology of the Reformation. While Luther was kept in hiding at the Wartburg in 1521/22, Bodenstein advanced the Reformation at Wittenberg. He wanted to establish it more firmly with a new city ordinance. For this reason he came into conflict with Luther, who wanted an open space for the proclamation of the Gospel, not any coercion that was regulated by new laws. The papal tyranny should not be replaced by an evangelical tyranny. Bodenstein did not understand this; instead he angrily left Wittenberg. Thus, a conflict flared up within the Reformation that burdened Luther more than the attacks by his enemies who were loyal to Rome. During the Peasants' War, Bodenstein came under unwarranted suspicion for having encouraged, along with Thomas Müntzer, violent action by the peasants. So he had to flee prosecution. He found a safe asylum with Luther. Katharina assumed the role of the hostess immediately after their wedding celebration. For eight weeks Bodenstein stayed at their home until Luther could help him move on.

Bodenstein began a long string of asylum seekers who were cared for by Katharina. Most of them were refugees who had run into danger because of their evangelical faith. There appeared runaway members of orders and expelled preachers who needed help but among them were also "thieves and rascals."[17] A few examples illustrate what kind of tragedies of fate Katharina confronted.

Conrad Cordatus was thrown into prison in Hungary for his Reformation sermons. He was able to flee and rushed—where else?—to Luther in 1526. He went to Liegnitz, from where he had to flee again. In March (?), 1528, Cordatus stopped again at Katharina's until 1529, when he became the second pastor at Zwickau. When he left there in 1531, he stayed once again at the Wittenberg Cloister until 1532. He began to jot down notes of Luther's conversations—especially at the table. When he found successors, a unique tradition of conversations with Luther emerged which help us to learn a great deal about Katharina.

Michael Stiefel, a fellow friar with Luther, who in 1522 praised him in a poem, found accommodation at the Wittenberg Cloister as early as 1523. In the beginning of 1525. Luther helped him to be called as a preacher in Austria. After Stiefel's friend Leonhard Kaiser was executed there as an evangelical preacher on August 16, 1527. Stiefel could no longer stay in Austria. Therefore he came to Luther in January, 1528, and was Katharina's guest until September when he began his ministry at Lochau (since 1573, Annaburg).

[17] WA Br 9:581.48 (3699 enclosure IV), Luther's Household Account [of 6 January 1542].

Ludwig Rabe, who had studied at Wittenberg from 1517, found a position at Halle. When he felt threatened by Cardinal Albrecht, Archbishop of Magdeburg and Mainz, in 1535 he fled to Luther, where he lived until June of 1538. Luther then provided him with the position of chancellor with Prince Wolfgang of Anhalt.

The *Hausfrau* Kete by Lucas Cranach.

On October 16, 1528, Duchess Ursula von Münsterberg, who fled from a Freiberg nunnery, became Katharina's guest for several weeks. Yes, even an electress availed herself of her care. Elizabeth von Brandenburg left her husband Elector Joachim I of Brandenburg in 1528 because he not only closed his mind to the Reformation but also made Katharina Hornung, wife of a Berlin patrician, his mistress. Elizabeth found refuge at Lichtenburg near the Elbe River and visited Martin and Katharina several times at Wittenberg. Taken ill, she stayed in Luther's house from mid-August, 1537. When she became childish, Katharina sat at her bed and calmed her.[18] In need of care, the electress and her entourage required more nursing than even Katharina and Martin were able to give her. From November he sought to have the electoral court of Saxony care for her elsewhere. But Elector Johann Friedrich beseeched Luther repeatedly to provide for her. She did not depart until the beginning of the new year.[19]

The reactions produced by the Reformation not only brought those men and women to the house of Katharina and Luther, who had to overcome their negative results, but many also arrived who wanted to get Luther's advice. Their stay was usually shorter. They

[18] WA Br 8:112.4 f.—the numbering 25 is questionable, a possible misprint for 5—(3170), Luther to Fürst Johann von Anhalt [on 20 August 1537 from Wittenberg].

[19] "Ein Brief Martin Luthers an Franz Burkhard [vom 7. November 1537 aus Wittenberg]: Edition nach dem Autographen," edited by Detlev Doering, *Lutherjahrbuch* 54 (1987): 94-99.

brought a great deal of positive news into the house about the dissemination of the evangelical message. As hostess, Katharina experienced vividly the light and dark sides of the Reformation.

The University of Wittenberg expected its professors to put students up in their houses, that is, to maintain a *Burse* [home for students]. There was sufficient room at the monastery which was built for about 40 friars. Katharina took care of the students' maintenance as well. A few young magisters moved in. One magister was responsible for the burse; in addition each magister looked after several students. Katharina not only had a great deal of work with them but at times also trouble when the payment for board had to be settled.

Occasionally Katharina and Martin offered refuge to friends. George Rörer was employed by the town of Wittenberg to see to it that the Wittenberg printings were delivered without mistakes. In 1525 Luther ordained him as a deacon of the Wittenberg town church. He was frequently in Luther's company to record his sermons and lectures. On October 2, 1527, he lost his wife to the plague. Thereupon Katharina and Luther took him and the family of Johannes Bugenhagen—a brother of the deceased Hanna Rörer—into their house. In 1539 Katharina and Martin received the four children of the couple Sebald and Anna Münster, whom the plague had snatched away, until Philipp Melanchthon's wife—a sister of Anna Münster—was able to provide for them at her home. Martin and Katharina did not let themselves be controlled by the fear of infection but by Christian charity with complete trust in God.

3. The Mother

Around the year 1529 Katharina accepted still another responsibility, that of a foster mother. Luther's sister Margarethe Kaufmann left behind six children who found a new home in Katharina's household. Also received were the children of another sister, who was married to Klaus Polner. That this was not entirely a matter of course can be seen by the fact that Luther's brother Jacob, who had inherited his parents' house, did not welcome any of his nieces and nephews. They not only had to be fed but also provided for. As a result of losing their parents, they were difficult to handle. When Luther was on a long journey, he asked his friends to help Katharina with the education of these children. From her own family, Katharina invited her nephew Florian von Bora into her home.

Katharina not only looked after her nieces and nephews but she also experienced joys and sorrows with her own children. On June 7,

1526, Johannes was born. On December 10, 1527, Elizabeth followed but she died as early as August 3, 1528—that is, in the first year of her life—which caused deep grief for her parents. On May 4, 1529, Magdalena came into the world. A day before Luther's forty-eighth birthday, on November 9, 1531, Martin was born. On January 28, 1533, Paul arrived and on December 17, 1534, Margarethe was born as the sixth and last child.

Katharina and Martin went through deep suffering with the death of their thirteen-year-old Magdalena on September 20, 1542. Through her friendliness Magdalena had conquered the hearts of many. It is moving to read the letters that reflect a wrestling between sadness and faith in God.[20] Since Magdalena died with a deep devotion to God's will, Luther knew that he had reason to thank God for her life and dying, but the grief over this loss silenced him. Therefore he asked his friend Justus Jonas to bring their thanks before God in their place as Magdalena's parents. Even later the sadness over this loss overwhelmed him and he reported that Katharina still cried over it.

The growing family of nieces, nephews and their own children, permanent guests, the magisters with their students, and occasional guests at mealtime filled the refectory that was built for 40 friars. They all wanted to be taken care of. How could that be accomplished economically and efficiently?

4. The Lady of the House

Several times in his letters Luther addresses Katharina as *Frau* (woman, Mrs.), virgin—which is to say, young woman—or *Hausfrau* (woman of the house). In those days these words had a different meaning than they do today. Where we use the word *Frau*, Luther's contemporaries used the word *Weib*. Furthermore, *Frau* was a term for the estate of a person befitting a woman of nobility who was addressed as ladyship (*Herrin*). Katharina filled the position of the Lady of the House perfectly. For Luther she continued to be his "dear" or "dearly beloved *Hausfrau*."[21]

Luther was the most successful author of the sixteenth-century. He could have earned a considerable amount of money for writing but he did not want it: "I will preach free of charge and write with disdain for the world, so that the world must see that a person can do some good not out of haughtiness but because he is a Christian."[22]

[20] See Helmar Junghans, "Martin Luthers letzte Jahre," *Luther* 67 (1996): 127-29.

[21] Stolt, 25.

[22] WA TR 2:24.20-22 (1284).

When the printers at Wittenberg offered him 400 Gulden annually—that was as much as he eventually received as a yearly salary—[he said] he does not want to sell God's grace—that is, what he has [freely] received from God.[23] Katharina, who had to concern herself with financing the expanding household, saw it differently but resigned herself to Luther's notions. She sought another solution: that of self-management as she had known it at Nimbschen.

First of all Katharina prepared the monastery garden, got a well dug, and had Luther procure seeds from out of town. In 1527 Luther acquired a small garden outside of the Elster Gate. Since the state of ownership was not clarified, he had to give it back. In 1531 he bought a garden with a strip of field and a barn. He was not very happy about the land purchase and emphasized that Katharina bought this garden for herself and not for him, indeed, against his will. Cordatus thereupon asks why he permitted this against his will. Luther's answer: "I could bear neither her pleas nor her tears."[24] Friends of Luther were convinced that Katharina changed her husband's mind not only in this case.[25]

On February 4, 1532 Elector Johann transfered the former monastery of the Augustinian Hermits along with its land to Luther and his heirs. In 1535/36 Luther acquired another garden with a *hufe* of land. The size of a *hufe* fluctuates, but would have been sufficient for the support of a farm family. In 1539 Katherina was successful in leasing the Boos farm with 3½ *hufen* southeast of Wittenberg under favorable conditions from the elector. In 1540 Luther bought the estate of Zölsdorf south of Leipzig that Katharina's brother could no longer manage. The elector undertook 600 Gulden of the 610-Gulden purchase price. In 1544 Luther acquired another garden and ordered 600 wine stakes and grafting twigs. Katharina evidently wanted to begin her own viticulture. In 1544 another field was added.

This land had to be farmed. By 1542 the farmstead on the north side of the cloister included five cows, nine calves, one goat with two kids, two sows and eleven other hogs. Luther also bought work animals—horses and oxen. Maids and farmhands helped in the house, in the stable, and in the field. It is true that Katharina included Luther in her management but the responsibility for the direction and supervision of this extensive household lay in her hands. Her aunt Magdalena von Bora, who fled with her from Nimbschen, was a big

[23] WA TR 4:431.29-432.1 (4690).

[24] WA TR 2:290.13-16 (1995).

[25] Ernst Kroker, *Katharina von Bora: Martin Luthers Frau; ein Lebens- und Charakterbild*, Edition 12 (Berlin: Evang. Verlagsanstalt, 1972), 274.

help until her death in the year 1537. After that Katharina had to work with strangers. This led to quite a few annoyances. A vagabond claimed to be an escaped nun, Rosina von Truchseß. Katharina put her in care of the kitchen, cellar and chambers. When in 1541 it turned out that Rosina lied, stole, and became pregnant, she fled. Four years later Katharina had to deal with a "second Rosina."

But Katharina also expended a great deal of energy taking care of her house. When she moved in after her wedding, she had to restore all the rotten straw mattresses and do a thorough cleaning. In the mostly-deserted monastery nobody had put things in order. She got the rooms whitewashed. After the cloister was lawfully transferred to Luther in 1532, he let Katharina adapt the house to the needs of the family. In 1532 a basement was added, but it caved in before it was completed and nearly killed Katharina and Martin. A brewery needed to be built. The renovation of the interior followed from 1535 to 1540. On this occasion a living room was built, which is preserved until this day as the *Lutherstube* (Luther parlor). From 1540 the *Katharinenportal* (Katherine door) graced the entrance. Besides that, stables and farm buildings had to be erected. Katharina occupied herself for years as a building supervisor.

III. The Years of Widowhood: 1546–552

On February 22, 1546, Katharina with her horsedrawn vehicle joined the funeral procession which accompanied the deceased Reformer through the Elster Gate to the Castle- and University-Church. There she heard the sermon of Johannes Bugenhagen and the funeral oration of Philipp Melanchthon. She witnessed the burial of her husband. A deep shadow fell on her life. For the present, it was a personal kind as all wives experience who stand at the graves of their husbands. But very soon the shadow of the Reformation would darken her life as well.

For the time being Luther's reputation helped her get her way with her plans. Luther had bequeathed to her in 1544 "all of his immovable and movable possessions as her property for the rest of her life."[26] He thereby prevented his inheritance from falling mostly to his children and Katharina's becoming dependent on them. At the same time he designated her as the guardian of the children. The former Chancellor Gregor Brück, who resided at Wittenberg, commented most critically in his legal opinion on Luther's testament and

[26] Pauline Puppel, "Zur Rechtsstellung der Katharina von Bora," *in Katharina von Bora, die Lutherin*, 43.

on Katharina to the Elector, but could not move him against Katharina's plans. Nevertheless, according to the law in force at that time, Katharina had to accept guardians for her children and for her legal transactions. She could, however, suggest persons whom the Elector Johann Friedrich generously considered during the appointment of guardians on March 24, 1546. He confirmed Luther's testament on April 11, 1546, in spite of its juristic faults. In his last will, Luther advanced a development that improved the widow's share of the inheritance. However, Brück recommended that the three sons be placed outside of Katharina's household because he considered Katharina unqualified for their education. On May 21, Katharina obtained an electoral decision that permitted the children to stay with their mother. In a surprisingly short time, Katharina's matters of inheritance and legal status were cleared up. Luther's effort to improve Katharina's situation after his death according to the then existing laws encouraged a development which grants to widows more rights regarding inheritance claims and guardianship over their children.[27]

Katharina used her newly-attained legal status to acquire the Wachsdorf estate south of Wittenberg. Since there were no provisions for widows and children of theologians until then, her efforts were understandable. For the purchase of the Wachsdorf estate, she could have sold the former Augustinian monastery. But, contrary to Brück's expectations, she wanted to keep it and to manage a *Burse*. She was indeed successful at it even though Luther could no longer be her center. Katharina prompted her guardians to make a request to the elector "for the sake of the Doctor ... to let the widow also have something."[28] Against Brück's advice, the elector supported the purchase with 2000 Gulden; the guardians and Luther's friend Nikolaus von Amsdorf raised the remaining 200 Gulden. On June 24 Luther's heirs became the owners of the Wachsdorf estate. Katharina believed that she had now provided well for herself and for her children. But she was mistaken. For one thing, it is questionable whether a rundown estate could be profitably managed without available capital. But the ensuing course of the Reformation also had catastrophic consequences.

Emperor Charles V decided to go to war against the Schmalkaldic League, a defense alliance of the Protestant estates of the Empire. The fighting began as early as 1546. Well-fortified Wittenberg prepared for a siege. The University disbanded at the beginning of No-

[27] Puppel, 44-46.

[28] Kroker, *Katharina von Bora*, 244.

vember. Katharina lost her students. Charles V succeeded in winning the support of Duke Moritz of Saxony. When his army drew near, Katharina fled with her children to Magdeburg. In the middle of November, Duke Moritz moved in close with an army that included unrestrained horsemen from Croatia, Walachia (Romania), and Poland. The beleaguered were able to ward off the charge upon Wittenberg on November 18. But they had to watch until after Christmas as the enemies plundered the area surrounding Wittenberg. Katharina's property outside of the walls was ravaged.

At the end of January 1547, Katharina returned with her family to Wittenberg. Emperor Charles V himself now advanced with his army. On April 24 he surprised the army of the Schmalkaldic League at the Lochauer Heide and took Elector Johann Friedrich prisoner. As a result, at the end of May Katharina fled with others from Wittenberg. They traveled with their children via Magdeburg to Braunschweig. From there they went to King Christian of Denmark who had continued to support her. Faced with marauding mercenaries, she returned to Braunschweig. Meanwhile the imperial army—likewise plundering—advanced toward Wittenberg without conquering it. Wittenberg capitulated on May 19. It fell to Duke Moritz of Saxony along with the electoral district and the Saxon electoral office.[29] Charles V entered the city but did not punish the Reformers or their families. Against the advice of the Emperor's councilors, Luther's grave remained untouched;[30] a pillage did not take place, since the army had to stay outside of the city.

Katharina could have stayed safely in Wittenberg as the Reformer Johannes Bugenhagen did. His house and yard remained intact. When the University was back in operation in the fall, Katharina re-opened her *Burse*, once again with success. But as far as her gardens and estates were concerned, she was reduced to poverty. Since she could not do without them, she had to go into debt to restore them. In the summer of 1548, she asked the Elector Moritz for a ratification of her property rights at Wachsdorf and also for the delivery of grain and wood, fifty Gulden annually and scholarships for each son,[31] all

[29] PKMS 3:412-16 (584), Wittenberg capitulation on 19 May 1547 to the imperial encampment at Wittenberg.

[30] Helmar Junghans, "Kaiser Karl V. am Grab Martin Luthers in der Schlosskirche zu Wittenberg," *Lutherjahrbuch* 54 (1987): 100-113.

[31] *Politische Korrespondenz des Herzogs und Kurfürsten Moritz von Sachsen,* Bd. 4: 26 May 1548–8 January1551, edited by Johannes Hermann and Guenther Wartenberg (Berlin: Akademie Verlag, 1992), 139 (95), Katharina Luther to Kurfürst Moritz von Sachsen on 16 September (?) 1548 from Wittenberg.

of which had been promised her by Johann Friedrich; no reply is extant. Quarrelsome neighbors involved her in lawsuits and, even though she did not lose them, they were worrisome for her. But before she could recover from the devastations of the Schmalkaldic War, a new shadow of the Reformation fell upon her: the city of Madgeburg did not submit to the religious politics of Charles V and therefore was besieged from the fall of 1550 until November of 1551. Once again armies traversed Saxon territory and devastated the area. Bugenhagen wrote to Christian III of Denmark: "It is indeed obvious that this year she and her neighbors have suffered great damages to their property." The estates that were to bring security to her in her old age, and to her children, were causing her great insecurity and worries.

In the summer of 1552 another outbreak of the plague occurred at Wittenberg. The University moved its lectures to Torgau. When in September the plague claimed casualties even in Katharina's house, she fled with her children to Torgau. On the way the horses took fright, Katharina jumped off the wagon, hit the ground hard, and plunged into a ditch filled with cold water. Paralysis and illness with a cold were the consequences. She lay bed-ridden at Torgau until death delivered her from all her cares and suffering on December 20, 1552. She found her last resting place at the Torgau town church, where until this day a stone epitaph, carved in relief, serves as a reminder of her.

IV. KATHARINA, AN EVANGELICAL SAINT

Who was this Katharina Luther nee von Bora? At the Leipzig Book Fair in spring 1999, Katharina was introduced by women of the "Workshop 'Katharina von Bora' of the Evangelical Academy Sachsen-Anhalt at Wittenberg" (*Arbeitsstelle "Katharina von Bora" bei der Evang. Akademie Sachsen-Anhalt zu Wittenberg*). They wanted to picture Katharina von Bora as a model for today's women. They characterized Katharina as an independent, strong, and courageous woman. The emphasis on independence reflected the interests of the lecturing women. The procedure amounts to making Katharina a symbolic figure of her own effort who fulfills her own wishes but does not ask questions. Was independence really so important for Katharina? Did she perhaps not let herself be guided by other motives? Is there not for us—that means men and women—still another point of view by which to remember her?

Katharina certainly was unusually capable and efficient. In her married life she mastered a barely-conceivable task and built as well as directed a substantial self-sufficient enterprise. She was a blessing for Luther; the marriage to him helped her find an exceptional field of activity and placed her into public view so that many still remember her today. However, her successes and the electoral support in her land purchases did not always find admirers. One has to question how she could finance all of this. It should be mentioned here that, besides his salary, Luther annually received a fixed amount of firewood, grain, as well as malt for beer brewing. From the elector also came presents of venison and wine. Other princes and people likewise brought presents to the Luther house. They were certainly aware of the hospitality Katharina showed in her home to the family of orphaned nieces and nephews, to Luther's Wittenberg friends, to refugees of the Reformation, and to those seeking advice. Nowadays Katharina would have had a legitimate claim for aid to dependant children, orphan compensation, nursing care, and official travel expenses. Many may have considered her to be greedy but she troubled herself personally over an economic base for her hospitable, obliging household. In his testament, Luther explicitly defended Katharina against the suspicion of having put aside cash. He said that he had "built, bought so much, and managed such an extensive and difficult household" that it is no wonder there was no cash left but rather [it was a miracle] that he had no greater debts.[32]

It is pointed out these days that Katharina was not so much in charge of a pastor's household as that of a professor. That is correct. However, one has to take into consideration that very few professors could have worked in such a turbulent household with so many persons. But this differentiation between a professor's and a pastor's household is unimportant for her significance. It is decisive that many Protestant parsonages have taken Katharina's household as a model and have maintained a hospitable, charitable home with many children. And with this we come to the heart of the evaluation.

Anyone studying Luther's teaching about marriage will soon come across his emphasis on marriage as an estate ordained by God himself. Marriage is the most distinguished estate and includes the household of an extended family. God himself has commanded it, whereas the estate of a monk is contrived by human beings and without promise. In a family, mutual relationships exist between the individual family members that allot to each one his tasks as described by Holy Scripture, but also care and love. From this grows the vocation for every Christian to make his contribution according to God's will

[32] WA Br 9:573.39-53 (3699), Luther's Testament of 6 January 1542.

who thereby preserves his creation and leads people to faith. Katharina and Martin endeavored to fulfill their tasks in the God-ordained estate of marriage. There was hardly any room left for reflections about self-realization.

In January 1533 Luther asked Katharina: "Do you believe that you are holy?" Completely surprised, she answered: "How can I be holy since I am a very great sinner?" And although she wanted thereby also to describe her standing before God, perhaps at the same time she was equally aware of having offended many a person with her self-confident behavior. Luther ordered her to believe that she was holy by virtue of her baptism.[33] More important for us than this general observation about being a Christian is the statement in Article 21 of the *Augsburg Confession* which is still valid in many evangelical Churches today:

> One must remember the saints ... that we strengthen our faith, seeing how grace has been given to them and how they have been helped by way of faith; besides, that everyone according to his calling take example by their good works ... .[34]

Katharina accepted her calling as the wife of the Reformer. Thus a fulfilled life was bestowed upon her. In this connection she took to heart the exhortation of Romans 12:13: "Practice hospitality" (*Übt Gastfreundschaft*). So it is written today in the revised Luther Bible. However Luther had probably not translated this accidentally in 1522: "Endeavor gladly to offer shelter" (*Strebt darnach das yhr gern herbergt*). Later he streamlined the sentence to the emphatic form: "Shelter gladly" (*Herberget gerne*).[35] With "gladly," Luther declares that God's commandments are to be kept not just in obedience but also with joy. At the same time, he is aware that the Holy Spirit must affect this willingness to serve out of Christian freedom. Katharina readily opened her house to many. The strength for her many-sided activities flowed from her faith in Christ. Therefore it is befitting to look upon Katharina as a gift of God for the Reformer Luther, to take notice of God's help in her many-sided activities, and to remember her as a model of faith; that is, to honor her as an evangelical saint.

Translated from the German by Rudolf K. Markwald

[33] WA TR 3:96.22-33 (2933 b).

[34] AC XXI:83. *Die Bekenntisschriften der evangelisch-lutherischen Kirche*[2] (Göttingen: Vandenhoeck &Ruprecht, 1955), 83b, 4-8; *Evangelisches Kirchengesangbuch* Nr. 807, Art. 21.

[35] WA DB 7:68f.

COMPARATIVE HERMENEUTICS: THE *GLOSSA ORDINARIA*, NICHOLAS OF LYRA, AND MARTIN LUTHER ON THE SONG OF SONGS

James G. Kiecker

Traditionally, medieval biblical interpretation has been divided into two major categories, literal and spiritual. Spiritual is often subdivided into allegorical (or figurative), tropological (or moral), and anagogical (or future). The literal with the tripartite spiritual sense, gives us the traditional fourfold sense of Scripture. But actually is this a successful categorization, in view of the fact that, at least in some scriptural books, there is a strong similarity between what gets labeled as literal and what as spiritual? It is often said that the *Glossa ordinaria* offers a spiritual interpretation of Scripture, while figures such as Nicholas of Lyra and Martin Luther provide a more literal interpretation. Is this really the case?

The goal of this essay is to compare three interpretations of the Song of Songs, that of the *Glossa ordinaria* from the early 1100s with those of Lyra in the early 1300s and Luther in the early 1500s. We will approach each interpretation historically, showing the impact of contemporary philosophy on the three interpretations. Then we will examine the hermeneutics of all three writers which were shaped by their various backgrounds. Next we will include samples of how each hermeneutic was put into practice in actual exegesis. Finally we will raise again the question whether or not a literal-spiritual dichotomy is useful when dealing with some portions of medieval, biblical commentaries.

I. Historical-Philosophical Background to the *Glossa ordinaria*

The dominant world-view from the beginning of Christianity to about the twelfth century was Platonism in one or another of its several manifestations. The cardinal doctrine of Platonic philosophy is the theory of archetypal ideas, according to which the fullest reality does not reside in the individual phenomenon, such as a particular man, but in the general idea of "man." Individual phenomena are only the fleeting, perishable semblances or shadows of the indestructible and essential ideas or forms.[1]

This Platonic and Neoplatonic world-view had a pronounced effect on literary interpretation. By the time of Christ, sophisticated Greeks were finding it hard to accept the surface literalness (that is, the text as it meets the eye) of the stories of Homer. Perhaps, they thought, the words of the text, the various characters and accounts, were insubstantial shadows of higher, spiritual realities (that is, something other than the surface literalness). On that premise the stories could be retained and utilized. Thus developed the technique of literary interpretation known as allegory, meaning "to say one thing, and signify something other than what is said."[2]

As first century Hellenistic society felt an embarrassment with its sacred literature, and the need to allegorize it, so Jews living in sophisticated centers such as Alexandria began to feel the same uneasiness with their Scriptures and their own need to allegorize. In the striking phrase of Beryl Smalley, "the allegorical interpretation marks a stage in the history of any civilized people whose sacred literature is 'primitive.'"[3] One of the first Jews to apply the method of allegory to Jewish Scriptures was Philo of Alexandria.

The early Christians soon followed suite. Paul used the word "allegory" in his interpretation of the two sons of Abraham (Genesis 16) in Galatians 4:22-26, though, since he did not deny the historicity of the account as allegorists often did, his method is more like what became known as typology.[4] Since so much of the Old Testament seemed to prefigure Christ, Paul's method was also christocentric. The author of Hebrews also used this method in his treatment of Melchizedek.[5]

To keep these background comments short, we will skip lightly through the centuries. In the second century allegory was the basic method of both Justin Martyr and Irenaeus.[6] Meanwhile, a Christian catechetical school was founded in Alexandria in which Clement and then Origen applied both typology and allegory to Scrip-

[1] A. H. Armstrong, ed., *The Cambridge History of Later Greek and Early Medieval Philosophy* (Cambridge: Cambridge University, 1967), 195-301.

[2] Ibid., 137-38.

[3] Beryl Smalley, *The Study of the Bible in the Middle Ages* (Notre Dame, Indiana: University of Notre Dame, 1964), 2.

[4] Robert M. Grant, *A Short History of the Interpretation of the Bible* (New York: Macmillan, 1948), 31-32, 75.

[5] See Genesis 14 and compare it with Hebrews 7.

[6] Armstrong, 164; Grant, 65, 70.

tures. Origen did not do away with the surface literalness of Scripture entirely. Where the level of the text made sense to him, he let it stand. Nevertheless, he elevated what he conceived to be the allegorical meaning behind the text over the basic literalness. All of Scripture had a spiritual sense, though not all of it had a literal sense.

In the fourth century, Ambrose followed Philo's Neoplatonic, allegorical interpretation of Genesis, which in turn inspired Augustine. Insofar as he was a Neoplatonist, Augustine put the meaning behind the text above the text's surface literalness. The words of Scripture reflected their divine author. "Divine illumination," as Augustine described it, enabled the reader to uncover the hidden meaning of the text. In general, Augustine began with the surface literalness of the text, giving this basic literal sense a wide enough meaning to include metaphor. But having ascertained the basic literalness, he preferred to attach a meaning beyond the surface literalness to the same text. There were cases, however, when one could not interpret literally at all: "Whatever appears in the divine Word that does not literally pertain to virtuous behavior or to the truth of faith you may take to be figurative,"[7] was his personal rule of interpretation.

Augustine set the tone for monastic exegesis that in many respects was a continuation of Neoplatonic, patristic, allegorical interpretation. Here we may mention such figures as Cassian (360–435), Cassiodorus (d. 575), Benedict (ca. 480–543), Gregory the Great (ca. 540–604), and in the sixth century Pseudo-Dionysius whose Neoplatonic writings profoundly affected biblical interpretation until the late Middle Ages.[8] The Venerable Bede (673–735) stated that if we follow only the letter of Scripture, and fail to draw out the allegories, we are not deriving what we should.[9]

In connection with the Carolingian revival of learning about 800 under Alcuin, there was the development of the *catena* or chain of exegetical extracts drawn from the Fathers. The *catena* assured the continuance of Neoplatonic, allegoristic, biblical interpretation.[10] During the ninth century the more original biblical commentaries continued to be in the Neoplatonic, allegoristic vein. This is true of

[7] Augustine, *On Christian Doctrine*, trans. D. W. Robertson, Jr. (New York: Bobbs-Merrill, 1958), 88.

[8] Armstrong, 467-72; David Knowles, *The Evolution of Medieval Thought* (New York: Random House, Vintage Books, 1962), 55-58; Etienne Gilson, *History of Christian Philosophy in the Middle Ages* (New York: Random House, 1955), 81-85.

[9] Smalley, 36.

[10] Grant, 116-17; Smalley, 37-38.

Radbertus (790–865), Erigena (ca. 810–877), Heimo, Heiric, and Remigius of Auxerre, and Angelom of Luxeuil. However, fragments of a new kind of exegesis started to make their appearance. Radbertus and Erigena were unafraid to question the Fathers. Rabanus Maurus (776 or 784–856) found a literal as well as a spiritual exposition for the books of Kings, and he consulted Jewish sources, which tended more toward the surface literalness than toward the allegorical interpretation.

During the tenth century there was a dearth of both *catenae* and original commentaries, due to the Viking invasions and to the interest in the liturgy of the Cluniac reformers.[11] After the year 1000 the gloss made its appearance. It was both marginal and interlinear.[12] It consisted of extracts from the Fathers and from more recent exegetes, generally anonymously. Under Anselm of Laon (d.1117), the gloss known as the *Glossa ordinaria* became standard after about 1100, serving chiefly as an aid to teaching in the schools.[13] Spicq characterizes the exegesis of the eighth to the eleventh centuries as "une exégèse essentiellement et universellement allégoric."[14]

To go just a bit beyond the gloss, the period of monastic exegesis is generally considered to end with Bernard of Clairvaux (1090–1153). Bernard not only compiled extracts from the Fathers, but was an exegete in his own right, given to finding the meaning of the text behind the text's surface literalness. "Abandon the carnal meaning for spiritual understanding, carnal slavery for the freedom of spiritual comprehension."[15] Like other monks, he commented on the Song of Songs in the form of sermons, which afforded an opportunity for purely spiritual exegesis. In this approach, Bernard stood in a direct line from Alexandria.[16]

[11] Smalley, 44-45.

[12] For the view that the author of the marginal glosses was Walafrid Strabo (d. 840), though the interlinear glosses were written by Anselm of Laon (d. 1117), see Frederick W. Farrar, *A History of Interpretation*, the Bampton Lectures, 1885 (Grand Rapids, Michigan: Baker Book House, 1961), 251.

[13] Smalley, 46-82.

[14] C. Spicq, *Esquisse d'une histoire de l'éxègese latine au moyen âge* (Paris: J. Vrin, 1944), 16.

[15] Quoted in Henri De Lubac, *The Sources of Revelation*, trans. Luke O'Neill (New York: Herder and Herder, 1968), 146.

[16] Knowles, 147-49; R. M. Southern, *The Making of the Middle Ages* (New Haven: Yale University Press, 1968), 215-17; Gilson, 164-67.

2. Hermeneutical Principles of the *Glossa ordinaria*

We turn now to the Preface for the Song of Songs in the *Glossa ordinaria.*[17] The Gloss's Preface plunges right into telling the interpreter how to understand the Song. We read that there are four personages in the Song—the bridegroom and his companions, and the bride and the young girls with her. In line with Platonic thinking and the whole tradition of biblical interpretation, we are told to understand the bridegroom to be Christ, and the bride to be the Church. The bridegroom's friends are the angels, and the bride's female attendants are potential brides.[18]

Furthermore, the reader is told that as a spiritual being he should spiritually hear sung the Song's words of love, and learn to transfer the impulses of his soul and the fire of natural love to "better things" (that is, spiritual things).[19] Later, the interpreter of the Song is told that the "subject-matter is the bridegroom and the bride, that is, the church and its head,"[20] and "in the manner of a marriage song he [Solomon, the Song's presumed author] sings mystically of the union of Christ and the church."[21] Finally we are told that the Song "reveals the unity of Christ and the church in the likeness of the bridegroom and bride."[22]

We must be very clear as to what we are being told in the Gloss's Preface. What can be called the surface literalness of the Song, the actual account of the Song as it appears to the eyes, is immediately to be leaped over into a spiritual sense, an allegory, the text saying one thing, but signifying something other than what is said in the text.

[17] *Glossa ordinaria, Pars 22, In Cantica Canticorum,* in *Corpus Christianorum, Continuatio Mediaevali* CLXX, ed. and trans. Mary Dove (Turnholti: Brepols, 1997). Hereafter this edition is referred to as Dove. The reader is invited to consult the *Biblia Latina cum Glossa Ordinaria,* Facsimile Reprint of the Editio Princeps: Adolph Rusch of Strassburg 1480/1481, intro. Karlfried Froehlich and Margaret T. Gibson, 4 vols. (Turnhout: Brepols, 1992). In her introduction to this work, Gibson cautions us that "an area still to be fully explored is the prefatory material to each book of the Glossed Bible" (vol. 1, ix). Though Gibson offers some suggestions as to the authors of the various statements in the Preface, we essentially do not know who gathered all the material together. All we can say is that it sets the tone for the Song's interpretation which follows.

[18] Dove, 72.

[19] Ibid., 74.

[20] Ibid., 76.

[21] Ibid., 78.

[22] Ibid., 80.

This thing, this "other than what is said in the text," becomes the true sense of the text. Again, this kind of interpretation is consistent with the prevailing Platonic world-view, which impacted biblical exegetes from the first century to the twelfth and, in fact, still has a certain appeal to this day.

3. The Exegesis of the Song of Songs in the *Glossa ordinaria*

We now look at some examples from the exegesis of the Song in the Gloss to see how well the hermeneutical directives of the Preface are carried out. Space forces us to be selective.

It is important to bear in mind what Mary Dove writes in her introduction to the *Glossa ordinaria*: "To speak of the 'glossator' is always a metaphor; there are many separate glossators, as well as a compiling glossator. The voices of the lovers in the Glossed Song of Songs embrace all the significances all these glossators draw out from them."[23]

Chapter 1:1—*Let him kiss me with the kisses of his mouth.*[24]

Gloss 6 —In line with Platonic-inspired interpretation, the Gloss moves directly from the level of the text to a spiritual interpretation of the text: "For just as two different bodies are joined in a kiss, so in the incarnation the two substances of divinity and humanity, utterly different, are united in an inseparable conjunction."[25]

Similarly:

Chapter 1:15—*Behold, you are beautiful, my beloved, and lovely; our bed [is] flowery.*[26]

Gloss 177—"Sometimes the church rests quietly in bed, as it were, with her bridegroom, in other words in times of peace when she perceives the beauty of God more clearly and gives birth by water and the Holy Spirit to a progeny of the faithful, redolent with the flower of faith. Sometimes, temptation rising up, she takes her place alongside her bridegroom in the line of battle."[27]

The *Glossa ordinaria*, while giving a spiritual interpretation to the text, nevertheless often discusses briefly the surface literalness of

[23] Ibid., 48.

[24] Ibid., 82. We shall try to follow as closely as possible the orthography of Dove.

[26] Ibid., 84.

[26] Ibid., 132.

[27] Ibid., 134.

the text, then almost imperceptively slides into a spiritual meaning. We find this in the glosses on chapter 2:8.

Chapter 2:8—"*The voice of my beloved; behold he comes leaping on the mountains, jumping over the hills.*"[28]

Gloss 54—

> The bride willingly receives the bridegroom's conjuration, and hearing the conclusion appended to it, "until she wishes" [ii, 7], notices that she is being implicitly instructed that she should wish voluntarily to rise. Therefore she proclaims that she is about to rise, and puts forward the kind of bridegroom for whose sake she wishes [to do so], and an appropriate time [for doing so].[39]

Now the switch from surface literalness to spiritual interpretation within the same Gloss:

> For after the apostles positioned in the primitive church of the nations had led themselves and others into such a state of perfection that they then took time off for contemplation, they once again realise[d] the duty imposed on them, that of traveling throughout the world and establishing new churches.[30]

In Glosses 56 and 57 there is a return to an exclusively spiritual interpretation:

Gloss 56—"He who is invisible visited us clothed in flesh, or 'came upon the mountains,' made himself visible in the scriptures, and from time to time has visited the hearts of the faithful with illumination."[31]

Gloss 57—"He made leaps from heaven to womb, from womb to cradle, from cradle to cross, from cross to tomb, and from the tomb he returns to heaven. He it is who is elevated above all mountains and hills, that is [all] saints both greater and lesser in stature."[32]

Another illustration of this approach is in chapter 3:2:

Chapter 3:2—"*I shall arise and go around the city, through the streets and squares; I shall seek him whom my soul loves. I have sought him and not found [him].*"[33]

[28] Ibid., 158.
[39] Ibid.
[30] Ibid.
[31] Ibid.
[32] Ibid.
[33] Ibid., 196.

The spiritual interpretation continues:

Gloss 11—

> [The Gentile church says:] "Because no angel, no prophet, no learned man whosoever reveals to me, the Gentile people, in [my] doubts the light of divine knowledge, and so I have not found where is to be learnt that which could not be found on my bed, I have proposed in my soul to rise up from the bed of carnal pleasures and to gird myself for the work of investigation into the means of salvation, and by land and sea, publicly and privately, throughout the world, to attend councils of men whom I have heard to be wise."[34]

Recall that the *Glossa ordinaria* dismisses the surface literalness, the bridegroom and bride, and turns directly to Christ and the Church. This third chapter delimits the Church to the "Gentile church," or rather, to the "Gentile people" (*gentilitati*), as the Dove translation shows, who will eventually form the "Gentile church." It is the Gentiles' struggle to become the "Gentile church" which the Gloss here describes. As the chapter proceeds, the Gentile Church takes shape, and, in keeping with Paul in Romans 11, it begins to call back the mistaken synagogue which had been called first to Christ by the apostles (ch. 3:4; Gloss 29).[35]

Eventually the Gentile Church is successful, and the Gloss states that "the Lord does not take less care of the assembled church of the Gentiles than of the church of the Jews, but contrives to take equal pains over the peace of both" (ch. 3:5; Gloss 41).[36] One might say that the *Glossa ordinaria* is interested in proselytizing the Jews, that there be one Church of Jews and Gentiles (again, Paul's hope).

Chapter 4:12—*"A garden shut up [is] my sister, bride, a garden shut up, a spring sealed."*[37]

On the surface level of the text, the bridegroom compares his bride to a garden, and to a spring. Immediately by allegory the bridegroom becomes Christ and the bride becomes the Church.

Gloss 115—"He [Christ] ... compares her [the church] to a garden on account of the copious fruits of [good] works"[38] which the Church produces. The glossator continues:

[34] Ibid., 196, 198.
[35] Ibid., 202.
[36] Ibid., 204.
[37] Ibid., 254.
[38] Ibid., 256.

Gloss 116—

> He puts "garden" twice, by which is signified the two states, that of the contemplatives and that of the actives, each of which is "shut up" because they cannot be despoiled or deprived of fruit by the adversary [viz, the devil]. There are many going about among the faithful who are in the power of the enemy, but they are not to be numbered among [those in] the fruitful garden, but thrown out like chaff.[39]

Then the glossator refers to the spring:

Gloss 117—

> The church is a 'spring' because it redounds with teaching bringing salvation, from which source it waters its neighbors, and 'sealed' because the spiritual sense is hidden in unworthy things [the literal sense], and because it is not disturbed by any attack.[40]

And so the *Glossa ordinaria* continues to the end of the Song. But let this be the end of examples from it. The glossators continue to employ spiritual interpretations along with the surface literalness of the Song. The bridegroom is Christ, the bride is the Church.

4. HISTORICAL-PHILOSOPHICAL BACKGROUND TO NICHOLAS OF LYRA

We have examined the historical-philosophical background to the spiritual interpretation, which culminates in the hermeneutical principles set forth in the Preface to the Song of Songs in the *Glossa ordinaria*. We have also looked at some examples of the Gloss's interpretation. Now, we turn to the historical-philosophical background to the so-called literal interpretation which will culminate in the hermeneutical principles of Nicholas of Lyra.

While the dominant world-view from the beginning of Christianity until the twelfth century derived from Plato, the subordinate world-view in this period derived from Aristotle. In place of Plato's doctrine of ideas which have a separate and external existence of their own, Aristotle proposed a group of universals which represent the common properties of any group of real objects. The universals, unlike Plato's ideas, have no existence outside of the objects they describe.[41]

[39] Ibid.

[40] Ibid.

[41] See Armstrong, note 1 above.

This Aristotelian world-view also had an effect on scriptural interpretation, though at first this effect was not as pronounced as that of the Platonic or Neoplatonic influences. The words of the text, the various characters and accounts, were not just insubstantial shadows of higher spiritual realities for Aristotelians. The words of the text had an intrinsic value and were worth examining in themselves. Scripture was not a mirror of something greater, but was the thing itself.

The Antiochene approach to scriptural interpretation, beginning in the second century, reflected the Aristotelian world-view. The members of this school set out to correct the abuse of the allegorical method, but they were not crude literalists. The literal sense covered the whole meaning of the writer, including metaphors and figures. They also accepted a spiritual sense which transcended the literal, but they restricted themselves to typology and they limited the number of types to be found in the Old Testament to a very few passages.[42]

Theodore of Mopsuestia (350–428) was the leading figure in the Antiochene approach. In his work on the Psalms he found that David was essentially a prophet for his own people. Only four Psalms—2, 8, 44(45), and 109(110)—were messianic. Such Psalms as 22(23) had an original historical meaning and could be understood only typically of Christ. The Song of Songs was composed by Solomon for his black Egyptian bride. Theodore reminded the Song's allegorical interpreters that there was no mention of God or the Church or the soul in it.[43] The general impression we get is that all Scripture has a literal sense, though sometimes in a limited way it may have a higher, spiritual sense. Note the difference here from Origen's earlier approach.

Theodore died in 428, and his work was burned at the Council of Constantinople in 553, supposedly for influencing Nestorius's errors. This is one reason why the Antiochene method did not influence the Middle Ages as much as the Alexandrine. Another reason for the lack of continuing Antiochene interpretation may be that the Alexandrine method "justified a paramount emotional need and corresponded to a world outlook while the [Antiochene method] struck [the medieval mind] as cold and irrelevant."[44] A further reason may be that the symbolic character of medieval consciousness may have predisposed the medieval student to allegorical methods.

[42] Smalley, 14; De Lubac, 47-49.

[43] Grant, 93-95; Smalley, 20-22.

[44] Smalley, 19.

Theodore's teachings influenced others, including John Chrysostom and Jerome. Similarly, Isidore of Seville (ca. 560–636) and the Irish scholars of the seventh century tended to follow Theodore and the Antiochene school, that is, their exegesis was more Aristotelian than Platonic.

We must step outside of monastic exegesis for a moment to take note of Boethius (480–525). His importance for us is that he translated a small number of Aristotle's works, which became a clear inroad into the basically Platonic and Neoplatonic philosophical mainstream. He was the first to apply Aristotelian methods to theological problems and to the elucidation of dogmatic statements, and thus became a direct ancestor of the scholastic method.

Late in the tenth century the balance began to tip from the Platonic world-view to the Aristotelian. The increasing use of Aristotle in the eleventh and twelfth centuries caused monastic exegesis, done along Neoplatonic lines, to wane; at the same time it caused scholastic exegesis to rise. Its way was prepared by what took place at the Abbey of St. Victor in Paris in the twelfth century. Beginning with Hugh of St. Victor (d. 1141) there was a turning away from spiritual to literal exegesis, that is, from the Alexandrine to the Antiochene approach, though Hugh and others probably did not realize it. Hugh found three senses in Scripture, the literal-historical, the allegorical, and the tropological. What was different about his method was the importance he placed on the literal. As Smalley says: "His great service to exegesis was to lay more stress on the literal interpretation *relative* to the spiritual ... ."[45]

With Richard of St. Victor (d. 1173) there was a return to the spiritual sense relative to the literal. But the next Victorine, Andrew (d. 1175), outdid Hugh in his stress on the literal. Though not the first to make use of Jewish exegesis, Andrew did so more than any exegete before him, believing the Jews would help him get at the literal and historical meaning of the text.

The Jewish exegete that Andrew used most often was Rabbi Solomon ben Isaac (1030-1105), better known as Rashi. Prior to Rashi's time, two methods of exegesis had been used by the Jews, the *halachic* and the *haggadic*. The former was the authoritative interpretation of the Old Testament in order to deduce the rule (*halacha*) of life. With the close of the Talmud in about 500, this method of exegesis ended. The *haggada* was a more informal treatment of the Old Testament employing imagery, allegory, moral stories, crude history,

[45] Ibid., 102; Knowles, 141-44.

and ingenious speculation. This method, found in the *Midrash*, continued up to Rashi's day. To these two methods Rashi added a third, the literal or rational interpretation of the text. He attended to grammar, syntax, comparative philology, chronology, and geography. The school which he founded, about 1070, continued these principles. Though Andrew did not follow Rashi slavishly, he felt that if one wanted the true literal sense, one had to study the Jews.[46]

The work of the Victorines was continued by the "masters of the sacred page," the doctors of theology in the University of Paris in the later twelfth and thirteenth centuries. Such masters as Peter Comestor (d. 1169), Peter the Chanter (d. 1228), and Stephen Langton (d. 1197) used Andrew's methods in a scientific study of Scripture. However, they were less literal than Andrew. As Peter Comestor expressed it in his *Historia Scholastica*: "History is the foundation ... allegory the wall ... tropology the roof ... ."[47] Spiritual exegesis was permissible, but it must be based on the literal.

We must not imagine a sudden shift from Plato-induced thinking to Aristotle-induced reasoning. The balance tipped slowly. Yet the change was unmistakable. Whereas Platonism directed one's thoughts from the surface literalness of the text to the meaning, Aristotelianism directed one's thoughts from the meaning to the surface literalness. Instead of acquiring knowledge by the illumination of the mind, one acquired knowledge by the use of one's senses. The Aristotelian exegete would view the spirit of Scripture as something not hidden behind the text or added to it but expressed directly in and through the text. At some point in the thirteenth century, commentators stepped out of the world of reflections into everyday life.

Scholastic exegesis was carried on by the new monastic orders of friars. Dominic (1170–1221) founded the Order of Preachers and Francis of Assisi (1182–1226) founded the Order of Friars Minor. The Franciscan Bonaventure (1221–1274), in his commentary on Ecclesiastes, laid emphasis on the literal sense.[48] However, in his *Itinerarium Mentis in Deum*, he emphasized the spiritual sense. The Dominican Albert the Great (1206/7–1280) concentrated on the surface literalness of the text.[49]

Albert's great pupil was the Dominican Thomas Aquinas (1225/6–1274). Aquinas took up the problem of the literal and spiritual

[46] Ibid., 172; see also Herman Hailperin, *Rashi and the Christian Scholars* (Pittsburgh: University of Pittsburgh, 1963).

[47] Ibid., 242.

[48] Ibid., 298; Knowles, 236-48.

[49] Ibid., 299.

senses in his *Summa theologiae*. God, he stated, is the principal author of Holy Scripture. Whereas, for human authors, words signify things; for the divine author, the things signified by the words signify still other things. When words signify things, the literal sense is intended. When the things signified by the words signify other things, the spiritual sense is intended. The spiritual sense may be divided into the allegorical, the moral, or the anagogical sense, but all are based on the literal sense. Furthermore, "the literal sense is whatever the author intends." The divine author may use a spiritual sense, but intend a literal sense. Therefore "the parabolic sense [that is, Scripture teaching in the form of a parable] is contained in the literal sense." Only by taking the literal sense seriously, and unlocking it by every means possible, can one hope to grasp the spiritual meaning. Without the literal sense there is no spiritual sense, only vagueness.[50]

5. HERMENEUTICAL PRINCIPLES OF NICHOLAS OF LYRA

It was in this milieu that Lyra appeared. He was born about 1270 in Normandy, and began studying in Paris about 1300, or possibly earlier. Meanwhile, Aquinas studied and taught in Paris off and on from 1245 to 1272. This proximity possibly accounts for Lyra's intimate acquaintance with Aquinas' methods of biblical interpretation.[51] Lyra knew Hebrew, either, as some suggest, because he was wholly or partly Jewish, or, more likely, because he studied in Évreux which was a center of Jewish biblical exegesis in the thirteenth century. Quite clearly he was influenced by Rashi, whom he quotes frequently. In 1300 or 1301 (perhaps 1291 or 1292) Lyra joined the Order of Friars Minor. He became a master of theology in 1308, and by 1309 he had an established position on the theological faculty at Paris. He then became involved in administrative duties, but in 1330 he resigned from them to devote more time to study. His Song Commentary was done about 1335. He died in 1349.

One must be careful when dealing with Lyra. Many standard references make such statements as the following: "As against the current allegoristic interpretations of the Bible, he set himself to ar-

[50] Thomas Aquinas, *Summa Theologiae*, ed. and trans. Thomas Gilby, O.P. (New York: Doubleday, Image Books, 1969), I.1.1.10, 59-61.

[51] Anonymous, "Nicholaus von Lyra und seine Stellung in der Geschichte der mittelalterlichen Schrift-Erklärung" (*Der Katholik* 2, Neue Folge, Mainz, 1859), 934-54.

rive at the exact and literal sense."[52] In a sense this is true enough. Lyra did concentrate on the surface literalness of the scriptural text. However, as we shall see in our examination of his commentary on the Song, he continues to insist he is doing a literal interpretation when in fact he is doing mostly what for centuries had been considered a spiritual interpretation.

Nicholas of Lyra.

Lyra commented on the Song twice, first literally (the *Postilla litteralis*) and then spiritually (the *Postilla moralis*). The *Postilla litteralis* is preceded by two Prologues, and the *Postilla moralis* by one; in all three he sets forth his hermeneutical principles.[53]

The thrust of the First Prologue is toward the spiritual interpretation of Scripture. Words are not flat and one-dimensional, and are, therefore, not to be taken only at face value. Rather, they are rich, many-sided, and pregnant with senses. Though Lyra does not mention Thomas Aquinas, he follows Aquinas almost verbatim: God is the principal author of the Scripture; he has the power not only to use words to signify things, but to use the things signified by the words to signify still other things. The first signification yields the literal or historical sense. The second yields the spiritual or mystical sense, which is subdivided into the allegorical, the moral or tropological, and anagogical senses. This sounds very much like the spiritual method employed in the *Glossa ordinaria*.

Lyra's emphasis in the Second Prologue is on the literal sense of Scripture. As he puts it, "Just as a building leaning off its foundation is in danger of collapsing, so a mystical interpretation disconnected

[52] *Oxford Dictionary of the Christian Church*, 2nd ed., "Nicholas de Lyra;" see also articles in the *New Catholic Dictionary*, 1929 ed., "Nicholas of Lyra" by Cyprian Emanuel; *New Catholic Encyclopedia*, 1967 ed., "Nicholas of Lyra" by J. J. Mahoney; *Encyclopedia Judaica*, 1971 ed., "Nicholas de Lyre" by Raphael Loewe; Spicq, 331; and the *New Schaff-Herzog Encyclopedia of Religious Knowledge*, 1963 ed., "Lyra, Nicholaus de" by R. Schmid.

[53] J.-P. Migne, *Patrologiae, Series Latina*, vol. 113, cols. 25-36, hereafter cited as *PL*. All translations are mine.

from the literal sense is to be considered unsuitable and improper."[54] Though Lyra does not mention Thomas Aquinas, he does mention Rashi. Not only will he make use of Catholic doctors, "but also of the Hebrews, especially of Rabbi Solomon, who among the Hebrew doctors spoke more reasonably in expressing the literal sense."[55]

In the course of the Second Prologue which deals with the literal interpretation of Scripture, Lyra refers with approval to seven rules for interpretation which stem from Augustine by way of Isidore of Seville. Lyra often gives what seems to be a spiritual interpretation of the scriptural examples which he uses to illustrate these rules. For example, the bridegroom and bride of the Old Testament reference in Isaiah 61:10 are understood as Christ and the Church. The daughters of Jerusalem and Solomon in the Song 1:5 are equated with the Church and God. In Isaiah 14:4, Lyra identifies the King of Babylon with a limb of the devil, and in Isaiah 14:12 he interprets Lucifer as the devil. Since the text itself does not make these identifications, it may seem that Lyra is giving spiritual interpretations. However, if Lyra assumes that the author of the text (ultimately God) *intends* these identifications, then in his own mind Lyra is giving a literal, not a spiritual interpretation.

Lyra is so caught up with the literal sense that he even speaks of a "double-literal sense" (*duplex sensus litteralis*).[56] In 1 Paralipomenon (1 Chronicles) 17:13, the Lord calls Solomon his son. This is literally so, according to Lyra, because Solomon was God's son by adoption and grace. At the same time, says Lyra, the author of Hebrews 1:5 finds this passage fulfilled in God and his Son. This is also literally so because Christ was God's Son by nature. Lyra grants that Solomon was "less perfectly" a son than Christ, and also concedes that Christ may be a spiritual interpretation of Solomon understood as a "type of Christ." But finally, for Lyra, this passage may be said to have no spiritual sense at all, only a literal. Solomon is literally God's Son.

The thrust of Lyra's Third Prologue (that is, his Prologue to the *Postilla moralis)* is, like his First Prologue to the *Postilla litteralis*, toward the spiritual interpretation of Scripture. The very designation *moralis* indicates that. This spiritual thrust is shown in Lyra's treatment of Judges 9:8 ("The trees went to anoint a king over them"), and Jesus' remark in Matthew 5:30 ("If thy right hand scandalize

[54] ... *sicut aedificium declinans a fundamento, disponitur ad ruinam: ita expositio mystica discrepans a sensu litterali, reputanda est indecens et inepta* ... . *PL* 113, col. 29.

[55] ... *sed etiam Hebraicorum, maxime Rabbi Solomonis, qui inter doctores Hebraeos locutus est rationabilius declarationem sensus literralis inducere. PL* 113, col. 30.

[56] ... *eadem littera aliquando habet duplicem sensum litteralem* ... . *PL* 113, col. 31.

thee, cut if off, and cast it from thee"). In each case Lyra shows there is no literal sense to these passages, only a spiritual. Surely, trees do not literally choose kings, and the Savior does not literally advocate self-mutilation.

Then, in a remarkable about-face, Lyra argues that the above two passages may be understood literally. Taking these passages as parables, Lyra's logic is as follows: When words signify things, the literal sense is present *first*, and if the things signified by the words signify other things, the spiritual sense (in this case the parabolic sense) is present *second*. When words do *not* signify things, that is, when there is no sense signified by the words, the literal sense is *not* present at all. However, in such cases, if the things signified by the words signify other things, the spiritual (parabolic) sense *is* present, and is in fact the only sense present. Now, whatever sense is present *first* is called the literal sense. Since the spiritual (parabolic) sense is the only sense present, it becomes perforce the *first* sense present. Therefore, the spiritual (parabolic) sense becomes the literal sense (*sensus parabolicus est litteralis*). In effect, Lyra is denying the existence of a spiritual sense of Scripture. There is only a literal.[57] But after this sortie into literal interpretation, Lyra returns to dividing the literal and spiritual senses, and continues in this vein until the end of his Third Prologue.

Before leaving Lyra's prefaces, we must be very clear about what Lyra is doing. We saw earlier that when the interpreters of the *Glossa ordinaria* encountered the surface literalness of the Song, they immediately leaped over that into an "other than what is said in the text" meaning, what we call the spiritual or allegorical sense. That became the true meaning of the text. We have shown the Platonic origin of that sort of thinking.

Now Lyra likewise encountered the surface literalness of the text and will leap over it, but in his mind, with its Aristotelian bias, he will not leap into a spiritual interpretation. Rather, since for him the whole text in itself was already an extended allegory, Lyra will leap into what he believes is the intention of the author, that is, the true literal sense of the text. Yet, the reader might well ask, are the glossator and Lyra doing the same thing? The only difference is that the glossator calls his interpretation spiritual, while Lyra in a convoluted way, calls his interpretation literal.

[57] *... aliqui doctores dicunt sensum parabolicum esse litteralem ...* . *PL* 113, col. 34.

6. THE EXEGESIS OF THE SONG OF SONGS ACCORDING TO LYRA

We now look at some examples from Lyra's exegesis of the Song to see how well the hermeneutical directives of the Prologues are carried out. Again space forces us to be selective.

Chapter 1:1—In line with Aristotelian and Thomistic-inspired interpretation, Lyra observes the surface literalness of the Song, which he deems a parable. For him, this means that his job is to go in search of the true literal sense. As he puts it: "The Song is a parable which speaks about the love between a bridegroom and his bride." However, "It is the literal sense which I intend to present ... . And the literal sense is this, *not* that which is signified by the words, but that which is signified by the things signified by the words ... . So then, in this book, it seems that the groom should be understood as God. The bride, then, is the Church, embracing the circumstances of both Testaments."[58] Note a difference here from the *Glossa ordinaria*. The bridegroom is not Christ, but God. The bride is not the New Testament, but the Church of both Testaments, that is all God's people of all time. No conversion of Jews is suggested. Contrast this with the *Glossa ordinaria*, chapter 3:2, Gloss 11, last sentence, above.

Chapter 1:15— *Behold thou art fair, my beloved, and comely*; of his fairness there is no end. *Our bed*, that is, the tabernacle where the bride through Moses and Aaron and other priests rested in quiet contemplation, *was bedecked with flowers*; for the inner covering of the tabernacle consisted of variously colored curtains, embroidered with a variety of beautiful flowers, Exodus 26.[59]

This passage illustrates Lyra's method. *Our bed* becomes immediately the tabernacle, which Lyra would consider not the spiritual meaning of *Our bed*, but the true literal meaning. He supports his

[58] James George Kiecker, *The "Postilla" of Nicholas of Lyra on the Song of Songs* (Milwaukee: Marquette University, 1998), 29, 31, 33. Latin and English on facing pages. In the case of Lyra, I am using the Douay-Rheims translation of the biblical text since this corresponds quite closely to the Latin Vulgate, and I am using my translation of Lyra's interpretation of the text. Hereafter referred to as Lyra.

[59] Lyra, 47. A matter of form should be pointed out. Whereas the *Glossa ordinaria* surrounds the text with various glosses, Lyra uses the "postilla" method. That is, he quotes from Scripture and immediately gives his explanation. *Postilla* probably comes from *post illa verba* ("after these words," that is, "after this, then this," that is, a "word by word" explanation, or a "running commentary"). The entire section of Scripture was usually still printed somewhere on the page. See Lyra, 12 and 126-28.

interpretation by reference to Exodus 26, where the curtains of the tabernacle are described as being embroidered with flowers. Note that the element of "rest" appears here; perhaps Lyra has the *Glossa ordinaria* open before him as he works, or this may be part of the traditional interpretation of the verse. Compare the *Glossa ordinaria*, chapter 1:15, Gloss 177, above.

Chapter 2:8—*The voice of my beloved.* This refers to the blessing of the giving of the Law, which was an especially gracious and noteworthy act, as it says in Deuteronomy 4[8]: "For what other nation is there so renowned that hath ceremonies, and just judgments and all the law, etc.?" Pertaining to this blessing the bride says: *The voice of my beloved*, pronouncing the precepts of the decalogue, Exodus 20[1-2]: "And the Lord spoke all these words: I am, etc." *Behold, he cometh leaping upon the mountains*, that is, descending upon Mt. Sinai, where he gave the precepts of the decalogue. Mt. Sinai is called "mountains" and "hills" in the plural because of the various parts of it; or perhaps here is a case of the use of the plural for the singular, as Scripture does frequently. For example, Exodus 32[4] states: "These are thy gods, O Israel, that have brought thee out of the land of Egypt." Yet there is only one idol.[60]

Lyra goes directly to what he considers is the true literal sense, beyond the surface literalness, that is, God giving his Law to the Old Testament believers and, by extension, New Testament believers as well. Notice that he supports his interpretation again by events in Scripture, which for him are unquestionably historic. The passage also illustrates Lyra's interest in grammar, a characteristic of Aristotle-based literal exegesis, noting that Scripture frequently employs a plural form for a singular, that is, synecdoche. Note that the *Glossa ordinaria* is also concerned about the literal interpretation of the same verse.

Chapter 3:2— *I will rise, and go about the city*, that is, I will wander in the desert for forty years, because, though a desert cannot be called a city in the usual sense, nevertheless it is here called a city because of the number of people wandering about in it. In this "city" there were 600,000 men, not counting women and children. *In the streets and the broad ways [I will seek him whom my soul loveth; I sought him, and I found him not],* because everywhere the people turned they implored the mercy of God.[61]

[60] Lyra, 51.
[61] Ibid., 57.

It is not the bride who speaks about searching the city for the groom. The true literal sense of the passage is the Israelites's wandering in the desert seeking God's mercy. But how can the desert be a city? According to Scripture, the Israelites numbered 600,000 men, plus women and children—surely, Lyra believes, enough people for a good-sized city. This passage shows the length that Lyra will go to turn surface literalness to true literalness.

Chapter 4:12—*A garden enclosed.* Here now is the second inducement to enter the Promised Land, namely, the fertility of the land and its pleasantness. The text continues, *O my sister, my spouse*, that is "O Church of Israel," which is called God's "spouse" in the sense that God espoused her by giving the Law on Mt. Sinai, and which is called God's "sister" when one considers the human nature of that nation. *A garden enclosed.* Inviting is the land promised to you, a "garden" because of its productivity, and "enclosed" because of its protection. For on the west it was bordered by the Mediterranean Sea, on the east by the Jordan River, on the north by Mt. Lebanon, and on the south by the Egyptian desert, which cannot be easily crossed. *A fountain sealed up*. Here the singular ("fountain") is used for the plural ("fountains"), as Scripture frequently does elsewhere. For the land has many fountains so clear that a person might think they were sealed off, so that neither animal or man could muddy the water.[62]

Dismissing the surface literalness and looking for the true literalness, Lyra turns again to Old Testament history to support his interpretation. In this case "garden" signifies the Promised Land, and "enclosed" signifies the geography which surrounds the Promised Land (geography being another concern of those interpreters influenced by Aristotle). Nor is Lyra deterred by the fact that the surface literalness contains "fountain," while the Promised Land had many fountains. Another example of synecdoche.

The rest of Lyra's Song commentary continues in the same vein. The surface literalness is dismissed, and, since the Song is considered a parable, the true literal sense must be found. The true literal sense is the intention of the author, and since, according to Thomas Aquinas, the ultimate author is God, it is with some *chutzpah* that Lyra claims to have arrived at the true literal sense.

[62] Ibid., 71, 73.

7. Historical-Philosophical Background of Martin Luther

Now that we have looked at the historical-philosophical background to spiritual interpretation practiced by the glossators of the *Glossa ordinaria*, and have done the same thing with the literal interpretation of Nicholas of Lyra, we turn to the same issue in the work of Martin Luther.

The influences of Lyra's literal method of interpretation lived on long after Lyra's death in 1349. According to Langlois, Lyra's *Postilla litteralis* still exists in several hundred manuscripts, in whole or in part.[63] Stegmüller, for example, lists twenty-four complete manuscripts.[64] There are fewer manuscripts of the *Postilla moralis* in existence.[65] Stegmüller lists twenty-two complete and partial manuscripts.[66]

The printed editions of the *Postilla litteralis*, in whole or in part, have been called innumerable.[67] It was the first Bible commentary to be printed, in Rome in 1471–2 with the last printing in Paris in 1660.[68] Parts of the *Postilla litteralis* were translated into French, German, and Italian, all before 1500.[69] It was translated into German as early as 1372.[70] Stegmüller lists ten complete editions of the *Postilla moralis*.[71] All of this attests to Lyra's popularity as well as the continuance of the Aristotelian-influenced literal method of interpretation.

An area ripe for research, which we will not enter here, is how far Lyra's literal method of interpretation spread among the biblical commentators of the later fourteenth to the early sixteenth century. Here we will confine ourselves to the impact of Lyra's method on Martin Luther.

There is ample evidence that Luther was impacted by Lyra's Aristotelian methodology. Luther refers to Lyra frequently, though ambivalently, throughout his writings. In his Psalm lectures (1513–

[63] C. V. Langlois, "Nicolas de Lyre, Frère Mineur." *Histoire littéraire de la France* 36 (1927): 374.

[64] Fridericus Stegmüller, *Repertorium Biblicum Medii Aevi* (Madrid, 1950–61), vol. 4: 90-91.

[65] Langlois, 381.

[66] Stegmüller, vol. 4:90-91.

[67] Hailperin, 138; Langlois, 375.

[68] Gosselin, 406-11; Stegmüller, vol. 4:52.

[69] *Dictionnaire de Théologie Catholique*, 1926 ed., vol. 9, pt. 1, col. 1421.

[70] Hailperin, 139; Langlois, 376.

[71] Stegmüller, vol. 4:90.

1515) Luther refers to Lyra several dozen times, overwhelmingly favorably.[72] On the other hand, in his Romans lectures (1515–1516) Luther's attitude toward Lyra is generally negative. Luther calls Lyra's interpretation foolish, false, in error, incorrect, pious but inept, and he dismisses Lyra sarcastically.[73]

By the end of the last decade of his life, Luther's attitude had changed again. In his Genesis lectures Luther refers to Lyra over one hundred times, generally favorably. The passage most often cited by those who wish to show Luther's attitude toward Lyra comes from these lectures: "I prefer him to almost all other interpreters of Scripture."[74] Luther's ambivalent attitude is summed up in his lectures on 2 Samuel (1543). Luther calls Lyra an "excellent man," a "good Hebraist," and a "fine Christian," except "whenever he follows his Rabbi Solomon." Then his work becomes "meaningless and unimpressive."[75]

Unfortunately, there is no direct evidence that Luther is influenced by Lyra's methodology in his Song of Solomon lectures. Luther never mentions Lyra at all. Yet it can be shown that in many passages Luther is following Lyra's interpretation quite closely, to the point that one may suspect that Luther has Lyra lying open before him on the table as he writes.[76]

8. LUTHER'S HERMENEUTICAL PRINCIPLES

Luther's lectures on the Song were given in 1530 and 1531.[77] In the preface he wrote for their publication in 1539, Luther states as his goal, "to get at the simplest sense and the real character of this book."[78] He goes on to tell us what he considers "the simplest sense" (*simplicissimus sensus*) to be:

[72] *Luther's Works*, 55 vols. (St. Louis: Concordia Publishing House, and Philadelphia: Fortress, 1955–1986), vols. 10 and 11. Hereafter this edition is cited as *LW*. For positive comments, see for example *LW* 10:38, 40, 104, 210. For more examples of positive comments, as well as occasional negative comments and other references to Lyra, see the Index to vol. 10:469, and the Index to vol. 11:562. See also *D. Martin Luthers Werke* (Weimar: Hermann Böhlaus Nachfolger, 1883 ff.), 3:34, 35, 104, 254. Hereafter this edition is cited as *WA*.

[73] *LW* 25:58, 60, 162, 435, 451; WA 56:65, 67, 181, 443, 458, 459.

[74] *LW* 2:164; WA 42:377: "... *Scripturae interpretibus eum antepono.*"

[75] *LW* 15:269; WA 54:30.

[76] This is the point I try to make in my *Postilla of Nicholas of Lyra on the Song of Songs.*

[77] *LW* 15:x-xi, 189-264; WA 31^2:586-769.

[78] *LW* 15:191; WA 31^2:586.

> I think it is a song in which Solomon honors God with his praises; he gives him thanks for his divinely established and confirmed kingdom and government; he prays for the preservation and extension of this his kingdom, and at the same time he encourages the inhabitants and citizens of his realm to be of good cheer in their trials and adversities and to trust in God, who is always ready to defend and rescue those who call upon him ... . Solomon ... wrote his song about his own kingdom and government ... . All this will become clear from the text itself, too.[79]

One is tempted to ask, "Where?" Luther explicitly says, "[The Song] does not treat a story of an individual ... but an entire permanent kingdom."[80] Lest anyone get the wrong idea about the true subject matter of the Song, Luther states:

> [Solomon] does not sing of these exalted matters in the common words that people ordinarily use, but he illustrates and adorns his theme with lofty and figurative words to such an extent that when

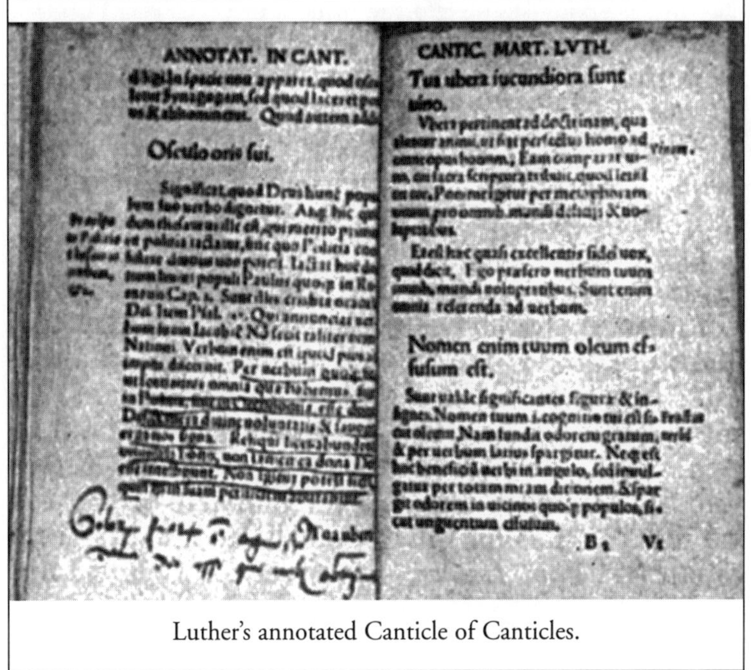

ANNOTAT. IN CANT.

Osculo oris sui.

CANTIC. MART. LVTH.

Tua ubera iucundiora sunt vino.

Nomen enim tuum oleum effusum est.

Luther's annotated Canticle of Canticles.

[79] Ibid. Though Luther claims the Song is about Solomon and his kingdom, the reader should be alert for implications Luther makes about what he believes should be the relationship between contemporary German rulers and their subjects.

[80] *LW* 15:192; WA 31^2:587.

> the crowd hears them, it supposes that the subject treated is something very different. For this is the custom with kings and princes; they compose and sing amatory ballads which the crowd takes to be songs about a bride or a sweetheart, when *in fact* [emphasis added] they portray the condition of their state and people with their songs ... . Solomon proceeds in just this fashion in this song of his. He uses magnificent words—words that are worthy of so great a king—in describing his concerns. He makes God the bridegroom and his people the bride ... .[81]

A little later Luther calls the Song "an encomium of the political order."[82]

Luther admits difficulty in the interpretation of the Song, calling it an "obscure" book. But "we shall never agree with those who think that it is a love song about the daughter of Pharaoh beloved by Solomon. Nor does it satisfy us to expound it of the union of God and the synagogue, or like the tropologists, of the faithful soul."[83] Luther even goes so far as to say, "if someone wants to add some allegories later, it takes no effort to invent them."[84]

Before leaving Luther's hermeneutical principles, pause and recall: the *Glossa ordinaria* follows Platonic lines. The surface literalness of the Song, dealing with a bridegroom and a bride, is leaped over into a spiritual sense, which turns out to be Christ and the Church. Skipping over Lyra's methodology for a moment, we find that by Luther's day Aristotelian interpretation has taken over. The surface literalness is immediately leaped over into what Luther calls the "simplest sense" of the text, the true sense, the sense that Luther believes the author of the text intends. And that turns out to be: God is the bridegroom and his people are the bride, with Solomon praising God for this pleasant kingdom. It seems that we do not actually have much real difference here at all. The Gloss leaps from surface literalness to spiritual sense, Luther leaps from surface literalness to "simplest sense," which for all the world looks like what the Gloss called the spiritual sense.

[81] *LW* 15:193; WA 31[2]:587.
[82] *LW* 15:195; WA 31[2]:591.
[83] *LW* 15:194; WA 31[2]:588, 589.
[84] *LW* 15:200: WA 31[2]: 610.

9. THE EXEGESIS OF THE SONG ACCORDING TO LUTHER

Chapter 1:1— *The Song of Songs.*

In line with Lyra's belief that the Song is a parable, for which the true literal sense must be found, Luther straightforwardly says: "The book derives its title either from the subject matter, because it deals with the greatest of all human works, namely, government: or else with the style, because it is written in the fashion of grand oratory. For the poem is entirely figurative, and figures of speech produce grand oratory."[85]

Luther then begins his search for the "simplest sense:"

Chapter 1:15 (16)— *Behold, you, too, are beautiful, my beloved, truly lovely.*

> Here is abundance of consolation. The Holy Spirit bears witness in the heart so that we are convinced we are pleasing and beautiful to God. The result therefore is that we in turn also confess that God is beautiful; that is, that He delights us, etc. However, this beauty is not obvious in time of tribulation.[86]

Similarly, he comments:

Chapter 2:8, 9—*The voice of my Beloved! Behold He comes, leaping upon the mountains, bounding over the hills. My beloved is like a gazelle, or a young stag.*

> This is the bride speaking: she means that she has heard the comforting words of the Groom and His exhortation to His attendants to be quiet and not to create any disturbance. "I perceive the sure effect of this exhortation," she says, "and His Word is not ineffective." For those who otherwise would have caused disturbances are called back to obedience and tranquility by the Word.
>
> That is, by means of His Word He leaps from one city to another so that everywhere the effect of His ministration may be felt among men. By the metaphor of the stag and the gazelle Solomon signifies the progress of the Word, because it spreads its effects to distant places with great swiftness.[87]

In Luther's mind, the simplest sense of this passage is not a bride calling her groom, but God's people calling on the true Groom, God

[85] *LW* 15:196; WA 31²:593.

[86] *LW* 15:209; WA 31²:631. As in the case of the *Glossa ordinaria* and Lyra, here with Luther we shall try to follow the orthography of our source, *Luther's Works.*

[87] *LW* 15:217, 218; WA 31²:654.

himself. This sounds like a spiritual interpretation. Within his simplest sense, Luther allows for a metaphor, the stag and the gazelle signifying the swift progress of God's Word throughout the world. The metaphor used within the simplest sense does not imply a switch to a spiritual interpretation. Here Luther is in line with Augustine, who allowed the literal sense of a text to contain such things as metaphors.

Chapter 3:2—*I will rise now and go about the city, etc.*

Luther comments: "These words similarly belong to his [Solomon's] description of the passion with which the good king and his whole people longed for tranquility and an end of evils in state and Church."[88] Since Luther makes short shrift of this passage, so shall we, noting only that he manages to remain in keeping with his fundamental approach: The simplest sense of the Song is Solomon, like a medieval monarch, concerned with good rulership of his state and the Church within it. But this simplest sense has no more to do with the surface literalness than the pure spiritual interpretation of the *Glossa ordinaria* or the true literal interpretation of Lyra.

Finally, Luther comments on verse 12 of chapter 4:

Chapter 4:12 – *A garden locked is My sister, My bride.*

> Another praiseworthy characteristic of this people! He commends the people because they are bound by most excellent laws, regulated by circumcision and other rites, and what is most important of all, sealed by the promises, by which they are distinguished from all other people. In the same way we Christians are now sealed by the Word, Baptism, and the Sacrament of the Altar, by which we are distinguished from all other races, not just before the world, but rather in God's own judgement.[89]

For Luther, Solomon is praising God for giving him a people which is indeed worthy of praise, since they abide by God's laws. Though Luther does not mention the part of 4:12 which speaks of the sealed fountain, he works in the idea of "sealed" by saying the people are sealed to God by God's promises. Then, going a step further, Luther applies the interpretation to the New Testament where God's people are sealed by Word and Sacraments. All this constitutes the simplest sense of the Song in 4:12. Or is this really an extension of spiritual exegesis?

[88] *LW* 15:223; WA 31^2:667.

[89] *LW* 15:234; WA 31^2:695, 696.

10. CONCLUSION

The goal of this essay was to compare three interpretations of the Song of Songs, that of the *Glossa ordinaria* from about 1100, that of Lyra in the early 1300s, and that of Luther in the early 1500s. To do this thoroughly we had to look at the historical-philosophical background to the writers of the three interpretations, to see where each one was coming from. Then we had to look at the hermeneutical principles which each of the interpreters claimed to follow. Finally, we were able to compare the exegesis of each interpreter.

We found that the *Gloss ordinaria*, so strongly influenced by Platonic thinking, readily dismissed the surface literalness of the Song to find the Song's true meaning in allegory, the bridegroom Christ and the bride the Church. Lyra, influenced by Aristotle, came at the Song from the opposite direction. The surface literalness of the Song was already an allegory, for which the true literal sense had to be found. This turned out to be God and the Church of all ages, God's believers in both the Old and New Testaments. In keeping with Lyra, Luther found the surface literalness figurative, for which the simplest sense had to be found. This turned out to be a song of Solomon praising God for his kingdom.

Though the three interpretations might seem divergent, they really are not. None of them is content to let the surface literalness of the Song stand as it is. It is, for them, the Word of God. Feeling, therefore, that the surface literalness of Scripture—a blatant love poem—is not worthy of Scripture, another meaning had to be found. We have seen this to be a more reverent meaning (the *Glossa ordinaria*), a more biblical-historical meaning (Lyra), and a more biblical-historical meaning with a generous dash of contemporary German-historical implication thrown in (Luther). But finally, the Song is *not* about Christ and the Church, nor about God and the Church of all ages, nor about Solomon's kingdom or anyone else's. Not really. All of this is imposed on the Song, though different terminology is employed. For finally the Song of Songs is only about a bridegroom and a bride—do with it what you will.

Dogma, Classical Rhetoric, Confession of Faith

LUTHER AS A CREATIVE WRITER:

The Explanation of the Second Article of the *Apostles' Creed* in the *Small Catechism*[*]

GOTTFRIED G. KRODEL

In his monumental commentary on Luther's catechisms, Albrecht Peters has given us thorough historical and theological insights into the text.[1] Occasionally Peters also deals with matters of writing, but they are not of major concern to him. Yet if one immerses oneself into the text of Luther's *Small Catechism* (*SC*),[2] one

[*] ABBREVIATIONS according to *International Glossary of Abbreviations for Theology and Related Subjects*, collected by Siegfried M. Schwertner (2d ed. rev. Berlin, New York: de Gruyter Verlag, 1992), with the following additions or modifications: *ApC*: *Apostles' Creed*.—*BC*: *The Book of Concord. The Confessions of the Evangelical Lutheran Church*, transl. and ed. by Theodore G. Tappert et al. (Philadelphia: Fortress Press, 1959).—*DC*: *Decree of the Council of Chalcedon*.—Denzinger: Heinrich Denzinger, ed., *Enchiridion Symbolorum, Definitionum et Declarationum de Rebus Fidei et Morum*, 31st ed. by Karl Rahner (Freiburg/Breisgau: Herder Verlag, 1957).—Dietz: Philipp Dietz, *Wörterbuch zu Dr. Martin Luthers Deutschen Schriften* (Leipzig: F. C. W. Vogel Verlag, 1870, 1872), 2 vols. (all that is available).—Götze: Alfred Götze, *Frühneuhochdeutsches Glossar* (5th ed. Berlin: de Gruyter Verlag, 1956).—Grimm: Jacob and Wilhelm Grimm, *Deutsches Wörterbuch*, 33 vols. (München: Deutscher Taschenbuch Verlag, 1984; repr. of the 1st ed., 1854–1971).—*LC*: Luther's *Large Catechism*; see n. 2.—*NC*: *The Nicene-Constantinopolitan Creed*.—Peters: Albrecht Peters, *Kommentar zu Luthers Katechismen*, 5 vols., ed. by Gottfried Seebaß (Göttingen: Verlag Vandenhoeck and Ruprecht, 1990–1994).—*SC*: Luther's *Small Catechism*; see n. 2.

[1] See Peters.

[2] Texts of *SC*: WA 30[1]:242-63, left column (this is the text of Michael Stiefel's manuscript copy [1530] of the *very first text* of *SC*, the one printed on posters); *BSLK* 501-41, left column; *BC* 338-56. In late spring of 1529, Bugenhagen arranged that the text of *SC* printed on posters was translated into low-German and published in Hamburg as a booklet; text: WA 30[1]:243-63, right column. The Stiefel and the Bugenhagen versions of *SC* may be considered to be the texts closest to Luther's first version. Texts of *LC*: WA 30[1]:125-238; *BSLK* 545-733, left column; *BC* 358-461. The following parenthetical references without siglum are to the WA text of *SC* and *LC*, with the spelling modernized. In other Luther texts the superscript 'e' has been replaced by the Umlaut. All translations are mine, unless otherwise noted. In the present context it is not necessary to deal with the nature of the relationship of *SC* to *LC*.

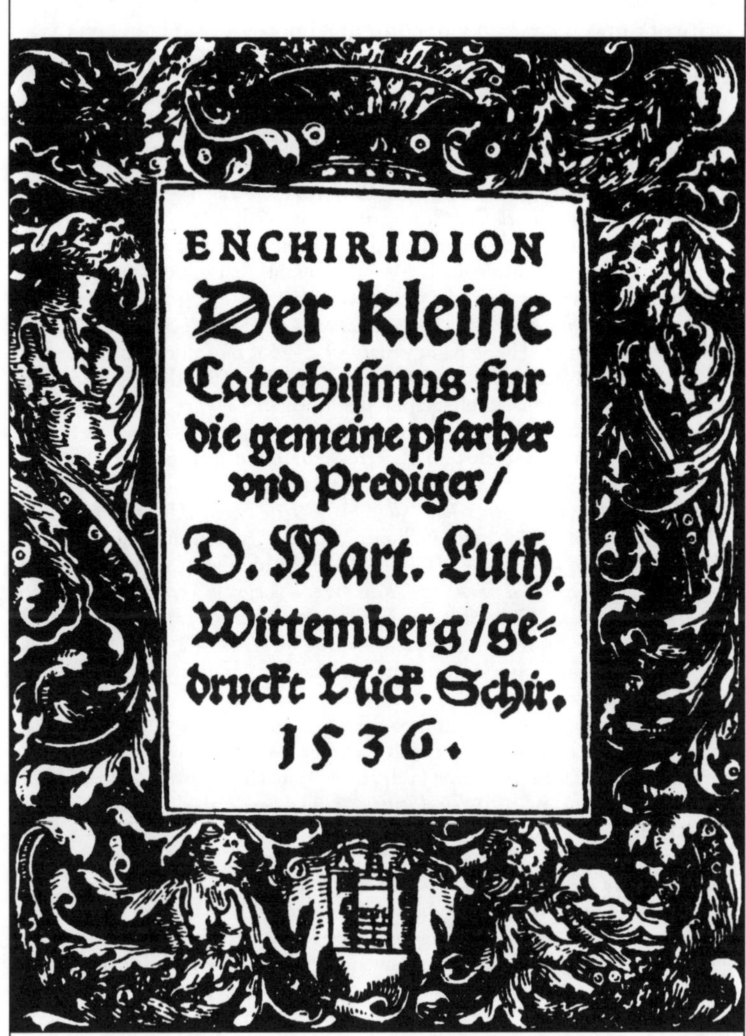

ENCHIRIDION
Der kleine
Catechismus fur
die gemeine pfarher
vnd Prediger/
D. Mart. Luth.
Wittemberg/ge=
druckt Nick. Schir.
1536.

The title page of Luther's *Small Catechism,*
Sixth Edition, Wittenberg, 1536.

swiftly becomes aware that it is a masterpiece of writing when viewed in terms of language, flow of the word-sounds, vividness of imagery, clarity of phrases, and flow of content.[3] Luther was able to create this literary masterpiece because he did not have to spend much time on thinking about *what* he wanted to say; his catechism sermons of 1528

[3] For Luther as a writer in German, see Herbert Wolf, *Germanistische Luther-Bibliographie* (Heidelberg: Winter Verlag, 1985); id., *Martin Luther. Eine Einführung in germanistische Luther-Studien* (Stuttgart: Metzler Verlag, 1980; this slender volume [172 pages of about four-and-a-half by seven-and-a-half inches] with citations of basic secondary literature is the indispensable first source for anyone who wishes to study the language of Luther's German writing); Karl Schottenloher, *Bibliographie zur deutschen Geschichte im Zeitalter der Glaubensspaltung*, 1517–1585, 6 vols. (2d ed. Stuttgart: Hiersemann Verlag, 1956–1958), 7 (Stuttgart: Hiersemann Verlag, 1966), 1: Nos. 13888-13929, 7: Nos. 56587-56601; the appropriate entries in the annual Luther bibliography published in *LuJ*. For the language and writing of *SC*, see WA 30^1:629-31; Peters 2:100; Ernst Göpfert, "Ueber die Sprache Luthers im Kleinen Katechismus," *Zeitschrift für den deutschen Unterricht* 2(1888):488-501; Walther Killy, "Die Sprache des Katechismus," in: Oliver Kohler, ed., *Aller Worte verschwiegenes Rot. Albrecht Goes zu Ehren* (Hünfelden: Präsenz Verlag, 1993), 111-33; Johannes Gillhoff, "Stil und Satzbau in Luthers Kleinem Katechismus," *Der alte Glaube* 9(1908):810-15. In his almost forgotten booklet, *Zur Sprache und Geschichte des Kleinen Katechismus* (Leipzig: Verlagsbuchhandlung Dürr, 1909), Johannes Gillhoff (a one-time teacher of future teachers) presented a wealth of materials on the language and writing of *SC* (13-62: "Zur Sprache des Kleinen Katechismus"). It is unfortunate that the form of his materials creates the impression that they are rather a labor of love than of scholarship. His materials deserve to be updated and then to become a fixed item for all who deal with *SC*. For Luther as a creative writer, see Martin Brecht, *Doctor Luther's Bulla and Reformation: A Look at Luther the Writer* (Valparaiso: Valparaiso University Press, 1991), and id., *Luther als Schriftsteller* (Stuttgart: Calwer Verlag, 1990); Heinrich Bornkamm, "Luther als Schriftsteller," in: id., *Luther: Gestalt und Wirkungen. Gesammelte Aufsätze* (Gütersloh: Gerd Mohn Verlag, 1975), 39-64; Heinz Dannenbauer, *Luther als religiöser Volksschriftsteller, 1517–1520* (Tübingen: Mohr Verlag, 1930); Peter Meinhold, *Luthers Sprachphilosophie* (Berlin: Lutherisches Verlagshaus, 1958); Stefan Sonderegger, "Die Reformatoren als Sprachgestalter," *Reformatio* 23(1974):94-108; Walter Schenker, *Die Sprache Huldrych Zwinglis im Kontrast zur Sprache Luthers* (Berlin: de Gruyter Verlag, 1977); Friedrich W. Kantzenbach, "Bild und Wort bei Luther und in der Sprache der Frömmigkeit," *NZSTh* 16(1974):57-74; Hermann Steinlein, "Luthers Anlage zur Bildhaftigkeit," *LuJ* 22(1940):9-45; Harry G. Haile, "Luther as Renaissance Writer," in: *The Renaissance and Reformation in Germany*, ed. by Gerhart Hoffmeister (New York: Ungar, 1977), 141-56; Johannes Ficker, *Luther als Professor* (Halle: Niemeyer Verlag, 1928), 15-18, 43; Hans Preuß, *Martin Luther der Künstler* (Gütersloh: Bertelsmann Verlag, 1931), 145-281. In general, see Heinz Bluhm, *Martin Luther: Creative Translator* (St. Louis: Concordia Publishing House, 1965); Heinz Otto Burger, "Luther als Ereignis der Literaturgeschichte," in: id., *"Dasein heisst eine Rolle spielen." Studien zur deutschen Literaturgeschichte* (München: Hanser Verlag, 1963), 56-74; Harry G. Haile, *Luther: An Experiment in Biography* (New York: Doubleday & Co., 1980).

and prior sermons and texts on the topics of the catechism[4] provided him with sufficient material; therefore he could concentrate on *how* to say what he wanted to say. In the following essay, I shall present some observations on Luther as a creative writer[5] by concentrating on the explanation of the Second Article of the *Apostles' Creed(ApC)* [6] in *SC*. First I shall focus on the structure and rhythm of Luther's text and then on its content and genre.[7]

I
STRUCTURE AND RHYTHM

The text under consideration (WA 30^1:248.18-249.22) consists of a title line and three sections of unequal length: the text of *ApC*, what we call the explanation of this text (which is connected with the text of *ApC* through the introductory phrase "Was ist das? Antwort"), and a closing sentence of affirmation.[8] The explanation is structured as one long sentence. It is made up of a comparatively brief main clause with which Luther begins his text; then follow three clauses in which he elaborates on this main clause: a relative clause, a consecutive clause, a clause of comparison. This long sentence is carefully

[4] See, for example, Gottfried G. Krodel, "Luther's Work on the Catechism in the Context of Late Medieval Catechetical Literature," *ConJ* 25(1999): 364, 372-74.

[5] For an example of the combination of theological argumentation and creative writing, see Kenneth Hagen, "The Testament of a Worm: Luther on Testament and Covenant," *Consensus. A Canadian Lutheran Journal of Theology* 8^1(1982):12-20.

[6] This excludes dealing with the whole of Luther's explanation of *ApC* as a text of Trinitarian theology. For details, see Peters 2:36-54.

[7] In the following materials I concentrate on the literary quality of the text. I am not concerned with problems of social history connected with Luther's literary productivity (propaganda, indoctrination), esp. with the question raised by Gerald Strauss whether Luther's catechisms contributed to the success or failure of the Reformation; see Gerald Strauss, *Luther's House of Learning. Indoctrination of the Young in the German Reformation* (Baltimore: The Johns Hopkins University Press, 1978). For a different context, see Mark U. Edwards, Jr., *Printing, Propaganda, and Martin Luther* (Berkeley: University of California Press, 1994). In general, see Wolfgang Weber, "Bemerkungen zu Luthers praktischem Beitrag bei der Ausbreitung und Durchsetzung seiner Lehre," *ZKG* 97(1986):309-33, esp. 316-19.

[8] In the Stiefel text (see n. 2) the last sentence ("Das ist gewißlich wahr") is separated from the preceding text by a *comma*, and the following "Das" begins with a capital letter. In the Bugenhagen text (see n. 2) we find a *period*, and the following "Dat" begins with a capital letter. For the use of the comma and its relationship to the connection of clauses and sentences in some of Luther's German writings, see Stolt, "Luthers rhetorische Syntax (as in n. 81)."

crafted, and one may suggest that Luther remembered his training in Latin well when he wrote this sentence.

Luther titles the Second Article: "Der andere Artikel [:] Von der Erlösung" (248.18). He quotes the text of the Second Article,[9] and then he uses the phrase "Was ist das? Antwort" (249.6) to connect the text of the Second Article with his own text. In the English versions of *SC* which are available to me, this phrase is translated as: "What does this mean? Answer." In my opinion this translation does not at all reflect what Luther says.

Luther does not say "What does this mean?" but "What is this?" There is a decided difference between these phrases. Today's common understanding of "to mean" and "meaning"[10] suggests that something can mean this or that, and therefore one can discuss what something means ("let's talk about it").[11] But the text following "Antwort" is not open for discussion. In the closing sentence Luther categorically designates his text as nothing other than truth (249.22) which, obviously, is beyond discussion. Since "das" refers back to the whole cited text, an appropriate translation of Luther's phrase would be: "What is this [that I have just said? To answer, I shall now elaborate on what I said, and this is my] Answer."

The transition between the text and explanation of the First Commandment in *LC* confirms the validity of this translation. Luther

[9] For Luther's text of *ApC*, see Peters 2:16-27.

[10] I am aware of the "scholarly" understanding of "meaning" presented, for example, in Webster's *Dictionary* and by Eric D. Hirsch, *Validity in Interpretation* (New Haven, London: Yale University Press, 1967), esp. chapt. 2 and Appendix I. But how many people do consult such texts? Therefore if the average person is to read "What does this mean?" with this scholarly understanding in mind, the phrase would have to be footnoted, for example, with a summary of Hirsch's argumentation or the appropriate entry in Webster. Otherwise the translation does not do justice to what Luther says. Whether such a footnote would help or hinder the pedagogical work would be another question.

[11] Were we living in Luther's time, the situation would be different. For Luther *Meinung* had a different content than it has for us today. He used *Meinung* for content, substance, intention, goal, plan, confession, and he even coordinated *Meinung* with *rechte Auslegung* (thus coming close to Hirsch's understanding of 'meaning'); see the conclusion of the section on the Ten Commandments in *LC* (180.23; *BC* 409): "Das ist ... die Meinung und rechte Auslegung." In his *Short Form of the Ten Commandments, the Creed, and the Lord's Prayer* (1520) Luther introduced the explanation of the individual sections of the Lord's Prayer with "Die Meynung"; WA 7:220-29. (In the case of the First Petition Luther wrote: "Die Meynung ist".) See further, Grimm 12: s.vv. "Meinen," "Meinung"; Hans Volz and Heinz Blanke, eds., *D. Martin Luther: Die gantze Heilige Schrifft Deudsch, 1545/ Auffs new zugericht* (München: Verlag Rogner and Bernhard, 1972), 351*, s.v. "Meinung"; Götze, s.v. "Meinung."

The title page of Luther's *Large Catechism*, printed by George Rhau, Wittenberg, 1529.

quotes the text of the commandment and then states: "Das ist,[12] du sollst mich allein für deinen Gott halten. Was ist das gesagt [see the suggested translation] und wie versteht man es? Was heißt einen Gott haben oder was ist Gott? Antwort:" And then follows the explanation (132.33-133.1). Luther's phrasing leaves no room for anything that would suggest "meaning" as this word is today commonly understood. He directly connects the quoted text with his explanation. Therefore, he uses "that is" in order to introduce what he intends to say about the text he has just quoted. And in his *Short Form* (1520) Luther connects the text of the three articles with his explanations through the phrase "Das ist," which is centered in the line.[13] This foreshadows the phrasing in *SC*, and is the phrasing of the transition from the text to the explanation of the First Commandment in *LC*. It is possible that for *SC* Luther abandoned the "that is" and adopted the question form of the transition from text to explanation because in 1522 he had seen this question form in the catechism of the Bohemian Brethren.[14]

Luther opens his text[15] with a weighty "curtain raiser" in the form of a simple sentence (*a*): "Ich glaube[,] daß Jesus Christus ... sei[16] mein Herr" (249.7.10f.). He introduces "I"[17] as the speaker of the text, and he combines declarative statements about two centers:

[12] See also, for example, the transition from the text to the explanation of *ApC* in the first Latin text of *SC* (1529): "Hoc est" (right col. of 292.9, 294.25, 296.23).

[13] WA 7:215.26, 217.5, 218.24. *Works of Martin Luther*. Philadelphia Edition, 2 (Philadelphia: Muhlenberg Press, 1943): 369, 370, 372 has a paragraph indentation, followed by "T h i s m e a n s – ". This letterspaced phrase followed by a dash does justice neither to Luther's text nor to the way the text appears on the page.

[14] For this catechism, and for Luther and the Bohemian Brethren, see Joseph Müller, ed., *Die deutschen Katechismen der Böhmischen Brüder* (Berlin: Verlag A. Hofmann and Company, 1887); Amadeo Molnár, "Luthers Beziehungen zu den Böhmischen Brüdern," in: Helmar Junghans, ed., *Leben und Werk Martin Luthers von 1526 bis 1546. Festgabe zu seinem 500. Geburtstag* (Göttingen: Verlag Vandenhoeck and Ruprecht, 1983), 627-39; Martin Brecht, *Martin Luther*, 3 vols., translated by James L. Schaaf (Philadelphia, Minneapolis: Fortress Press, 1985–1993), 2:75-77.

[15] For observations on the composition of Luther's text, see Gillhoff, *Sprache und Geschichte* (as in n. 3), 39f.

[16] "Sei" is a grammatical subjunctive, dependent on "daß" ("quod ... sit" in the earliest Latin text; 294.26.29) but not a subjunctive of content (possibility or wishful thinking). For the content of the clause, see the *LC* text (186.11f. 22-28, 187.4f.; *BC* 414.27, 30, 31), where Luther makes clear (esp. 187.4f.; *BC* 414.31) that he is thinking in terms of things which have happened. See also nn. 36, 55.

[17] See also below, 150.

I, Jesus Christ—*I believe, Jesus Christ is my Lord.* The center of this opening sentence is the combination of I and Jesus Christ.

Luther at once qualifies "Jesus Christus" by creating an appositional clause; it consists of two sections, (*a*.1, *a*.2), constructed in parallel form and connected by "und auch" (249.7-10): "wahrhaftiger Gott vom Vater in Ewigkeit geboren und auch wahrhaftiger Mensch von der Jungfrau Maria geboren." With this clause Luther shifts the weight of the sentence from the combination 'I and Jesus Christ' to Jesus Christ. (*A*.1) has to be considered Luther's attempt to place Jesus Christ into the context of the Trinitarian God, though in *LC* this is clearer than in *SC*.[18] In the process of creating this clause, Luther reshapes the two phrases of the Creed's relative clause ("who was conceived by the Holy Spirit, born of the Virgin Mary"), and he expands the Creed's appositional phrase "his only Son." He also takes the other appositional phrase, "our Lord," out of its appositional position and makes it the subject of the clause which is dependent on "ich glaube"; in addition, he reshapes the text to read: "sei mein Herr."[19]

(*A*) shows a skillful author who seamlessly weaves together the opening phrase of the Second Article of *ApC*, the basic materials presented in the opening phrase of the Second Article of *Nicene Creed(NC)*,[20] and the two-nature Christology of *Chalcedonian Definition(DC)*.[21] Luther places the opening statements of *ApC* ("Jesus Christ, his only Son, our Lord,

[18] (186.1-3.); *BC* 413.26: "Here [in the Second Article] we learn to know the second person of the Godhead, and we see what we receive from God over and above the temporal goods mentioned above [in the First Article]—that is , how he has completely given himself to us, withholding nothing." See also the closing section of the explanation of the Creed in *LC* (191.28-192.34); *BC* 419.63-420.70.

[19] For the role of 'Lord' in the whole text, see Peters 2:111-15.

[20] *BC* 18: from "And in one Lord Jesus Christ" to "being of one substance with the Father." For *NC*, see Reinhart Staats, *Das Glaubensbekenntnis von Nizäa-Konstantinopel. Historische und theologische Grundlagen* (Darmstadt: Wissenschaftliche Buchgesellschaft, 1996).

[21] Denzinger No. 148; *Readings in Church History*, ed. by Colman J. Barry, O.S.B. (Westminster: The Newman Press, 1960): 103-105, esp. 104. For the texts, see also Eduard Schwartz, "Das Nicaenum und das Constantinopolitanum auf der Synode von Chalkedon," *ZNW* 25(1926):38-88. For details, see Aloys Grillmeier, S.J., *Christ in Christian Tradition. From the Apostolic Age to Chalcedon (451)*, transl. by J.S. Bowden (New York: Sheed and Ward, 1965), 480-92; Hermann Sasse, "The 1,500th Anniversary of Chalcedon," in: id., *We Confess Jesus Christ*, 1, transl. by Norman Nagel (St. Louis: Concordia Publishing House,1984):55-70; I. Ortiz de Urbina, S.J., "Das Glaubenssymbol von Chalkedon: sein Text, sein Werden, seine dogmatische Bedeutung," in: Aloys Grillmeier, S.J., and Heinrich Bacht, S.J., eds., *Das Konzil von Chalkedon. Geschichte und Gegenwart*, 3 vols. (2d printing, corrected. Würzburg: Echter Verlag, 1959), 1:389-418.

who was conceived by the Holy Spirit, born of the Virgin Mary") in the context of the dogmatic decisions of the early Church.[22] He adopts the reality which stands behind the *homoousios*,[23] and he adopts the two-nature Christology.[24] He reduces the complex formulations to a few simple statements, and then he follows up these statements with "is my Lord." In this process "Lord" receives a weight which it did not have in *ApC, NC*, or *DC*. [25] "Lord" both closes (*a*) and opens the door to the following text.[26] That text is now solidly grounded[27] in the affirmation of the *homoousios* and two-nature Christology: Lord is Jesus Christ, the one person who is both true God, born of the Father in eternity (and therefore very God of very God), and true man, born of the Virgin Mary, the one person in whom the divine

[22] For Luther and the dogmas of the early Church, see Bernhard Lohse, *Luthers Theologie in ihrer historischen Entwicklung und in ihrem systematischen Zusammenhang* (Göttingen: Verlag Vandenhoeck and Ruprecht, 1995), 223-27, 235-39, 249-52. For Luther and the christological dogma of the early church, see also Theodosius Harnack, *Luthers Theologie mit besonderer Beziehung auf seine Versöhnungs- und Erlösungslehre*, 2: *Luthers Lehre von dem Erlöser und der Erlösung*, new ed. by Oskar Grether (München: Kaiser Verlag, 1927); Albrecht Peters, "Luthers Christuszeugnis als Zusammenfassung der Christusbotschaft der Kirche," *KuD* 13(1967):1-26, 73-98; Marc Lienhard, *Luther's Witness to Jesus Christ. Stages and Themes of the Reformer's Christology*, transl. by Edwin H. Robertson (Minneapolis: Augsburg Publishing House, 1982), 307-58, 371-87; Dorothea Vorländer, *Deus Incarnatus. Die Zweinaturenchristologie Luthers bis 1521* (Wittenberg: Luther Verlag, 1974). See also nn. 23, 124, 125, 126.

[23] Luther did not like the term, though he affirmed that it was useful and necessary. For details, see for example, WA 8.117.33-118.9 (*Against Latomus*, 1521); 18:741.34-742.3 (*The Bondage of the Will*, 1525); 39²:20f. (disputation on John 1:14, Jan. 11, 1539 [argumentum 15, both versions]); 39²:304.10-305.26 (doctoral disputation of Georg Major and Johannes Faber, Dec. 12,1544); 50:572.13-573.5, 600.20-602.24 (*On the Councils and the Church*, 1539); WA.B 7:35.254-260 (Luther to Nikolaus von Amsdorf, ca. March 11, 1534).

[24] For Luther texts and secondary literature dealing with Luther and the two-nature Christology, see also Peters 2:170f.

[25] In *ApC* "our Lord" is an apposition to "Jesus Christ," following the apposition "his only Son," and in *NC* and *DC* "Lord" is used as a title for Jesus Christ.

[26] See also *LC* (186.4-8.): "Dieser Artikel ist nun sehr reich und weit, aber daß wirs auch kurz und kindlich handeln, wollen wir ein Wort uns vornehmen und darinnen die ganze Summa [des Artikels] davon fassen, nämlich ... das man daraus lerne, wie wir erlöset sind, Und soll stehen auf diesen Worten 'An Jesum Christum, unseren HERRN'."

[27] See also Ernst Kinder, "Soteriological Motifs in Early Creeds," *Lutheran World* 8(1961):16-23, esp. 16: "[Reformation theology] completely understood the teaching of justification as resting upon an *already existing substructure* [italics by Kinder], the Christology of the ancient church. Article IV of the Ausgburg Confession with the words 'propter Christum' points back to Article III, where the christological decisions of the ancient church are expressly adopted ... ."

and human natures coexist, the God-man. But this God-man is Lord not in a general, collective sense ("*our* Lord"), but in a very personal sense—he is "*my* Lord". At this point the *homoousios* and the two-nature Christology are no longer complicated theories[28] developed in a distant past, or religious rules to be obeyed, and 'Lord' is no longer a general statement, an apposition, or a title qualifying Jesus Christ. *"Lord" now describes a situation resulting from actions which touch "I" directly*, and these actions are inseparably linked with the God-man. The way Luther works with the appropriate materials from *NC* and *DC* shows that for him these materials present realities which concern "I" in the most concrete way: *Jesus Christ is my Lord, because he is who he is, the God-man,*[29] *and (therefore) did what he did*—as will be described in the next sections of Luther's text.

At the end of (*a*) Luther has set the stage for the following materials. Already one can now see an arch beginning to form, which leads toward the closing statement. Because whatever has been said thus far, and will be said in the following text, deals with the God-man, it is most certainly true.

[28] See also Hans Preuß, *Martin Luther der Christenmensch* (Gütersloh: Verlag Bertelsmann, 1942), 32f.

[29] At the end of (*a*) "sei mein Herr" would stand as a 'nude' phrase, were it not for the qualifications which precede the phrase. "True God ... true man" qualifies "Jesus Christ," and through Jesus Christ it qualifies "my Lord." Therefore though "true God ... true man" is 'only' an apposition, it is of fundamental significance for the text. Jesus Christ is the Lord of "I"; but "my Lord" is not just anyone, he is true God and true man. Therefore the affirmation of Christ's lordship *includes*—not presupposes or assumes—the affirmation of his being both true God and true man—for Luther one does not exist without the other. Karl Knoke presented a valuable analysis of the text in an effort critically to discuss Albrecht Ritschl's view. Yet at the end he (and he is not alone) underestimated the significance which the phrase "true God ... true man" has for the text. He wrote ("Zur Sicherstellung des ursprünglichen Sinnes der Lutherischen Erklärung des zweiten Artikels," *NKZ* 2[1891]:93-108, esp. 107): "In der That treten jene Prädikate, welche auf Christi beide Naturen hinweisen, *nur* in einem nebensätzlichen Gewande, nämlich in der Form der Apposition auf; sie deuten *nur* auf eine *vorausgesetzte Vorbedingung unseres Glaubens, nicht auf den Inhalt des Glaubens selbst.* Dieser liegt doch in dem 'sei mein Herr' mit der Finalbestimmung: 'auf daß ich in seinem Reiche unter ihm lebe und ihm diene'." (Italics mine.) He goes so far (ibid.) as to consider the two-nature doctrine in Luther's text as something which is of secondary importance ("etwas Untergeordnetes"). While it is true that "my Lord" is the key to the text, one may not isolate it from "true God ... true man" and treat that phrase as if it were only an unimportant apposition or a presupposition for "my Lord." The earliest Latin text (1529) makes such an underestimating of that phrase impossible. Here (294.26-296.1, right col.) we read: "Credo, quod Iesus Christus sit verus Deus ..., credo quoque quod sit verus homo ..., quod sit Dominus meus." Here, contrary to Knoke's argument, both natures are a part of the content of "I believe".

Following the end of (*a*) one long clause begins which is carefully structured in three sections, (*b*), (*c*), and (*d*). Luther continues by qualifying "mein Herr" with the relative clause (*b*): "der mich verlorenen und verdammten Menschen erlöset hat[,] erworben [und] gewonnen ...[30] von allen Sünden, vom Tod und von der Gewalt des Teufels[,] nicht mit Gold oder Silber[,] sondern mit seinem heiligen[,] teuren Blut und mit seinem unschuldigen Leiden und Sterben" (249.11-17). With "Mensch" and the way he qualifies this noun Luther tries to build a bridge to the First Article,[31] and in terms of writing he is not very successful. But on the basis of the *LC* text it is clear that with "Mensch" the Second Article is connected to the First, a connection which summarizes all of Genesis 1 through 3 in a few words.[32]

In this relative clause Luther deals with the Creed's sections from "suffered under Pontius Pilate" to "descended into Hell." He picks up the relative clause of *ApC*, which is now shortened of the two opening phrases ("who was conceived by the Holy Spirit, born of the Virgin Mary"). Yet Luther's clause looks quite different from the one in *ApC*, and one is struck by the freedom with which Luther treats the materials of the Creed: not a word about Pilate, or about Christ having been buried, or about Christ having descended into Hell.[33] Further, the verbs of *ApC*, which—in continuation of the opening statements that Jesus Christ was conceived by the Holy Spirit and born of the Virgin Mary—report the major stages in the Jesus story ("suffered," "crucified," "[has] died") are replaced with weighty nouns qualified by adjectives ("teures Blut," "unschuldiges Leiden und Sterben"). What Luther presents is not a commentary (as we understand this technical term) on the text of *ApC* or a paraphrase of that text. He presents *his understanding* of this text. And that understanding is shaped by the statement in *NC*: "who for us humans[34] and for our salvation came down from heaven."[35] Already the title which Luther gives to the Second Article ("Der andere Artikel [:] Von der

[30] See n. 44.

[31] It is interesting to note that Luther does not use "Geschöpf" or "Kreatur" but "Mensch."

[32] *LC* (186.16-19); *BC* 414.28.

[33] For the Descent into Hell, see Peters 151-57.

[34] "Homines" in the Latin text (*Missale Romanum*) for *anthropous*, "Menschen" in the German text of *BSLK* 26.13.

[35] Denzinger No. 86; *BSLK* 26.13; *BC* 18. In *LC* (186.19-22) Luther paraphrases this passage: "Da war kein Rat, Hilfe noch Trost, bis daß sich dieser einige und ewige Gottes Sohn unseres Jammers und Elends aus grundloser Güte erbarmte und vom Himmel kam[,] uns zu helfen."

Erlösung" [248.18]) points toward the dominant role of this passage, granted that one may question Luther's "Erlösung" when one places it in the context of *NC's soteria*. With a radical phrasing one could say that Luther's text shows that for him the Second Article deals not with the highlights of the Jesus story, as recorded in *ApC*, but with Redemption. As the text will establish, Redemption is not an idea but an event which is enacted by the Redeemer.[36] There is, then, an ever-so-slight shift in emphasis from the Jesus story to Redemption and the Redeemer, and that shift in emphasis is interesting; for in the *Short Form* of 1520 Luther placed the text and his explanation under the simple title "Jesus" and used for the individual articles only "Das erste Teil des Glaubens," "Das andere Teil," "Das dritte Teil."[37]

(*B*) consists of two coordinated but not verbally connected subsections, (*b*.1) and (*b*.2). Each subsection has its own center.[38] In (*b*.1) "I" is the center of the statements, and "I" is defined with two adjectives (derived from verbs) and a noun.[39] In (*b*.2) Christ is the center of the statements. The shift from (*b*.1) to (*b*.2) is signaled only by the thought that "my Lord" did what he did not with gold or silver, but any verbal connection is missing. The abrupt shift from "I" to Christ, and then the construction of (*b*.2) as a contrast ("nicht mit ... sondern mit ...") gives speed to the text.

Using three verbs[40] and three nouns,[41] Luther structures (*b*.1) as a statement about "I". He structures (*b*.2) as a contrast,[42] and he connects this contrast with the three verbs of (*b*.1)—but he does not repeat the verbs, he presupposes them. The contrast is expressed in two sets of nouns. The first set consists of two unqualified nouns

[36] See also *LC* (186.29-187.5): "Das sei nun die Summa dieses Artikels, daß das Wörtlein HERRE auffs einfältigste soviel heiße als ein Erlöser, das ist[,] der uns vom Teufel zu Gott, vom Tod zum Leben, von [der] Sünde zur Gerechtigkeit gebracht hat und dabei erhält. Die Stücke aber, so nacheinander in diesem Artikel folgen, tun nichts anderes, denn daß sie solche Erlösung verklären und ausdrücken, *wie und wodurch sie geschehen sei*, ... was er daran *gewendet und gewagt hat, daß er uns gewönne* und zu seiner Herrschaft *brächte*, nämlich[,] daß *er Mensch geworden [ist]*, ..., *auf daß er der Sünden Herr were*, ... *daß* er für mich *genug täte* und *bezahlte*, was ich verschuldet habe, ... Und dies alles darum, daß er mein HERR würde." (For my italics, see n. 55.) See also *BC* 414.31. For Luther texts and secondary literature dealing with Christ as the Redeemer, see Peters 2:171f.

[37] WA 7:214.23, 215.23, 216.30, 218.20.

[38] Below, in the quotation of the text, these centers appear in capital letters.

[39] Below, in the quotation of the text, this appears in bold typeface.

[40] Below, in the quotation of the text, the verbs appear in italics.

[41] Below, in the quotation of the text, the nouns appear in small capitals.

[42] Below, in the quotation of the text, this contrast is marked by underlining the appropriate words.

connected by "oder." The second set consists of one noun qualified three times and of two additional nouns qualified twice, and the three nouns are connected by "und": Not with gold or silver, but with (1) his (2) holy (3) precious blood and with (1) his (2) innocent suffering and death. "Oder" of the first set of nouns suggests that both nouns are only alternatives for the same thing and therefore have the same weight.[43] On the other hand, the two occurrences of "und" in the second set of nouns signal coordination of things which are sufficiently weighty that the author feels he has to list them separately. (*B*.2) is, then, not only a simple contrast of two things, but the two things contrasted are related to each other in gradation: from the lower to the highest, from material things to the most personal thing, one's death. This, then, is Luther's text, with my emphases:

> mein Herr[,] der (*b*.1) MICH **verlorenen** und **verdammten Menschen** *erlöset hat*[,] *erworben* [und] *gewonnen*,[44] von allen SÜNDEN, vom TOD und von der GEWALT DES TEUFELS[,]"—(*b*.2): [mein HERR, der mich erlöset, erworben und gewonnen hat] "nicht mit GOLD oder SILBER[,] sondern mit seinem heiligen[,] teuren BLUT und mit seinem unschuldigen LEIDEN und STERBEN,

The sequence (*b*.1): 1[45] - 2[46] - 3[47] - 3[48] - (*b*.2): 1[49] - 2[50] - 3[51] - 3[52] creates a rhythmic, swiftly flowing text; it reaches its peaks in the three verbs and in the two sets of three nouns.[53]

Luther continues (249.17-20)[54] with the consecutive clause (*c*), introduced with "auf daß."[55] It consists of three coordinated subsec-

[43] See, however, also n. 99.

[44] In the earliest German texts is inserted: "und." Already the earliest Latin version (1529) smooths the text in a way which justifies our version (296.2-4, right col.). For the passage in the 16th century prints and possible explanations of this rather awkward "und", see WA 30^{1}:366, n. 2.

[45] *Mich*.

[46] *Verlorenen, verdammten*.

[47] *Erlöset, erworben, gewonnen*.

[48] *Sünde, Tod, Teufel*.

[49] *Mein Herr*, presupposed.

[50] *Gold oder Silber*.

[51] *Erlöset, erworben, gewonnen*, presupposed.

[52] *Blut, Leiden, Sterben*.

[53] *Erlöset, erworben, gewonnen—Sünden, Tod, Teufel—Blut, Leiden, Sterben*. In the phrase "Gewalt des Teufels", "Gewalt" strengthens "Teufel" the way an adjective qualifies a noun; therefore the phrase can be considered one noun.

[54] For the appearance of the quotation below, see nn. 38, 40, 41.

[55] See Carl Franke, *Grundzüge der Schriftsprache Luthers in allgemeinverständlicher Darstellung*, 3. *Luthers Satzlehre* (Hildesheim, New York: Georg Olms Verlag, 1973; repr. of the second ed. rev. 1922): 318, 320.k, 321.f and 3, 327.i and

k, 356, 357.k, 365.a; Johannes Erben, *Grundzüge einer Syntax Luthers* (Berlin: Akademie Verlag, 1954), 114f. ("damit," "daß"), 116 ("daß"); id., *Abriss der deutschen Grammatik* (9th ed. München: Hueber Verlag, 1966), 187f. Luther uses "daß" or "auf daß" to introduce dependent clauses of purpose, intention, goal, consequences, or accomplishments (final and consecutive clauses), with the verb(s) in such a clause in the subjunctive. On the basis of grammar alone it is impossible exactly to identify the nature of such a clause, and one has to use the content and context for arriving at such a decision. (*B*) is a relative clause, but it is also the clause on which (*c*) is dependent. (*C*) is not a final clause (as has been suggested, for example, by Knoke [see n. 29], Gillhoff [*Sprache und Geschichte* (as in n. 3), 39], and others), introduced by "auf daß," in which the content of (*c*) is the goal, intention, or—it is hoped—the eventual outcome of (*b*). (For examples of final clauses introduced by "auf daß," see some of the materials presented in Franke.) (*C*), introduced with "auf daß," presents *the ongoing results of the completed actions* which are expressed in the verbs of the prior clause (*b*.1), on which (*c*) is dependent; conversely, the verbs in (*b*.1) express the actions which necessarily had to occur for creating the ongoing situation which is described in (*c*). (Therefore Luther sometimes introduces such a consecutive clause also with "damit" in the sense of 'with these actions' [in stead of "auf daß"], which refers back to the verbs of a prior clause.) (*C*) expresses the actual—not wished or hoped for—*ongoing results* of a situation which was created in (*b*). In such a case, most of the time Luther uses the present subjunctive for the verbs which describe the ongoing results of an action which had been completed in the prior clause. (See also Franke, 321.3.) "Sei," "leb," and "diene," introduced by "auf daß," are subjunctives expressing dependency on the verbs of (*b*.1), which, in turn, signal the past completion of a situation ("erlöset *hat*, ..."). Therefore they are not subjunctives of meaning or content, expressing assumed, or wished for, or speculated about possibilities. The phrasing in *LC* makes clear beyond a doubt that Luther thought in the indicative and not the subjunctive mood (italics mine): "Also *sind* nun jene Tyrannen und Stockmeister alle *vertrieben* und *ist* an ihre statt *getreten* Jesus Christus, ein Herr des Lebens, ... und *hat* uns arme, verlorene Menschen aus der Hölle Rachen *gerissen*, gewonnen, frey gemacht und wiedergebracht in des Vaters Huld und Gnade und als sein Eigentum unter seinen Schirm und Schutz *genommen*, *daß er uns regiere* [consecutive clause with the verb in the present subjunctive, describing the ongoing result of the prior verbs, for example, *hat gerissen* and *genommen*] durch seine Gerechtigkeit, ..." (186.22-28; see also ibid., 35 ["gewagt hat, daß er uns gewönne," as in n. 36].) Further, the idea of the 'blessed exchange,' developed by Luther in his book on Christian freedom, strengthens the argument that in (*c*) Luther thinks or speaks of ongoing results of Christ's actions. *The outcome of whatever Jesus Christ did was a new situation for "I"*. Luther does not deal with the problem whether "I" in his or her daily life puts this new situation into operation, and here the catechist has the task of developing Luther's statement. But this does not change Luther's affirmation expressed in this sentence that the result of Christ's actions, described in (*b*), is a new reality and not a possibility, or something wished for or eventually, hopefully to be accomplished. As a result of what Jesus Christ did for and to me, *he has a claim on me and I am his property*. It is another problem whether I affirm this! (Marginally: In *BC* 345.4, "*sei* mein Herr," dependent on "ich glaube, daß," is translated as "*is* my Lord." On the other hand, "ich sein eigen *sei*," dependent on "auf daß," is translated as "I *may* be his [own]"!)

tions, (*c*.1), (*c*.2), (*c*.3), which are connected by "und." These subsections have only one center, that is, "I":

> (*C*) auf daß (*c*.1) ICH sein *eigen sei*[56] (*c*.2) und in seinem REICH unter ihm *lebe* (*c*.3) und ihm *diene* in ewiger GERECHTIGKEIT[,] UNSCHULD und SELIGKEIT,

The result of the events listed in (*b*) is now described in three steps, expressed through three present tense verbs: "(sein eigen) *sein*, (in seinem Reich) *leben*, (ihm) *dienen*." This is the result of whatever Christ did: "I" is Christ's property, "I" lives under him in his kingdom, and "I" serves him in eternal righteousness, innocence, and blessedness.

As the text stands now, "in ewiger Gerechtigkeit[,] Unschuld und Seligkeit" is connected with "und ihm diene." It is possible that this connection was Luther's intention. But in light of all of Luther's theology one may wonder whether "in eternal righteousness, innocence, and blessedness" could or should not be connected also with (*c*.1) and (*c*.2). If indeed this were the case, then a comma would probably have separated the phrase from the preceding three verb phrases. Had we Luther's manuscript available,[57] and thus could see how he punctuated the text, we could make a definite statement about this matter.[58]

The rhythm of this clause is the result of the tripartition of the text and of the gradation inherent in the three subsections: from being—to living—to doing. If one takes (*b*) and (*c*) together, then a unique sequence exists, which binds both clauses together: three verbs –three nouns–three nouns–three verbs–three nouns: *erlöset, erworben, gewonnen*—SÜNDEN, TOD, TEUFEL—BLUT, LEIDEN, STERBEN —*eigen sein, leben, dienen*—GERECHTIGKEIT, UNSCHULD, SELIGKEIT. Just as Luther structures the whole sentence dependent on "is my Lord" in

[56] "Eigen sei" in the sense of *Eigentum sein*. *BC* 345.4 (*SC*) and 414.30 (*LC*) and other English versions use only "his" or "his own." This weak phrasing tiptoes around what Luther says. The *LC* text (186.26) makes clear that when Luther writes "eigen sei" he thinks in terms of the stronger and precise word, "Eigentum" or property. As a result of whatever Christ did for and to "I," *Christ has a claim on "I". "I" belongs to Christ the way one owns something*, a piece of land, a part of one's body, or even a human being the way a medieval lord could own a serf. See also Dietz 1: s.v. "eigen"; Götze, s.v. "eigen"; *Trübners Deutsches Wörterbuch*, 2 (Berlin: de Gruyter Verlag, 1940): s.vv. "eigen," "Eigentum." For Christ and his property, that is, his people, see, for example, Hans Joachim Iwand, *Luthers Theologie. Nachgelassene Werke*, 5, ed. by Helmut Gollwitzer et al. (München: Kaiser Verlag, 1974): 105-10 ("Christus und die Seinen"), 131-176 ("Wer sind die Seinen?").

[57] See also below, 147.

[58] The *LC* text does not help in this matter.

the three sections (*b*), (*c*), and (*d*), so he expresses what is important to him in groups of three words, and this gives the text solemnity and rhythm.

At this point it is possible that the reader might expect that Luther is, at least for the time being, at the end of what he wants to say about the phrase "is my Lord." But Luther is not at the end. In the following (249.20-22), he deals[59] with the Creed's statements: "on the third day he rose from the dead, he ascended into heaven, and is now sitting at the right hand of God, the Father almighty, and from there he will come to judge the living and the dead." One is again struck by the freedom with which Luther treats the text.

Luther ignores the Ascension; apparently he considers "he reigns in eternity" sufficient to explain "he ascended into heaven and is now sitting at the right hand of God, the Father almighty." He also ignores the last clause, "from there he will come to judge the living and the dead."[60] Luther concentrates on the Resurrection and the now living Christ and his eternal ruling, an activity connected with power.[61] In *ApC* Christ is risen from (among) the dead; for Luther, Christ is risen "vom Tod."[62] The Resurrection is not an event which takes place among the dead.[63] *It is a personal encounter between Christ and death*, in which death is the loser, and with it all the demonic forces. Says Luther in *LC* (187.5): "Danach ist er wieder aufgestanden, [hat] den Tod verschlungen und gefressen[.] Und endlich [ist] er gen Himmel gefahren und [hat] das Regiment genommen zur rechten des Vaters, daß ihm der Teufel und alle Gewalt muß untertan sein und zu Füßen liegen ... ." Luther's hymn, *Christ Jesus Lay in Death's Strong Bands*, illustrates the full dimension of this shift from "the dead" to "death." And this shift creates a connection with the statement in (*b*.1) that Christ has redeemed "I" from the slavery in which death holds "I".

Luther uses[64] "gleich wie" to connect (*c*) with (*d*). This phrase[65] introduces new materials which are related to the materials presented

[59] See also Peters 2:157-70.

[60] Luther saves that clause for the explanation of the Third Article (250.14-17). Here, in connection with the very last statement of the Creed ("resurrection of the body and life everlasting"), he somewhat deals with that clause, without, however, focusing on Judgment Day explicitly. See also Peters 2:166-70.

[61] See also the *LC* text (187.5-8); *BC* 414, toward the end of 31.

[62] The English text in *BC* 345.4 (*SC*), and also 414.31 (*LC*), does not do justice to Luther's text.

[63] According to the *Short Form* (1520), Christ rose from *the dead*; WA 7:218.4.

[64] For the appearance of the quotation below, see nn. 38, 40, 41.

[65] The earliest Latin text reads "quemadmodum" (296.11). The parallel text in *LC* is constructed differently (187.5-8); *BC* 414 toward the end of 31.

in (*c*) by way of comparison ("just as").[66] The text consists of two subsections (*d*.1, *d*.2), which are coordinated though not verbally connected. In both subsections Christ is the center of the statements. (*D*.1) consists of one verb connected with one noun, (*d*.2) consists of two verbs connected by "und," and both verbs are connected with one noun:

> gleich wie (*d*.1) ER *ist auferstanden* vom TOD[,] (*d*.2) *lebet*[67] und *regiert* in EWIGKEIT,

The rhythm of the text[68] is the result of the gradation which exists between the two subsections: Luther moves from Christ's Resurrection (*d*.1), an event located in time and space, to Christ's eternal life and reign (*d*.2). (*D*.2) consists of two verbs and one noun—but what verbs and what a noun! He LIVES and REIGNS in ETERNITY! With (*d*.2) Luther's text forms a grandiose arch, stretching from *eternity* (*a*.1), *past* ([*a*.2], [*b*.2], [*d*.1]), *presence* ([*a*: "*Ich glaube* ... mein Herr"], [*b*.1], [*c*]), to *eternity* (*d*.2):

> Jesus Christ, born of the Father *in eternity*
>
> and also born of the Virgin Mary (that is, *in time and space*), is *now my Lord*, because he has done all that is described in (*b*), with the result that I am his property, live in his kingdom, and serve him in *eternal* righteousness, innocence, and blessedness
>
> now lives and reigns *in eternity*!

The adjective "eternal" in (*c*.3), connected with *statements about "I"*, is picked up as a noun in (*d*.2), but now connected with *statements about Jesus Christ: He* lives and reigns in eternity. What is said about "I" in (*c*), is heightened by what is said about Christ: as Christ is risen from death and lives and reigns in eternity, so "I" lives now and shall live eternally in Christ's kingdom and serve him now and in eternity in righteousness, innocence, and blessedness because Jesus Christ made "I" his property. The text following "gleich wie" guarantees what is said in (*c*) about "I", [69] and at the same time it sets the stage for the closing sentence (*e*): "Das ist gewißlich wahr."

[66] See Dietz 2: s.v. "gleich § 7"; Götze, s.v. "gleich." There are several words and ways with which Luther introduces a clause of comparison; "wie" would be one of them. Usually he uses it alone. It seems that when he wants to speak emphatically, he adds "gleich" to "wie." See Erben, *Syntax* (as in n. 55), 103, and ibid., n.1 ("wie"), 117, and ibid. n. 2 ("wie").

[67] In a paraphrase of the text, Luther's theology would justify adding "now" at this point.

[68] Sequence: 1 verb - 1 noun - 2 verbs - 1 noun.

[69] Therefore a freer translation of Luther's "gleich wie" would be: "just as he *indeed* is risen from death."

This sentence, which we find at the end of the explanation of each of the articles, is a summarizing statement of affirmation. The sentence suggests solemnity, and it brings to mind the weighty opening, "Ich glaube." While the text does not say so, obviously the statement is made by the speaker who in (*a*) has introduced himself or herself with "I believe." Is he or she the center of the sentence? Further, to what does "Das" refer? What is covered by the affirmation spelled out in this sentence? These questions are not quite as superfluous as it might appear at a first glance at the text. We do not have Luther's manuscript. Therefore in matters of the punctuation preceding or following a word and capitalization of the first letter of a word following a mark of punctuation, we have to work with the text as it has come down to us through the tradition, and that textual tradition is not as clear[70] and uniform as we want it to be. We need not go into these technical details. If we look at the sentence as it is, then "Das" refers first of all to the content of (*d*). But since (*d*) is 'only' a part of the text which begins in (*b*), the affirmation spelled out in (*e*) also applies to that whole text. And if there is any value in the image of the arch, mentioned above, then (*e*) is the terminal anchoring point of the arch, while (*a*) is the beginning anchoring point[71] of the arch: (*E*) it is most certainly true that Jesus Christ is my Lord—as (*a*) I believe—because of (*b*) through (*d*). In (*a*) "I" and Christ are the combined center of the sentence. Now in (*e*) the order is reversed to Christ and "I": Christ is my Lord, and this is most certainly true, as I believe. While "I" is the speaker, "I" is not the center of the statement but Christ and "I" together are the center.

Two additional observations:

If we look at the text as a unit—not the individual sections—we find a rhythm in the text, which is the result of the shifts in what I have called the center of the statements: I and Christ[72]—Christ[73]—I[74]—Christ[75]—I[76]—Christ[77]—Christ and I.[78] If we use numbers (2 for Christ, 3 for I, 1 for I and Christ or Christ and I) then the text is structured in the following sequence: 1-2-3-2-3-2-1; *note* the central

[70] See, for example, WA 30^1:243, left col., n. 1.

[71] See above, 139, 146.

[72] (*A*).

[73] (*A*.1, 2).

[74] (*B*.1).

[75] (*B*.2).

[76] (*C*).

[77] (*D*).

[78] (*E*).

position of Christ. This rhythm makes the text flow swiftly and easily so that it can be quickly memorized, and it justifies the suggestion that Luther intended the text to be spoken rather than only read.[79]

Further, if we precede the text's declaratory statements with questions, then Luther would deal with six questions: Who is Jesus Christ? Who am I? What did Jesus Christ do? What was the result of what Jesus Christ did? How, or with what means, did Jesus Christ do what he did? And finally, why is what is being said in this text true?

II
CONTENT AND GENRE

Classical rhetoric can further help us understand Luther's text.

The role of Luther and Melanchthon in the academic reforms of Wittenberg University in the years 1517 to 1520/21 and the promotion of humanistic studies, especially rhetoric, in these reforms is known, and we need not deal with these events.[80] Luther was thoroughly familiar with classical rhetoric and used it in his lectures, writing, and preaching.[81]

[79] See also Johannes Erben, "Die sprachgeschichtliche Stellung Luthers. Eine Skizze vom Standpunkt der Syntax," *BGDS* 76(1954):166-79, esp. 171f.; Peters 2:100; Stolt, "Luthers rhetorische Syntax" (as in n. 81). The value of this suggestion gains weight if one considers the level of literacy in Luther's days (esp. in the rural areas), and also the fact that the 'first edition' of *SC* was printed on posters; they were to be exhibited to people and then read by someone who could read and help the people memorize and recite the text. For the language of Luther's literary productivity as a spoken language, and for rhythm in Luther's sentence construction, see also Erben, *Syntax* (as in n. 55), 23, n.2, 155-57.

[80] See, for example, Brecht, *Luther* (as in n. 14), 1:275-82; Karl Bauer, *Die Wittenberger Universitätstheologie und die Anfänge der Deutschen Reformation* (Tübingen: Mohr Verlag, 1928); Ernest G. Schwiebert, *Luther and his Times* (St. Louis: Concordia Publishing House, 1950), 293-302; id., "New Groups at the University of Wittenberg," *ARG* 49(1958):60-79; Wilhelm Maurer, *Der junge Melanchthon zwischen Humanismus und Reformation*, 1. *Der Humanist* (Göttingen: Verlag Vandenhoeck and Ruprecht, 1967):171-198; Robert Rosin, "The Reformation, Humanism, and Education: The Wittenberg Model for Reform," *ConJ* 16(1990):301-18; Junghans, *Der junge Luther*, as in n. 81.

[81] For Luther and rhetoric, see Reinhard Breymayer, "Bibliographie zum Thema 'Luther und die Rhetorik'," *LingBibl* 3(1973. Heft 21/22):39-44; Wolf, *Luther-Bibliographie* (as in n. 3), Nos. 1345-1356, and Wolf *Einführung* (as in n. 3), 95-101; Lischer, as in n. 90; Ulrich Nembach, *Predigt des Evangeliums: Luther als Prediger, Pädagoge und Rhetor* (Neukirchen-Vlyn: Neukirchner Verlag 1972; for this book, see *LuJ* 44[1977]: 39f.); Birgit Stolt, *Wortkampf: Frühneuhochdeutsche Beispiele zur rhetorischen Praxis* (Frankfurt: Athenäum Verlag, 1974), 31-119; id., "Rhetorische Textkohärenz—am Beispiel Martin Luthers," *Rhetorik* 10(1991):89-

In terms of classical rhetoric,[82] what follows "Antwort" is a text of the *genus deliberativum*. In the speech or text the author presents a

99; id., "Martin Luthers rhetorische Syntax," in: Gert Ueding, ed., *Rhetorik zwischen den Wissenschaften: Geschichte, System, Praxis als Probleme des 'Historischen Wörterbuchs der Rhetorik'* (Tübingen: Niemeyer Verlag, 1991), 207-20; Helmar Junghans, *Der junge Luther und die Humanisten* (Weimar: Verlag Hermann Böhlaus Nachfolger, 1984), 31-62, 207-35, 240-73; id., "Martin Luther und die Rhetorik," *SSAW*. Philologisch-historische Klasse 136^2(1998); id., "Die Worte Christi geben das Leben," in: *Der Mensch Luther und sein Umfeld. Wartburg Jahrbuch*, Sonderband 1996:154-75; Karl-Heinz zur Mühlen, "Rhetorik in Predigten und Schriften Luthers," *LuJ* 57(1990):257-59; Dieter Gutzen, "'Es ligt alles am wort'. Überlegungen zu Luthers Rhetorik," in: Ueding, *Rhetorik zwischen den Wissenschaften*, 229-35; Klaus Dockhorn, "Luthers Glaubensbegriff und die Rhetorik: Zu Gerhard Ebelings 'Einführung in die theologische Sprachlehre'," *LingBibl* 3(1972. Heft 21/22):19-39; Wolfgang Maaser, "Rhetorik und Dialektik. Überlegungen zur systematischen Relevanz der Rhetoriktradition bei Luther," *Luther* 69(1998):25-39; Ursula Stock, "Spes exercens conscientiam. Sprache und Affekt in Luthers Auslegung des 6. Psalms in den Operationes in Psalmos," *AWA* 5(1984):229-43; Neil R. Leroux, "Luther's *Am Neujahrstage*: Style as Argument," *Rhetorica* 12(1994):1-42; Heiko A. Oberman, "Immo. Luthers reformatorische Entdeckung im Spiegel der Rhetorik," *AWA* 5(1984):17-38; Oswald Bayer, "Vom Wunderwerk, Gottes Wort recht zu verstehen. Luthers letzter Zettel," *KuD* 37(1991):258-79; Susanne Dähn, *Rede als Text. Rhetorik und Stilistik in Luthers Sakramentssermonen von 1519* (Frankfurt: Peter Lang Verlag, 1997; for this book, see *LuJ* 65[1998]:155, and *SCJ* 29[1998]:195-97); for a rhetorical analysis of Luther's explanation of the First Article of *ApC* in *SC*, see Krodel, as in n. 4, Appendix. Only recently has scholarship started to deal with details in the topic 'Luther and rhetoric', and much work still has to be done. In terms of Luther's biography, one of the problems which has to be solved is the question of Luther's sources; Stolt and Junghans have made important observations on this question. For this question, Eberhard Ockel, "Martin Luther und die rhetorische Tradition," in: *Martin Luther: Annäherungen und Anfragen*, ed. by Willigis Eckermann and Edgar Papp (Vechta: Vechtaer Verlag, 1985), 58-75, is not very helpful.

[82] In the following rhetorical materials I deal with basics only and ignore the many variations and fine points which one can find in the texts of classical rhetoric. Therefore I list only basic references. Some initial information can be found in C.Hugh Holman and William Harmon, *A Handbook to Literature* (5th ed. New York: Macmillan Publishing Co., 1986), s.vv. "Amplification," "Argumentation," "Confession," "Contrast," "Description," "Invention," "Narration," "Oration," "Persuasion." The standard works are: Heinrich Lausberg, *Handbook of Literary Rhetoric. A Foundation for Literary Study*, transl. from the second ed., 1973, by Matthew T. Bliss et al., ed. by David E. Orton and R. Dean Anderson (Leiden: Brill, 1998); *Historisches Wörterbuch der Rhetorik* (*HWR*), ed. by Gert Ueding et al. (Tübingen: Niemeyer Verlag, Darmstadt: Wissenschaftliche Buchgesellschaft, 1992), incomplete. For the rhetorical materials used in the following analysis, see Lausberg, *Handbook*, §§ 224 (*genus deliberativum*), 260 (*inventio*), 289, 346f (*propositio*), 289-347 (*narratio*; 289, 290: literary narrative [event, *persona*, *historia*, *fabula*]; 1107-1110: *fabula*; 289, 290, 323, 328: *res, causa* [for other definitions, see § 1244, s.vv. "causa," "res"]; 289, 290, 328: *elementa narrationis*; § 1244, s.v. "expositio"),

case for the public to ponder. The author hopes that the public will eventually take a specific action because of the content of what he or she has presented. The opening phrase, "*I* believe that Jesus Christ is *my* Lord," and the closing affirmation make clear that the case presented by the author does not deal with a theoretical person "I", but with the author himself, and by extension with myself. The case presented is the story of *my* life.[83] And the audience addressed through this case is first of all I myself, and then the listener or reader. The goal of the text is the affirmation expressed in (*e*), which is derived from (*a*).

"Was ist das? Antwort" connects the quoted text with Luther's own text; that text is an *explanatio dicti superioris* and may be considered a long epexegetical statement[84] by way of *amplificatio*.

Luther deals with a given text. Therefore he does not have to search for, or discover, or invent (*inventio*) the materials to be treated in his speech or text. From the given text he formulates in (*a*) the *propositio*, the introductory listing of the points which in the following materials have to be treated in detail.[85] And in that listing Luther moves from me, the author or speaker, to Jesus Christus whom he qualifies with the two appositions ("wahrhaftiger Gott," "wahrhaftiger Mensch"), to "sei mein Herr." A short version of the *propositio* would read: "*I believe that Jesus Christ is my Lord.*" As any freshman learns in

400-409 (*amplificatio*), 257.1, 261, 262, 289, 295 (*argumentatio*), 413 (*affirmatio*). For the required features of a *narratio*, of which some can be found in Luther's text, see ibid., §§ 290, 293-298, 307, 309, 326-334 (*docere, movere, delectare, brevitas, non plus dicere quam oportet*), 528-537 (*perspicuitas*), 326, 845, 1055-1062, 1074 (*aptum*, familiarity, appropriateness), 312, 322-334 (*probabilitas, credibilitas*). See also *HWR* 1(1992): s.vv. "Affirmatio," "Amplificatio" A, B.I, "Angemessenheit," "Argumentation" 1.B.I.*b*, "Autobiographie"; 2(1994): s.vv. "Brevitas," "Confessio," "Confessiones," "Delectare," "Descriptio," "Docere," "Epexegese"; 3(1996): s.vv. "Explanatio", "Exposition".

[83] It is possible that, as Peters has argued (2:27-29), this concentration on "me" is the result of the medieval setting of *ApC*, the confession of sins.

[84] See also the suggested translation of the connecting phrase, above, 134, 136. For a short epexegetical statement, see, for example, Rom. 7:18: "... nothing good dwells within me, *that is*, in my flesh."

[85] According to some theoreticians of classical rhetoric, this listing may be placed at the end of the text, as a summary of sorts. Were one to apply this possibility to Luther's text, one would have an interesting version. Luther would start his text with (*b*), but he would have eliminated the relative connection of (*b*) and reshaped the text as a direct statement: "What is this that I have just said? Answer: Jesus Christ has redeemed me, a lost and condemned creature, ..." Then would follow (*c*) and (*d*) in their present form. The end of Luther's text might read: "This (that is, [b], [c], and [d]) is most certainly true. In sum: [or: "Therefore:"] I believe that Jesus Christ, true God ..., true man ..., is my Lord."

his or her composition class, at the end of the introduction the theme or thesis for what follows has to be formulated and set forth. "I believe that Jesus Christ is my Lord" is the thesis, the *cantus firmus* which governs all that Luther will say in the following lines, and which is the key to understanding it.[86]

(*B*) through (*d*) is a *narratio*,[87] a story about events or actions as Luther sees them being implied in his thesis. In *LC* Luther expresses this idea of events or actions in a clearer way. He writes (*BC* 414.27.31, italics mine): "I believe that Jesus Christ ... *has become my Lord.*" And then he at once asks: "*What is it to 'become a Lord*'?" And now he develops in broad strokes a vivid picture of all that Jesus Christ did in order to create this lordship. He concludes these materials by coming back to his original question, but now he summarizes his answer: "[He did] all this *in order to become my Lord.*"[88]

Luther's *narratio* is an *expositio* of the thesis. The concreteness of the content,[89] the simplicity of the writing, and the rhythm of the clauses in this story place its author among the great tellers of biblical stories.[90] The story does not deal with a *fabula* but a *historia*, and it is that *historia* which is to explain the quoted text. In classical rhetoric the subject matter (*res*, *causa*) of a *historia* can be an event, idea, person, thing, problem (sometimes even a crime). In our text, the *res* is the *personae*, or rather the *descriptio personarum*. In five steps Luther executes this *descriptio personarum*—I, Jesus Christ—by way of *amplificatio* of the thesis.

[86] See also Peters 2:111: "Der Versuch, mit Hilfe dieser Wendung [*ApC's* apposition 'our Lord'], den gesamten Artikel in den Griff zu bekommen, ist vor [Luther] nirgendwo gemacht worden, ..."

[87] In the introduction to his explanation of *ApC* in the *Short Form* (1520) Luther writes: "Der Glaube teilt sich in drei Hauptstücke, nach [denen] die drei Personen der heiligen, göttlichen Dreifaltigkeit ... *erzählet* werden"; WA 7:214.25f., italics mine. See also Peters 2:20: "Im Stil der 'narratio', des rühmenden Nacherzählens der großen Heilstaten Gottes, lenkt vor allem die entfaltete Form des Textus receptus [of *ApC*] unser Augenmerk auf die Stellen, an welchen Gottes Wirken hineingreift in das Sicht- und Faßbare unserer Erdenwelt." Peters footnotes *narratio* with a general reference to Augustine's *De catechizandis rudibus*.

[88] See also n. 36.

[89] See esp. (*b*.1) and (*b*.2).

[90] For Luther the storyteller, see the delightful collection of texts, *Wie Luther den Deutschen das Leben Jesu erzählt hat*, ed. by Walther Köhler (2d ed.rev. Leipzig: Verlag Heinsius Nachfolger, 1934). See also Ficker and Preuß (esp. 202f.), as in n. 3; Richard Lischer, "'Story' in Luthers Predigten: Ein Beitrag zur Beziehung zwischen Rhetorik und Anthropology," *EvTh* 43(1983. Heft 6):526-47. Many of the images which Luther suggests (sometimes only with a word or two) in the explanation of *ApC* in the catechisms we find fully developed in the *Wartburg Postilla*.

Step one: Already in his weighty opening statement ("I believe that Jesus Christ is my Lord"), Luther begins developing his story by elaborating (*amplificatio*) on one of the persons mentioned in this statement, Jesus Christ. Who is he? Answer (*a*.1, *a*.2): the God-man—true God, born from the Father in eternity, true man, born from the Virgin Mary. At this point the emphasis is on Jesus Christ as a person. The connection with the other person mentioned, I, is established through the fact that it is I who believes that this God-man is my Lord.

Step two: In (*b.1*) Luther elaborates on me, and he does it in two statements. They are related to each other in such a way that the second statement qualifies the first by transcending it. Who am I? First statement: A lost and condemned human being;[91] second statement: a lost and condemned human being who, nevertheless, has been redeemed, acquired, and rescued from all sins, from death, and from the power of the Devil. Who did all this?

Step three: To answer this question, Luther returns in (*b.2*) to Jesus Christ, on whom he has elaborated in (*a*.1) and (*a*.2), emphasizing Christ as a person. Luther continues to unfold his story by further elaborating on Jesus Christ, now emphasizing the fact that he is my Lord. Luther does this in two ways. First: he places what he says in (*b.1*) about me in a relative clause dependent on "is my Lord" ("... sei mein Herr, *der* mich erlöset hat ..."). It is Jesus Christ who did all this for and to me and thus became my Lord. Second: In (*b.2*) he describes how, or with what means, Jesus Christ did for and to me what he did. Using the rhetorical device of contrast ("not with ... but with"), Luther creates a feeling for the tremendous price Christ paid in order to become my Lord. At the end of (*b*) Luther indirectly returns to the end of (*a*). In (*a*) Luther says that I believe that Jesus Christ is my Lord. Now, having arrived at the end of (*b*), Luther has made clear that *Jesus Christ indeed has become my Lord because of what he has done for and to me.*[92]

At this point the *amplificatio* of the thesis in the form of the *descriptio personarum* has led Luther beyond the text of *ApC*.[93] *The Jesus story recorded in ApC has become the story of my Redemption, enacted by the God-man*, that is, I am placed into this Jesus story. From the *homoousia* of the Father and the Son and the two-nature Christology, that is, ontological statements, Luther draws action and

[91] See above, 140.

[92] See n. 36.

[93] How far Luther has moved from the text of *ApC* can be seen if one compares the explanation of the Second Article in the *Short Form* (WA 7:217.5-218.19) with that in *SC*.

event statements in which he elaborates on the few action and event statements of *ApC*. He develops the few statements of *ApC* into a swiftly moving, highly dramatic story, in which I am incorporated into those few statements of *ApC*. Luther's text is filled with actions (the rhythm of the text underscores this element), and the text suggests a wide radius of human experiences.

(*B*) has to be seen against a colorful background. There is the buying of someone's freedom who has been jailed for not paying his or her debts. There is bargaining going on for that person's freedom. There is battling going on between the demonic forces (sin, death, Devil) and Jesus Christ. In *SC* Luther presents his ideas as briefly as possible, in *LC* (186.11-15, 22-28, 187.1-4)[94] he paints a vivid picture. The text of *SC* pictures me as the eternal prisoner of sin, death, and Devil. In order to change this picture, Christ appears on the scene. He bargains with the demonic forces for my freedom by offering gold or silver, to no avail. He must battle with them, a "strange war"[95] indeed.[96] "The Lord of Sabaoth" succeeds and "holds the field for ever."[97] Jesus Christ defeats sin, death, and Devil, and through this victory he redeems me[98] in the same way an indentured servant is redeemed. He frees me from the captivity in which I am being held by sin, death, and Devil—but at what cost! The most precious of material things, gold, accomplishes nothing.[99] Christ has to pay the highest price that can be paid, his blood and life. The person who pays that price in order for me to be freed from those demonic forces which have enslaved me has *a rightful claim on me*—indeed, *he is my Lord and I am his property*![100]

[94] *BC* 414.27. 30. 31. See also Luther's hymn, *A Mighty Fortress is our God.*

[95] See Luther's Easter hymn, *Christ Jesus Lay in Death's Strong Bands*; WA 27:108.23-31 (sermon for Apr. 11, 1528).

[96] A different image (well-known in the tradition and often used by Luther) would be that of cheating the Devil out of his prey, or death and Devil being fooled by Christ (in an effort to devour Jesus Christ, both bit into him, but Christ's divinity was too strong for their teeth). See, for example, WA 20:360.28-30 (sermon for Apr. 3, 1526 [see n. 124]; 23:714.1-6. 18-24 (sermon for May 31, 1527); 27:117.2-14 (1. sermon for Apr. 12, 1528); Hagen, as in n. 5; Martin Brecht, "Zum Verständnis von Luthers Lied 'Ein feste Burg'," *ARG* 70(1979):110.

[97] Jesus Christ is victorious because he is "the right man" for the battle to be fought; see below, 160f.

[98] For Luther texts and secondary literature dealing with this battle and victory, see Peters 2:171f.

[99] If gold does not accomplish anything, what could silver accomplish?! *Note* Luther's sequence: not with gold or silver! Following the *LC* text (187.3), *BC* 345.4 turns this sequence around and replaces Luther's "oder" with "and." Do we have in Luther's text an echo of the buying of indulgences with a small silver coin?

[100] See nn. 36, 55, 56.

In (*b*) past and present are merged, and Luther is ready to take *step four* in developing the story. He confronts himself with the question: What is the result of Christ having become my Lord? In dealing with this question, Luther moves his story to a new level.

Luther returns to "I believe" of the thesis, as I have now been qualified through the statements in (*b*). In (*c*) he elaborates on what Christ's actions have accomplished for me: Having a (new) Lord,[101] I am no longer lost and condemned. I am freed from being a lost and condemned person, and I am freed to be a new person. That freed, new person is not something esoteric. Though Luther does not spell it out, that new person is a reality which receives its *Gestalt* in the daily drowning of the Old Adam and the obedience to the commandments.[102] If ever there is a text in which Luther's understanding of the essence of the Christian's existence is presented in a nutshell, then (*b*) and (*c*) together are that text; the dogmatic statements developed in (*a*) and (*b*) lead seamlessly in (*c*) to statements of ethics. Luther describes this new person in three brief statements which are related to each other by way of gradation—from being, to living, to doing: I am Christ's property, I live in his kingdom under his authority, I serve him in everlasting righteousness, innocence, and blessedness; I am Christ's property by living in his kingdom and serving him. Therefore Luther's brief statements implicitly involve the exhortation: "Be now, live now, enact now, what Christ has made you." They also open the door to eternity: service to my Lord Jesus Christ in righteousness, innocence, and blessedness is not a temporary but an eternal matter.

In (*d*) Luther takes the *fifth* and final *step* in the development of his *narratio*. Rhetorically seen, this section has two functions:

(*D*) is the final *amplificatio* of the thesis by way of the *descriptio personarum*. Having dealt with me in (*c*), Luther now turns again to Jesus Christ. Presupposing (*a*.1.) and (*a*.2), Luther makes final statements about

[101] See the text of *LC* (186.13-15. 22-27); *BC* 414.27. 29. 30: "Before this [that is, before Jesus Christ became my Lord] I had no Lord and King but was captive under the power of the devil. ... Those tyrant and jailers now have been routed, and their place has been taken by Jesus Christ, the Lord of life ... ." For (*b*) and (*c*) as the unity of Christ's work of Redemption and Reconciliation, see Peters 2:122-39.

[102] Here the catechist has to connect the explanation of the Second Article with the explanation of Holy Baptism and the commandments, and also with the Table of Duties. As early as in the *Short Form* (1520) Luther had spelled out some details about this connection; see WA 7:204.5-205.7, and Krodel (as in n. 4), 374f., 376f., 402, nn. 153, 156. For *Gestalt*, see Reinhard Hütter, "The Twofold Center of Lutheran Ethics: Christian Freedom and God's Commandments," in: Karen L. Bloomquist and John R. Stumme, eds., *The Promise of Lutheran Ethics* (Minneapolis: Fortress Press, 1998), 31-54.

"Lord". "Lord" signals that the God-man has escaped the clutches of death; in so doing he has destroyed the power of sin, death, and Devil.[103] More: "Lord" signals that the God-man lives and rules in eternity. The lordship of the God-man combines past, presence, and future, or Easter, Ascension, and Second Coming, and it signals power. The God-man has broken the power—or kingdom—of sin, death, and Devil, has created his own kingdom, and now rules over his own kingdom.[104] These events guarantee the truth of what has been said, specifically in (*c*), but generally in all sections. Hence (*e*): "Das ist gewißlich wahr."

With this first function of (*d*) is combined a second one. Luther is at the end of his *narratio*. In classical rhetoric the *narratio* is to lead to the *argumentatio*. Here truth or untruth of the presented *historia* is proven so that, it is hoped, people will act upon it. (*D*) is not only the final *amplificatio* of the thesis by way of the *descriptio personarum*, it is also the *argumentatio*—of sorts. (*D*) and (*e*) are not an *argumentatio* in the strict sense of the term. Luther does not *prove* anything. Rhetorically he engages in a dangerous strategy by assuming that the audience accepts that the proof of truth rests in the *historia* itself because that *historia* deals with the God-man. If Jesus Christ is not true God and true man, and if Jesus Christ has not risen from death and does not live and reign eternally, then the story is not true—but then I am still a lost and condemned human being.[105] But I affirm that Jesus Christ is true God and true man, has done all that is narrated in (b) and (c), even more, has risen from death, lives and reigns eternally, and therefore is my Lord. In sum: (*e*) the *historia* is true insofar as I am concerned. Picking up on the weighty "I believe" of (*a*), Luther turns the *argumentatio* into an *affirmatio*, and his *narratio* ends in a clear 'either-or,' even though Luther does not spell this out. My *affirmatio* is—I hope—to accomplish that I maintain the truth of the *historia* (come Hell or whatever may!). My *affirmatio* is also to solicit my audience's joining me in accepting and maintaining the truth of the *historia* and thus making it their own *historia*. This clear 'either-or' and the *affirmatio* reflect the *genus deliberativum* of the text. In literary terms Luther's *narratio* is an autobiography of sorts; in theological terms it is a *confessio*. Each statement narrating

[103] Or their kingdom; so in *LC* (187.8). In order to get a feeling for the drama which stands behind (*d*), and of the weight which (*d*) has in the whole text, see the *LC* text (186.22-28, 187.5-10); *BC* 414.29.31.

[104] It is noteworthy that Luther does not deal with details in the nature and functioning of this kingdom and rule. See also below, 156f.

[105] See also 1 Cor. 15:14-18, esp. 17f.

the *historia* says something both about me and about Jesus Christ. Each statement defines and expresses my existence in a final sense; it puts a stamp on me, so to speak, the way in which in Baptism the sign of the Cross is placed upon me. And each statement defines Jesus Christ; it puts a stamp on him, so to speak. The two processes of defining result in the now to be slightly enlarged thesis: *I believe that Jesus Christ is the God-man who has become my Lord because he is my Redeemer, and therefore I am his property.*[106]

The *amplificatio* in the form of a *descriptio personarum* does not create a 'wild' story. Luther abides by the rule of brevity (*brevitas*). He does not say more[107] than has to be said (*quantum satis est*, or [*non*] *plus dicere quam oportet*) in order to make the *historia* he presents—or rather the text of the Second Article which his story is to explain—clear (*perspicuitas*) and credible. He creates a simple and yet highly dramatic story with the title "My Redemption," with me and my Redeemer as the main characters in this story. Rhetorically Luther accomplishes this *brevitas* by selecting from the *elementa* which could structure a *narratio* only those which he can directly derive from the thesis. The *elementa* which govern his *amplificatio* are some of those "W" questions,[108] with which students have to deal in their freshman composition course: *Who*? Who is Jesus Christ? Who am I before Jesus Christ acted upon me? After he acted upon me? *What*? What did Jesus Christ do? What was the result of what he did? *How*, or with *what means*, did he do what he did? *Why* is what is being said in this text true? Luther's answers to these questions in the form of brief, swiftly moving statements give his text the quality of simplicity and of drama.

Luther does not deal with some questions: *What is the nature of Christ's lordship*? *How does Christ's rule function*? *Where is Christ's kingdom*? How, or *by what means am I*[109] *able to say: I believe that Jesus Christ is my Lord*? *How*, or by what means, *is it possible that I come under Christ's lordship*? *How can I bridge the gap between what happened, as this is narrated in ApC, and my presence*? *How can this story become my own story*?[110] In light of the proposition it would seem necessary that Luther deal with these questions, and we feel that at

[106] See the text of *LC* in n. 36.

[107] For Luther it was "Kunst und große Tugend" to say many things with few words, and do it "fein" (see Wolf, *Einführung* [as in n. 3], 93)—and this notwithstanding his so often criticized *verbositas*.

[108] See also above, 148.

[109] Or those whom I "entreat" (2 Cor. 5:20) to join me in that confession of faith.

[110] For details, see Martin Stallmann, "Der zweite Artikel als katechetisches Problem," in: id., *Die biblische Geschichte im Unterricht. Katechetische Beiträge* (Göttingen: Verlag Vandenhoeck and Ruprecht, 1963), 28-38.

this point there is a lacuna in Luther's story. But what may appear to us to be a lacuna is for Luther the bridge which connects the Second and Third Articles. Therefore he deals with these questions in his explanation of the Third Article, especially the opening lines (250.1-11; *BC* 345.6).[111] Here the answer to our questions is grounded in the work of the Holy Spirit, which in turn is tied to the Word as a means of grace.[112] Our questions lead from Christology to Pneumatology and Ecclesiology.

Luther's story deals with things with which his listeners or readers could be thoroughly familiar.[113] To begin with, *ApC*, the Commandments, and the Lord's Prayer had a fixed place in the lives of people, especially in their confessional practice.[114] Further, sermons and art works in their churches could impress upon the people a profound feeling for the Virgin Mary and for Christ's birth, childhood, Passion, and Resurrection. Further, there is the phrase "my

[111] The situation is identical in *LC*. If at this point we compare *SC* with the *Short Form* (1520), we can observe how Luther's thinking developed over the years. In the *Short Form*, in the explanation of the Second Article, Luther mentioned in connection with Christ's Resurrection the following: Christ rose from the dead in order to give me and all his believers a new life; in this way Christ has awakened them together with himself in grace and the Spirit so that henceforth they sin no more but serve him alone (WA 7:218.4-7). The new life—in terms of the present questions, this would be the belief that Jesus Christ is my Lord—is connected with the Resurrection and the Holy Spirit, even though Luther did not develop this connection in detail. In the opening lines of the explanation of the Third Article (ibid., 218.25-32), faith in Jesus Christ and God Father is solidly grounded in the work of the Holy Spirit. (In this passage we find already phrases that are similar to those in *SC*, and the passage as a whole reminds one of the closing passage of the explanation of the Creed in *LC* [191.28-192.34]; *BC* 419.63 to the end.) But in this opening section that work of the Holy Spirit is not yet solidly connected with the gospel as a means of grace. Luther mentions Word and sacraments in the section on the church; here he says that the church is gathered, preserved, and governed through the Holy Spirit and daily multiplied "in the sacraments and Word of God" (WA 7:219.4f.). Regardless how we understand "in", the phrase is not yet as precise as the one in the opening section of the explanation of the Third Article in *SC* ("... the Holy Spirit *has called me through* the gospel ..."). When Luther wrote *SC* he eliminated any reference to the Holy Spirit from the explanation of the Second Article, and in the explanation of the Third Article he explicitly connected the work of the Holy Spirit with the gospel. Perhaps one may suggest that this development was the result of the controversy with the *Schwärmer*, at least in part.

[112] For details, see Peters 2:188-204.

[113] That the modern reader or listener might feel differently is one of the problems with which the catechist has to deal. For the medieval religious mentality, see also Arnold Angenendt, *Geschichte der Religiosität im Mittelalter* (Darmstadt: Wissenschaftliche Buchgesellschaft, 1997).

[114] For some materials, see Krodel (as in n. 4), 365-72.

Lord." In *ApC*, "Lord" is a theological term. On the basis of the last clause of the Second Article ("from there he will come to judge the living and the dead"), the peoples' understanding of Christ being Lord was dominated by Christ being the final judge. This understanding was very often strengthened by fire-and-brimstone sermons; or it was impressed upon the minds of the people whenever they entered a church, because the doors to many churches were crowned with the figure of Christ the judge and a depiction of the Last Judgment. For Luther's audience "lord" had also a social content, and that content made the phrase "I believe that Jesus Christ is *my Lord*" concrete in a way which is difficult for modern man to grasp.[115] From everyday living, people knew what a condemned person was, what being in bondage and being redeemed from bondage was, and what the value of gold or silver was. The majority of the people in Luther's audience was preoccupied with Judgment Day and therefore with dying as a personal encounter with death.[116] The Devil[117] with his great guile and might was everywhere, and not even holy persons, things, or doings were safe from him.[118] And finally, the church's confessional practice, combined with fire-and-brimstone sermons,

[115] See Grimm 10: s.v. "Herr" I. For example, there was the lord of the serf or servant, the lord of the manor, the lord of the castle, the lord of the court, the lord of the city, the lord (or *patronus*) of the local church, the lord of the shop or household. In all these cases 'lord' implied degrees of ownership, of authority to command, and of the duty to obey.

[116] See the *ars moriendi* literature.

[117] For the Devil in Luther's thought, see Wolf, *Luther–Bibliographie* (as in n. 3), Nos. 3463-3471.

[118] While gargoyles were to keep the demonic forces away from the interior of sanctuaries, this did not at all prevent the Devil from being around holy men, things, or activities. Among the many works of art which illustrate this situation, one excellent example comes to mind, a painting by Michael Pacher (1435[?] to 1498) in the Alte Pinakothek in München. The painting is a part of an altar of which only parts are extant, and it is titled: *St. Wolfgang and the Devil.* It shows a street scene with St. Wolfgang, vested as a bishop, standing at a house and being confronted by a most horrifying monster of a Devil. The Devil is holding a book for the bishop to read, probably a lectionary, or a prayer book, or maybe a theological book, but in any case a book dealing with something which the bishop, the holy man, is doing. The bishop does not look at the book, his eyes are fixed on the Devil; the right hand of the bishop shows that he is apparently making the sign of the Cross. One may see in the position of the eyes and this sign an effort of the bishop to protect himself against the Devil by subduing the Devil. The Devil appears to be totally unimpressed by whatever the bishop is doing. The painting illustrates a situation in which not even the holy man is safe from a confrontation with the Devil, and that not even the act of reading what may be considered a holy text, or meditating upon it, can be done without the Devil being around. If this can happen to a bishop, what chances do I have not to be harassed by the Devil?!

made certain that people were aware that they were condemned sinners. There existed, then, many contact points between Luther's text and the audience, and the text was solidly grounded in everyday living. The materials presented in Luther's story were appropriate (*aptum*)[119] in terms of the listeners' or readers' experiences. Therefore the story was probable, and even more, credible.

III
Conclusion

Luther's text shows that he has grasped the *Sitz im Leben* of the earliest form of *ApC*; and that was Baptism, the act of transition from Old to New Adam.[120] *ApC* was therefore not only the recitation of the highlights in the Jesus story derived from Bible passages, but it was also, and primarily, a statement about himself or herself made by the person to be baptized; that is, *ApC* was a verbal expression of a person's existence, a confession in the strictest sense of the word. Guided by the soteriological component of *NC*, the affirmation that Jesus Christ came down from heaven for the sake of our salvation, Luther turned the Jesus story of *ApC* into the dramatic[121] story of my

[119] For *aptum*, see also Wolf, *Einführung* (as in n. 3), 96f. "Die Fähigkeit, situativen Erfordernissen sprachlich Rechnung zu tragen, kommt in der Schlagkraft und Unmittelbarkeit [Luthers] Schriften zum Ausdruck. Im Zusammenhang damit ist seine adäquate Einstellung auf das jeweilige Publikum zu nennen," 96. See also Weber, as in n. 7.

[120] For details, see Peters 2:15f. One may even argue that Luther rediscovered that *Sitz im Leben* (and the understanding of *ApC* connected with it), which seems to have been lost in the medieval church; for some details, see Krodel (as n. 4), 369f. In the *Short Form* (1520) the connection between Creed and Baptism is clearly expressed; in the opening lines of the explanation of the First Article Luther mentioned the renunciation of the Devil; WA 7:215.27f.

[121] See Ficker (as in n. 3), 16: "[Luther] malt ... mit den Worten, und hierbei mit dem Stift wie mit dem Pinsel, dem feinen und dem breiten; manchmal ists, als wenn er, der selber drechselte, in Holz schneidet oder formt wie ein Bildhauer. ... seine Schilderung wird zum Drama"; ibid., 18: "Das rhetorische Ich wird zum dramatischen Ich: er ist als Zuschauer bei den [biblischen] Geschichten, die er zu erklären hat, er erlebt sie mit: 'so unmittelbar ist mir Christus gegenwärtig, als wenn er in dieser Stunde sein Blut vergossen hätte'." For more similar materials, see Ficker, 42-45. If we disregard "verlorenen" and "verdammten" (used as adjectives), and the two "geboren" in (*a*.1 and 2), then we find no verbs in the passive voice, but eleven verbs in the active voice. See also Wolf, *Einführung* (as in n. 3), 35: "[Luther's] Satzgestaltung ist von dynamischen Zügen durchdrungen. Das kommt etwa in der Verlagerung von der nominalen (vgl. Scholastik, Kanzleien!) zur verbalen Aussage zum Ausdruck, ... In Verbindung damit ist auch das Zurücktreten des passiven Genus ... zugunsten der Tätigkeitsform anzuführen; ... ."

life, titled "My Redemption," with me and Jesus Christ as the main characters in this story. Using the rhetorical device of *amplificatio* by way of the *descriptio personarum*, he developed statements about my existence as it was before Christ entered my life, and then as it has been shaped by Christ, "[God's] only Son." In developing the story, Luther worked with the content of the dogmatic decision regarding the *homoousia* existing between the Father and the Son, and regarding the two natures co-existing in the one person Jesus Christ. He used these ontological statements in such a way that they were the part of my life's story which made that story possible: *Only because Jesus Christ was the "rechte Mann,"*[122] *the right man,*[123] *was he able to do whatever he did for and to me,*[124] *and therefore became my Lord —*

Gillhoff, *Sprache und Geschichte* (as in n. 3), 18-21 presents observations about the ratio of verbs to nouns and the use of verbs in the active voice throughout *SC*.

[122] At this point I am indebted to Brecht, "Zum Verständnis von Luthers Lied 'Ein feste Burg'" (as in n. 96), 110-114.

[123] See Luther's hymn, *A Mighty Fortress*. (The English version, "the valiant one," does not do justice to Luther's text.) For "right man," see also Luther to Caspar Müller, chancellor of Mansfeld: Nov. 24, 1534: WA.B 7:118.29-32; Preuß, *Luther der Christenmensch* (as in n. 28), 38-40. In general, see Klaus Burba, *Die Christologie in Luthers Liedern* (Gütersloh: Bertelsmann Verlag, 1956).

[124] See, for example, the sermon for April 3, 1526: WA 20:360.3: "So spricht auch der alte lerer der Kirchen, Joannes Damascenus lib 4. cap. 3. von Christo: Caro secundum sui naturam non est adorablilis, adoratur autem in incarnato Deo verbo, non propter seipsam, sed propter coniunctum ipsi secundum hypostasin Deum verbum. Et non dicimus, quod carnem adoramus nudam, sed carnem Dei, id est, increatum Deum. Das ist warlich ein schöner gewaltiger spruch, ... denn die beide naturn in Christo wollen unzertrennet und ungescheiden sein. ... Denn das were gar ein schlechte, ja gar keine erlösung gewesen, ... wenn nur allein der Mensch Christus und nicht zu gleich gott oder gottes Son in diese person vereiniget, gecreutziget und gestorben wer, ... Ob Christus gleich wird sterben und leiden, sol er doch nicht im tod bleiben, sonder wider erstehen, grünen und lebendig werden, warumb denn das? Darumb, denn er ist nicht ein schlechter mensch, sonder warhafftiger Gott. Wenn er ein schlechter Mensch were gewesen, wie wir, so were er dem tode und Teuffel vil zu schwach gewesen. Dieweil er aber Gott ist, und gott das leben ist und das leben, abs gleich stirbet, kan es nicht im tod bleiben, denn leben mus leben bleiben, ... Der halben so mus dieser Gott, der Mensche ist, vom tode wider erstehen, grunen und lewendig werden, domit er brenge vorgebung der sunde, gerechtigkeit, leben und seligkeit allen, die an ihn gleuben. Das heist dann Infernus ex morsu depascitur. Die helle hat die zene an diesem Christo, der das leben ist stumpff gebissen und hat ire krafft darüber verloren"; sermon for April 11, 1528: WA 27:108-112, esp. 109.11: "Christus est verus peccator qui nullum fecit et tamen reus omnium. Da wird er zuthuen haben gehabt Satan. ... Sic enim facit peccatum et mortis timor. Nemo potests hoc facere qui stat in agone, ut sich zu got gebe. Ideo magna res, quod Christus in tanta angustia ad deum confugit. Alius homo qui venit in veram mortis angustiam et diu manet in ea, diffidit. Exempla: Iob not potuit facere, quod Christus et tamen non tam profunde. Non

right man, that is, true God and also true man, the God-man. He was the one who was born of the Father in eternity and was *homoousios* with the Father, very God of very God, who was also born of the Virgin Mary, and in whom the divine and the human natures were united, "unconfusedly, immutably, indivisibly, inseparably."[125] There-

est hominis pugna cum morte ringen, unicae personae gehorts, Christo. An das exempel und werck mogen wir uns halten"; sermon for April 12, 1528: WA 27:116.18: "Audistis de passione Christi, ... de resurrectione dicemus. Da sthet, das Christus unter dem tod erfur kriecht und uberhebt sich uber Satan, peccatum et diabolum conculcat, ad hoc utitur sola persona sua et corpore, non viribus aliorum exercituum. ... nullus angelus, creatura possunt ista ... vincere. Sed illa persona potuit, quomodo? Est naturalis dei filius, item verus homo, ex his naturis unum factum id est una persona. Sicut dicimus: leib und seel sunt unterschiedlich natur et tamen una res vel persona. Peccatum in illum positum et illud vult personam hanc damnare, quasi ipse fecisset. Ibi pugna maxima. Cogitandum, quanta res peccatum mundi. Peccatum facile vicisset Christum, si mera humanitas in eo fuisset, sed peccatum ghet die gotheit so wol an als humanitatem, quae divinitas est eterna iustitia, quam nemo potest damnare. Das geneust die menscheit, das sie mit got ein person ist. Sunde, du hast mich angreiffen, tu hast kein recht zu mir. Ita in sich et per seipsum vicit peccatum et non erat alius modus vicendi peccatum. ... [117.18] Das heist uberwinden peccatum, mortem in sich selbs und durch etc. si non fuisset deus, non potuisset enden. ... Ex utrisque naturis facta una persona, secundum divinitatem non est mortuus"; *Postilla for the Home*, 1544: WA 52:656.21: "Aber wer mit Petro recht auff das Ambt sihet, das Christus in der welt füren und mit uns außrichten soll, der muß mit Petro schliessen, das Christus müsse Got sein in gleicher almechtigkeyt. Denn Sünd, Todt und Teuffel uberwinden und das ewige leben geben, das kan kein mensch, wie wir sehen, Die Sünd und der Todt halten sie alle gefangen. So nun diser mensch, da Petrus mit redet, der rechte Christ ist, der uns sol vom fluch, von der sünde, vom todt und des Teuffels reich heffen, So muß er auch Gottes Son sein, der das leben in jm selbs hab und Allmechtig sey wie Gott, Mit den Menschen ist es verloren. Das heißt nun Christum recht erkennen und bekennen, das man nicht allein die worte sage: Du bist Christus, Gottes Son, sonder es im hertzen dafür halte, das dieser Jhesus, von der junckfrawen Maria geboren, sey Gottes Son, der darumb auff erden kummen unnd mensch sey worden, das er dem Teuffel auff den kopff tretten, den fluch, da alle menschen der sünden halben unter sind, wegk nemen Und dagegen uns zu gnaden bringen will, Wo das hertz solches vestigklich glaubt, für der Sünde und dem Todt nicht erschrickt, darumb das er Christum hat, das heißt recht bekennen und glauben." Luther could also argue that because Christ *in propria sua persona* overcame the law, therefore he has to be the Son of God: WA 40^{I}:569.5-7 (*Second Lecture on Galatians*, 1531) and ibid., 25 (the published text): "Cum autem Christus in propria sua persona legem vicerit, necessario sequitur eum esse natura Deum. Nemo enim, sive sit homo sive Angelus, est supra legem, praeter solum Deum. At Christus est supra legem, quia vicit ac iugulavit eam, igitur est filius Dei ac natura Deus." In general, see *Lecture on Hebrews*, 1517/18: WA 57:128.9-130.11.

[125] Barry, *Readings* (as in n. 21), 104; Denzinger No. 148. – For Luther and *DC*, see nn. 22, 124; sermon for Apr. 30, 1525: WA 16:217.30: "Also haben in [that is, Jesus Christus] die Sophisten gemalet, wie er Mensch und Gott sey, zelen seine beine und arm, mischen seine beiden Naturen wünderlich in einander, welches

fore he was able to complete the drama of my Redemption successfully. Luther derived action statements from the ontological statements of the dogmas, whereby the statements about Christ's person and those about Christ's *Amt* or *Werk* are interdependent: A statement about Christ as person—true God, true man—leads to a statement shaped by whatever Christ did (Christ's *Werk*), and vice versa. Christ *is* my Lord because he did what is described in (*b*) and (*d*); in *LC* Luther is more precise, though he uses more words: "I believe that Jesus Christ, true Son of God (person) *has become* my Lord (action, work); and now follows the picturesque description of the actions through which Christ became my Lord (186.10-28). In sum: my Redemption is real and true because the one who worked out my Redemption, my Redeemer, is the Second Person of the Trinity, as defined in *NC*, incarnate, as defined in *DC*.[126]

denn nur eine Sophistische erkenntnis des HErrn Christi ist, denn Christus ist nicht darümb Christus genennet, das er zwo Naturen hat, was gehet mich dasselbige an? Sondern er treget diesen herrlichen und tröstlichen Namen von dem Ampt und werck, so er auff sich genommen hat, dasselbige gibt im den Namen. Das er von natur mensch und Gott ist, das hat er für sich, aber das er sein Ampt dahin gewendet und seine liebe ausgeschüttet und mein Heiland und Erlöser wird, das geschiet mir zu Trost und zu gut, es gilt mir darümb, das er sein Volck von Sünden los machen wil. Matthei am 1. Capitel wird angezeiget vom Engel Gabriel, **das er sol Jhesus heissen**, Nicht darümb das er Gott und Mensch ist, Sondern das er das Ampt sol füren und in das Werck treten, **den Leuten von Sünden und Tode zu helffen**. Das machet in zu einem Manne, dafür sollen wir in auch halten, das er das Heubt und Oberherr des Christenthums und aller Gottseligkeit ist" [bold letters according to the text]; WA TR 2: No. 2159: "Physica tractat de motu rerum, mathematica vero de quidditate et formis earum. Ideo non est loquendum de Christo mathematice nec physice, sed magis, quis sit *usus eius*, quid nobis attulerit etc." (italics mine); *Against Latomus*, 1521: WA 8:126.23-29; disputation on John 1:14 (argumentum 15), Jan. 11, 1539: WA 39²:20.15-21.11; *On Psalm 45*, 1532: WA 40²:517.3-518.9 (manuscript text), 516.23-518.17 (published text). – See also Harnack, *Luthers Theologie* (as in n. 22), 2:160: "... mit der gesamten Kirche [hält Luther] streng an den chalcedonischen Bestimmungen über die beiden Naturen in der Person Christi, überwindet jedoch den herrschenden Dualismus, indem er besonders die Menschheit Christi in der Zeit seines irdischen Lebens und Wirkens betont, aber nicht bei ihr stehen bleibt, sondern von da aus die ganze volle Person betrachtet"; Peters, "Luthers Christuszeugnis (as in n. 22)," 6: "... Luther ... läßt ... die seinshaften Formeln des Chalkedonense hinter sich und dringt zur existentialen Innenschau der Moderne vor."

[126] For the (reverse) argumentation from Christ's *Werk* to his person, see, for example, n. 124 (sermon for Apr. 12, 1528; *Postilla for the Home*, 1544; *Second Lecture on Galatians*). Our observations lead us to the scholarly debate about the topic 'Luther and the dogmas of the early church'. The issue in this debate is not Luther's affirmation of *NC* and *DC*—it seems that no one doubts this affirmation—but his understanding and use of both texts and the actual and possible

In terms of genre, Luther's text belongs to the *genus deliberativum*. This is reflected especially in the sharp either-or which is implied in the end of Luther's text. In a narrow sense, I am addressed in this text, my life's story is at stake. In a wider sense, whatever is said by, to, and about me, is an invitation to join in this, my life's story.

Above[127] I suggested that Luther intended the text to be spoken.[128] Only to read and study the text would not do justice to it—I live the story of my life. In terms of actions, I do this through what

implications which this understanding and use had for his theology. To deal with this debate would demand much more space than is allowed for this contribution. Therefore the listing of the important references has to suffice: Friedrich Loofs, *Leitfaden zum Studium der Dogmengeschichte* (4th ed. rev. Halle: Niemeyer Verlag, 1906), 724, 747-52; Adolf von Harnack, *Lehrbuch der Dogmengeschichte* (Darmstadt: Wissenschaftliche Buchgesellschaft, 1964; repr. of the 4th ed. rev., 1909, 1910), 3:808-63, esp. 814-20, 834-38, 857-63; Karl Holl, *Gesammelte Aufsätze zur Kirchengeschichte*, 1. *Luther* (6th ed.rev. Tübingen: Mohr Verlag, 1932): 69, n. 4; Yves M.-J. Congar, O.P., "Regards et réflexions sur la christologie de Luther," in: Grillmeier-Bacht (as in n. 21), *Konzil*, 3: 457-86; Axel Schmidt, *Die Christologie in Martin Luthers späten Disputationen* (St. Otilien: Eos Verlag, 1990); Werner Elert, *The Structure of Lutheranism*, 1, transl. by Walter A. Hansen (St. Louis: Concordia Publishing House, 1962): 200-236; Lohse, *Luthers Theologie* (as in n. 22), 245-48; Johannes von Walter, "Luthers Christusbild," *LuJ* 21(1939):1-27, esp. 5-7; Knoke, as in n. 29; Wilhelm Maurer, "Die Anfänge von Luthers Theologie. Eine Frage an die lutherische Kirche," in: id., *Kirche und Geschichte. Gesammelte Aufsätze*, ed. by Ernst Wilhelm Kohls and Gerhard Müller (Göttingen: Verlag Vandenhoeck and Ruprecht, 1970), 1:22-37, esp. 25f.; Peters, "Luthers Christuszeugnis (as in n. 22)," esp. 10, 96, n. 147 (see also n. 125); Vorländer, *Deus Incarnatus* (as in n. 22), 11-22, 107f., 222-29; Lienhard, *Luther's Witness* (as in n. 22), 18-26, 153-94, 307-58, 371-82; Kinder, "Soteriological Motifs (as in n. 27)," esp. 16-18, 22f.; Franz Posset, *Luther's Catholic Christology According to His Johannine Lectures of 1527* (Milwaukee: Northwestern Publishing House, 1988); Peter Manns, "Fides absoluta – fides incarnata. Zur Rechtfertigungslehre Luthers im Großen Galater-Kommentar," in: *Reformata reformanda. Festgabe für Hubert Jedin zum 17. Juni 1965*, ed. by Erwin Iserloh and Konrad Repgen, 1 (Münster: Verlag Aschendorff, 1965):265-312, esp. 278, n. 58.

[127] 147f.

[128] Gillhoff, *Sprache und Geschichte* (as in n. 3), 38: "Wir schreiben leise, Luther schreibt laut. Bei uns riecht jeder Satz nach Papier und Tinte; der Katechismus ist mündlich aufgebaut, ist mehr eingestellt aufs Sprechen, Beten und Hören als aufs Lesen." In general, see Adam Weyer, "'Das Euangelium wil nit alleyn geschrieben, ßondern viel mehr mit leyplicher stym gepredigt seyn'. Luthers Invocavit-Predigten im Kontext der Reformationsbewegung," in: Heinz Ludwig Arnold, ed., *Martin Luther* (München: *Text und Kritik. Zeitschrift für Literatur*. Sonderband, 1983), 86-104; this article does not deal with the catechisms, but it presents important observations which can substantiate the validity of my suggestion. See also Wolf, *Einführung* (as in n. 3), 51-53, for materials on the role which speaking plays in Luther's theology and literary creativity.

Luther describes in (*c*).[129] In terms of the text, I do this through daily prayer and meditation.[130] In its most original form *ApC* was the prayer made by the person to be baptized. On the basis of the literary quality in general, the rhythm of the text in particular, Luther's explanation is a text which easily lends itself to memorization, meditation, and prayer. Certainly, then, the text should be rescued from a situation in which it is—one hopes—memorized in Confirmation instruction, but is then all too often ignored and then forgotten.[131]

[129] Or in the explanation of the commandments, of the Lord's Prayer, and Baptism, and in the Tables of Duties.

[130] See Brecht, *Luther als Schriftsteller* (as in n. 3), 35: "... Luther hat die Katechismusstücke tatsächlich betend meditiert." See further, Martin Nicol, *Meditation bei Luther* (2d. ed. rev. Göttingen: Verlag Vandenhoeck and Ruprecht, 1991), 150-167 ("Katechismusmeditation"); Philipp Bachmann, "Zu Luthers Katechismen, 1: Für wen und wozu sind die beiden Katechismen geschrieben?" *NKZ* 26(1915):244-253, 311-320; Brecht, *Luther* (as in n. 14), 2:120.

[131] If indeed Luther wrote 'my' life story, to be used in meditation and prayer, then perhaps our parish educational system ought to be rethought in an effort to help people live within this story. In general, at the present, Sunday school and the first year of Confirmation instruction concentrate on the biblical stories. And then in the second year of Confirmation instruction a doctrinal system is developed along the line of *SC*, backed by proof texts, that is, *individual biblical passages isolated from their context* (that is, the biblical story as a whole) and added on to the text of *SC*; it is hoped that all these materials will be memorized by the Confirmands. Perhaps the individual sections of the *SC* materials should be adjusted to the intellectual levels of different grades in Sunday School and absorbed into the biblical stories of the Sunday School, whenever possible or appropriate. Conversely, perhaps the instruction in a specific paragraph of *SC* should be framed by an appropriate story so that paragraph and story support each other. In this connection 'story' need not be a biblical story, though using a biblical story would probably be the rule; but under certain circumstances 'story' could very well be taken from daily life. And finally, perhaps a program of adult education should be developed based on a combination of materials derived from Scripture, *SC* and *LC*, and daily life. One could follow Luther's example and implement such a program through series of sermons on the topics of the catechism, or one could implement such a program through special education hours; if one uses special education hours, then the parents of the Confirmands could be a natural audience for such a program in an effort to build a spiritual unity between parents and children. For some of the problems connected with an approach to Christian education in which catechism and Bible story are united, see Stallmann, *Biblische Geschichte* (as in n. 110).

CONTEMPORANEITY: A HERMENEUTICAL PERSPECTIVE IN MARTIN LUTHER'S WORK

Timothy Maschke

Martin Luther employed a variety of principles for interpreting Scripture which reflected his recognition of the depth and richness of the biblical texts. His hermeneutical principles are clearly articulated in numerous articles and books.[1] Kenneth Hagen, to whom this volume is dedicated, has spent much of his professional life leading many of us to see Luther's practice of these principles of interpretation more clearly and more concretely.[2] It is not necessary to review Luther's principles in this essay, nor to reiterate Hagen's articulate and detailed work in this area. In this essay, I would merely like to draw attention to a somewhat peculiar approach by Luther which particularly relates to what is occurring in biblical hermeneutics today.[3] The concept or phrase, *hermeneutic of contemporaneity*, seems especially suited to describe Luther's perspective on Scripture as a living voice of the Gospel. Let me explain what I mean.

Over two centuries ago, G. E. Lessing described a modern dilemma, which all contemporary Bible readers encounter, when he spoke of "the ugly great ditch"[4] between faith and history. Lessing

[1] A. Skevington Wood, *Luther's Principles of Biblical Interpretation* (London: The Tyndale Press, 1960), gives a rather concise overview. See also Ralph Doermann's chapter, "Luther's Principles of Biblical Interpretation," in *Interpreting Luther's Legacy*, edited by Fred W. Meuser and Stanley D. Schneider (Minneapolis: Augsburg, 1969); Gerhard Ebeling's article, "Die Anfänge von Luthers Hermeneutik," in *Zeitschrift fur Theologie und Kirche* 48 (1951); Jaroslav Pelikan's *Luther the Expositor: Introduction to the Reformer's Exegetical Writings*, a supplement to Luther's Works (St. Louis: Concordia, 1959); and James Samuel Preus, *From Shadow to Promise: Old Testament Interpretation from Augustine to the Young Luther* (Cambridge: Harvard University Press, 1969).

[2] Kenneth Hagen, *Luther's Approach to Scripture as seen in his 'Commentaries' on Galatians 1519–1538* (Tübingen: J.C.B. Mohr [Paul Siebeck], 1993); "Luther, Martin (1483–1546)," in *Historical Handbook of Major Biblical Interpreters*, ed. Donald K. McKim (Downers Grove: Inter-Varsity Press, 1998).

[3] Anthony C. Thiselton, *New Horizons in Hermeneutics* (Grand Rapids, MI: Zondervan Publishing House, 1992), describes many of the newer approaches, particularly that of Gadamer and Ricoeur as well as that of Barth and Derrida.

[4] G. E. Lessing, "Über den Beweis des Geistes und der Kraft," in *Gotthold Ephraim Lessings sämtlichen Schriften*, vol. 13, ed. Karl Lachmann (Berlin: Goeschen'sche Verlagshandlung, 1897), 4.22, as cited in Alister E. McGrath, *Christian Theology: An Introduction*, Second edition (New York: Blackwell, 1997), 363.

was describing what he perceived as an insurmountable gap between historical events and faith-full responses to those events. The modern viewpoint among many biblical scholars today is that history is irretrievable and that the texts which we have are so historically bound that they are not reliable.

Although Luther never faced that concept as articulated in the Enlightenment, he did encounter the need to hear God's word directly for his own day and age. To those of us who face the daily dilemma of bridging the gap of history, Luther offers some helpful insights for our own biblical hermeneutics. Luther utilizes what I am calling in this essay a hermeneutic of contemporaneity, that is, hearing God speak to us in the present time. Gordon Isaac stated this perspective well in his dissertation on Luther's *enarratio* on Psalm 90:

> One of the surprising things to the modern ear is that there seems to be no sense of historical gap in Luther's view ... . Luther can speak of Epicurus, Cicero, Moses and scholars loyal to the Papacy all in one breath.[5]

Luther's concern for communicating the Gospel clearly and for applying biblical texts to his German hearers compelled him to employ this particular hermeneutic of contemporaneity.[6]

In the following sections of this essay, I will explain what gave rise to my observation of contemporaneity in Luther's work. Then we will see Luther's own understanding of Scripture and history. The major part of this essay will illustrate this hermeneutic of contemporaneity in several of Luther's commentaries. At the end of

[5] Gordon Isaac, *In Public Defense of the Ministry of Moses: Luther's Enarratio on Psalm 90, 1534–1535* (Ph.D. dissertation, Marquette University, 1996), 21-22. Among five characteristics of *enarratio*, Isaac mentions: "3. *Enarratio* displays no sense of historical gap, or positively, this connotes the contemporaneity of the Word"(Isaac, 159). Isaac illustrates this more thoroughly when he writes: "Mention has already been made of the incredibly diverse cross section of individuals and groups that Luther calls upon in his comments on verse one. Seemingly in one breath, Luther can use the names of Moses, Anselm, Paul, and Adam and Eve without differentiation. These diverse personalities from very different eras are woven into the fabric of Luther's presentation with remarkable ease"(Isaac, 163-64).

[6] Scott Hendrix, "Luther Against the Background of the History of Biblical Interpretation," *Interpretation* 37 (July 1983), 238, might question this as an actual hermeneutic approach. Hendrix suggests, "His [Luther's] own way was, however, not a hermeneutical method in the sense of much modern biblical criticism," but he does admit that "Luther ... is in a category by himself," in regards to his hermeneutic approach. Thiselton, 322, says that "Hermeneutics concerns *all* human enquiry," but earlier, 6, suggested a concept of "*new* horizons" for an approach which is similar to what I am proposing as "in actualizations of understanding or encounter between readers and texts ... ."

the essay, my concluding comments seek to apply Luther's pre-modern view of Scripture as an aid in our post-modern cultural need for communicating the Gospel clearly.

A Liturgical Reality

The sense of contemporaneity was first evident to me in my studies of Luther's liturgical renovations. In 1523 and again in 1526, Luther offered the congregation in Wittenberg a revised liturgy of the Mass in his *Formula Missae et Communionis* and his *Deutsche Messe*. An interesting feature in both of these services is not merely that he reintroduced the distribution of both elements (the wine along with the bread), but how he described their distribution. The peculiar feature in light of present-day practice is that the distribution of the cup is distinct and separated from the distribution of the host. When describing this practice in the 1523 *Formula Missae*, Luther explains:

> This is the order Christ seems to have observed, as the words of the Gospel show, where he told them to eat the bread before he had blessed the cup ... thus you see that the cup was not blessed until after the bread had been eaten. [7]

In his *German Mass* three years later, Luther shows the same innovative approach:

> It seems to me that it would accord with the Lord's Supper to administer the sacrament immediately after the consecration of the bread, before the cup is blessed; for both Luke and Paul say, "He took the cup after they had supped, etc." [8]

When analyzing this practice, I saw that Luther was exhibiting this hermeneutic of contemporaneity. He brings the ritual reality of the New Testament record into the present experience of his congregation.[9]

[7] Martin Luther, "An Order of Mass and Communion for the Church at Wittenberg, 1523" in *Luther's Works* 53, translated by Paul Zeller Strodach, revised by Ulrich S. Leupold (Philadelphia: Fortress Press, 1965), 30 (cf. WA 12: 214,8-10). Cited hereafter as LW 53.

[8] Martin Luther, "The German Mass and Order of Service, 1526," in *Luther's Works* 53, translated by Augustus Steimle, revised by Ulrich S. Leupold (Philadelphia: Fortress Press, 1965), 81 (cf. WA 19:99,5-8).

[9] The Reformed theologians would emphasize a repristinating experience of going back in time, while Luther recognized the Gospel as a living, contemporary Word. I thank Dr. Timothy Wengert of the Lutheran Theological Seminary at

From the altar of the city church of St. Mary, Wittenberg.
Lucas Cranach the Elder, 1547.

This sense of Christ being present in Wittenberg is evident in more than the ritual actions prescribed by Luther. Regarding the proclamation of the Gospel, Luther explains: "The Gospel is the voice crying in the wilderness and calling unbelievers to faith."[10] For Luther, the image of John the Baptist is made contemporary in the actual proclamation of the Gospel. Later in the service, when Luther discusses the exchange of peace using the *Pax vobiscum,* Luther declares that "faith holds to these words as coming from the mouth of Christ himself."[11]

Philadephia for pointing out an illustration of this contemporaneity in art. In the Wittenberg altarpiece by Lucas Cranach Luther is depicted as receiving the Lord's Supper as one of the disciples and a sixteenth century layman is distributing the cup. Christ has thus come into the present.

[10] LW 53:25 (WA 12:211,8-9).

[11] LW 53:28-29 (WA 12:213,10-11).

Again, we see no historical discontinuity and disparity in Luther's mind, but instead he perceives a contemporaneity of the believers with Christ.

Even Luther's perspective on the architectural structure of church buildings, particularly the placement of the altar, gives evidence of this hermeneutic of contemporaneity. In his *German Mass,* he makes reference to a specialized service for true believers. He then adds this comment about the placement of the altar at such a service:

> In the mass, however, of real Christians, the altar should not remain where it is, and the priest should always face the people as Christ doubtlessly did in the Last Supper.[12]

Here, again, we can see that Luther's concern is not to establish some kind of legalistic rituals, but he seems intent upon bringing the Wittenberg worshipers into the very presence of Christ. Thus, in his conservative liturgical renovations,[13] we see a bridging of the perceived gap between the biblical events and the present participants with a hermeneutic of contemporaneity.

LUTHER'S HERMENEUTICS

Having recognized this perspective by Luther in his liturgical work, I went back to look at Luther's understanding of Scripture, particularly as evident in his commentaries. Luther's hermeneutics grew out of the long tradition of the *quadriga*. The *quadriga* was the dominant medieval view that Scripture had a fourfold sense—the literal, allegorical, moral, and anagogical.[14] This medieval monastic approach resulted in the view that Scripture was indeed *sacra pagina* (sacred page) and *sacra scriptura* (sacred writing) but also the very *verbum Dei*. As Kenneth Hagen points out, the sacred page bore the clear and recognized imprint of God as God's Word was recorded for future generations.[15] The collected writings were indeed sacred be-

[12] LW 53:69 (WA 19:80, 28-30).

[13] Frank C. Senn, *Christian Liturgy: Catholic and Evangelical* (Minneapolis, MN: Fortress Press, 1997), chapter 8 "Luther's Liturgical Reforms," 267-298.

[14] Nicholas of Lyra repeated a monastic poem on the *quadriga* (*Littera gesta docet; quid credas allegoria; Moralis quid agas; quo tendas anagogia*) in one of his glosses. It has been translated as follows: The letter shows us what God did; allegory shows where our faith is hid; The moral meaning rules our life; anagogy shows where we end our strife.

[15] Hagen, *Luther's Approach to Scripture*, 35-48. Similarly, Brian A. Gerrish, "Biblical Authority and the Continental Reformation," *Scottish Journal of Theology*, X, 346, cites several of Luther's exegetical principles, including the historical

cause God himself authored them. Not only that, but they brought the reader into the very presence of God.

Luther came to understand the Scriptures as the most effective vehicle through which God communicates his love and grace in Christ to the world. Although he sought to plumb the deeper spiritual truths of Scripture, Luther always worked with the text as God's revelation and communication. The Holy Spirit had brought these words to human writers and continued to communicate God's sacred truths through these writings.

Luther's view of Scripture, however, is not merely a medieval monastic view of Scripture. Both medieval and renaissance interpreters faced a sense of history's distance and its irretrievability even in the use of the *quadriga*. James S. Preus notes the following about medieval commentators:

> The *sensus litteralis* tended to be reduced to the *sensus historicus*, especially as regards the Old Testament, and hence irretrievably past. The *historia* by itself, and therefore the words that narrated and interpreted it, bore no message for any time beyond its own—and what it said to its own time even tended to be deceiving because it was *figura*. The letter was without spirit, without theological meaning for the future. And thus, for the situation in which the Christian exegete found himself centuries later, it was "unedifying."[16]

The search for contemporary meaning was directed beyond the literal text of Scripture into a variety of alternative senses.

The humanists of Luther's day were interested in the texts of Scripture, the authorship and the languages used. Yet, they saw a distance between their time and the biblical age. It is into this context that Luther drew out his own approach to Scripture and its contemporary relevance for God's people. Martin Brecht explains that for Luther "interpretation of Scripture must not be antiquarian, but

dimension. To the principle "Scripture alone," Luther adds the further principle "the historical sense alone." That Luther understood Scripture as being of divine origin is evidenced in the literally hundreds of statements to that effect made by Luther and gathered by Francis Pieper, *Christian Dogmatics* (St. Louis: Concordia, 1950) I, 278.

[16] Preus, *From Shadow to Promise*, 269-70. Similarly, Hagen, 32, says that "In Luther's day, the sense of cultural distance between the world of the Bible and the contemporary world was beginning to emerge among some of the Humanists."

contemporary."[17] Contemporaneity, therefore, was Luther's stance toward Scripture. The plain words of Scripture brought the living experience of the Spirit and the presence of Christ into Luther's own contemporary circumstances.[18]

John Headley clarifies this unique perspective which Luther brought to the hermeneutic task:

> Traditional exegesis sought contemporaneousness with the past by imitation and repetition of the past ... . Since the Christ event cannot be repeated and revelation is a revelation in the past, an imitation which seeks contemporaneousness is impossible, for imitation cannot go beyond the outer appearance of this event. Consequently, one's relation to Christ can only be concealed, never visible, for it is not the work but faith that constitutes contemporaneousness with Christ, because the first attempts the impossible task of copying the example of Christ, while the second appropriates the gift of Christ.[19]

It was Luther's study of the Old Testament which made him aware of how similar his own situation was to that of the people of the Old Testament.[20] He recognized that the ancient, yet sacred text was still speaking to him in his own time. Thus, the *quadriga* was not a satisfactory solution to interpreting the Scriptures. In addition, as Kenneth Hagen explains Luther's approach to the biblical text, "The humanist sense of the distance of Scripture from the present was not accepted."[21] Something more was necessary in order to bring the Scriptures to life in the present. That more comes in the work of the Holy Spirit.

[17] Martin Brecht, *Martin Luther: His Road to Reformation 1483–1521*, trans. James L. Schaaf (Philadelphia: Fortress, 1985), 289-90.

[18] Ernst-Wilhelm Kohls, "Luther's Aussagen über die Mitte, Klarheit und Selbsttätigkeit der Heiligen Schrift," *Lutherjahrbuch* 1973 (Hamburg: Friedrich Wittig), 56.

[19] John M. Headley, *Luther's View of Church History* (New Haven: Yale University Press, 1963), 24-25.

[20] In a recent article, "Men are From ~~Mars~~ Judah, Women are from ~~Venus~~ Bethlehem: How a Modern Bestseller Illuminates the Book of Ruth," *Bible Review* (August 1998), 34-41, 54, Denise Dick Herr voices the recognition of contemporary characteristic differences between men and women in conversations recorded in the story of Ruth.

[21] Hagen, "Luther, Martin (1483–1546)," 215.

From the title page of a 16th-century Bible. The spectators at the crucifixion include David, Moses, and some prophets, all wearing sixteenth-century garb as do the figures surounding Christ.

Luther's View of History

In order to understand Luther, we also need to look briefly at his understanding of history. Luther saw all of history as God's activity for accomplishing his will through people. History was the knowledge, albeit indirect, of this divine activity in time, which was recorded for the purpose of bringing people to know God, particularly as revealed in the life, death, and resurrection of Jesus. Because the events of Scripture were past, they were not recoverable. Yet, the text of Scripture provided the vital link for the hearer and preacher which could lead one to faith in Christ.[22]

A sense of contemporaneity arises from the relationship of Christ with the Word and the Spirit, "an insight of supreme significance not only for the theology of the Reformation in respect to its Scholastic past but more particularly for Luther's view of history," notes John Headley. "This insight is the continuing presence of Christ in time."[23] Christ's Spirit caused the Scriptures to be written. He continues to speak through these Scriptures. Therefore, Christ continues to speak through the Spirit-ed (the Greek word in 2 Timothy 3:16 is *theopneustos*) Word.

Another way of saying this is that, for Luther, the historicity of Scripture was closely tied with its divine-human origin as well as to the presence of Christ in Scripture. The nineteenth century Lutheran dogmatician, Francis Pieper notes:

> Luther was well aware of the human side of Scripture, but only in the sense that God caused His Word to be written by men in a human tongue. He is horrified at people who dare assert that Scripture is not entirely and in all its parts the Word of God, because the writers, such as Peter and Paul, after all were men.[24]

Thus, the Bible is both a human and a divine Word. God is the divine author and the human writers were moved by God to communicate his word in human terms and in human times. Luther viewed Scripture, while more than either mere letter or mere spirit, as soundly historical.[25] Gordon Isaac expands upon this idea when he says, "Since Luther's concern is to speak the truth, and the one

[22] Headley, 42-55.

[23] Headley, 23.

[24] Pieper, *Christian Dogmatics* I, 278.

[25] Brian A. Gerrish, *The Old Protestantism and the New: Essays on the Reformation Heritage* (Chicago: The University of Chicago Press, 1982), 57, citing LW 1:233 and LW 2:164.

who is himself the truth is living, all ages converge into the present, into the 'today' to which the sacred page addresses itself."[26]

One other way of viewing this perspective grows out of John Headley's comment when he speaks about "the continuing presence of Christ in time." This continuing presence, he notes, "... rests upon the virtually sacramental nature of the Word made visible to faith in Scripture."[27] In Luther's thinking and writing, there is a sacramental understanding of Christ's contemporary presence even in Scripture. This is not, however, some kind of a transubstantiation of the text into something other than the text, but rather this is the characteristic Lutheran perspective of the presence of Christ "in, with, and under"[28] the text of Scripture. The Christ of the New Testament continues to speak a contemporary word and to be present through the text to contemporary readers by the power of the Spirit working in the biblical text. History is always the story of God's activity in the world, and particularly through his Word in the Church.

Contemporaneity in Luther's Commentaries

This contemporaneous presence of Christ in Scripture provided Luther with many opportunities for specific applications of the biblical text, as evidenced in many of his biblical commentaries. The contemporaneous Christ also speaks a present word to the contemporary reader.

Under Kenneth Hagen's guidance, I have enjoyed working particularly in Luther's lectures and commentaries on Paul's epistle to the Galatians. It is therefore with these works that I wish to explore more specifically this look at Luther's perspective of contemporaneity. In his Galatians commentary of 1519, Luther cites Isaiah 63 and 64 and concludes, "In this prayer Isaiah has depicted the appearance of the church today in such a way that it cannot be depicted more aptly."[29] For Luther, the Old Testament spoke to the contemporary situation. Here, in what most modern biblical scholars would consider an anachronistic view, Luther shows his perspective of contemporaneity by

[26] Isaac, 21-22.

[27] Headley, 23.

[28] Formula of Concord, Solid Declaration, article VII "The Lord's Supper," 35, in *The Book of Concord*, edited and translated by Theodore G. Tappert (Philadelphia: Fortress Press, 1959), 575.

[29] Martin Luther, "Lectures on Galatians 1519," in *Luther's Works* 27, translated by Richard Jungkuntz (St. Louis: Concordia, 1964), 410. Hereafter cited as LW 27 (Cf. WA 2:617,42-618,1).

claiming that Isaiah spoke of the reality of the Christian Church in the sixteenth century.

Earlier in that same commentary, Luther hears Paul's words as being addressed to his own day and age as he remarks: "You see, therefore, how very soundly *Paul instructs us*, lest we be deceived by a title, a name, a face, or a person, and neglect his counsel" [emphasis added].[30] Although he acknowledged that Paul was writing to the Galatians, Luther recognizes that Paul was also speaking a contemporary word to Luther's own time.

There are numerous other examples of such comments of a similar tone to Luther's auditors and readers which show the contemporaneity of Scripture.[31] In his comments on Galatians 5:26, Luther shows how this hermeneutical approach works:

> For if Divine Scriptures are treated in such a way as to be understood only with regard to the past and not to be applied also to our own manner of life, of what benefit will they be? Then they are cold, dead, and not even divine. For you see how fittingly and vividly, yes, how necessarily, this passage applies to our age.[32]

Luther could not let the Scriptures remain a dead-letter of historic irrelevance, but felt compelled to recognize and report a contemporary word for himself and his hearers.

Even clearer comments of Scripture's contemporaneity are heard in Luther's commentary which grew out of his later lectures on Galatians and which were printed in 1535.[33] For example, in commenting on Galatians 3:23, Luther states:

> Paul is referring to the time of fulfillment, when Christ came. But you should apply it not only to the time but also to feelings; for what happened historically and temporally when Christ came—namely, that he abrogated the Law and brought liberty and eternal life to light—this happens personally and spiritually every day in any Christian, in whom there are found the time of Law and the time of grace in constant alternation.[34]

[30] LW 27:206 (WA 2:480,26-27).

[31] LW 27:156, 167, 172, 187, 206, 221, 223, 235, 249-50, 254, 282, 283, 289, 321, 326, 330, 335, 347, 351, 362, 374, 397-8, 404 (Cf. WA 2 corresponding pages).

[32] LW 27:386 (WA 2:601,19-23).

[33] Martin Luther, "Lectures on Galatians 1535," in *Luther's Works* 26, translated by Jaroslav Pelikan (St. Louis: Concordia, 1963), 16, 30, 32, 33-36, 46, 48, 51, 59, 62, 154, 215, 221, 232, 234, 321-22, 331, 351. Hereafter cited as LW 26 (Cf. WA 40[1]).

[34] LW 26:340 (Cf. WA 40[1]: 523,31-524,16)

Here we note an additional element in Luther's approach. It is in the application of another of Luther's hermeneutical principles, that of the distinction between Law-Gospel, that a personal and spiritual sense of the text was contemporaneously applicable for Luther. This contemporaneity of the text is even more evident in a comment he makes just a few verses further:

> ... Christ came once for all at a set time ... . In addition, Christ comes spiritually every day; through the Word of the Gospel faith also comes every day ... .[35]

In effect, Luther is showing that the text is a living, vibrant and contemporary Word, which brings the Good News of God's grace in Christ for all time to those of faith. The text brings the presence of Christ to the contemporary reader.

But this understanding of Scripture's contemporaneity is not merely an outgrowth of Luther's love for Paul's letter to the Galatians. This hermeneutics of contemporaneity is evident in many of his other commentaries or lectures, particularly on the Psalms.

Scott Hendrix, in commenting on Luther's principles of biblical interpretation, shows that this contemporaneity is also evident in his interpretation of the Psalms. "Luther concluded that, because the Word of God is eternal, it should apply to people of all times. Since attitudes of godliness and ungodliness remain the same throughout all ages, Luther argued that Psalm 1 could be applied to his contemporaries (WA 2, 34.9-35.11; LW 14, 290-91)."[36] Although the Psalms were composed over several centuries, Luther found that the texts brought a contemporary word to his own hearers.

Similarly, Isaac explains Luther's approach to another Psalm, Psalm 90, in this way:

> The exposition [of Psalm 90], while recognizing the difference between Moses' day and the present, does not show an awkwardness or modern consciousness of an historical gap between what the text meant in its day and what it may mean for today. For Luther, there is no hesitation between those boundaries, if indeed, he even recognized them as boundaries. The exposition of the text resides in the present because the word of the text brings with it the Spirit of the living Word.[37]

[35] LW 26:351 (Cf. WA 40[1]: 538,29-31).

[36] Hendrix, 232-33.

[37] Isaac, 85.

Therefore, the text of Scripture is capable of bridging the historical gap between the biblical times and the contemporary hearer.

In an exposition of Psalm 118, Ronald M. Hals refers to Luther's interpretation. He finds this same concept of contemporaneity of the Psalter in Luther's exposition of Psalm 118. Hals writes:

> What Luther does with Psalm 118 is to make it his own. He calls it "my own beloved Psalm" and interprets it as speaking directly to his situation. Thereby, of course, in one sense he misunderstands it almost totally, for the psalm knows nothing of sixteenth century German Christendom. In another sense, though, he opens the door to the only true understanding. He recognizes that here is not "mere literature" (*Lesewort*), but the "words of life" (*Lebewort*).[38]

The Psalter thus is a book in which Christ speaks contemporaneously, because he is really present in the text and his Spirit makes him present to the readers and hearers.

Another favorite biblical text for Luther was the book of Genesis, having lectured on it numerous times in his life. Luther's comments on Genesis 3:7 show how Luther distinguished no temporal separation between Adam and Eve and Luther's own contemporary society. He describes how Adam and Eve hid from God and then recalls:

> Now, after sin, we not only shun the glance of men when we are naked; but we are also bashful in our own presence, just as Moses states here about Adam and Eve. This shame is a witness that our heart has lost the trust in God which they who were naked had before sin.[39]

In a contemporary way, the word of the Law continues to function among the people of Luther's own time, he notes. People today still feel shame as a result of a loss of trust in God.

A little later in Genesis, Luther commented about how similar human nature is after the Fall. After stating how stupid Adam was in trying to hide from God and excuse himself, Luther continues:

> However, we must not think that this happened to Adam alone. We, each one of us, do the same thing; our nature does not permit us to act otherwise after we have become guilty of sin.[40]

[38] Ronald M. Hals, "Psalm 118," *Interpretation* 37:3 (July 1983), 277.

[39] Martin Luther, "Lectures on Genesis, chapters 1-5," in *Luther's Works* 1, translated by George V. Schick (St. Louis: Concordia, 1958), 167 (Cf. WA 42:125,15-18).

[40] LW 1:175 (WA 41:137,15).

Thus, the biblical story is not merely a historical record of the past, but an account that describes the human condition to this day. The biblical text brings the readers face to face with the reality of their contemporary condition before God. It brings them into God's presence and God into their contemporary life.

This hermeneutic of contemporaneity is evident in many other comments on Scripture by Luther. Besides the Psalms and Genesis, Luther also saw the present relevance of the biblical message in the New Testament. In a lecture on 1 Corinthians 15, Luther stated how Paul's words were not merely for the Corinthians, but for Luther's own hearers:

> Behold, thus the apostle at the very outset wants to lead us away from all disputation and tutelage of reason and direct us solely to the Word, which he had received from Christ and had proclaimed to them [the Corinthians].[41]

The text of Scripture leads all who hear it back to Christ, whether in Paul's day or in the present.

Contemporaneity is also evident as Luther understood the possibility and responsibility of hermeneutics leading to proclamation. Interpretation by itself is an exercise of the letter only, he knew. Only when hermeneutics connects to homiletics and the active life of the Church, does the Spirit come into his prominent role and Christ becomes really present. Headley gives a helpful reminder in the following comment:

> The proclamation of Christ does not concern simply a past, historical event but is a gift and a bestowing which endures forever. The story contains its own outgoing contemporaneousness, which is appropriated in faith by the believer.[42]

Thus, Luther's approach grew out of his own interest and intent for the Word of God as it was preached from the German pulpits of his day.

This emphasis upon the contemporaneity of Scripture and preaching also has a devotional dimension. When commenting on the *Magnificat*, Luther stressed the fact that in her song Mary was expressing her own experience. But this experience is also the continuing experience of the reader through the working of the Holy Spirit as the Holy Scriptures are read. Luther states: "No one can receive [a proper interpretation] from the Holy Spirit without expe-

[41] Martin Luther, "Commentary on 1 Corinthians 15," in *Luther's Works* 28, translated by Martin H. Bertram (St. Louis: Concordia, 1973), 68 (cf. WA 36:492).

[42] Headley, 24.

riencing, proving, and feeling it. In such experience the Holy Spirit instructs us as in his own school, outside of which naught is learned save empty words and idle fables."[43] This devotional approach certainly is best described in Luther's famous adaptation of the monastic discipline—prayer, meditation, and testing (*oratio*, *meditatio*, and *tentatio*) make a theologian.[44] It is the Spirit, working through the Word, who makes the text contemporary with the reader. Luther reiterates the crucial point of this hermeneutic of contemporaneity. The Scriptures become contemporaneous with us because the Spirit works through that Word, speaking a word of Gospel to a sinner in need of good news.

There are innumerable other examples of this perspective in Luther's lectures and commentaries. The material gathered in this section merely illustrates the breadth of this concept in Luther's writings. By way of conclusion, one final comment by Luther is in order. Again, in his 1535 Commentary on Galatians, we hear how Luther underscores the contemporaneity of the Spirit's activity in and through Scripture.

> Therefore let us permit the Holy Spirit to speak, as He does in the Scriptures, either about abstract, bare, and simple faith or about concrete, composite, and incarnate faith.[45]

The Holy Spirit continues to speak through Scripture to the Church and the contemporary reader, just as he had in the very beginning.[46]

CONTEMPORARY HERMENEUTICS AND LUTHER SCHOLARSHIP

What does Luther's approach to the text of Scripture say to biblical interpreters and expositors today? Lessing's gap of history con-

[43] A. S. Wood, 15, citing the Holman Edition of Luther's Works, III, 127.

[44] The classic location of this advice is in Luther's "Preface to the Wittenberg Edition of Luther's German Writings, 1539," in *Luther's Works* 34, translated by Robert R. Heitner, edited by Lewis W. Spitz (Philadelphia: Muhlenberg Press, 1960), 279-288 (cf. WA 50: 657-661). In his 1535 Galatians commentary, Luther adverts to this idea briefly (LW 26:65; cf. WA 40^{1}:130).

[45] LW 26:266 (cf. WA 40^{1}:417,12).

[46] Luther, "Lectures on Genesis, chapters 1-5," 262: "Moses says that these words [Genesis 4:6] were spoken by the Lord, because Adam had now been accounted just and had been endowed with the Holy Spirit. What he now says in accordance with the Word of God and through the Holy Spirit is correctly declared to have been said by God. Similarly today, those who preach the Gospel are not themselves directly the preachers, but Christ speaks and preaches through them" (cf. WA 41:194,16-20).

tinues to plague modern biblical scholarship (just the use of that word "modern" shows the continuing effect of such a concept). Most practitioners of contemporary biblical hermeneutics consider three particular and distinct elements—the text, the writer, and the reader.[47] Almost half a millennium ago, Luther saw the relationship of the text, the writer, and the reader as being linked to each other in a dynamic way. He also bridged the historical "ditch" between history and faith.

From Luther's perspective, the text is the actual vehicle for bringing the biblical author or writer (or even the reported-event) forward in history so that the text links the writer and reader as contemporaries. Kenneth Hagen has correctly and succinctly noted, "For Luther, Paul was contemporary. In Luther's mind, there was no intellectual or human progress from Paul's day to his that would alter the theological task."[48]

Although many scholars have mentioned this contemporaneity in Luther, few have clearly made it a key in Luther's hermeneutics. In this section, we will hear from a few other writers who have described Luther's approach in light of this peculiar perspective.

Following the model of Paul Ricoeur, Hans Frei described the uniqueness of Luther's approach in this way: "There is no proper understanding of texts from the past, "distanced" or released from their original moorings, except on the model (or, rather, more than the model) of a temporally present event, an event in and of contemporary consciousness."[49] Thus, Luther was ahead of his time in seeing the contemporary relevance of the text as a present reality.

Gerhard Ebeling has done much in the area of hermeneutics, particularly in Luther's own understanding of Scripture. He remarked about Luther's approach that:

> The word-event in human language is the most suitable form of God's communication with man ... . The hermeneutical result is, therefore, that the very word as such is of hermeneutical importance and is able to illumine, to bring about clarity, and to give life. The hermeneutical task can only consist of the fact that we

[47] Dan McCartney and Charles Clayton, *Let the Reader Understand: A Guide to Interpreting and Applying the Bible* (Wheaton, IL: Victor Books, 1994); W. Randolph Tate, *Biblical Interpretation: An Integrated Approach* (Peabody, MA: Hendrickson Publishers, Inc., 1991), and James W. Voelz, *What Does This Mean?* (St. Louis: Concordia, 1995), 16-20, provide similar perspectives on these issues.

[48] Hagen, *Galatians*, 33.

[49] Hans W. Frei, "The 'Literal Reading' of Biblical Narrative in the Christian Tradition: Does It Stretch or Will It Break?" in *The Bible and the Narrative Tradition*, ed. by Frank McConnell (New York: Oxford University Press, 1986), 52.

> devote ourselves to the service of the word-event in such a way that the word becomes truly word, and that it occurs as pure word in the fullness of its power.[50]

This word-event is another way of speaking of the contemporaneity of Scripture. Christ's presence comes into the present through the very Word of God.

Another Luther scholar, Gerhard Forde, emphasized this proclamational element of the word-event by reminding us that "for Luther proper preaching is the solution to the problem of interpretation."[51] He suggests that, for Luther, preaching the letter was speaking in the imperative mood, while preaching the spirit was in the declarative mood. Such proper preaching of the Word of Law and Gospel brought the reality of God's Spirit to the listeners as well as the interpreter. Thus, the experience of the Word brought a "second immediacy" (to use a recent hermeneutic phrase) with the reality which the Word communicates.[52] Again, we can note the connection between the Word, the Spirit, and the reality which the Word brings into the present. This is none other than a recognition of Luther's hermeneutic of contemporaneity.

Several years ago, Scott Hendrix came to a similar conclusion when he stated the following:

> Luther was unwilling to make the sharp distinction encouraged by modern criticism between what the text meant and what it means. He did not ignore this distinction and could leave the meaning of a text at the level of historical or theological analysis. At the same time, he often utilized personal experience and his

[50] Gerhard Ebeling, "The New Hermeneutics and the Early Luther," trans. by Mrs. James Carse, *Theology Today* XXI:1 (April 1964), 46.

[51] Gerhard O. Forde, "Law and Gospel in Luther's Hermeneutic," *Interpretation* 37:3 (July 1983), 241.

[52] Martin Warner, "Introduction," *The Bible as Rhetoric: Studies in Biblical Persuasion and Credibility*, Warwick Studies in Philosophy and Literature (New York: Routledge, 1990), 21, cites Paul Ricoeur, *Freud and Philosophy: An Essay on Interpretation*, trans. by D. Savage (New Haven: Yale University Press, 1970), 28: "The contrary of suspicion, I will say bluntly, is faith. What faith? No longer, to be sure, the first faith of the simple soul, but rather the second faith of one who has engaged in hermeneutics, faith that has undergone criticism, postcritical faith. Ricoeur is here drawing on his work in *The Symbolism of Evil* [trans. E. Buchanan. (Boston: Beacon Press, 1969) especially the "Conclusion"] where he distinguished between a 'first' or 'primitive naïveté,' which involves an 'immediacy of belief' to which an educated twentieth-century reader cannot with integrity return, and a 'second naïveté,' in and through criticism' which allows a 'second immediacy'." This second immediacy seems to be a contemporary illustration of what Luther experienced.

> diagnosis of the contemporary church to make the text speak immediately to his own day and thus to reveal its meaning.[53]

Thus, Luther bridged Lessing's ditch or the Kantian gap by recognizing that the very Scriptures themselves brought him into a vital, living relationship with the eternally gracious God who sent his Son and continues to send his Spirit.

SOME CONCLUDING THOUGHTS

Although Luther's hermeneutics grew out of the long tradition of the *quadriga*, throughout his life, he was being influenced by the very text he studied. Although he was a teacher of the Old Testament, he was especially moved by the Pauline literature of the Scriptures. From the Old Testament Scriptures and Paul, he developed his hermeneutic principles.

Contemporaneity, as it has been used here in this essay, describes Luther's dynamic recognition of the relationship of Scripture to the contemporary reader. The plain, clear words of Scripture brought the living experience of the Christ's Spirit into Luther's own contemporary circumstances.

Luther bridges Lessing's ditch of history with the living, life-giving Spirit-filled Word which both brings God's power and presence into the present as well as draws the reader into the experience of the text. Luther understood the biblical text as the vehicle for bringing Christ into the contemporary experience of the reader. The text itself is the locus for a contemporary interchange with the ultimate Reality, who is the Word-made-flesh. This is Luther's legacy.

[53] Hendrix, 238.

MARTIN LUTHER CONTRA MEDIEVAL MONASTICISM: A FRIAR IN THE LION'S DEN

Heiko A. Oberman

I. Barriers beyond the Breakthrough

During the second part of the last century, a concerted effort was made to reorient the quest for the time and content of Luther's Reformation Breakthrough. Carefully steering a course between the Scylla of presenting Luther as a *Deus ex machina*, the unprecedented Discoverer of the Gospel, and the Charybdis of creating a golden chain of medieval witnesses to the Truth (*testes veritatis*), the so-called 'Forerunners,' the 'library' of the young Luther was scrutinized in order to reconstruct the earliest stages in his development. Once it was realized that Luther unfolded his program as a professor of biblical theology, the scriptural commentaries that were—or could have been—at Luther's disposal were drawn into consideration in order to place Luther 'in context' (Heinrich Bornkamm, Martin Brecht, David Steinmetz). This advance could only be achieved after the characteristics of Luther's new hermeneutics were established (Gerhard Ebeling, Samuel Preus). Moreover, a concerted effort was made to transcend the earlier boundaries of a limited canon of philosophical and theological academic 'authorities' by extending the scope of research to include that not necessarily 'mystical,' wide-ranging world of devotional literature variously influenced by (pseudo-)Bernard, (pseudo-)Bonaventura, Gerson, Tauler and the Modern Devotion (Christoph Burger, Berndt Hamm, Steven Ozment).

Amidst a growing awareness that the Books of the Bible were not primarily resources for doctrinal information but sources for meditation, Luther's development could be charted anew by closely following the breathtaking development from the *Dictata super Psalterium*, the early Psalms commentary of 1513-1516 (Scott Hendrix), through the *Operationes in Psalmos*, the second commentary on the Psalms of the years 1519-1521 (Gerhard Hammer), abruptly broken off when the Luther case (*causa Lutheri*) had become so politically explosive that the reformer was cited to appear in April 1521 before the Emperor in Worms (Kurt-Victor Selge, Eike Wolgast). As yet no agreement has been achieved in the ongoing debate about an early (1514) or a late (1518) dating of the Reformation Breakthrough (Ernst Bizer, Bernhard Lohse, Martin Brecht, Otto Hermann Pesch). Nevertheless all scholars involved in this exacting and meticulous research-project are in agreement that along a seven-year trajectory (1513-1519) Luther developed a new biblical dictionary pursuing what he called 'the theological grammar' of the Scriptures.[1]

Trained in Erfurt in the tradition of William Occam (†1349), Gregory of Rimini (†1358), Peter d'Ailly (†1420), and Gabriel Biel (†1495), the reformer stood on the shoulders of innovators who had declared the words of human language to be 'natural signs' rather than reverberations of the eternal *Logos*. These Nominalists—the *nominales* or *moderni*—had shouldered the task of cleansing the scholarly vocabulary of its former speculative connotations: in the battle cry 'words are free' (*nomina sunt ad placitum*) swings the tone of liberation that should be heard as a Declaration of Independence. Accordingly, in the field of philology and linguistics the definition of terminology 'in context' had to be attended to with a new insistence on precise formulations and forms of argumentation (the 'modus loquendi' as 'dicendi proprietas'). This would prove to be the congenious plank in the platform of Nominalism making it an attractive coalition partner for Renaissance humanists in their enthusiastic pursuit of rhetoric—and vice versa (Charles Trinkaus, Helmar Junghans).

It is this search for the unique vocabulary of Scripture that propels Luther on a path of ever new discoveries, focused on the growing awareness that the biblical God communicated with the Prophets and Apostles in ways and words not respected or reflected in the traditional scholastic speculative grammar saturated with definitions drawn from 'Aristotle.' This is what Luther means when he insists on the need of "the eyes and ears of faith." God's words and ways are so unexpected and so far beyond our ken that, without the Spirit, "no human being will be able to grasp them."[2] In the earliest notes

[1] "... quae contra omnium hominum sensum, praesertim sapientium, sapiat. Sed primo grammatica videamus, verum ea theologica," *Operationes in Psalmos*, Ps. 1:1a (1519); D. Martin Luther, *Operationes in Psalmos 1519-1521*, Teil II: *Psalm 1 bis 10 (Vulgata)*, ed. Gerhard Hammer and Manfred Biersack, Archiv zur Weimarer Ausgabe der Werke Martin Luthers. Texte und Untersuchungen [= AWA], vol. 2 (Cologne: Böhlau, 1981), 29, 2-4.

[2] "Fidei oculis et auribus opus est, ut haec verba ['Beatus vir qui non abiit in consilio impiorum et in via peccatorum non stetit in cathedra pestilentiae non sedit', Ps. 1:1] spiritus audias et eorum rem videas. Homo enim non potest ea intelligere." Ibid., AWA 2.37, 5f.

we have from Luther's hand (1509), Aristotle is already designated as an unreliable gadabout ('fabulator,' *Schwätzer*)[3]—not as concerns his impressive, wide-ranging analysis of the physical world, but when used as court of appeal in interpreting the Word of God.[4] This Augustinian tenet, in keeping with the *via Gregorii* named after the nominalist platform of Gregory of Rimini (Manfred Schulze), did not fail to cause tensions between the theological and philosophical wings of Erfurt's Nominalism (Adolar Zumkeller). In his May 1518 letter to Erfurt's prominent nominalist logician, Jodocus Trutfetter (†1519), Luther roundly blamed his one-time philosophical teacher for a fatal lack of critical distance from Aristotle. By that time, Luther had already launched his attack against scholastic theology (4 September 1517), writing Aristotle out of the book of theology even more bitingly than any of his Augustinian predecessors: "Aristotle is for theology darkness at noon: Against the scholastic doctors (*Contra scholasticos*)."[5]

Whereas for this reason Luther's May 1518 critique of Aristotle could not have come as a surprise to Trutfetter, all the more noteworthy is Luther's expression of lasting indebtedness to his former schoolmaster: "You were the first to teach me that only the Scriptures deserve belief, whereas all other authorities have to be read with dis-

[3] WA 9.23, 7. In 1517, Luther uses the seemingly synonymous term 'illusor.' WABr 1.88, 4-89, 30 (no. 34); 8 February 1517, Luther to Johannes Lang. It is to be noted, however, that the 'illusor' is the characteristic Gestalt of the Devil in the End Time. Though not established for 1517, in 1521 Luther repeatedly suggests this identification by invoking II Peter 3:3: "Venient in novissimis diebus in deceptione illusores ..." WA 8.644, 1-3; "O tempora, o regna, o facta et omnia Satanae!" WA 8.651, 2f.

[4] As Adolar Zumkeller has shown, sharp critique of Aristotle is a strong tenet in the Erfurt *studium*, the 'seminary' of Luther's order, the Augustinian Observants: *Erbsünde, Gnade, Rechtfertigung und Verdienst nach der Lehre der Erfurter Augustinertheologen des Spätmittelalters*, Cassiciacum, 35 (Würzburg: Augustinus-Verlag, 1984); see the substantial review by Wolfgang Urban in *Theologische Revue* 83 (1987), 37-40; here particularly the documentation for the *via Gregorii*, and for the impact of Gregory of Rimini as the *doctor authenticus* on the Erfurt Augustinian Johannes Klenkok (†1374), the renowned blaster of the 'Sachsenspiegel.' For the history of the *via Gregorii*, see Manfred Schulze, "'Via Gregorii' in Forschung und Quellen," in *Gregor von Rimini. Werk und Wirkung bis zur Reformation*, ed. Heiko A. Oberman, Spätmittelalter und Reformation. Texte und Untersuchungen, 20 (Berlin: de Gruyter, 1981), 1-126.

[5] Despite the laborious punctuation of the text as a consequence of the nineteenth-century ideal of 'diplomatische Treue', I refer here to the best annotated edition of the *Disputatio contra scholasticam theologiam* by Helmar Junghans in *Martin Luther: Studienausgabe*, ed. Hans-Ulrich Delius, vol. 1 (Berlin: Evangelische Verlagsanstalt, 1979), 169, 16f.

cernment."[6] This statement should not be understood as the later Protestant maxim of 'Scripture alone'—after all *sola scriptura* is the fundamental principal of the entire scholastic disputation tradition. What is intended here is something else, and for our purposes far more important: in the Scriptures God defines his own vocabulary or—to coin a phrase not used by Luther—*nomina sunt ad placitum Dei*, God defines his own terms. The good interpreter will attend to His way of speaking (*modus dicendi*); only the Scriptures can introduce the reader to the 'Grammar of God' if he expects to crack the code of key terms, the nuggets of biblical theology. Consequently Reuchlin's introduction to Hebrew (1506) became a prized tool (Siegfried Raeder), and ten years later the publication of Erasmus' groundbreaking *Novum Instrumentum* an event (Anne Reeve, Michael Screech, Cornelis Augustijn, Johannes Trapman).

It is the uncontested merit of an international phalanx of historians to have zeroed in on one of the most central terms in this new theology, unfolded by Luther in his lectures on the Letter to the Hebrews (April 1517-March 1518). As in the amazing case of the invention of movable type simultaneously in Haarlem and Mainz, unbeknownst to one another scholars on both sides of the Atlantic in three different language areas (Joop Boendermaker, Kenneth Hagen, Oswald Bayer) started to pursue the crucial terms 'covenant' or 'pactum,' together with the revealing variants 'testament' and 'promise.'[7]

[6] "... ex te primo omnium didici, solis canonicis libris deberi fidem, caeteris omnibus iudicium ..." WABr 1.171, 72f. (no. 74), 9 May 1518. Luther's second most important Erfurt teacher in philosophy, Bartholomäus Arnoldi von Usingen (1464/65-1532), was inspired by Luther to join the Augustinian Observants in Erfurt. However, he did not follow Luther's 'second turn,' and died as a convinced opponent of the Reformation. Cf. for biography and bibliography on Usingen the introduction to *Bartholomaei Arnoldi de Usingen O.S.A. Responsio contra Apologiam Philippi Melanchthonis*, ed. Primoz Simoniti, Cassiciacum. Supplement, 7 (Würzburg: Augustinus-Verlag, 1978), esp. xii.

[7] Johannes P. Boendermaker, *Luthers Commentaar op de Brief aan de Hebreeën, 1517-1518*, Van Gorcum's Theologische Bibliotheek, 38 (Assen: Van Gorcum, 1965); Kenneth Hagen, *A Theology of Testament in the Young Luther: The Lectures on Hebrews*, Studies in Medieval and Reformation Thought, 12 (Leiden: Brill, 1974), esp.117-19.

In pursuing the theological center of Luther's reformation 'breakthrough,' Oswald Bayer traced the significance of *pactum* (or *testamentum*) back to the early Luther and noted that a key text (Mark 16:16) is interpreted by Luther "im Einklang mit der nominalistischen Tradition." *Promissio. Geschichte der reformatorischen Wende in Luthers Theologie,* Forschungen zur Kirchen- und Dogmengeschichte, 24 (Göttingen: Vandenhoeck & Ruprecht, 1971), 119. For the function of *pactum* in the unfolding of Luther's doctrine of the Eucharist, see ibid., esp. 241-53.

Luther's focus on covenant proved to be the essential conduit of his discovery that God is not the Thomistic 'Highest Being' but the bonding 'God who acts in history,' not an Unmoved Mover but the highly mobile Granter of testament and promise, the God of faith and fidelity.[8]

Today we see clearly the extent to which this covenant-theology is already firmly moored in the thought of the earliest Luther, and how along the path of exploring the testament of God he came to discover the doctrine of justification by faith alone, as well as its ecclesiological and sacramental implications.[9] Whereas traditional Luther scholarship treats the doctrine of justification under its own heading and presents the Eucharist in a separate chapter, Luther's passionate rejection of Zwingli's symbolic doctrine of the Lord's Supper (Marburg 1529: *significat*) proves to be directly related to the fact that he regarded the words of institution of the Eucharist as the reliable covenantal promise which cannot, without peril, be adjusted to fit the categories of human ratiocination. The God-who-acts cannot be figured out by reason but makes himself known in Word and Deed, through preaching, absolution, water, bread and wine.

This noteworthy interconnection between Luther's confrontation with Erfurt's Trutfetter and Zurich's Zwingli alerts us to the considerable limitations of the time-honored concept of the Reformation 'breakthrough'—irrespective of whether its dating should be closer to 1514 or 1518, and irrespective of whether its content is best defined as the transformation of the 'Justice of God' (*Iustitia Dei*)

[8] Berndt Hamm explored the theological foundation of this 'theology of piety' in *Promissio, Pactum, Ordinatio. Freiheit und Selbstbindung Gottes in der scholastischen Gnadenlehre*, Beiträge zur historischen Theologie, 54 (Tübingen: J.C.B. Mohr, 1977), esp. 361, 366, 375, 379. Cf. id., *Frömmigkeitstheologie am Anfang des 16. Jahrhundert: Studiën zu Johannes von Paltz und seinem Umkreis*, Beiträge zur historischen Theologie, 65 (Tübingen: J.C.B. Mohr, 1982). For a concise introduction to Hamm's concept of this 'theology of piety', see id., "Normative Centering in the Fifteenth and Sixteenth Centuries: Observations on Religiosity, Theology, and Iconology," translated by John M. Frymire, *Journal of Early Modern History* 3 (1999), 309-54, esp. 325-30; for the demanding task of finding the English equivalent for these terms see Frymire, 307-9.

[9] The *pactum* makes the sacramental element into a reliable sign "... quo comprehenderet deum nec vagaretur aut fluctuaret in suis speculationibus ... Nec est periculosius in homine aliquid ratione, quae pro sua curiositate non potest non evagari ..." "Sermo de Testamento Christi" (8 April 1520), WA 9.448, 35-449, 5. The covenantal view of God is already firmly in place with the earliest Luther: "*Et hoc placitum*: i.e., pactum," (marginal to Augustine's *De Trinitate* I.3; c. 1509), WA 9.16, 4; "... pepigit nobiscum fedus ..." (Ps. 118:88; c. 1514) WA 4.350, 13.

into the 'Justice of Christ' (*Iustitia Christi*), as I have argued.[10] Such a one-time 'breakthrough' is an unrealistic, romantic concept which misleadingly suggests that through the mighty arms of a Divine Bulldozer, all barricades on 'The Road to Reformation' were removed—once and for all. As a consequence, insufficient attention has been paid to subsequent momentous developments in Luther thought. After what the reformer described, from the perspective of nearly three decades later, as the awesome turning point in his quest for the merciful God, some major decisions still awaited him. One of the most important among these was simultaneously the most existential one, the right approach to the life he was leading as an Observant Augustinian Friar,[11] the life of dedicated service to God under the eternal vows of obedience, poverty and chastity.

2. TO BIND FOR LIFE IS TO BLIND FOR LIFE: THE MONASTIC VOWS

It has long been suggested that Luther's reevaluation of the monastic vows in the year 1521 marks a watershed in Europe's religious and cultural life. Indeed, the 1521 attack on monastic life by rejecting the eternal vows (*De votis monasticis iudicium*) cannot be understood in any other terms than as a frontal assault, implying a complete reinterpretation of the whole moral fibre of medieval Christianity, namely its high road to perfection, the 'freeway' (*via securior*) to salvation, the life of 'regular,' untrammeled dedication to the service of

[10] Heiko A. Oberman, "'Iustitia Christi' and 'Iustitia Dei': Luther and the Scholastic Doctrines of Justification," *The Harvard Theological Review* 59 (1966), 1-26. Reprinted in German translation: "'Iustitia Christi' und 'Iustitia Dei'. Luther und die scholastischen Lehren von der Rechtfertigung," in *Der Durchbruch der reformatorischen Erkenntnis bei Luther*, ed. Bernhard Lohse, Wege der Forschung, 123 (Darmstadt: Wissenschaftliche Buchgesellschaft, 1968), 413-44.

[11] Though we limited our purview to the yield of Luther scholarship in the second half of the twentieth century, an exception must be made for the groundbreaking work of the immensely learned Dominican, Heinrich Denifle: his whole *oeuvre* testifies to the fact that Luther-hatred can be as fruitful as the Luther-love motivating the majority of Luther scholars. Because of the understandable need to counter his—indeed nefarious—personal attacks on the reformer, his richly documented illumination of Luther's 'Sitz im Leben,' specifically his analysis of Luther's spirituality as a member of Augustinian Observants, has not been sufficiently 'received.' On 10 June 1905, Heinrich Denifle O.P. died just two weeks after completing the preface to his *Quellenbelege. Die abendländischen Schriftausleger bis Luther über Justitia Dei (Rom. 1,17) und Justificatio*, published as volume I of the *Ergänzungen zu Denifle's Luther und Luthertum* (Mainz: Verlag von Kirchheim, 1905).

God.[12] In recent research this treatise of Luther has even been held up as "the most radical critique of monasticism ever formulated," and said to have unleashed a "mass movement" of monks, friars and nuns who experienced a second conversion; the monastic vision which once had been the very *raison d'être* of their way of life had become obsolete—indeed, to combat it could now be embraced as "the new vocation."[13] Such an articulation, especially when dramatized as a clean and clear cut with the past ('klarer Schnitt'), sounds very much like the proud Protestant profile of a previous period. Or is it? Before Luther's *apertura*—his breaching of the monastic walls—is properly assessed, we are well advised to take a serious look at the stages in which Luther came to terms with the cowl on his own body, which he was not yet prepared to shed for another three years (9 October 1524). On closer consideration the heralded 'clear cut' proves to display a lucidity shot through with intriguing, opaque streaks.

The Monastery as Teacher and Tyrant

As our point of departure we choose a time *after* the latest date computed for the Reformation Breakthrough (1518). In 1519, Luther still had an open mind as far as the viability of the monastic life is concerned. At the beginning of his second Psalms commentary (1519), he already started to sketch the dialectic of Christian freedom and secular service that he would present in 1520 as a powerful, pastoral manifesto in the "Freedom of the Christian" (*De libertate Christiana*). Taking up the theme of his grand Gotha sermon of 1 May 1515 on the divisive sin of backbiting—the homily preached on the festive occasion of his election as vicar over ten Augustinian houses in

[12] Still fundamental is the study of Bernhard Lohse, *Mönchtum und Reformation. Luthers Auseinandersetzung mit dem Mönchsideal des Mittelalters* (Göttingen: Vandenhoeck & Ruprecht, 1963). See further the descriptive chronological listing of Luther's treatment of the vows by Heinz-Meinolf Stamm, *Luthers Stellung zum Ordensleben*, Veröffentlichungen des Instituts für Europäische Geschichte Mainz, 101 (Wiesbaden: Franz Steiner, 1980).

[13] "Ideale und Hoffnungen, die einstmals den Einsatz des ganzen Lebens wert gewesen waren, galten nun als obsolet, ja der Kampf gegen sie konnte als neue Lebensaufgabe erscheinen." Bernd Moeller, "Die frühe Reformation in Deutschland als neues Mönchtum," in *Die frühe Reformation in Deutschland als Umbruch. Wissenschaftliches Symposion des Vereins für Reformationsgeschichte 1996*, ed. id. with Stephen E. Buckwalter, Schriften des Vereins für Reformationsgeschichte, 199 (Gütersloh: Gütersloher Verlagshaus, 1998), 76-91; 86. For a critical evaluation and further literature, see my review article in *Archive for Reformation History* 91 (2000), 477-87; 481-85.

On Applas von Rom
kan man wol selig werden/durch
anzaigung der götlichen hailigen geschrifft.

Frater Martinus
(1519).

Thüringen and Saxony[14]—in 1519 Luther turned this transgression of extreme Observants into a typical characteristic of all the Godless (*impii*). The few deviators from the Rule of St. Augustine have now become the massive opposition to the faithful (*populus fidelis*); they assault all those who in Christian freedom do not restrict true service to liturgical 'ceremonies.' They are so mesmerized by holy days, special times, set works and sacred places that even "if a neighbor is dying from hunger, they will stick to their ways and not move an inch."[15] In contrast, the true Christian practices charity at all times, with all kind of action, wherever needed and towards everyone, irre-

[14] WA 1.44-52; 50, 12-20. See my article, "Teufelsdreck: Eschatology and Scatology in the 'Old' Luther," *The Sixteenth Century Journal* 19 (1988), 435-50. Cf. my *Luther: Man Between God and the Devil*, trans. Eileen Walliser-Schwarzbart (New Haven, Conn.: Yale University Press, 1989), 106-10.

[15] "*In tempore suo*. O aureum et amabile verbum, quo asseritur libertas iustitiae Christianae! Impiis stati sunt dies, stata tempora, certa opera, certa loca, quibus sic inhaerent, ut, si proximus fame esset moriturus, non ab illis divelli possint." AWA 2.49, 7-10. Otto Hermann Pesch called attention to the nearly contemporary *Taufsermon* of Luther (1519) in one of the most theologically perceptive evaluations of Luther's position on monasticism. Pesch follows received opinion when he regards Luther's position in 1521 as the endpoint: "Luthers Kritik am Mönchtum in katholischer Sicht," in *Strukturen Christlicher Existenz. Beiträge zur Erneuerung des geistlichen Lebens*, ed. H. Schlier, E. v. Severus, J. Sudbrack, A. Pereira (Würzburg: Echter-Verlag, 1968), 81-96, 371-74. For the *Taufsermon*, see WA 2.727-37.

spective of whether this is a Jew, Gentile, Greek or Barbarian; the Christian "is truly a man of all seasons."[16]

For our understanding of what is often (in tune with modern sensitivities) anachronistically called Luther's 'polemics,' it is important to highlight that in 1519, he returns once more to his favorite theme of backbiting. The Godless, the *impii* or enemies of God, are a gated community locking themselves up in their own prison of holy space, holy work, and holy time, systematically degrading the outside world as a cesspool of evil. Accordingly, they fall over everything and on everyone, furiously driven to backbiting critiques, always ready to condemn. Thus they achieve the same intensity in malevolence that true Christians achieve in virtue: "If they would invest all that evil energy in truly good works, there would not be a shorter highroad to true piety."[17] When Richard Marius (†1999) presents the Reformation as a disaster for Western civilization unleashed by Luther's irrational fury, he psychologizes—and therewith trivializes—the voice of prophetic protest against the systemic fury of the anti-Church.[18]

If Luther had left the matter with this attack on divisive self-righteousness, we might well have concluded that in 1519 he merely 'upped the ante' after initially targeting just the opposition of some extremely 'Observant' friars. For the Augustinian Vicar, the Frater Martinus of 1515, these had been a fanatical group of 'pharisees,' anxious and therefore aggressive sticklers to the letter of the *Constitutiones*—the regulations defining everyday monastic life for

[16] "At beatus hic vir liber in omne tempus, in omne opus, in omnem locum, in omnem personam. Utcumque sese obtulerit casus, tibi serviet; quodcumque invenerit manus eius, hoc faciet. Non est Judaeus neque gentilis neque Graecus neque Barbarus, nullius prorsus personae, sed *dat fructum suum in tempore suo*, quoties opus sit eius opera deo et hominibus. Ideo neque fructus eius habet nomen, neque tempus eius habet nomen, neque ipse habet nomen, neque rivi aquarum eius habent nomen; unus non uni nec uno tempore, loco, opere, sed omnibus ubique per omnia servit estque vere vir omnium horarum, omnium operum, omnium personarum et imagine sui patris omnia in omnibus et super omnia." AWA 2.49, 10-19.

[17] "Impii vero, sicut Ps 17 [,46] dicitur: 'Clauduntur in angustiis suis', seipsos captivant et in operibus, temporibus, locis a se electis torquent, extra quae nihil rectum geri putant. Unde suorum fructuum aestimatores nihil faciunt, quam ut alienos fructus mordeant, iudicent, damnent, liberrimi, et in quocumque tempore prompti alios reprehendere, et omnino tales in malo faciendo, quales pii sunt in bono. Sunt enim et ipsi omnium horarum viri, non uno modo, non uno tempore, non uni homini, sed utcumque sors obtulerit, aliis detrahentes ac nocentes. Quae studia si verterent ad bona, nullo meliore compendio pii fierent." AWA 2.49, 20-50, 4.

[18] Richard Marius, *Martin Luther: The Christian between God and Death* (Cambridge, Mass.: Harvard University Press, 1998); see my critical review article under the gentle title "Varieties of Protest," in *The New Republic* 221 (16 August 1999), 40-45.

his Augustinians:[19] deviating from the Rule, they clung to the rules. We would have readily granted that by 1519 the previous demarcation line had deepened and sharpened into the radical rift between the Godless and the Faithful (*impii* and *pii*): the miserable deviators had become mighty demons. We would not, however, have dared to go so far as to suggest that Luther's critique could be interpreted as an assault on the monastic life. Yet Luther himself felt that he had come so close to this very inference that he had to deny explicitly any implied dismissal of monasticism as such:

> I do not say this because I object to the rules and rituals (*caerimoniae*) of churches and monasteries. To the contrary, from the very start it has been the essence of the monastic life that one enters a monastery in order to learn obedience by sacrificing one's own will, prepared to serve everyone in every respect. The monasteries were the very training centers to learn and grow in Christian liberty, as they are still today (*sicut adhuc sunt*) wherever they serve this original intention ... .[20]

This *sicut adhuc sunt*—'as they still are'—is still strikingly conservative as compared to later statements. Yet this explicit appreciation and legitimation does not imply that monasticism is a permanent feature of Christianity, one of its essentials and part of its life throughout the End. Monasticism can be abolished, just as the ceremonial part of the Old Testament law was abrogated:

[19] "Constitutiones fratrum Eremitarum sancti Augustini apostolicorum privilegiorum formam pro reformatione Alemanniae," ed. Wolfgang Günter, in Johann von Staupitz, *Sämtliche Schriften. Abhandlungen, Predigten, Zeugnisse*, ed. Lothar Graf zu Dohna and Richard Wetzel, vol. 5, Spätmittelalter und Reformation, 17 (Berlin: de Gruyter, 2001). For a well-documented reconstruction of what it meant to belong to the *Ordo Eremitarum Sancti Augustini* (O.E.S.A.; today O.S.A.), particularly in Germany and specifically in late medieval Erfurt, see Eric L. Saak, "The Creation of Augustinian Identity in the Later Middle Ages," *Augustiniana* 49 (1999), 109-64; ibid., 251-86. Though I received this bipartite article after completion of the text of this article, I should like to acknowledge that my understanding of daily life in the Order (O.E.S.A.) was much enhanced by directing Saak's dissertation entitled "Religio Augustini: Jordan of Quedlinburg and the Augustinian Tradition in Late Medieval Germany," University of Arizona, 1993—to be published in revised form in Studies in Medieval and Reformation Thought (Leiden: Brill, 2001).

[20] "Non sane haec dico, quod caerimonias ecclesiarum et monasteriorum reprobem, immo haec fuit prima religiosorum institutio, ut, qui monasterium ingressus esset, maiori subiectus disceret nihil proprie operari, sed promptus omnibus servire. Erantque monasteria vere quaedam gymnasia Christianae libertatis exercendae et perficiendae, sicut adhuc sunt, sicubi priscam servant institutionem; hic, inquam, erat finis et modus caerimoniarum." AWA 2.50, 5-10.

> After all, the ceremonies of the Old Law were eminent forms of practicing true and genuine piety. Yet when by evil design they started to undermine freedom and when, under the pretext of sticking to ceremonial propriety, they started to douse the flame of true piety and consequently perverted liberty into slavery, it became necessary to abolish all such ceremonies—just as today every faithful pastor will do away with that rage of rules (*tumultus caerimoniales*), wherever these become traps of souls and scandalous obstacles to genuine piety.[21]

Yet in 1519 'they still are' centers of inspiration: the monastic life is still functional and functioning.

The Prophet of the Last Days

In 1521 the time of that 'Faithful Pastor' has come. Vows have to be abolished because they prove not to be "based on the Word of God," but rather (*immo*: to the contrary) "militate against the Word of God."[22] *De votis monasticis* is so rich that Luther scholars understandably had their hands full with summarizing its contents. However, if we want to do more than list Luther's positions, we must discover what exactly made Luther change his mind on such an existential issue. In general terms, we know that it occurred sometime during those two decisive years of growing confrontation between the end of 1519 and November 1521 when *De votis monasticis* was committed to paper on the Wartburg. Fortunately, we can be far more precise, as a matter of fact, quite definite. Though there may well have been a variety of factors unbeknownst to him, or us, for Luther one is of overriding significance, the ticking clock of eschatological urgency. Once this is clear, we can narrow down the

[21] "Nam quid sunt ipsa quoque caritatis et misercordiae opera quam liberae quaedam caerimoniae, cum et ipsa sint externa et corporalia? Et veteris legis caerimoniae itidem erant utilissimae exercitationes verae et liberae pietatis. At ubi coeperunt perversitatis studio in libertatis iniuriam usurpari, et earum praetextu vera pietas exstingui, iamque pro libertate servitus tyrannisaret, opus erat, ut universae tollerentur, sicut et nunc quoque pastorum piae sollicitudinis esset tumultus caerimoniales abrogare, ubi nonnisi in laqueos animarum et in offendicula liberae pietatis grassantur." AWA 2.50, 11-18.

[22] WA 8.578, 4f. For Luther's characteristic use of 'immo,' see my article "'Immo'. Luthers reformatorische Entdeckungen im Spiegel der Rhetorik," in *Lutheriana. Zum 500. Geburtstag Martin Luthers von den Mitarbeitern der Weimarer Ausgabe*, ed. Gerhard Hammer and Karl-Heinz zur Mühlen, AWA 5 (Cologne: Böhlau, 1984), 17-38.

time this occurred to him: it is towards the end of February 1520 that Luther had become acutely aware of living in these Last Days.[23]

Reformation scholars interested in establishing Luther as the Father of international Protestantism have highlighted the message of religious and social emancipation from the medieval two-tiered morality; for the common folk, the general standard of Christian decency (*praecepta*) sufficed, whereas those under vows, the heroic counsels (*consilia*) of the Sermon on the Mount obeyed the call to 'turn one's cheek' and 'go the extra mile' (Matt. 5:39; 42). According to this reasoning, Luther provided modern times with its emancipated awareness of prime responsibility to a society in need, the world outside the monastic walls; thus Luther lifted medieval Christianity over the threshold to 'modern times.' De facto, however, Luther does not live on the eve of modern times but at the End of Time.[24] With

[23] On 24 February 1520, Luther shared with his intimate friend, Georg Spalatin (†1545), a breathtaking, chilling thought. He had just completed reading the annotated edition (Mainz, n.d. [1520]) by the poet laureate Ulrich of Hutten (†1523) of Lorenzo Valla's 1440 treatise (distributed originally in Italy in just a few manuscript copies) in which the *Donation of Constantine* was unmasked as forgery. At that point a horrifying awareness dawned on him: "I am deeply filled with anxiety that there is hardly any reason to doubt that the Pope is really the 'Antichrist' so widely expected": "Deus bone, quante seu tenebre seu nequitie Romanensium & quod in Dei iuditio mireris per tot secula non modo durasse, Sed etiam prevaluisse ac inter decretales relata esse. tam Impura tam crassa tam impudentia mendacia inque fidei articulorum (nequid monstrosissimi monstri desit) vicem successisse. Ego sic angor, ut prope non dubitem papam esse proprie Antichristum illum, quem vulgata opinione expectat mundus." WABr 2.48, 22-49, 28 (no. 257).

Though Luther refers explicitly only to Valla, the Hutten edition entitled *De Donatione Constantini quid veri habeat*, s.l., s.a., also contained the critique advanced by Nicolas of Cusa and Antonius of Florence; cf. *Ulrichi Hutteni Equitis Germani Opera quae reperiri potverunt omnia*, ed. Eduardus Böcking; Ulrichs von Hutten Schriften, 1 (Leipzig: B.G. Teubner, 1859), 18*. Cf. WA 50.65f. Whereas Böcking surmises ("wie ich glaube"; ibid.) that the year of publication is early 1518 in Mainz, the WA-editor can establish—on the basis of the Adelmann correspondence—that the first edition (second edition, 1522) is to be set in 'Anfang, 1520.' See the quoted letter no. 257, WABr 2.51, n. 14.

[24] For the origins of the systematic neglect of Luther's realistic eschatology, see below note 68. For the presentation of Luther as harbinger of modernity, see B. Moeller, "Die frühe Reformation in Deutschland als neues Mönchtum" (see above note 13), 89f. As concerns Moeller's related suggestion that the Reformation can be characterized as a new form of monasticism ("neues Mönchtum"; ibid. 88) based on the contention that Protestantism in all its variances would display 'congregational features' ("in jeder seiner Spielarten ein kongregationalistischer Zug zu eigen" ist; ibid. 89), it is relevant to recall the sustained, pan-European effort of the mendicant orders to challenge the parish, its cohesion and privileges. Whereas in Moeller's view of fifteenth century piety there is hardly any place for heresy, the escalation of the public debate about the inquisitional cases brought against John of Wesel, Wessel

extreme urgency the reformer jumps to the defense of the Church Catholic, now caught 'in these Last Days' in the Babylonian cage, enslaved and suffocating under the yoke of justification by works. This new urgency is for Luther documented by the fact that vows prove to be devastating weapons of the Devil assailing Church and society at the End of Time. He perverts the best we have, our highest aspirations, fooling us with the spectre of his 'Highway to Heaven.'

The preface to his father Johannes climaxes in the statement that "the Day of the Lord is near."[25] In the body of his manifest, this message is brought home by going right to the top, to the Apostles St. Paul and St. Peter. St. Paul is invoked to show that we live in 'dangerous times' (*periculosa tempora*: 2 Tim. 3:1).[26] St. Peter is the

Gansfort and Johannes Reuchlin—not to mention Martin Luther—feeds on the constantly fermenting tension between 'fratres' and 'curati'; cf. "Luther and the *Via Moderna*," see esp. n. 71. See the ample evidence presented in a rich scholarly tradition reaching from Luzian Pfleger (*Die elsässische Pfarrei. Ihre Entstehung und Entwicklung. Ein Beitrag zur kirchlichen Rechts- und Kulturgeschichte*, Forschungen zur Kirchengeschichte des Elsaß, 3 (Strasbourg: Gesellschaft für Elsässische Kirchengeschichte, 1936), esp. 146-79) through Wolfgang Günter's careful 'Einleitung' to Johannes Staupitz' *Decisio quaestionis de audentia missae* (1500). Herein this mendicant breaks ranks by defending the rights of the parish priest, only to be attacked by Caspar Schatzgeyer O.F.M. (†1527), later a vocal opponent of Luther; see Staupitz, *Sämtliche Schriften*, 5 [above note 19], 5-8.

Though uncomfortable with—and indeed, apologizing for—Luther's identification of the papacy with the Antichrist, Bernhard Lohse's impressive grasp of the morphology of Luther's thought allowed him to highlight the central role of the Last Judgment, so that at least the end of the rule of the Antichrist is done full justice: Lohse, *Luthers Theologie in ihrer historishen Entwicklung und in ihrem systematischen Zusammenhang* (Göttingen: Vandenhoeck & Ruprecht, 1995), 276; cf. 345f.

For further literature, see the excellent survey by Willem van 't Spijker in *Eschatologie. Handboek over de christelijke Toekomstverwachting*, ed. W. van 't Spijker (Kampen: De Groot Goudriaan, 1999), 201-42; cf. the essay on the eschatology of the 'Zestiende-eeuwse Radicalen' by Willem Balke, ibid. 243-58.

[25] "Confido enim instare diem illum ..." *De votis monasticis iudicium*; Preface addressed to his father from the Wartburg ('ex eremo'), 21 November 1521; WA 8.576, 23. For the popular impact of this Latin treatise-for-the-well-trained, particularly through the elaboration in the German Epiphanias-sermon published in the sought-after Christmaspostille, see the well-documented essay of Hans-Christoph Rublack, "Zur Rezeption von Luthers De votis monasticis iudicium," in *Reformation und Revolution. Beiträge zum politischen Wandel und den sozialen Kräften am Beginn der Neuzeit. Festschrift für Rainer Wohlfeil zum 60. Geburtstag*, ed. Rainer Postel and Franklin Kopitzsch (Stuttgart: Steiner, 1989), 224-37.

[26] "O vere tempora periculosa, de quibus Paulus praedixit. Nunc vero, cum votum et institutum suum in hoc verbum dei: 'Vovete et reddite,' fundent, ego pronuncio, morem istum dispensandi esse impium, et perditionis et operationis errorem. Vel eo tandem cogam, ut vota omnia prohibita et libera esse evincam, quod ut plenius et copiosius faciam, videamus primum causas levissimae suae

prophet forecasting the horrible chaos to come in the Last Days (*in novissimis diebus*: 2 Peter 3:3); in the End Time we will be misled by 'deceivers' (*illusores*) who gut the Gospel.[27] Whereas Luther had long since identified Aristotle as the deceiver (*illusor*), the perverter of scholastic theology,[28] now this deception has come to encompass all the diabolical forces which subvert Christian freedom and suppress the Gospel. There is no time to be lost: the Good Pastor is to be the prophet of the End Time. The dialectic of 1519, softened by the 'not yet' (*adhuc*), has grown into the clarion call for full mobilization and has become the platform for resistance.[29] St. Peter's and St. Paul's forecast of the demonic threat 'in these Last Days' dawned upon him in a first horror by February 1520 and is spelled out in November 1521. Luther wrote this manifesto in Latin and initially reached only the educated elite; yet even a mediocre Latinist was bound to be captivated by the power of his passionate prose.[30]

dispensationis in aliis partibus regulae et rigoris crudelis in retinendae castitatis voto." WA 8.635, 15-21. Cf. the discourse on 2 Tim. 3:1-9 in the German *Weihnachtspostille*, wherein the vices and problems of the clergy are listed from the pope down to the parish priests. The main thrust is less anti-clerical than anti-Roman, anti-mendicant and critical of Cathedral chapters. Throughout, though only until 1540 (see below note 68), the meaning of 2 Tim. 3 is interpreted in the context of the End Time, 'in novissimis diebus': "Ich meyne, S. Paulus hatt alhie keyn blat fur den mund genommen und gleych mit fingern auff unser geystliche herrnn und Herodis heyligis gesind zeyget. Ist doch keyn buchstab hie gesetzt, den nitt yderman sihet offentlich ym geystlichen stand weldigen ... Drumb mussen wyr den reychen text Pauli eyn wenig bedencken und eben ansehen, das wyr den Herodem recht wol erkennen." WA 10 I.1.634, 20-635, 7. That is, "... syn [Paul's] wort sind klar und dringen auff das platten- unnd kappenvolck, auff das geystliche regiment." Ibid., 635, 13f. "Wo ist geystlich leben, gottisdienst, heylige stend, denn bey den stifften und klostern? Item, das er sagt, sie lauffen durch die hewßer und furen die weyber gefangen und leren sie ymer, ist yhe klerlich von den lerern und predigern gesagt, ßondern von den bettellorden und landleuffernn. Item, das sie der warheytt widerstehen, wie Jannes und Mambres Mosi ..." Ibid., 635, 17-21. The extensive application of 2 Tim. 3 in the *Weihnachtspostille* presents the abomination of the Mass as the climax of the millennial horrors: "Ich acht, das solcher mißprauch des hohen sacraments dißem stand halten ist, als dem ergisten, vorderblichsten und grewlichsten, der auff erden komen ist, und unter den boßen der grossist und letzt seyn wirtt." Ibid., 706, 20-22.

[27] "Et Petrus: 'Venient in novissimis diebus, in deceptione illusores, secundum propria desideria ambulantes.'" WA 8.644, 1-3.

[28] See above note 3.

[29] WA 8.635, 15-18; cf. above note 26.

[30] We can identify one of those very first readers of the Latin original of *De votis monasticis*. Thanks to a 1540 transcript of Luther's Table Talk by Johannes Mathesius, we learn that 'Prince Frederick,' as Luther vividly recalled, read 'the whole treatise immediately upon receipt throughout the night so assiduously that he was knocked out for two days': "... nam meum librum de votis legit per totam

Notwithstanding all innovation, we should not overlook that for Luther there is still the possibility of a genuine evangelical monastic life—he himself would stay on for another three years. Provided the conscience is free from seeking gain before God, one can embrace the vows. It is to be absolutely clear, however, that the monastic life is in no sense a higher state than any secular profession. And as soon as Christian love (*charitas*) calls to duties outside the monastic walls, "you would commit a grave sin if you would cling to your vows."[31] It can indeed be a conscientious decision to stay or to enter the monastery for schooling and discipline, in keeping with the original foundation of the monasteries. However, to be certain that one enters—

noctem, ita ut biduum esset infirmus." WAT 4.624, 19f. (no. 5034). The Elector's command of Latin was more than rusty, fair and usable, though not displaying any Humanist splendor; see Ingetraut Ludolphy, *Friedrich der Weise. Kurfürst von Sachsen 1463-1525* (Göttingen: Vandenhoeck & Ruprecht, 1984), 46. In contrast with most other German 'princes' of his time, the Elector could therefore grasp forthwith (*statim*) what 'evangelical freedom' implied for the reformer's appearance in the public forum, sending Luther a fine piece of cloth for a new robe: for once the Elector thought faster than Luther could act.

Frederick the Wise (†1525) continued to enact the traditional Saxon policy of support for the conciliar program of reformation 'in head and members' by seizing initiative to reorder Church and society, consistently favoring the growth of observance in the O.E.S.A. For this strategy as well as its significance for the state of the German Empire on the eve of the Reformation, see the documentation provided by Manfred Schulze, *Fürsten und Reformation. Geistliche Reformpolitik weltlicher Fürsten vor der Reformation*, Spätmittelalter und Reformation, Neue Reihe, 2 (Tübingen: Mohr Siebeck, 1991).

[31] "Ita si voveas religionem, ut cum hominibus eiusmodi vivas ea conscientia, ut nihil hinc commodi vel incommodi petas apud deum, sed quod vel casus hoc vitae genus obtulerit amplectendum vel ita visum tibi sit vivere, nihilo te meliorem hinc arbitratus eo, qui vel uxorem duxerit vel agriculturam apprehenderit, neque male voves neque male vivis quantum ad voti rationem attinet. Nam quo casu charitas exigat cadere votum, non sine peccato in voto pertinax fueris, ut dicemus." WA 8.610, 5-12. Cf. "Er spricht [2 Tim. 3:5]: 'hutte dich und meyde dieselbigen', darynn er uns warnett, das wyr uns fur dem geystlichen regiment und stand fursehen, und gibt urlaub, ia gepeutt eraußtzulauffen, wer auff yhre weyße drynnen ist, wie wyr horen werden, sperret alle stifft und klöster auff, macht pfaffen unnd munche loß. Wie auch Christus Matt. 24 [:23, 26]: man soll von yhn flehen unnd sie meyden." Turning to 2 Tim. 3:6-7: "Wer mag das anders deutten, denn auff die bettelorden, wilch der Apostel hie klerlich vorsehenn hatt, sie sind es yhe, die durch die hewßer lauffen." WA 10 I.1.662, 5-15. Cf. "O herrgott, wie sicher blind ist die wellt! Wie ists vorkeret, die wellt ist izt geystlich, die geystlichen sind die wellt. Wie starck ist des Endchrists regiment!" Ibid., 688, 11-13. At the same time evangelical monasticism is still an option: "Darumb allen den tzu ratten ist, das sie platten und kappen, stifft unnd kloster lassen und auffhoren yhr gelubd zu hallten, odder fahen von newes an, ynn Christlichem glawben unnd meynung tzu geloben solchs leben." Ibid., 687, 20-23.

or stays—without ulterior motives, is a tall order. As a matter of fact, "in these dangerous times," it is extremely risky to draw the right demarcation line.[32] Yet one thing should be clear to everyone: by their very nature vows are temporary. Beware—be prepared! *To bind for life is to blind for life.*

Open those Gates: Sola fide

In 1528, Luther's gestation process is definitely completed. The one manuscript containing fifteen German theses about the monastic life ("*Das Closter leben unchristlich sey*") carries as its date '1528' and presents itself as an extract from *De votis monasticis*. The title of the three early prints of 1531 suggests that someone else may have drawn up this list of fifteen propositions, but—as the editor properly points out—the 1528 theses contain too many fresh formulations to think in terms of a mere scribal extract. The occasion may well have been a widely broadcast event, the dramatic decision of Duchess Ursula of Münsterberg to leave her St. Magdalen Cloister in Freiberg on 6 October 1528—Luther wrote a postscript to her *Apologia pro vita sua*.[33]

Yet even if written to legitimize escape or 'Klosterflucht,' to use that loaded term for the trek out of the monastery into the world, it is clear that Luther not only reinterpreted his own vows but also abandoned the 'not yet' (*adhuc*) of 1519; the evangelical option of risking the monastic life by entering or staying in good conscience

[32] "Rursum fieri potest ut aliqui spiritu fidei haec apprehendant citra scandalum at foeliciter impleant, ut de sanctis credimus. Et cum hos non liceat damnare nec illos laudare, fit ut periculosa sint omnia et nihil possit certo definiri." WA 8.652, 23-26. Cf. "Ach gott, hymlischer vatter, deyneß grewlichen tzornß und schrecklichen gerichts ubir die welt yn dißen ferlichen, elenden zeytten, und leyder das niemandt erkennen will." WA 10 I.1.640, 1-3.

The possibility of an evangelical monastic life is articulated in the section of the *Weihnachtspostille* suppressed in 1540 (see below note 68): "... auff das wyr allen iungen munchen und nonnen mugen weyber und menner geben und widerumb weltlich machen, wo es yhn nott ist und nit halten konnen mit gutem gewissen und gottlichem gefallen und willen, damit wyr die klöster widderumb bringen ynn yhr allt, erst, ursprunglich reformacion und weßen, das sie seyen Christlich schulen, darynnen man die knaben und meydlin lere tzucht, ehre und den glawben, darnach sie drynnen mugen frey bleyben biß ynn den todt, oder wie lang sie wollen, und gott hatt sie auch nie anders angesehen noch gewolt." Ibid., 700, 13-20.

[33] For the introduction to the fifteen theses, see WA 59.93-103; 93f. Luther's postscript for the 'Apology' of Duchess Ursula, WA 26.623-25.

has been left behind as well. All the arguments of *De votis monasticis* are now refashioned into fifteen sharp hammer-blows against the monastic life. In one formidable summary of his entire position, Luther throws the whole weight of the doctrine of justification against the vows; contrary to faith "they rely more on the quality of their life than on Christ."[34]

The year 1521, then, did not bring the surgical incision for which it is all too readily acclaimed. We encounter Luther in *De votis monasticis* upon a path of clarification on which he has made enormous strides—its ongoing trajectory, however, is still shrouded in the expected yet unpredictable clouds of the End Time. The dramatization of the 'clear cut,' even when born out of admiration, does not enlarge but diminishes the stature of such a towering but real historical person groping for answers before acting on his convictions. Throughout most of 1524, three years after his frontal assault on the vows, Luther was not yet ready for what should have been a triumphant ritual, a festive farewell to arms. Notwithstanding his growing convictions, Luther was not prepared to shed his cowl, not for a long time; not until the Sunday service on 9 October 1524 did he appear for the first time in public without his Augustinian robes—a week later never to don them again.[35]

Martin Brecht is prepared to accept Luther's explanation that he had retained his cowl 'out of consideration for the weak.'[36] This may well be part of the reason; the other part Luther later recalls: He found it 'difficult to shed his habit' (*difficulter cucullam meam deposui*).[37] This hovering hesitation about such a momentous step is all the more credible in view of Luther's other testimony that he had entered the order not for gain, but for his soul's sake. For twenty years, he had been a highly motivated friar, living "in every respect conscientiously in keeping with our *Constitutiones*" (*salutis meae causa vovebam et rigidissime servabam nostra statuta*).[38]

[34] "Das sie den wercken gerechtigkeit für Got geben wider den glauben und auff ihr leben sich verlassen mehr den auff Christum. Das sie wider die Christliche freyheit sünde und gewissen machen yn speise, kleider, stet, wercken, da keine für Got sind." WA 59.101, 10-13.

[35] See the concise description by Martin Brecht, *Martin Luther, vol. 2: Ordnung und Abgrenzung der Reformation 1521-1532* (Stuttgart: Calwer Verlag, 1986), 99 with n. 2 on p. 453.

[36] Ibid.

[37] WAT 5.657, 19f. (no. 6430).

[38] WAT 5.303, 16f. (no. 4414); for these 'statuta,' see above note 19.

The correct understanding of Luther's crucial May 1524 letter to Wolfgang Capito, the Strasbourg reformer, and indirectly to Martin Bucer, proves to be more complex than the lucid Latin would lead one to expect. On first sight the central clause does give verbatim support to the interpretation that Luther, though long clear about the 'right attitude' in his own mind, retained the cowl out of pastoral concern that the 'weak' could be scandalized. However, the apologetic context of this statement should not be overlooked. Realizing that he must seem 'slow' in comparison with the quickly evolving, robust evangelical movement in southern Germany, Luther has to explain the 'two-speed' advance of the Reformation, so much faster abroad and, when measured in terms of the issue of the vows, obviously strikingly successful in Strasbourg. This is the context for his admission: "We have long enough catered to the weak." Luther goes on to agree that it is time for action: "Accordingly, even I finally start to stop wearing my cowl. I kept it on to respect the weak and ridicule the Pope."[39] Only thereafter follows the phrase that will not have convinced any of the Southern Reformers—nor should it mesmerize his modern interpreters. The very choice of words 'even I myself' (*et ego*) and 'finally' (*tandem*) alerts us to the fact that Luther belonged to those weak ones himself. Even at this late date, it took him another half year to make good his intention "to stop wearing my cowl" in public.

This conclusion removes the reformer from the high pedestal of the 'neutral' umpire; instead it returns him to the fold of existential participants in a fast-moving series of contingent, constantly surprising historical events. Ultimately, far more important than the invocation of the 'weak' is Luther's ridiculing of the Pope. Capito and Bucer will not have been even less impressed by this explanation. They were already well on the way to Protestantism, intent on organizing a new church combating the grasp of a medieval Antichrist, blocking access to modern times. The Prophet of the End Time is convinced that only the Gospel can slacken the hold of the Evil One; at stake is the defense of Catholicism—the mightiest weapon is the only one left, the irony of truth.

[39] "Nam et ego incipiam tandem etiam cucullum reiicere, quem ad sustentationem infirmorum et ad ludibrium pape hactenus retinui." WABr 3.299, 23-25 (no. 748). For the 'amazing' (*mirifice*) nature of the events sparking off *De votis monasticis*, see below note 66.

3. The Holy Highway: From St. Antony to St. Francis

What makes the Last Days so dangerous is the total loss of moral orientation and the inversion of all values. A particularly pernicious case in point is the exploitation of the intimate connection between 'saint' and 'monk' in exemplary persons such as St. Anthony (†356), St. Bernard (†1153) and above all St. Francis (†1226). Their very lives are constantly used to prove that God himself legitimized monastic vows and approved of their path to perfection. The shift from 1519 to 1521 could not be achieved without scaling a formidable barrier, the power of precedent set by those great saints who had written Rules and successfully established the mighty, omnipresent Orders.

The easy part was the acknowledgment of the value of monastic houses as 'gymnasia for the youth.' In 1519, Luther had articulated his appreciation of this important pedagogical and societal function; his respect for the 'original intention' with its programmatic potential is fully retained in 1521. Luther's own order had cherished this educational role (*docere verbo et exemplo*), today regarded as a characteristic of the Praemonstratensian Renaissance during the extended incubation period of the Augustinian Hermits; it was to become an essential part of the dowry for their Great Union, approved in 1258.[40] Accordingly, the monastery as a center of learning and discipline might need reform but could be retained without any need for concession or compromise.

[40] For 1519, see above note 19. Far from being omitted in 1521, the educational function of monasticism is elaborated and presented as *conditio sine qua non* for its genuine Christian character exemplified by the *Vitas Patrum*—in the various Luther editions consulted not identified as the influential Collection of Saints' Lives. "Proinde ego ausim pronunciare cum fiducia: Nisi monastica obedientia voveatur et servetur temporaliter tanquam rudimentum ad Christianam et Evangelicam obedientiam, ut iuvenilis aetas in ea exercitata discat sic omnibus in omnibus cedere, sicut per votum cedit suo maiori in monasterio in aliquibus, quemadmodum in Vitis Patrum quaedam etiam probant exempla, esse plane impiam et mox deserendam. Sic et puerorum paupertas est, ne res administrent, quo discant frugales esse qui propter aetatem prodigi et dissoluti fierent, si statim in manu eorum res traderentur." WA 8.646, 39-647, 6. For the Praemonstratensian ideal of teaching as the combination of the *vita contemplativa* and the *vita activa*, see Caroline Walker Bynum, *Docere verbo et exemplo. An Aspect of Twelfth-Century Spirituality*, Harvard Theological Studies, 31 (Missoula, Mont.: Scholars Press, 1979); quoted by Saak, "The Creation of Augustinian Identity in the Later Middle Ages," (see above note 19), 118.

The 'Holy Fathers,' the *sancti* who had established rules and lived accordingly, were a problem of quite a different dimension—and in 1521 Luther had to come to terms with this formidable obstacle. He himself was brought up in a religious world saturated with the saints' lives, the *Vitas Patrum* and the *Legenda Aurea* (1260); his own order had extended these two rich resources of saintly lore with the stories of St. Augustine's miracles, performed by their 'Pater Noster,' as well as the Great Deeds of the later 'sons of St. Augustine,' forming together the true City of God. In Luther's own *studium* in Erfurt, Jordan of Quedlinburg (†1380) had completed his *Lives of the Brothers* (*Liber Vitasfratrum,* 1357), ready to be recited by a reader (*lectio*) during the silent meals in the refectory.[41] While studying his Bible, Luther was daily surrounded by that living voice of the Gospel, the cloud of witnesses stretching from the Desert Fathers to 'modern times,' all of them in unison proclaiming the high road to perfection. Cracking the code of the Saints was therefore no mean task. In 1521 Luther had to labor page after page to solve the riddle of the Rule, trying to come to terms with the evident power of the Spirit operative on that mighty monastic trajectory from St. Anthony to St. Francis and his beloved Vicar General, John of Staupitz O.E.S.A. (†1524), the self-confessed Forerunner of the Gospel (*precursor evangelii*)—perhaps not mentioned at this time because he had already stepped down as Vicar General at the 1520 chapter meeting in Eisleben (St. Augustine's Day, 28 August 1520).[42]

The red line of *De votis monasticis*, the theme to which Luther returns ever anew, is the miraculous operation of the Spirit calling forth saints to live the life of the Gospel. Accordingly, he chooses as his point of departure St. Anthony, the very Father of all monks and founder of the monastic life. St. Anthony withdrew from the world

[41] For the function of the *Vitasfratrum* as the Augustinians' *Legenda aurea*, see Saak,"The Creation of Augustinian Identity in the Later Middle Ages," (see above note 19), esp. 269-86. For the *lectio* in the refectorium, see the "Constitutiones," *Johann von Staupitz.Sämtliche Schriften*, (see above note 19), cap. 21, 12 along with editor's note 7.

[42] See the still most reliable reconstruction by Thedor Kolde, *Die deutsche Augustiner-Congregation und Johann von Staupitz. Ein Beitrag zur Ordens- und Reformationsgeschichte* (Gotha: Friedrich Andreas Perthes, 1879), 327f. Cf. my articles "Captivitas Babylonica: Die Kirchenkritik des Johann von Staupitz," *Reformatio et reformationes. Festschrift für Lothar Graf zu Dohna zum 65. Geburtstag*, ed. Andreas Mehl and Wolfgang Christian Schneider, THD-Schriftenreihe Wissenschaft und Technik, 47 (Darmstadt, 1989), 97-106; and "*Duplex misericordia*: Der Teufel und die Kirche in der Theologie des jungen Johann von Staupitz," *Festschrift für Martin Anton Schmidt zum 70. Geburtstag*, Theologische Zeitschrift, 45 (1989), 231-43.

and lived a spotless life in keeping with the Gospel (*iuxta formam Evangelii*; WA 8.578, 20).[43] His successors, however, turned the Gospel into the law and insisted on a Rule instead of obeying the command "listen to Christ" (cf. Matt. 17:5). In a next step Luther then turned to St. Francis, that truly great man deeply driven by the Spirit (*vir admirabilis et spiritu ferventissimus*). Citing the Rule confirmed in 1223, Luther points out that St. Francis wanted no rule other than the Gospel.[44]

By deciding to give nevertheless his own Rule to the *minores*, he made a human error; after all, a Franciscan friar cannot pledge more than what he already vowed in his Baptism, namely the Gospel (*nempe Evangelium*). If then their Rule is declared to be the Gospel, and if following this Gospel is claimed as typically Franciscan, what else do they say than that only the Franciscan friars are Christians![45] The consequent loss of Christian liberty is pernicious, and particularly so in the case of the Observant Franciscans. For this group Luther creates the special derogatory term 'super-Franciscans' (*Franciscanissimi*). Two years earlier he had already debated them in a dramatic Wittenberg disputation;[46] now he completely cuts the umbilical cord by anathematizing the Observants in no uncertain terms: "No one is today less like St. Francis!"[47]

[43] For the momentous pilgrimage of Staupitz from Eisleben (O.E.S.A.) to Salzburg (ultimately O.S.B.) as well as the continuity in Staupitz' theological position, see Johann von Staupitz, *Sämtliche Schriften. Abhandlungen, Predigten, Zeugnisse*, ed. Lothar Graf zu Dohna and Richard Wetzel, vol. 2: *Lateinische Schriften* II: *Libellus de exsecutione aeternae praedestinationis*, ed. Lother Graf zu Dohna and Richard Wetzel, Spätmittelalter und Reformation. Texte und Untersuchungen, 14 (Berlin: de Gruyter, 1979) 8f. with notes 30f. Cf. Lothar Graf zu Dohna in his 'Einleitung' to the *Consultatio super Confessione Fratris Stephani Agricolae*, in vol. 5 (see above note 19).

[44] The formulation in the Franciscan Rule 'sanctum Evangelium observare' is rendered by Luther as: "Regulam suam esse Evangelium Ihesu Cristi." WA 8.579, 26f.

[45] WA 8.380, 13-15.

[46] The point of departure of the amazing, recently discovered Disputation of 4 October 1519 (between representatives of the Saxon chapter of the Franciscan reformed conventuals, that is, the 'Martinianer', convened in Wittenberg and members of the Wittenberg theological faculty) is the fundamental '*prima propositio*' advanced by the Franciscan side: "Gratiose decrevit divina benignitas senescente mundo novam quandam ecclesiae suae militantis militiam demonstrare." See the exemplary edition by Gerhard Hammer, "Franziskanerdisputation," WA 59.606-97; 678, 5-7. In the context of the ensuing debate about the stigmatization of St. Francis, Luther returns to the opening thesis: "Martinus [Luther] opposuit quaerens sic, an ideo haereticus sit, si non credat Francisci religionem a deo esse institutam." Ibid. 686, 29f. It is noteworthy that on the far-advanced age of the world (*senescente mundo*), Luther and his Franciscan opponents were in full agreement.

[47] WA 8.590, 18f.

In order to cope with St. Francis—as well as St. Bernard and St. Anthony before him—Luther invoked the precedent of Daniel in the Lion's Den (Daniel 6; cf. 3:19-23), imprisoned in the Babylonian pit of destruction; there the great saints survived by divine intervention (*miraculose*).[48] St. Francis and his fellow saints erred in claiming the Gospel for themselves; yet at the same time they were driven by such a power of the Spirit that "though they might not have possessed the Kingdom of God in word, they did in deed."[49] St. Bernard and many other great monks were so full of the Spirit that the poison of the vows could not touch them (*venenum hoc non nocuit*).[50]

[48] The monastic life is as risky as the Babylonian pit: "... in qua electi miraculose, ceu tres pueri in fornace, serventur." WA 8.586, 31f.

In his *Weihnachtspostille* Luther unfolds the 'Den' in a series of exempla: "Eyns haben sie, das sie auffwerffen: Es seyen heylige vetter ynn geystlichem stand geweßen. Aber dagegen sollt sie erschrecken, das Christus spricht, die außerweleten mugen vorfurett werden von yhn [Matt. 24:24; 2, 1 ff.], wie alhie die Magi von Herodes vorfurett wurden. Und der exempell viell mehr: die drey kinder Ananias, Azarias, Misael blieben ym fewroffen Babylonis, Naaman auß Syrien bleyb frum ym tempell des abtgotts alleyn. Joseph bleyb frum ynn Aegypto. Was soll ich sagen: sanct Hagnes bleyb keusch ym gemeynen frawenhawß, und die merterer blieben heylig yn kerkern, und noch teglich bleyben Christen frum, ym fleysch, ynn der wellt, mitten unter den teuffelln; *sollt er denn nitt auch Francis., Bernhard und yhr gleychen mitten ym yrthum behalten haben kunden, und ob [sie] mitunter geyrret hetten, widder erauß furen?* [author's italics] Er hatt fast keynen grossen heyligen on yrthum leben lassen, Mosen unnd Aaron und Mariam, David, Salomon, Ezechias und viel mehr hatt er lassen strauchlen, auff das yhe niemandt auff die blosse exempell der heyligen unnd werck on schrifft sich vorlassen sollt, aber wyr plumpen eynhynn, was wyr nur sehen und horen von heyligen, da fallen wyr auff und treffen gemeynicklich das, da sie als menschen geprechlich geyrret haben. Da muß denn der yrthum uns eyn grundliche warheytt seyn ..." WA 10 I.1.705, 21-706, 12.

God does not always intervene 'miraculose.' See in the *Weihnachtspostille*: "... der Bapst lest sie fliessen, brennen und martern, wie sie konnen, das ich acht, es sind die kinder, die dem fewrigen abgott Moloch ym volck Israel geopffertt und vorbrennet wurden." WA 10 I.1.693, 20-22.

[49] "Non enim in sermone, sed in virtute regnum dei habebant." WA 8.587, 39.

[50] "Atque demus, ut fide pura miraculose serveris vovens et vivens in votis, sicut Bernhardus et multi alii servati sunt, quibus propter fidem Christi, qua pleni erant, venenum hoc non nocuit." WA 8.600, 26-29. For Bernard of Clairvaux, see Erich Kleineidam, "Ursprung und Gegenstand der Theologie bei Bernhard von Clairvaux und Martin Luther," in *Dienst der Vermittlung. Festschrift zum 25jährigen Bestehen des philosophisch-theologischen Studiums im Priesterseminar Erfurt*, Erfurter Theologishe Studien, 37 (Leipzig: St. Benno Verlag, 1977), 221-47; Theo Bell, *Divus Bernhardus. Bernhard von Clairvaux in Martin Luthers Schriften*, Veröffentlichungen des Instituts für Europäische Geschichte Mainz. Abteilung für Religionsgeschichte, 148 (Mainz: P. von Zabern, 1993 [Dutch original, 1989]); Franz Posset, *St. Bernard's Influence on two Reformers: John von Staupitz and Martin Luther*, Cistercian Studies, 25 (1990), 175-87. Id. "Bernhard von Clairvauxs

In short, Luther does not question at all that "these saints lived *under* the vows;" his point is that "they did not live *out* of them."[51] They survived in the Lion's Den thanks to the miraculous intervention of God.

The imagery of the 'Babylonian Den' came readily to mind—for Luther and his readers. As one of the choice mnemonic devices in sermons, stained-glass windows, and catechetical instruction, the connection was obvious; the seven mortal sins corresponded to the seven temptations of Christ, with the seven sacraments ... and the seven lions in Daniel's Den. The life-context of 'the Friar in the Den' was crystal clear—the early humanists would be quick to call it *luce clarius*—as immediately understandable as a modern lampoon.[52] The 'prison in the den' set Luther free from his 'Holy Past'; thus empowered he could make a major step ahead on the winding Road to the Reformation—the Day of the Lord, the final survival of the Church Catholic. It was a step not easily taken. Even three years later, it was "with difficulty" (*difficulter*), or as put elsewhere in the Table Talk, "with pain in the heart" (*aegre*) that he shed his cowl. He himself had been a Friar in the Den and there discovered God's sustaining intervention, a place not easily erased from memory ... or ripped away like rags from the body.[53]

4. OPEN THE SCRIPTURES: *Sola Scriptura*

In three giant steps we have reached the end in tracking Luther's effort to tackle the wrenching question of the monastic vows well after the so-called Reformation Breakthrough. This does not mean that we have come to the end of unexpected findings in *De votis*

Sermone zur Weihnachts-, Fasten- und Osterzeit als Quellen Luthers," in *Lutherjahrbuch*, 61 (1994), 93-116; Id. *Pater Bernhardus: Martin Luther and Bernard of Clairvaux* (Kalamazoo: Cistercian Publications, 1999); Bernhard Lohse, "Luther und Bernhard von Clairvaux" in *Bernhard von Clairvaux. Rezeption und Wirkung im Mittelalter und in der Neuzeit*, ed. Kaspar Elm, Wolfenbütteler Mittelalter-Studien, 6 (Wies-baden:Harrassowitz, 1994), 271-301.

[51] "Non disputo, ut sancti vixerint sub instituto isto, sed de ipso instituto." WA 8.617, 27f.

[52] See Craig Hairline and Eddy Put, *A Bishop's Tale. Mathias Hovius among his Flock in Seventeenth-Century Flanders* (New Haven, Connecticut: Yale University Press, 2000), 10. For a critical assessment of relevant recent research, see Craig Hairline, "Official Religion—Popular Religion in Recent Historiography of the Catholic Reformation," *Archive for Reformation History* 81 (1990), 239-62.

[53] "Difficulter cucullam meam deposui." WAT 5.657, 19f. (no. 6430); cf. "... aegre et difficulter deposuisset habitum." WAT 4.303, 17f. (no. 4414). See above note 37.

monasticis, that rich, at once private and frank,[54] passionate and profound capstone on the Reformation writings of the previous year. Luther's campaign to open the monastic doors for service to the world 'outside' is the religious and social application of his discovery of the doctrine of justification by faith, the so-called formal principle of the Reformation. Yet in the execution of this task Luther comes at the same time to a redefinition of what has often been called the 'material principle' of the Reformation, Scripture alone (*sola scriptura*).

This theme forces us to return to our point of departure, Luther's quest for the 'Grammar of God.' In his effort to come to terms with such saintly heroes as St. Francis, Luther developed the narrative of 'the Friar in the Den.' Notwithstanding the 'poisonous' condition of the monastic life, St. Francis survived thanks to God's mighty intervention. All those impressive monks lived under extremely dangerous conditions—out of this den of evil God salvaged them miraculously (*in qua electi miraculose ... serventur*).[55] Though Christ neither taught nor lived the monastic life, He spoke and lived through His saints so powerfully (*mirabiliter*) that, though under the vows, they lived without vows.[56] The exceptional survival of these great saints cannot establish a precedent for the Christian life; they are extraordinary, living acts of God (*nam sanctos semper excipio in suis mirabilibus*).[57]

[54] "Ego ipse in me et multis aliis expertus sum, quam pacatus et quietus soleat esse Satan in primo anno sacerdocii et monachatus, ut nihil iucundius esse videatur castitate, sed hoc in tentationem et in laqueum insidiosissimus hostis facit, cui cooperantur insani monastici et annum probationis non solum non ex spiritu, sed neque ex re ipsa, verum ex calendario et numero dierum metiuntur, ut probent nihil sani neque pensi apud se esse, incedentes in rebus istis spiritualibus et periculosissimis ceu bruta (ut Petrus ait [II Peter 2:12]) irrationalia, naturaliter in mactationem genita." WA 8.660, 31-38. Cf. the striking frankness in the *Weihnachtspostille*: "... verleucke du nur nit, das du eyn mensch seyest, der fleysch und blutt hatt, laß darnach gott richten tzwisschen den Engelischen starcken hellten unnd dyr krancken, vorachten sunder! Ich hoff, ich sey tzo fernn kommen, das ich von gottis gnaden bleyben werd, wie ich bynn, wiewol ich noch nit byn ubirn berg und den keuschen hertzen mich nit traw tzuvorgleychen, were myr auch leydt, und gott wollt mich gnediglich dafur behutten." WA 10 I.1.707, 24-708, 4.

[55] WA 8.586, 30-32.

[56] "... licet in sanctis sub votorum instituto captivis operatus sit et locutus mirabiliter sine votis." WA 8.656, 26-27.

[57] WA 8.660, 6. To put this in the vocabulary of the *via moderna* so familiar to him, Luther argues that the exceptional intervention of God *de potentia absoluta* does not de-legitimize the established order (lex stans*) de potentia ordinata*. See my essay "Luther and the *Via Moderna*: The Philosophical Backdrop of the Reformation Breakthrough" in the *The Journal of Ecclesiastical History*, forthcoming (2001).

The three vows do not lead to a higher but to a hindered Christian life. As far as *poverty* is concerned, here applies the proverb "desperation makes the monk."[58] The vow of *obedience*, already addressed in the Latin Preface to father Hans, is in the German vernacular

[58] "Es hat die wahrheit das sprichwort erfunden: vortzweyffeln macht eyn munch; denn wieviel ist yhr, die nit alleyn darumb geystlich werden, das sie ßorgen, sie mugen sich nit erneeren oder musten mit erbeyt und muhe sich erneeren?" WA 10 I.1.639, 6-9; cf. WA 10 III.229, 20 (Sermon 1522); WA 29.65, 12f. (Sermon 1529); WA 32.319, 35 (Sermon 1530/32). One year earlier Luther had invoked this proverb in a comparatively milder version, confirming our findings as to the stage Luther reached in 1520 (*adhuc*—'das mehrer teyl'—not all monks—de-emphasizing the sole focus on the cowl by the inclusion of the parish priests): "Ich befind das sprichwort warhafftig, das vorzweyffeln machet das mehrer teyl munch unnd pfaffen: drumb gaht und staht es auch, wie wir sehen." *An den christlichen Adel deutscher Nation* (1520), WA 6.468, 5-7. For "Verzweiflung macht Münch," see *Deutsches Sprichwörter-Lexikon. Ein Hausschatz für das Deutsche Volk*, ed. Karl Friedrich Wilhelm Wander, vol. 4 (Darmstadt: Wissenschaftliche Buchgesellschaft, 1964 [Leipzig, 1876]), col. 1625.

Luther admired the wisdom of vernacular market-place proverbs as much as Erasmus treasured his classical *adagia*. Although a timeless favorite, this genre is particularly precious for the historian of late medieval and early modern mentality as a revealing form of communication. Proverbs can best be characterized as vivid caricatures transporting information in the abbreviated, suggestive form of modern cartoons or television-spots. It is interesting that in the Latin version our proverb has a wider societal scope, reflecting perhaps its urban-civic matrix: 'Desperation produces three M's: a Monk, a Medical aide, and a Military soldier' (*Desperatio facit tria 'M': Monachum, Medicum, Militem*); Wander, s.v. 'Verzweiflung.' In 'spotting' the monk Luther can employ a reductionist caricature because he has amply articulated the basis of his critique in assailing monasticism as the final and ultimate outgrowth of justification 'by works.'

At the same time we should touch on the other side of the coin, the mentality and response of those who read and pondered Luther, but decided to remain in their cloisters (for further literature, see my review article of Moeller, *Die frühe Reformation* [see above note 13], 483f.). Since the myth of the 'mass-movement' has tended to drown out the numerous decision makers 'on the other side,' it is pertinent to give voice to at least one eloquent and influential member of the opposition: Johann Justus Landsberg (1490-1539), a member of the Carthusian Order which, when compared with O.E.S.A. and O.F.M., proved strikingly impervious to Lutheran 'poison.' This younger contemporary of Luther entered the Cologne 'Carthuse' in 1509 and was a mighty voice in that crucial region which in the 1540's stood between the confessions. For background see Karl-Heinz zur Mühlen, the editor of the "Akten der Reichsreligionsgespräche" (in 1540-41, 1546, and 1557), "Die Edition der Akten und Berichte der Religionsgespräche von Hagenau und Worms 1540/41," in id., *Reformatorisches Profil. Studien zum Weg Martin Luthers und der Reformation*, ed. Johannes Brosseder and Athina Lexutt (Göttingen: Vandenhoeck & Ruprecht, 1995), 310-24.

In one of his many tracts and sermons dedicated to the monastic life, Landsberg provided a sober answer to the widely circulated critique of the 'vorzweiffelte munch':

extensively shown to undermine the cornerstone of societal cohesion by subverting the Fourth Commandment.[59] Yet the reformer still has to crack the emotionally and socially toughest question of all, the precarious issue of the perennial vow of *chastity*. Without ado Luther addresses a sexual taboo by invoking St. Paul (Romans 7:18ff) to argue that there is an indelible desire in the law-of-our-members militating against the law of the Spirit. St. Paul himself exemplifies that libido is forgiven and accepted by God as part of the life of

"Meministis ut olim ex Aegypto eduxerit Deus filios Israel, et quoties in veteri lege praeceperit, ut essent memores tanti beneficii. Idem facit Deus, quando hodie certos quosdam electos suos ex hoc seculo nequam vocat ad vitam monasticam quae sanctorum virorum testimonio velut quaedam paradisus terrestris est: esto quod quidam illic non bene vivant; quod nihil illi vitae derogat, quando etiam nemo propterea damnat matrimonium, quod multi sint adulteri ..."; "In solemnitate SS. Apostolorum Petri et Pauli," *D. Joannis Justi Lanspergii Cartusiani opera omnia. In quinque tomos distributa juxta exemplar Coloniense anni 1693 editio nova et emendata*, vol. 2 (Monsterolii: Typis Cartusiae Sanctae Mariae de Pratis, 1889), "Sermo secundus," 404-8; 405, cols. 1-2. John Frymire kindly called my attention to the impressive nineteenth-century edition of this widely read opponent of Lutheranism. For further literature on Landsberg (Landsberger), see Joseph Greven, *Die Kölner Kartause und die Anfänge der katholischen Reform in Deutschland*, ed. Wilhelm Neuß, Katholisches Leben und Kämpfen im Zeitalter der Glaubenspaltung, 6 (Münster i.W.: Aschendorff, 1935), 27-49; for Landsberg's writings, see ed. Wilbirgis Klaiber, *Katholische Kontroverstheologen und Reformer des 16. Jahrhunderts. Ein Werkverzeichnis*, Reformationsgeschichtliche Studien und Texte, 116 (Münster i.W.: Aschendorff, 1978), 164-66 (nos. 1753-1766). The Carthusians were well prepared to function as 'counter-elite' when the pivotal Cologne Archdiocese was kept in the Catholic camp after Emperor Charles V tipped the scales by conquering Guelders and Zutphen (1543). For the influence of the Cologne Carthusians, see Gérald Chaix, *Réforme et Contre-Réforme Catholiques: Recherches sur la Chartreuse de Cologne au XVI Siècle*, Analecta Cartusiana, 80 (Salzburg: 1981), 1:157-63, 175-202; and the lucid interpretation by Sigrun Haude, *In the Shadow of "Savage Wolves." Anabaptist Münster and the German Reformation during the 1530s*, Studies in Central European Histories (Boston: Humanities Press-Brill, 2000), 60-69.

[59] "Darumb sage ich: der Bapst nympt yhm fur auß lautterm frevel munch und nonnen auß den klosternn tzihen und hatt seyn nitt macht; Die eltern haben des macht und mugen yhr kind lassen drynnen odder erauß nehmen, wenn und wie sie wollen, odder wie sie sehen, das den kindern nutz ist." WA 10 I.1.641, 12-16. Cf. "... ßo mach nur nit viel disputirnß, gang frey hyn und tzeuch das kind auß dem kloster, auß kutten, auß blatten, und woreyn es geschlossen ist. Sihe nit an, wenn es hunderttausent gelubd than hette, und alle Bischoffe auff eynen hawffen dran gesegnet hetten! Deyn kind ist dyr befolhen von gott tzu regirn ..." Ibid., 640, 28-641, 4. For the growing emphasis on paternal authority and civic obedience in the later Middle Ages and early modern period, see Robert James Bast, *Honor Your Fathers. Catechisms and the Emergence of a Patriarchal Ideology in Germany 1400-1600*, Studies in Medieval and Reformation Thought, 63 (Leiden: Brill, 1997).

faith.[60] Hence it cannot be legitimate that a vow of chastity—which is after all a human invention and not part of the law of God—cannot be broken without the penalty of mortal sin.

Now Luther goes on to take a further, decisive step. As we know from the Book of Acts, during the 'Council of the Apostles' (Acts 15:6-30—the First Council of the Church) the Apostle Paul defended Peter's plea for baptizing Gentiles without circumcision by invoking the mighty acts of God, 'all the signs and miracles through which God had worked among the Gentiles' (Acts 15:12). Luther points out that St. Paul thus legitimized the revolutionary move to universalize mosaic Judaism by opening the doors of the Church with reference to God's miraculous mass conversion of Gentiles. Such disregard for the Law of Moses could not but appear to deviate from the Truth: "Against nearly the complete—and completely erring—earliest Church, Peter, Paul and Barnabas stood shoulder-to-shoulder in upholding the doctrine of freedom by appealing to the liberating acts of God."[61] They spoke up 'against everyone' (*adversus omnes*)—exactly the formula Luther had used to abjure scholastic theology four years earlier (1517).[62]

Then follows Luther's momentous conclusion: "From this we learn that in cases where there is no evidence of Scripture to appeal to, we should rely on certain works of God and accept them in place of the testimony of Scripture."[63] Luther had already touched on the

[60] "... propter fidem in spiritu repugnantem ignoscitur et non imputatur ..." WA 8.653, 30-32. Luther can be quite frank—amazingly frank as compared with our 'modern' times—about the application of these words to himself: WA 10 I.1.707, 24-708, 4; see above note 54. As compared to the medieval, consistently negative view of 'libido'—located in the 'lower', 'female' part of the soul—Luther's reevaluation has unexpected implications that call for further treatment.

[61] "Apostolus Paulus Act. xv. [15:12] ex operibus dei demonstravit libertatem Evangelicam, quod spiritus dabatur gentibus absque circuncisione et lege Mosi, licet tota ferme Ecclesia illa primitiva erronea conscientia contrarium sentiret, solus autem Petrus, Paulus et Barnabus autoritate divinorum operum, libertatis sententiam tulerunt et firmaverunt adversus omnes." WA 8.654, 5-9.

[62] "Contra omnes"; see the *Disputatio contra scholasticam theologiam* (see above note 5), 168, 10.

[63] "In qua re nos erudimur ut, ubi scripturae testimonia non suffragantur, illic certis operibus dei nos niti oportere et vice testimoniorum ea sequi." WA 8.654, 9-11.

We touch here upon an aspect of Luther's thought which proved to be highly explosive in 'the years of decision' at the end of the Weimar Republic and the rise of Adolf Hitler, when this 'God-given reversal' turned into a central plank in the platform of the *Deutsche Christen*. Divorced from a firm grasp of the biblical Luther of the Last Days, such extra-scriptural revelation can feed into a malleable doctrine of Providence which not only the Führer liked to invoke but which paved the path of such an influential Luther scholar as Emanuel Hirsch (†1972) to a Nazi ideology he would never foreswear. The key words signifying for him the mighty hand

issue of 'new revelation' in arguing that the vows had neither a basis in Holy Scripture nor the support of "any sign or miracle to establish that they carry divine approbation."[64] This time he invokes God's revealing intervention as explicit proof and decisive evidence. We do not want to overlook that such divine acts must be 'certain' in order to be understood and obeyed as if it were Scripture. Nevertheless, already during the Leipzig Disputation (1519), Luther had mentioned the possibility of a 'new revelation,' adding that any such revelation stood to be tested and approved (*nova et probata revelatio*).[65] This time he makes far more than a passing comment and argues his case against 'nearly the complete Church' on the basis, we must assume, of the amazing acts of God in the course of the Reformation, particularly mindful of the wave of friars flooding out from his monastery in Wittenberg.[66] This wave is not the heralded 'mass movement'

of Providence (*Gottes Lenkung*) are 'Volksschicksal' and 'nationale Wiedergeburt'—entailing the recovery of a 'Deutscher Volksordnung und Volksart' as the basis of a virtue designated by Hirsch as 'Deutsche Humanität,' not easy to translate yet soon afterwards spelled out throughout Europe. For the explicit appeal to extra-scriptural revelation, see Emanuel Hirsch, *Das kirchliche Wollen der Deutschen Christen* (Berlin-Steglitz: Evangelischer Preßverband für Deutschland e.V., 1933), 6. For his unmitigated, profound account ('Rechenschaft') after the end of the Thousand Years, see "Meine theologische Anfänge," *Freies Christentum* 3 (1951), Nummer 10, 2-4; "Mein Weg in die Wissenschaft (1911-16)," Nummer 11, 3-5; "Meine Wendejahre (1916-21)," Nummer 12, 3-6. Hirsch saw more clearly than his modern admirers that scholarship and politics are closely, in this case indissolubly intertwined. *Intiis obsta!* Beware! Luther's doctrine of justification is abused when invoked to justify a man, his thoughts, his generation, his country—or anyone, anywhere in space or time.

[64] "... [monastica institutio] nullum habet testimonium de scriptura, neque ullum signum aut prodigium quo sit coelitus comprobata ..." WA 8.617, 18f.

[65] WA 59.466, 1062.

[66] WABr 2.404, 6f. (no. 404); 22 November 1521, Luther (from the Wartburg) to Spalatin. Luther wrote his *De votis monasticis* in response to reports from Wittenberg that a considerable number of his *confratres* (probably as many as thirteen) had shed the cowl. The WA-editor quotes Kaspar Cruciger as reporting that monks 'everywhere' (*passim*) had left their monasteries; ibid., note 4. These must have seemed 'Mighty Acts' to Luther even while being so concerned (*timor*) about the right motivation that he took up his pen and started writing. The exclamation 'wonderfully' (*mirifice*, 'wunderbarlich') pertains to the progress of the Reformation in south Germany and the Alsace three years later, yet articulates exactly the surprised joy which Luther associates with the Mighty Acts of God: "Mirifice placent nuptie sacerdotorum et monachorum et monalium apud vos; placet appellatio maritorum adversus satane episcopum, placent vocati ad parochias." WABr 3.299, 16-18; (no. 748), to Capito and Bucer; cf. above note 39.

The 'mass movement' which Protestant historians later were to hail as the measure of Luther's success is exactly—and properly—what Luther was originally concerned about most. As he wrote on the High Feast of the Assumption of the Virgin Mary, a conscientious decision is not easily reached in a 'crowd' (*turba*). WABr 2.380, 33f.; 15 August 1521, Luther (from the Wartburg) to Spalatin.

unleashed by *De votis monasticis*, but the one preceding its conception and sparking off Luther's mind. Once again the Reformation movement is ahead of Luther's thinking.[67] And exactly this constellation leads to his stunning conclusion.

The parallel is too striking to ignore: just as St. Paul 'read' the mighty *immigration* of Gentiles into the Church, Luther is legitimized to 'read' the amazing *emigration* from the monastery—both are telling, liberating signs from God. His fear (*timor*) is that this constellation is not properly understood and that not all the implications have been fully grasped. One of these implications is that the canon is open in as much as the acts of God recorded in Scripture continue to take place and are to be reckoned with. Luther does not elaborate on the safeguards implied in the word 'certain,' but it cannot be wrong to say that such new guidance is to be accepted when in keeping with the acts of God as revealed in the Scriptures.

As it is well known, Luther's insistence on the testimony of Scripture forced his early opponents to de-emphasize scholastic authorities and increase their appeal to biblical passages. The obverse consequence in this dialectical relationship has not been pursued, namely that Luther, intent on unfolding the biblical basis of the 'Gospel,' came to de-emphasize the 'extracanonical' acts of God, so as not to undermine that crucial twofold function of *sola scriptura*, namely to interpret itself (*sui ipsius interpres*) *and* to test (*lex divina*) the validity of all ecclesiastical legislation. Doubtlessly, any appeal to 'new' acts of God (*vice testimoniorum*) could be all too readily invoked to legitimize either the 'inner word' of the Radical Reformation or the 'outer word' of the Counter Reformation.

What Luther came to de-emphasize, Lutherans erased and Protestants dismissed. In the very process of dissemination, the full scope of Luther's stance on the vows was severely curtailed. Whereas Luther's platform—far more daringly innovative than hitherto supposed—opened not only the gate of the monasteries but also the canon of the Scriptures, this second aspect of his *apertura* did not outlast his life-

[67] Luther took up his pen to write *De votis monasticis* on the basis of 'vague and not-verified rumors' that 'some of ours [Augustinian friars]' have shed their cowl (*vaga et incerta relatione didici deposuisse*): "I am filled with fear (*timui*) that their action might not have been taken with that profundity which makes for a firm decision (*forte non satis firma conscientia*). It is this grave concern which forced my hand to write this treatise ... (*Hic timor extorsit mihi eum libellum ...*) in the hope that they themselves take heart and those of goodwill are heartened;" cf. above note 39. WABr 2.404, 6-405, 11 (no. 441); 22 November 1521, Luther (from the Wartburg) to Spalatin. Cf. preceding note 66.

time. Luther's 1521 attack on the vows, originally addressed in Latin to sophisticated, well-trained *confratres*, was divulged to the German-speaking world in the vivid vernacular of the *Weihnachtspostille* (1522) and the *Predigten von Advent bis auf Ostern* (1525), by 1544 promulgated in more than twenty-three editions. In the Wittenberg editions of Hans Luft (1540) and Nikolaus Wolrab (1544), however, two crucial sections were omitted, namely the distinct discourse on the three vows—and precisely here the message of God's ongoing acts was embedded—as well as the extensive unfolding of Luther's vision of the End 'in these Last Days' (*in novissimis diebus*; 2 Tim. 3:1-9).[68] If it is correct to define a biblical prophet not as forecaster but as interpreter of divine intervention in history, we must conclude that, with these omissions, in one single and momentous blow, the powerful profile of Luther's prophetic eschatology *and* his prophetic extension of the canon was obfuscated, if not erased. In short, we witness here the emergence of an expurgated Luther that would shape his historical profile until our own day.

The Tridentine reception of the late medieval solution—namely that the Bible supports postcanonical or extracanonical doctrine implicitly (*implicite*) or silently (*silenter*)—would invoke the 'unwritten traditions' (*sine scripto traditiones*) as deserving 'equal respect with the Bible' (*pari pietatis affectu*). Thus the Council proclaimed a continuous oral tradition reaching *back* to Jesus and the apostles.[69] In

[68] In the wide vernacular popularization of *De votis* the horrors of the End Times are spelled out in the application of 2Tim. 3:1-9—only to be suppressed in 1540. Cf. "Das Evangelium am tage der heyligen drey künige. Matthei 2[:1-13]"; WA 10 I.1.555, 16-728, 24, *Weihnachtspostille*, 1522; then in *Predigten von Advent bis auf Ostern*, 1525ff., at least twenty-three editions by 1544. Together with the extensive discussion of the monastic vows (681, 24-709, 9) this section was *not* included in the Wittenberg editions by Hans Luft, 1540, and Nikolaus Wolrab, 1544. See WA 10 I.1.viii f; cf. above note 24.

It is noteworthy that there is evidence that in England the original intention of Luther was 'received.' See Frank Engehausen, "Luther und die Wunderzeichen: Eine englische Uebersetzung der Adventspostille im Jahre 1661," *ARG* 84 (1993): 276-88. In the context of his discussion of radical "Puritanismus," Engehausen refers to an English version (*Signs of Christ's coming, And Of the last day* ... London: n.p., 1561) of excerpts from Luther's *Adventspostille* (1522). It should be noted that this translation is not based on the purged German text, but on the unpurged Latin Basel edition of 1546: *Enarrationes seu Postillae ... maiores, in Lectiones, quae ex Evangelicis historijs*. This English version highlighted the sermon for 2. Advent, based on Luke 21: 21-33 (WA 10 I.2, 93-120).

[69] See Hubert Jedin, *Geschichte des Konzils von Trient*, vol. 2 (Freiburg: Herder Verlag, 1957), 61. Cf. my "*Quo vadis, Petre?* Tradition from Irenaeus to *Humani Generis*," in *The Dawn of the Reformation. Essays in Late Medieval and Early Reformation Thought* (Edinburgh: T.&T. Clark, 1986), esp. 286-89.

contrast, Luther looks *forward* accounting for the ongoing post-biblical acts of God.

Such extracurricular interventions of God do not convey a new 'Gospel' but provide marching orders for the Church Militant. They would be misunderstood—and will continue to be ignored—as long as we overlook the realistic eschatology at the very center of Luther's prophetic faith. Those new acts of God serve to protect the Church Catholic 'in these Last Days,' amidst the struggle for survival in the decisive battle between God and the Devil.

"ROCK" AND "RECOGNITION"

Martin Luther's Catholic Interpretation of "You are Peter and on this rock I will build my Church" (Matthew 16:18) and the Friendly Criticism from the Point of View of the "Hebrew Truth" by his Confrère, Caspar Amman, "Doctor of the Sacred Page"

FRANZ POSSET

The interpretation of Jesus' word to Simon in Matthew 16:18, "You are Peter ... " was at times quite controversial in the history of Christianity. Today, however, the controversy appears to be settled as the *Catechism of the Catholic Church* (1994) declares: "Moved by the grace of the Holy Spirit and drawn by the Father, we believe in Jesus and confess: 'You are the Christ, the Son of the living God.' On the rock of this faith confessed by St. Peter, Christ built his Church."[1] Differences over the interpretation of Matthew 16:18 climaxed in the early sixteenth century when scholars searched for the "gospel truth," *evangelica veritas*,[2] based upon the original biblical texts. Luther joined them in this endeavor, always searching for the "Christian evangelical truth."[3]

[1] Number 424. It is conspicuous that the verse, Matthew 16:18, does not play any role whatsoever in the contemporary Lutheran approach to papal primacy. No mention is made of it by Harding Meyer, "'Suprema auctoritas ideo ab omne errore immunis': The Lutheran Approach to Primacy," in James F. Puglisi, ed., *Petrine Ministry and the Unity of the Church. Toward a Patient and Fraternal Dialogue: A Symposium Celebrating the 100th Anniversary of the Foundation of the Society of the Atonement. Rome, December 4-6, 1997* (Collegeville, MN: The Liturgical Press, 1999), 15-34. We may ask with Geoffrey Wainwright: *Is the Reformation Over?* (The Père Marquette Lecture in Theology 2000; Milwaukee: Marquette University Press, 2000). That the Reformation is not over, is shown in the study of the history of the image of Peter in John's Gospel in the past one hundred years: Manfred Diefenbach, "Ökumenische Probleme infolge johanneischer Auslegung: eine wirkungs- und rezeptionsgeschichtliche Betrachtung des johanneischen Petrusbildes," *Catholica* (1998): 44-66.

[2] This expression is found, for instance, in the correspondence of the year 1523 between the two humanists, the Augustinian Caspar Amman and the Benedictine Veit Bild; see Alois Wagner, "Der Augustiner Kaspar Amman," *Jahresbericht des Historischen Vereins Dillingen* 7 (1894): 42-64, here 60.

[3] Luther: *die Christliche Ewangelisch warhait*, WA 10^3:210.17.

I. REVIEW OF THE HISTORY OF THE UNDERSTANDING OF MATTHEW 16:18

Up to about 250 A.D., the early Church did not use Matthew 16:18 in support of the authority of the papacy. Neither Tertullian (c. 160–c. 225) nor Origen (c. 185–c. 253) derived from this verse any juridical primacy of the successors of Peter in Rome. Tertullian thought that Matthew 16:18 was directed to the Apostle Peter personally and was not transferred to anyone else.[4] In the controversy over baptism by heretics of the third century, Matthew 16:18 appears to have been used for the first time in support of the position of the Bishop of Rome, who claimed sovereign authority on the basis of it, according to the correspondence of Cyprian (d. 258).[5] In the fourth century, Bishop Optatus of Milevis in North Africa (approx. 380) argued with (mistaken) linguistic skills for papal primacy because Peter was called *Cephas* in John 1:42[6] (falsely translating *cephas* with *caput* [head] in thinking perhaps of the Greek *kephale* which means head).

In the history of Bible interpretation, the opinions of the Church Fathers played a key role. They were mindful of the statement that the rock is Christ according to 1 Corinthians 10:4 *(petra autem erat Christus,* "and the rock was Christ"). In his thinking in this area Augustine (354–430) was influenced occasionally by Cyprian, when Augustine taught that the Church is founded on Peter the rock.[7] However, Augustine also has the other understanding. In his homily 244 on John 20, he quoted Matthew 16:18 and then stated that "the rock was Christ" and that the name Peter is derived from that rock. "The rock rose [from the dead] so that he may make Peter firm, for

[4] See Kurt Guggisberg, "Matthäus 16,18 u. 19 in der Kirchengeschichte. Ein geschichtlicher Überblick über die Entwicklung der Primatslehre," ZKG 54 (1935): 276-300; see Hans von Campenhausen, *Ecclesiastical Authority and Spiritual Power in the Church of the First Three Centuries*, trans. J. A. Baker (Stanford: University Press, 1969).

[5] See *Saint Cyprian's Letters*, trans. Rose Bernard Donna, The Fathers of the Church, vol. 51 (Washington: Catholic University of America Press, 1964), 75; Klaus Schatz, *Papal Primacy: From Its Origins to the Present*, trans. John A Otto and Linda M. Maloney (Collegeville: The Liturgical Press, 1996), 13f.

[6] *Petro primo Cathedram episcopalem esse collatam, in qua sederit omnium Apostolorum caput Petrus; unde et Cephas appelatus est: in qua una cathedra unitas ab omnibus servaretur.* PL 11:947; see Schatz, *Papal Primacy*, 92.

[7] See G. R. Evans, entry "Catholic, Church as" in Allan D. Fitzgerald, ed., *Augustine through the Ages: An Encyclopedia* (Grand Rapids and Cambridge, U.K: William B. Eerdmans, 1999), 150.

Peter would have perished if the rock would not live."[8] In his *Reconsiderations* Augustine offered both interpretations and left the preference up to the reader.[9]

In his zeal for getting at the truth according to the Hebrew original (*Hebraica veritas*[10]) the Church Father Jerome (340/50–420) wanted to make sure that *Petrus* is understood in the Hebrew and Syriac languages as *Cephas,* which in Greek and Latin means *petra.*[11] In the fifth century Pope Leo the Great (440–461) declared that the Church is built on the firmness of faith as Simon expressed it.[12] Unchallenged at that time, he also claimed that the Roman Church always had the primacy over the others.[13] At the end of the ninth century, the Frank cleric Auxilius declared that the Church is built on

[8] *Petra erat ipse Christus, ille autem a petra Petrus. Ideo surrexerat petra, ut firmaret Petrum: nam perierat Petrus, nisi viveret petra,* PL 38:1148.

[9] *In quo [libro contra epistulam Donati] dixi quodam loco de apostolo Petro, quod in illo tamquam in petra fundata sit ecclesia. qui* [sic] *sensus etiam cantatur ore multorum in uersibus beatissimi Ambrosii, ubi de gallo gallinacio ait: 'hoc ipsa petra ecclesiae, canente culpam diluit'. sed scio me postea saepissime sic exposuisse, quod a domino dictum est: 'tu es Petrus et super hanc petram aedificabo ecclesiam meam', ut super hunc intelligeretur, quem confessus est Petrus dicens: 'tu es Christus, filius dei uiui', ac sic Petrus ab hac petra appelatus personam ecclesiae figuraret, quae super hanc petram aedificatur et accepit 'claves regni caelorum'. non enim dictum illi est: tu es petra, sed: 'tu es Petrus'. 'petra autem erat Christus' quem confessus Simon, sicut et tota ecclesia confitetur, dictus est Petrus. harum duarum autem sententiarum quae sit probabilior, eligat lector. Retractationes,* 1.1. c. 20 (21) n. 2 (1), CSEL 36:97f; see Franz Gillmann, "Zur scholastischen Auslegung von Mt 16,18," *Archiv für katholisches Kirchenrecht* 104 (1924), 41-53, here 41.

[10] Jerome appears to have coined the expression *Hebraica ueritas;* he used it in his *Epistola LVII* [57] *ad Pammachium de optime genere interpretandi*: *quod Iohannes euangelista sumpsit iuxta Hebraicam ueritatem,* CSEL 54:513,23. In his *Epistola CVI* [106], he used it seven times, see CSEL 55:247.9, 249.8, 252.6, 253.22, 254.19, 267.12, 270.2; see Gianfranco Miletto, "Die 'Hebraica Veritas' in S. Hieronymus" in Helmut Merklein, Karlheinz Müller, and Gunter Stemberger, eds, *Bibel in jüdischer und christlicher Tradition: Festschrift für Johann Maier zum 60. Geburtstag* (Frankfurt: Anton Hain, 1993), 56-65. Adam Kamesar, *Jerome, Greek Scholarship and the Hebrew Bible: A Study of the "Quaestiones Hebraicae in Genesim"* (Oxford: Clarendon Press; New York: Oxford University Press, 1993).

[11] *Non quod aliud significet Petrus, aliud Cephas: sed quod quam nos Latine et Graece petram vocemus, hanc Hebraei et Syri propter linguae inter se viciniam, Cephan nuncupent. Commentariorum in epistolam ad Galatas lib. 1 cap. 2,* PL 26:341 (on Gal 2).

[12] See Leo I on Matthew 16:18: *Tantumque in hac fidei sublimitate complacuit, ut beatitudinis felicitate donatus sacram inviolabilis petrae acciperet firmitatem, super quam fundata Ecclesia portis inferi et mortis legibus praevaleret, sermo* 51,1: PL 54:308-9; *et pro soliditate fidei, quam erat praedicaturus, audiret: Tu es Petrus* (Matthew 16:18), *sermo* 62,2: PL 54:350-51; *sermo* 83,3: PL 54:431-32; *sermo* 4,3: PL 54:150-52.

[13] *Ecclesia Romana semper habuit primatum*; see Guggisberg, 286.

the rock that is Christ, referring to 1 Corinthians 10:4, and that Peter is entrusted to lead the Church. His contemporary Vulgarius insisted that Jesus did not speak of Rome on which to build the Church, nor on Peter, but on *petra* and on the solidity of this rock.[14]

The standard medieval *Glossed Bible* known since the twelfth century as the *Biblia Latina cum Glossa ordinaria* incorporated several exegetical/theological sources, including especially Augustine.[15] Thomas Aquinas (1224/25–1274) and Martin Luther used this valuable source.[16] The *Glossa ordinaria* declared with Bede and Hrabanus Maurus that "Simon" means "the obedient one" and "Peter" means the "recognizer".[17] Throughout the Middle Ages the *Glossed Bible* was the definitive reference edition of the Bible that provided easy access to the Church Fathers' opinions and that could be consulted in every good library of the then-known world. In church politics, with Pope Gregory VII and his *Dictatus Papae* of 1075, the supreme authority of the Roman pope was firmly established and the declaration was made that the papacy will never err because of the biblical testimony (*scriptura testante*).[18]

At about 1150 Peter Lombard taught—relying on Ambrose and Augustine—that Christ is the "foundation of the foundations".[19] Thomas Aquinas, *magister in sacra pagina,* kept following the exegetical tradition declaring Christ to be the foundation of the Church.[20] In his *Catena Aurea* (the Latin term for anthology) which Pope Urban IV had commissioned, Thomas wrote on the basis of comments by Jerome, Chrysostom, and the *Reconsiderations* of Augustine, that the "rock was Christ whom Peter confessed". Thomas, too, brought 1 Corinthians 10:4 into play here: "For as from Christ proceeded that light to the Apostles, whereby they were called the light of the world, and those other names which were imposed upon them by the Lord, so

[14] ... '*etra autem erat Christus*', *ecclesia super petram, id est Christum, fundata et Petro ad regendam commissa* .... *In defensionem sacrae ordinationis papae Formosi I,* as found in E. Dümmler, *Auxilius und Vulgarius* (Leipzig, 1866), 59f and 130; see Gillmann, 42.

[15] See Margaret T. Gibson, "The Glossed Bible" in *Biblia Latina Cum Glossa Ordinaria: Facsimile Reprint of the Editio Princeps Adolph Rusch of Strassburg 1480/81*. Introduction by Karlfried Froehlich and Margaret T. Gibson (Turnhout: Brepols, 1992), VIII-IX.

[16] See XI.

[17] Bede on Matthew 4:5 (not on 16:18): *Simon interpretatur obediens; Petrus agnoscens,* PL 92:22; Hrabanus: *Simon enim interpretatur obediens, Petrus agnoscens,* PL 107:789.

[18] See Guggisberg, 291. On the *Dictatus*, see Schatz, *Papal Primacy*, 85-89.

[19] *Fundamentum fundamentorum*, on Ephesians 2; PL 192:186.

[20] *Christo, qui est Ecclesiae fundamentum, Summa Theologiae, supplementum, Tertiae Partis, quaestio 6, articulus 6, ad 2*; see Gillmann, 42 (note).

upon Simon who believed in Christ the Rock, he bestowed the name of Peter (Rock) ... But the rock was Christ" [1 Corinthians 10:4].[21]

Nicholas of Lyra (c. 1270–1349), the foremost authority in medieval biblical exegesis, interpreted the Bible according to the *Hebraica veritas* (the Hebrew original). He actually used this notion in his *Postilla litteralis* on Genesis 4.[22] He taught that Simon received his name Peter as the confessor of the *petra*. The Lord promised to build his Church on the rock which Peter recognized to be Christ himself.[23] Lyra's *Biblia cum postillis* appeared in print in three volumes in 1482.[24] Martin Luther praised Lyra for his exegetical work, especially because he was able to reconcile places in Scripture that seem to be at odds. "Lyra is very good."[25] Without Lyra, Luther said, we would understand neither the New nor the Old Testament.

From the history of Western church law we learn that the canon lawyer and Bishop, Ivo of Chartres (died 1117), argued from 1 Corinthians 10:4 in his sermon on the *cathedra S. Petri* and declared that Peter's name was derived from Christ as the *petra* on the basis of the solidity of Simon's confession in Matthew 16:18.[26] Petrus Cellensis, also a Bishop of Chartres (died 1183), argued in the same way from 1 Corinthians 10:4.[27] Similarly, the *Decretum Gratiani* spoke of Christ as

[21] *Catena Aurea. Commentary on the four Gospels collected out of the works of the Fathers by Saint Thomas Aquinas. Volume I St. Matthew, English translation first published in 1841 edited by John Henry Newman with a new introduction by Aidan Nichols OP* (Southampton: The Saint Austin Press, 1997), 584f.

[22] See Franz Boehmisch's article on the internet: "Raschi und Nicolaus de Lyra," http://www.ktf.uni-passau.de/mitarbeiter/boehmisch/lyra.html, Passau 1995. Lyra wrote on the difference between the Vulgate and the Hebrew Bible in his *Tractatus de differentia nostrae translationis ab Hebraica littera in Veteri Testamento*; see Herman Hailperin, *Rashi and the Christian Scholars* (Pittsburgh: University of Pittsburgh Press, 1963), 283f.

[23] ...*Quia tu es Petrus, i. e. confessor petre vereque Christus factus est [petra];* Gillmann, 49, n. 3. *Et super hanc petram, quam confessus es, i. e. Christum edificabo ecclesiam meam;* Gillmann, 49, n. 4. See John E. Bigane, *Faith, Christ, or Peter: Matthew 16:18 In Sixteenth Century Roman Catholic Exegesis* (Washington: University Press of America, 1981), 90.

[24] Printed by Franciscus Renner in Venice; see James George Kiecker, *The Postilla of Nicholas of Lyra on the Song of Songs* (Milwaukee: Marquette University Press, 1998), 13.

[25] *Lira ist sehr gut,* WA 48:691 (no. 7118).

[26] *Felix vocabuli denuntiatio, ut a petra de qua scriptum est, "Petra autem erat Christu," Petrus denominetur, nominis Christi participatione decoretur, ipso Christo sibi nomen imponente, ut Petrus sit, et Petrus vocetur. Super hance etiam petram Dominus Ecclesiam suam aedificandam providit, quatenus cujus fidei confessio pro sui soliditate Petrae comparanda erat, nominis etiam sui applauderet appellationi,* PL 162:595f; see Gillmann, 43, n. 1.

[27] *[Cathedra] fundata enim est super petram, id est Christum, qui cum Patre et spiritu sancto vivit et regnat Deus per omnia saecula saeculorum. Amen; Sermo LIX De S. Petro seu cathedra S. Petri,* PL 202:821f.

the rock and that it was Christ as the *petra* who imposed the name Peter on the apostle.[28] The great canonist Huguccio[29] held the same position; that the "rock" means Christ or the solid faith of the apostle who recognized Christ as the Son of God; and that the Church is built on Christ according to 1 Corinthians 10:4. Peter is the servant (*minister*).[30]

Around 1300, Guido de Baysio (Archdeacon at Bologna) repeated that Christ had spoken of himself as the rock and then gave Simon the name Peter. The rock is Christ in the first place as found in Peter's confession. Guido declared that Matthew 16:18 is to be understood in the light of 1 Corinthians 10:4. He apparently used Jerome's linguistic expertise when he said that the Latin and Greek languages call *petra* what the Hebrews and Syriacs call *cepha*. Guido appears to have also relied on Bede, saying that Peter is the "recognizer" (*agnoscens*). Guido, however, (mis)understood the Hebrew *cepha* as the Greek *cephale* which in Latin means *caput* (head).[31]

At about the same time, Jacobus de Viterbo, an Augustinian friar (died c. 1308), spoke of *petra* as Peter in his book *De regimine christiano (ad Bonifacium)*, but he also declared Christ to be the rock by alluding to1 Corinthians 10:4 and quoting Augustine who left the understanding up to the reader's discretion.[32] As the principal teacher for the Augustinian order in the Middle Ages (although otherwise a

[28] *A se petra Petri sibi nomen imposuit,* Gillmann, 43.

[29] See Wolfgang P. Muller, *Huguccio: The Life, Works, and Thought of a Twelfth-Century Jurist* (Washington: Catholic University of America Press, 1994).

[30] *Nam a petra dictus est Petrus, de qua petra dicitur: Petra autem erat Christus . Tu es Petrus, dictus a me petra, et super hanc petram, i. e. super me, edificabo ecclesiam meam principaliter, quasi auctorem, set secundario et quasi ministrum;* see Gillmann, 45 with n. 1.

[31] On 'confession': ... *'Tu es Petrus, quod latini et greci dicunt petram, hebrei et syri cepham. Item: Ergo es cephas et super hanc petram, a qua diceris Petrus, edificabo ecclesiam meam. Vel: super hanc petram, quam confessus es, que sola fundamentum est.* On 'Petrus': *Petrus a petra, i. e. Christo nomen acceptit, super quem, scil. Christum fundata est ecclesia ... Petrus interpretatur vocatus vel agnoscens, hebraice cepha, i. e. agnoscens vel vocatus,... et ipse cephas dictus est, quod in capite sit constitutus apostolorum. Cephali enim grece, latine dicitur caput... quod ipse erat, i. e. ab eo, quod ipse dominus erat, scil. petra, de qua dictum est: 'Petra autem erat Christus* [1 Corinthians 10:4], as quoted in Gillmann, 47, n. 4. When it comes to transliterations of Hebrew and Greek words in medieval Latin texts or in Luther's and Amman's texts, I usually follow the transliterations given in these sources which may differ from the modern way of transliterating.

[32] Jacobus de Viterbo: ...*Petra erat Christus* [see 1 Corinthians 10:4]. *Vel: super hanc fidem et confessionem...,* as quoted in Gillmann 47f, n. 4. Adolar Zumkeller, *Theology and History of the Augustinian School in the Middle Ages,* John E. Rotelle, ed. (Villanova: Augustinian Press, 1996), 94-104, treats Jacobus' book, but does not mention any interpretation of Matthew 16:18.

papalist who proclaimed that "the pope is the Church"), Aegidius Romanus (Giles of Rome, c. 1245–1316) also preferred to understand Christ as the rock.[33] Blessed Simon Fidati of Cascia (died 1348), also an Augustinian friar, wrote the often-reprinted book on the four gospels, *De gestis Domini salvatoris*. He wanted the word "rock" in Matthew 16:18 not to be applied to Peter, but to Christ.[34] With that he did not deny the primacy of Peter but simply intended to adhere to the interpretation of Augustine. Alvarus Pelagius (died 1350), in his *de planctu ecclesiae* of 1335, held that the rock in Matthew 16:18 may mean either Peter (and his successors) or the Christ whom Peter confessed. The latter (Christ, the rock) is more probable, he declared, relying on 1 Corinthians 10:4 and the *Glossa ordinaria*.[35]

Cardinal Pierre d'Ailly (died about 1420) noted the various interpretations of *petra* in the holy fathers of old. He hinted at Augustine's two basic interpretations, that is, Peter as the rock and Christ as the rock. Although Augustine left the issue undecided, the cardinal himself preferred to speak with 1 Corinthians 10:4 of Christ as the rock, reasoning that nobody would want to build the Church on the human weakness of Peter at the time of Christ's crucifixion. Christ built his Church on himself as the foundation rock, and he made Peter firm on it.[36] Finally, besides interpreting the rock to mean Peter or Christ according to the literal sense, he noted that one may also understand the rock in the spiritual sense to mean Sacred Scripture and the doctrine of Christ on which the Church is founded.[37] This spiritual reading will appeal to Luther, as we shall see.

Since the middle of the fifteenth century, Roman humanists at the service of the papacy developed their theories in support of papal supremacy.[38] Others, however, developed their own opinions. The

[33] *Aegidius da Roma in prologo sententiarum q. 3*, as referred to in the sixteenth century by Caspar Amman in his pamphlet against Murner; see Otto Clemen's edition, "Eine Abhandlung Kaspar Ammans," ARG 4 (1906): 162-83, text on 167-80, here 173. On Aegidius Romanus, see entry by Eric. L. Saak in *Augustine through the Ages*,14f.

[34] See Zumkeller, *Theology and History*, 39.

[35] ... *Potest autem intelligi uno modo hanc petram super te et successores tuos, vel super hanc petram, i. e. super hunc, quem confessus es, quia petra erat Christus, ad I Cor X* [1 Corinthians 10:4]; Gillmann, 49, n. 5 and n. 6.

[36] See *Recommendatio sacre scripture*, as quoted in Gillmann, 49f, n. 1 and n. 2.

[37] ... *tamen secundum spiritualem intellectum per hanc petram divinam scripturam et sacram Christi doctrinam signare possumus...*, as quoted in Gillmann, 50, n. 3.

[38] Typical for the papalist position were treatises such as the *Summa de ecclesia* of 1453 by the Dominican and Cardinal Johannes Turrecremata, or the *Tractatus de cause immediata ecclesiastice potestatis* by the two Dominicans Petrus de Palude and Guillaume de Pierre Godin. Another treatise was called *De potestate pape et*

Spanish exegete and later Bishop of Avila, Alfonso Tostado (died 1455), largely followed d'Ailly as Tostado preferred to read Matthew 16:18 with 1 Corinthians 10:4 in mind and to understand Christ as the rock whom Peter recognized. After all, *Petrus* is not *petra*. He recommended following Augustine's second opinion, namely that Christ is the rock.[39]

The canonist Cardinal Johannes Antonius de Sancto Georgio (died 1509) also argued from 1 Corinthians 10:4 and taught that Christ is the rock. Simon received the name Peter as derived from *petra* because he was the first to recognize Christ as the Son of God. This Cardinal even claimed that all authorities *(secundum omnes)* interpret *petra* to mean Christ and that on him (Christ) Peter is founded as his vicar.[40] He may have had in mind the authorities that Thomas Aquinas had listed in his *Catena Aurea* which was printed at that time in Rome in 1470, and reprinted twenty times between 1501 and 1520. German and Spanish translations were already made available in the fifteenth century. Luther may have had access to them.

II. Luther's Understanding of Matthew 16:18 in the Midst of the Controversy Over Authority

We do not know whether Luther was aware of all of the Church Fathers' contributions to this subject, and whether he knew of the conviction of Cardinal Johannes Antonius de Sancto Georgio that all previous authorities interpreted *petra* in Matthew 16:18 to mean Christ. Nor do we know for sure whether he knew of all the opinions that had developed within his own religious order (for example,

termino eius by Bishop Domenico de' Domenichi, written in Rome in 1456 (Domenico died 1478); see Heribert Smolinsky, "Papstgewalt ohne Grenzen? Papalistische Theorie im Zeitalter der Renaissancepäpste und des römisch-italienischen Humanismus," *Rottenburger Jahrbuch für Kirchengeschichte* 11 (1992): 71-83. One of the extreme papalists was the Spaniard Rodrigo Sanchez de Arevalo (died 1470), called the "champion of the papacy," see Richard H. Trame, *Rodrigo Sanchez de Arevalo 1404-1470. Spanish Diplomat and Champion of the Papacy* (Washington: Catholic University Press, 1958).

[39] See Gillmann, 51.

[40] *Nota, quod ecclesia dicitur fundata in Petri soliditate. Veritas est, quod fundata est in Christo iuxta illud; 'et super hanc petram edificabo ecclesiam meam'. Exponitur illa litera secundum omnes: 'Et super hanc petram', i. e. Christum, ... Debet ergo iuxta sanum intellectum sic intelligi, quod ecclesia est fundata in Petro tanquam in vicario illius, qui est ecclesie fundamentum,* Gillmann, 52, n. 4; J. A. de S. Georgio published his *Commentaria super Decreto* at Pavia in 1497, printed by Leonardus Gerla.

Jacobus de Viterbo or Aegidius Romanus). Luther certainly must have known Augustine's reflections on this issue, and he apparently sided with the concept of Christ as the rock. Luther also must have been familiar with the position of his superior Johann von Staupitz (died 1524), professor of the sacred page at Wittenberg, although Staupitz had not published his opinion at that time. What Staupitz thought of Peter as the rock he proclaimed in sermons in 1512 at Salzburg of which nuns took notes: "One may see and recognize that one needs to build upon Christ alone as the rock, and on nobody else."[41] Luther certainly was convinced that he had the right understanding of this verse, in agreement with the Catholic tradition.

At that time, a major controversy developed over the Roman tradition of how to understand the Petrine office in the Church.[42] In spring 1518 the Dominican theologian at the papal court, Silvester Prierias, wrote his reaction to Luther's theses on the indulgences of 1517, that is his *Dialogue on the power of the Pope against Luther's conclusions,* in which he focused on the infallibility of the pope. He declared Luther's teachings erroneous, false, presumptuous, or heretical.[43] Luther responded immediately with his *Ad dialogum Silvestri Prieriatis de potestate papae responsio* (1518); and Prierias followed in turn with a *Replica.*[44] Later on Luther wrote another response to Prierias as part of his response to Ambrosius Catharinus,[45] in which Luther entered his polemic against the use of Matthew 16:18 in support of the power of the Roman Church over the other Churches.[46] Luther concluded "that Christ's word in Matthew 16 does not pertain to any person, but alone to the Church which is built in the Spirit upon Christ the Rock, not upon the pope nor on the Roman

[41] Sermon 5, in *Johann von Staupitz: Salzburger Predigten 1512: Eine textkritische Edition* (Tübingen: Neuphilologische Fakultät, 1990), 57-64, here 64.

[42] See Remigius Bäumer, "Die Auseinandersetzungen über die römische Petrustradition in den ersten Jahrzehnten der Reformationszeit," *Römische Quartalschrift* 57 (1962): 20-57; Scott H. Hendrix, *Luther and the Papacy: Stages in a Reformation Conflict* (Philadelphia: Fortress Press, 1981).

[43] Prierias' expert opinion is known under the title *In praesumptuosas Martini Luther conclusiones de potestate papae dialogus;* see Remigius Bäumer, "Der Lutherprozess," in idem, ed., *Lutherprozess und Lutherbann: Vorgeschichte, Ergebnis, Nachwirkung* (Münster: Aschendorff, 1972), 26, n. 29.

[44] WA 1:644-86. See *Replica F. Silvestri Prieriatis ad F. M. Luther*, with Luther's Preface, WA 2:50-56.

[45] *Ad librum eximii Magistri Nostri Magistri Ambrosii Catharini, defensoris Silvestri Prietatis acerrimi, responsio* (1521), WA 7:698-778.

[46] See WA 7:708,15-719,6.

Church."[47] And Luther set the record straight that *cephas* means rock and not head.[48]

In 1519 Luther published his *Commentary on Galatians* which he understood as a "testimony" of his faith in Christ,[49] and also his sermon on the feast day of Saints Peter and Paul (29 June 1519) with its prescribed gospel text, Matthew 16:12-19, which he had preached at the time of the Leipzig Debate. This German sermon was published in 1520 at Basel under the title "A comforting sermon on the grace of God and free will. And on the power of the keys of St. Peter."[50] The same printer at Basel brought Luther's *Commentary on Galatians* to the market in 1520, after it had already appeared in 1519 at Leipzig.[51] Luther's work on Galatians is of interest here insofar as his confrère, the biblical humanist Caspar Amman,[52] liked it very much (see below), presumably because Luther showed himself a linguist as he worked with the original text which Erasmus provided, and as he paid attention to the Hebrew background of words of the New Testament.[53] On Galatians 2:14 Luther focused on "Cephe" (for Peter). He sided with Jerome's hint at the Hebrew and Syriac meaning of *cephe*, which means *pétros* or *pétra* in Greek, and *saxum* (a rock or large stone) or *soliditas* (firmness, solidity) in Latin. Luther rejected the interpretation of *cephe* to mean head, the Latin *caput,* which would make Peter the head of the Church in addition or competition with Christ. Luther pointed out that there is a difference

[47] *Concludo ergo adversus te, demonstrative convictum, verbum Christi Matt xvi. ad nullam personam pertinere, sed ad solam Ecclesiam in spiritu aedificatam super Petram Christum, non super Papam nec super Romanam Ecclesiam.* WA 7:709,25-28.

[48] See WA 7:718,4-7.

[49] See Kenneth Hagen, *Luther's Approach to Scripture as seen in his "Commentaries" on Galatians 1519–1538* (Tübingen: J. C. B. Mohr [Paul Siebeck], 1993), 8.

[50] *Ein trostlich predig von der gnaden gottes vnd fryen willen. Vnd von dem gewalt der schlussel sant Petri. Beschrieben durch D. Martinum Luther* (Basel: Adam Petri, 1520); WA 2:244-49.

[51] *In epistolam Pauli ad Galatas, F. Martini Lutheri Augustiniani commentarius* (Basel: Adam Petri, 1520; Leipzig: Melchior Lotther, 1519). Later editions were printed in 1523, 1535, and 1538. A German version came out in 1525. See Hagen, vii with notes and 6-8.

[52] For a biographical sketch, see Franz Posset, art. "Amman, Caspar," *Biographisch-Bibliographisches Kirchenlexikon* (Herzberg: Verlag Traugott Bautz, 2000), vol. 16:49-52.

[53] *Sed et graeca vox, autore Erasmo*; or: *ut enim Erasmus hic dicit in Graeco,* WA 2:481.23-25; 482.8f; 18-22. Erasmus translated the Greek New Testament into Latin by being truthful to the Greek (*ad graecam veritatem*). Luther saw, for instance, in Galatians 2:7 a "hebraism" at work (*dextras societatis*); on this he referred to Erasmus.

between the Hebrew/Syriac *cephe* and the Greek *kephalé* which is the proper word for head. Evidently he understood Simon as *Cephas* (Galatians 2:14) to mean rock, and not head, and he referred to "the decretals taken from Leo and Ambrose" for his support.[54] On Galatians 5:7 (against being misled) Luther wrote about the proper understanding of John 21:17 and Matthew 16:18. The Lord's mandate in John does not mean that prelates may dominate their congregations, and the Lord's word in Matthew does not mean earthly power, but that the Church is built on the solidity of the faith in Christ.[55]

In his sermon on Matthew 16 at Leipzig Luther was not much concerned with the issue of the meaning of the "rock". His main topic was "grace" that makes a person divine; and that God's grace deifies man.[56] Almost in passing he indicated that Peter is to be understood as representing the entire Church,[57] following Origen whose opinion Luther may have read in Erasmus' New Testament edition and annotations of 1519.[58] The printed version of Luther's sermon provides the gospel text in German in which Luther inserted in parenthesis the explanation after the name Peter: "that is, a rock". He also used the traditional word *Kirche* for "Church" while at other times he preferred to translate the Greek/Latin *ecclesia* with German *gemeyne* or *Gemein[d]e* (that is, community).[59]

In the aftermath of the Leipzig Disputation (August 1519), a lively correspondence took place that tried to compete for the favors of the Elector Frederick the Wise. Andreas Bodenstein von Karlstadt

[54] ... *'Cephale' graecum caput significat, non 'Cephe' Syrum* ... . WA 2:488.25-31; LW 27:218. In his later commentary (1531/1535) Luther ignored the name *Cephe* and only spoke and wrote of Peter (see on Galatians 2:14).

[55] See WA 2:568,24-33; LW 27:338.

[56] *Gottformig und vergottet*, WA 2:248.2. See Franz Posset, "Deification in the German Spirituality of the Late Middle Ages and in Luther: An Ecumenical Historical Perspective," *Archiv für Reformationsgeschichte* 84 (1993): 103-26.

[57] See WA 2: 248f.

[58]Erasmus: *In quem haud hunc dubie competunt inprimis velut in Christianae fidei principem. At non in hunc vnum, sed in omnes Christianos, quod eleganter indicat Orige[nes] Omelia prima harum quas habemus,* as also Amman quoted these words in his Latin pamphlet against Murner; Clemen, 172f.

[59] On this issue, see for instance H. C. Erik Midelfort, "Social History and Biblical Exegesis: Community, Family, and Witchcraft in Sixteenth-Century Germany" in David C. Steinmetz (ed.), *The Bible in the Sixteenth Century* (Durham: Duke University Press, 1990), 7-20, here 9f. Midelfort, however, is not aware of Luther's consistently inconsistent use of his own translations, as Luther translates Matthew 16:18 with either *Kirche* or *Gemeinde*. Here is Luther's original wording of Matthew 16:18 in German in 1519 including Luther's original parenthesis: *Du bist Petrus (das ist ein fels), und auff dissen fels will ich bawen meine Kirche* (You are Peter [that is a rock] and on this rock I will build my Church). WA 2:246.17f.

(1480–1541) and Luther formed a united front against Johann Eck (1486–1543). They objected to Eck's one-sided interpretation of the rock to mean Peter, and they maintained that Matthew 16:18 must be read with 1 Corinthians 10:4 in mind. They explicitly relied on Augustine in this regard for their own support.[60] Eck charged Luther that even if Augustine and all the Fathers would have understood Peter as the rock, Luther still would have objected to them.[61] Eck wrote on 8 November 1519 to the Elector that nobody had denied that the rock in Matthew 16:18 is to be understood as Christ, following Augustine. However, he insisted that it also means Peter as the vicar on which the Church is built, and that he certainly did not disregard the biblical text as the evil-minded Doctor Martin had alleged. Eck for his position referred to Cyprian, Origen, Augustine, Hilary, Chrysostom, Bede, Leo, Ambrose, Gregory, Cyril, Ignatius, Maximus, and to Church councils.[62] After the Leipzig Disputation Eck decided to write a book about this issue against Luther. Finished in February 1520, he gave the manuscript to the printer Conrat Resch in Paris, who published it under the title *De primatu Petri adversus Ludderum Ioannis Eckii libri tres* in September 1521 together with a letter by Pope Leo X. His favorite authority appears to have been Cyprian to whom Eck referred to more than fifty times.[63]

After the fruitless interrogation in October 1518 by Cardinal Cajetan (1468–1534) at Augsburg, Cajetan (the Prior General of the Dominican friars) had made the Augustinian Friar Martin his target with a polemic writing (published in 1521 in three places—Rome, Cologne, and Milan).[64] In April 1520 at Leipzig the Franciscan Bible

[60] Luther: *Item: 'tu es Petrus, et super hanc petram etc.' hab ich mit St. Aug. und der ganzen Gschrift durch petram Christum verstanden, als Paulus sagt: 'petra autem erat Christus'* [1 Corinthians 10:4]. *Doctor Eck hat Petrum haben wollen;* in: *Doctor Martinus Luther und Doctor Carlstat [sic] Antwort auf Doctor Johann Eck Schreiben an mein gnädigisten Herrn Herzog Fryderichen zu Sachsen Kurfürsten. ...* WA Br 1:468.93-96 (no. 192).

[61] See WA 2:278.3.

[62] *Doctor Eckius' Ableinen des falschen, irrsaligen Schreiben D. Ludders und Carlestat an meinen genädigisten Herrn, Herzog Fryderich, Churfursten etc.* WA Br 1:481.72-83.

[63] See Anette Zillenbiller, "*Legi saepius et relegi Cyprianum*: Johannes Ecks Cyprianrezeption in seinem Werk *De primatu Petri*" in Leif Grane, Alfred Schindler, and Markus Wriedt, eds., *Auctoritas Patrum II. Neue Beiträge zur Rezeption der Kirchenväter im 15. und 16. Jahrhundert. New Contributions on the Reception of the Church Fathers in the 15th and 16th Centuries* (Mainz: Philipp von Zabern, 1998), 295-306.

[64] Luther: *Resolutiones lutherianae super propositionibus suis decima tertia de potestate papae* (1519). Cajetan: *De divina institutione pontificatus Romani pontificis super totam ecclesiam a Christo in Petro.* See Bigane, 108.

scholar Augustinus Alveldt (died after 1532) wrote against Luther, who retorted with his *Concerning the Papacy in Rome against the very famous Romanist at Leipzig*, that is, against Alveldt who favored the interpretation of *petra* as Peter, the person. Luther preferred the understanding of *petra* as Christ and faith in Christ. He further explained that the "rock" cannot mean "authority" (*ubirkeit*) because no authority is able to stand against hell, but only Christ and the faith. The Church is built "on strong, right faith, on Christ, the rock".[65]

In November 1520 the Franciscan Thomas Murner (1475–1537)[66] at Strasbourg came to the defense of his confrère Alveldt and published his "Christian and fraternal" correction of Luther,[67] which was his first anti-Lutheran pamphlet. Murner was one of the most clever, witty, and popular writers of his time.[68] Immediately after this first pamphlet, Murner edited his "On the papacy that is the highest authority of the Christian faith against Doctor Martin Luther."[69] This

[65] Luther: *drumb musz 'der felsz' nit heyssen ubirkeit, wilch nicht mag widder die pfortten der helle bestehen, sondern allein Christum und den glauben,...sondern in einem festen rechten glauben, auff Christo, dem fels, erbawet*, in *Von dem Papsthum zu Rom wider den hochberühmten Romanisten zu Leipzig*, WA 6:314.26-28 and 315.8-12. See Reinhard Schwarz, *Luther* (Göttingen: Vandenhoeck & Ruprecht, 1985), 79; Heribert Smolinsky, *Augustin von Alveldt und Hieronymus Emser* (Münster: Aschendorff, 1984), 81 (on Alveldt who likes the equation Rock=Peter). Idem, "Papstgewalt ohne Grenzen?" 71-83.

[66] See Linda L. Gaus, "Thomas Murner," in James Harolin and Max Reinhart, eds., *German Writers of the Reformation* (Detroit: Gale Research, 1997), 184-97. On Murner and his anonymous pamphlets, see Thomas Kaufmann, "Anonyme Flugschriften der frühen Reformation" in Stephen E. Buckwalter and Bernd Moeller, eds, *Die frühe Reformation in Deutschland als Umbruch* (Gütersloh: Gütersloher Verlagshaus, 1998), 208-12. It remains noteworthy that Murner in 1512 made some sarcastic remarks about the trafficking in indulgences: "If the pope wants to grant an indulgence, then the prince wants to have his share. If one won't let him have his share, then the indulgence must be given up." Wolfgang Pfeiffer-Belli, ed., *Thomas Murners Deutsche Schriften* (Berlin: Walter de Gruyter, 1926), vol. 2:249.

[67] *Ein christlich und briederliche ermanung an den hoch gelerten doctor Luther*, printed by Johann Grieninger at Strasbourg on 11 November 1520; Pfeiffer-Belli, *Thomas Murners Schriften* (Berlin: Walter de Gruyter, 1927), vol. 6:29-87.

[68] In 1522 Murner published his satirical epic, *Vom Lutherischen Narren*. In 1525 Murner was expelled from Strasbourg and went to Lucerne in Switzerland, where he took up his pen against the Swiss reformers. Murner thought he could turn public opinion against Luther simply by translating Luther's *Babylonian Captivity* into German without comment; see Erwin Iserloh, Joseph Glazik, and Hubert Jedin, *Reformation and Counter Reformation*, trans. Anselm Biggs and Peter W. Becker (London: Burns & Oates, 1980), 71 and 203.

[69] *Uon dem babstenthum das ist von der hochsten oberkeit Christlichs glauben wyder doctor Martinum Luther*, printed by Johann Grieninger at Strasbourg on 13 December 1520; *Deutsche Schriften*, vol. 7:3-55.

was the time when Luther burned the papal bull that threatened him with excommunication. Luther in his explanation for burning the bull included his understanding of Matthew 16:18 in the light of 1 Corinthians 10:4, both in the Latin and in the German version.[70] In contrast, in his "On the papacy" the Franciscan Murner utilized Matthew 16:18 and John 1:42 for his specific purposes of cementing the centralist papal position.

As soon as the Augustinian Prior of Lauingen Caspar Amman became aware of Murner's polemics, he stepped in; that is, on 12 February 1521, with his refutation of Murner's opinion—in favor of Luther. Amman called his own pamphlet the "True exposition of the words of Christ, 'You are Peter and on this rock I will build my Church'," and he declared that his position is fed from the "Hebrew font".[71] By this he meant the "Hebrew truth" of Christ's wording in the original language, which Amman said was spoken in Hebrew.

[70] WA 7:170,10-12 (German); 24-26 (Latin).

[71] *M. Gasparis Amman vera expositio verborum christi* [sic] *Tu es Petrus et super hanc petram edificabo ecclesiam meam Tu Vocaberis cephas quod Interpretatur Petrus Et tibi dabo claues regni celorum Contra falsam expositionem doctoris Thome Murner Ex fonte Hebreo hausta frater Gaspar Amman Augustinianus Gaspari Haslachio sacerdoti et Theologo salutem optat plurimam.* Edited by Otto Clemen, "Eine Abhandlung Kaspar Ammans" ARG 4 (1906): 162-83, text on 167-80. On the issue of "Hebrew truth"/ *Hebraica veritas* in the history of Bible interpretation, a number of studies appeared in recent years (however, without any mention of Amman); for instance, Miletto (as quoted above). S. Kamin, "The Theological Significance of the *Hebraica Veritas* in Jerome's Thought" in Michael A. Fishbane and Emmanuel Tov, eds, *Sha'arei Talmon: Studies in the Bible, Qumran, and the Ancient Near East presented to Shemaryahu Talmon* (Winona Lake, Ind.: Eisenbrauns, 1992), 243-53. On this issue in the Middle Ages, see Ary Grabois, "The *Hebraica Veritas* and Jewish-Christian Intellectual Relations in the Twelfth Century" *Speculum* 50 (1975): 613-34. Grover A. Zinn, "History and Interpretation: 'Hebrew Truth,' Judaism, and the Victorine Exegetical Tradition" in James H. Charlesworth, ed., *Jews and Christians: Exploring the Past, Present, and Future* (New York: Crossroad, 1990), 100-122. Friedrich Lotter, "Das Prinzip der 'Hebraica Veritas' und die heilsgeschichtliche Rolle Israels bei den frühen Zisterziensern" in Merklein et al. (1993), 479-517. On this issue in the fifteenth and sixteenth centuries, see R. Gerald Hobbs, "*Hebraica Veritas* and *Traditio Apostolica*: Saint Paul and the Interpretation of the Psalms in the Sixteenth Century" in David C. Steinmetz, ed., *The Bible in the Sixteenth Century* (Durham: Duke University Press, 1990), 83-99. Heiko A. Oberman, "The Discovery of Hebrew and the Discrimination of the Jews: The *Veritas Hebraica* as Double-Edged Sword in Renaissance and Reformation" in Andrew C. Fix and Susan C. Karant-Nunn, eds, *Germania Illustrata: Essays on Early Modern Germany presented to Gerald Strauss* (Kirksville: Sixteenth Century Journal Publishers, 1992), 19-34. Oberman also studied the issue in Wessel Gansfort (died 1489) in "Gansfort, Reuchlin and the 'Obscure Men': First Fissures in the Foundations of Faith" in Johannes Helmrath, Heribert Müller, and Helmut Wolff, eds, *Studien zum 15. Jahrhundert: Festschrift für Erich Meuthen* (2 vols., Munich: R. Oldenbourg Verlag, 1994), vol. 2:717-35, here 732-34 ("Wessel Gansfort: The Challenge of the *Veritas Hebraica*"). Thomas Willi,

The search for the "Hebrew truth" gained momentum in the 1520s,[72] when the issue was also debated whether Saint Peter had been in Rome at all, whether he had died there, and whether the popes may call themselves successors of Peter. This controversy had started anew at that time with a book published in 1519 by the Bohemian humanist Ulricus Velenus.[73] Luther had read it but was not convinced by the arguments presented in it.[74]

Back to the Amman/Murner controversy: Amman declared Murner's understanding of the biblical verses a "false interpretation of the foundation of the Catholic Church" and questioned whether the rock has to mean the person of Simon.[75] He also objected to Murner's translation of *cephas* (John 1:42) as head and that Peter supposedly was placed as the head over the other apostles.[76] Amman

"Basel und die Kontroverse um die *Veritas Hebraica*" in *Theologische Zeitschrift* 53 (1997): 165-76. On this issue as a systematic and exegetical problem, see Klaus Haacker and Heinzpeter Hempelmann, *Hebraica Veritas: Die hebräische Grundlage der biblischen Theologie als exegetische und systematische Aufgabe* (Wuppertal and Zurich: R. Brockhaus Verlag, 1989).

[72]As may be seen, for instance, from the preface to *The Psalter of David in Englishe Purely and Faithfully Translated after the Texte of Feline* of 1529/1530 (by Martin Bucer, translated by George Joye; Antwerp 1530) in which we read that "the trowthe [truth] of the Psalms must be fetched more nigh the Hebrew verity"; as quoted by Hobbs, "*Hebraica Veritas* and *Traditio Apostolica*," 99.

[73] *In hoc libello gravissimis certissimisque et in sacra scriptura fundatis rationibus variis probatur, Apostolum Petrum Romam non venisse, neque illic passum, proinde satis frivole et temere Romanus Pontifex se Petri successorem iactat et nominat etc.* (1519; no location given), see Bäumer, "Auseinandersetzungen," 24; A. J. Lamping, *Ulrichus Velenus (Oldrich Velensk) and his treatise against the papacy* (Leiden: Brill, 1976).

[74] *Sed non evincit,* Luther wrote about it to Spalatin on 3 February 1521, WA Br 2:260.

[75] Clemen 196. Amman quoted Murner's vernacular sentence with which Murner had dismissed Saint Augustine's interpretation of the Matthew 16:18 as follows: Murner: *Ich lass mich ober von nemandss, er sey wer er wol, dar von tringen, dass ich die wortern Cristi anderss verstandt dan das er petrum ain felsen genant hat vnd auff den selbenn felsenn, das ist auff petrum, seyne kirchenn gefundiret, dan die wordt Christi lauttenden sein klerer dan die sunne ... Ich sich nit, dass dar auf ottwass vnradtss oder nachtailss entstan kondt oder mog, dass man sprecht, der Text trag disen sin auff im.* Clemen 169f and 172. Pfeiffer-Belli (vol. 7:17f) has a slightly differing spelling which makes the following translation more likely: "Nobody —whoever he may be—can take away from me the understanding of the words of Christ [in Matthew 16:18], that he called Peter a rock and that on this rock, that is on Peter, he founded his church, because the words of Christ are clearer than the sun. I don't see that from this [understanding] could or may come any garbage or disadvantage ... ."

[76] Amman quoted Murner's vernacular as follows: *was wollend die worter auf in tragen, das Im die vrstend Christi in sunderhayt verkundet wardt, das er cephas, das ist ain haupt genendt wirt für die andern alle.* Clemen 174. Pfeiffer-Belli (vol. 7:26) has a slightly differing spelling.

exclaimed: "O you poor Murnar [sic][77], what have you studied! Where have you [learned to] read *cephas* to mean head if not from those who along with you are delirious because of their defective knowledge of the noble languages?"[78] The learned Amman knew, of course, that the latinized *cephas* is the transliteration of the Semitic *képhá* (rock), and that it does not have anything to do with the Greek *kephalé* (head).

There existed at that time a certain battle front of the Augustinians against the Dominicans and Franciscans. However, the front was not delineated as clearly nor as permanently as it seemed at first. The Augustinian Egidio da Viterbo (1469–1532), who up to February 1518 was the Prior General of the order to which Amman and Luther belonged, but now living in Rome having been made a cardinal by Leo X, crossed the line and began to side with the Dominicans and thus with the Roman court's position. After Luther had burned the canon law book and the bull that threatened him with excommunication on 10 December 1520, the Roman authorities proceeded with their call upon the emperor to act on behalf of the Church against Luther. During the pope's deliberations with his cardinals on 6 February 1521 the pope asked them to work on ways to approach the emperor in this regard. Cardinal Egidio now became actively involved against his subordinate, Friar Martin. Egidio's opinion is known as *Informatio pro concilio contra Lutheranos.*[79] He turned out to be a proponent of the universal primacy of the papacy. This learned Cardinal quoted Matthew 16:18 in support for his opinion and relied also on Chrysostom, Augustine, Origen, Jerome, Ambrose, Gregory, Leo, Bede, the *Glossa ordinaria*, Thomas Aquinas, Albert the Great, and those conciliar decrees that support the primacy of the popes. However, he did not make use of canons from the Church's law books in order to avoid, as he stated, "that Martin burn them up again".[80] Interestingly, Egidio pointed out that Luther was correct in interpreting the rock of Matthew 16:18 to mean Christ as the "principal foundation" *(principale fundamentum)*. Simultaneously Egidio insisted that Peter was given the place of a secondary basis (after Christ) by divine decree. The biblical text has several meanings, Egidio pointed

[77] Amman played with Murner's last name here and throughout his pamphlet: Mur-nar(r) = Mur-fool (*Narr* in modern German means fool).

[78] *O du armer Murnar, wass hastu gestudirt! Vbi legisti cephas significare caput nisi apud illos, qui tecum ex linguarum nobilium defectu delirant?* Clemen, 174.

[79] The content of the booklet has little to do with a plea for a council; see Hermann Tüchle, "Des Papstes und seiner Jünger Bücher," in Bäumer, ed., *Lutherprozess*, 49-68, here 51.

[80] *Ne Martinus iterum illos comburat,* as quoted by Tüchle, 57.

out.[81] Luther most likely was not aware of his superior's *Informatio* in which he was called "the father of lies, [and] minister of Satan".[82]

Luther was officially excommunicated on 3 January 1521. Around that time he eagerly worked on texts in Latin[83] and in German[84] in defense against this Roman bull of excommunication. In them he dealt with Matthew 16:18 at length. In the Latin text he used the Vulgate version of Matthew 16:18 and rejected the idea that "rock" would mean the pope's *monarchia*; such an interpretation he considered "most impious and intolerable,"[85] because Christ alone is the "rock".[86] Luther, however, did not quote 1 Corinthians 10:4 at this point in his Latin text while in his vernacular text he did;[87] and he translated Matthew 16:18 in the traditional way.[88]

After the imperial diet of Worms in the spring of 1521 he was confined at the Wartburg Castle, that is from May 1521 on. There he began to translate the New Testament into German, which is known as his *September Testament* because it was first published on 21 September 1522 (without Luther's name) by a printer at Wittenberg. It carried the simple title: *Das Newe Testament Deutzsch* (*The New Testament [in] German*). The twenty-five-year-old Philip Melanchthon, professor of Greek at Wittenberg, had ameliorated Luther's draft over the summer months of 1522 before it went to the press. It made history as it marked the beginning of a new epoch in vernacular Bible versions which no longer were translated exclusively from the Vulgate version.[89]

Matthew 16:18 in Luther's translation reads as follows: *du bist Petrus, vnnd auff disen felss will ich bawen meyne gemeyne*[90] (You are Peter and on this rock I will build my community). Luther here left

[81] See Tüchle, 57.

[82] *Contra patrem mendacii, ministrum sathanae, Martinum; Informatio* as edited in part by Tüchle, 67 (Appendix).

[83] *Assertio omnium articulorum M. Lutheri per Bullam Leonis X. novissimam damnatorum* (1520), WA 7:91-151.

[84] *Grund und Ursach aller Artikel D. Martin Luthers, so durch römische Bulle unrechtlich verdammt sind* (1521), WA 7:299-457.

[85] WA 7:128,33-39.

[86] *Per petram, qua solus Christus,* WA 7:129,14f.

[87] *Darausz folget, dasz dyszer felsz ist Christus selbs, wye yhn sant Paulus nennet i. Cor. x. und der baw ist die glewbige kirche,* WA 7:412,16f.

[88] *Christus spricht Matt. xvi. zu sanct Petro: 'Du bist Petrus (das ist ein felsz), und auff den felsz wil ich bawen meine kirchen...',* WA 7:409,35f.

[89] See Schwarz, *Luther*, 118. Wycliffe's English translation in the 14th century, as well as the first printed Bibles in German of 1466, the Italian version of 1471, the Catalan version of 1478, the Czech version of 1488, and the French of 1530 had Jerome's Latin version (Vulgate) as their basis.

out, of course, the explanatory note in parenthesis (*das ist ein fels*) which he had included in the sermon text of 1519. Luther added instead his marginal note on Matthew 16:18 about the name Peter, namely that it means rock, an opinion which he had already published in his *Commentary on Galatians* in 1519. The marginal note on Matthew 16:18 reads as follows: "(Petrus) *Cepha* in Syriac, *Petros* in Greek, means *fels* [rock] in German, and all Christians are peters [rockers] because of the confession which Peter makes here, [the confession] which is the rock on which Peter and all peters [rockers] are built … . "[91]

After Luther had returned from the Wartburg Castle in March 1522, he preached again on Matthew 16:13-19, for the feast of Saints Peter and Paul, and he called this gospel text "almost the best piece and main sentence"[92] of the entire Gospel of Matthew. Luther expanded the verse again by adding "and a rock" after the name Peter as he had done in his 1519 sermon. He did not use the same German version of Matthew 16:18 which he had used in that sermon nor the one which he offered in his *September Testament* (1522). There is no difference in meaning, only in the wording and spelling. Here is his wording from the 1522 sermon on the power of Saint Peter: *du bist Petrus und ain Felss, und auff den Felss will ich bawen mein Kirchen*[93] (You are Peter and a rock, and on the rock I will build my Church). Luther insisted that Christ is "the entire rock" of which Peter is only "a piece," just as Jesus is called Christ and we are called "Christians" after him because of our fellowship with him and faith in him.[94]

Luther presented basically the same position which the fifteenth century churchmen, the French Cardinal Pierre d'Ailly and the Spanish Bishop Alfonso Tostado had held (without Luther mentioning

[90] WA DB 6:76 (1522), no lines given, as this is a marginal note on "Petrus". One may disregard the differing spelling, as no rules for spelling were known at that time.

[91] *(Petrus) Cepha Syrisch, Petros kriechisch heyst auff deutsch eyn fels vnd alle Christen sind petri vmb der bekentnis willen, die hie Petrus thut, wilche ist der felss, darauff Petrus vnd alle petri bawet sind, gemyn ist die bekentnis also auch der name.* WA DB 6:76 (1522). The same marginal note is kept with different spelling in the edition of 1546 (WA DB 6:77).

[92] *Sermo von Gewalt Sanct Peters,* WA 10^3:208. 4f. *Und ist auch fast das beste stuck und der hauptspruch.*

[93] *Sermo von Gewalt Sanct Peters,* WA 10^3:210.6f. See Reinhard Schwarz, "Der Felsgrund der Kirche. Ein christlicher Sermon von Gewalt S. Peters … ," *Luther* 66 (1995): 2-10.

[94] *Das muest also verston, das hie Petrus ain felßen haist, und Christus hayst ain felß, dann Christus ist der gantze fels, Petrus aber ist ain stuck des felsenß, gleich wie er Christus hayst, wir aber hayssen von jm Christen der gemainschaft und glaubens halben,* WA 10^3:213.11-16.

any names here) and the contemporary Canon Lawyer Cardinal Johannes Antonius de Santo Georgio, who had declared that all the authors of the past always had understood *petra* in Matthew 16:18 to mean Christ. Luther preached that the rock means Christ, or his "word," or "the Christian evangelical truth". He thus sounded here like Cardinal Pierre d'Ailly one hundred years earlier. Luther rejected the equation, rock = Peter and the popes.[95] Although Luther translated "Peter" with "rock" he rejected the idea that this would mean to build the Church on Peter the person. The rock is Christ, he insisted, by following the preferential interpretation of many Catholic Bible scholars and canon lawyers before him. Up to the end of his life Luther maintained that the rock is Christ, and Peter is the "rocker" (*Felser*) because of his profession of faith in the Son of God; and this understanding is, according to Luther, the simple and certain meaning of the words of Matthew 16:18.[96] When in December 1523 Luther corresponded with the Grand-Master of the Teutonic Knights, he included a lengthy passage on his view of Peter and the papacy. He wrote that Peter and the pope cannot possibly be the "foundation" or the "rock" (*petra*) of the Church, and gave his known reasons for maintaining this position.[97] In Luther's revision/translation of the Latin Bible on which he worked during the 1520s, nothing changed in the wording of Matthew 16:18. Luther's Latin Bible reads the same as the traditional Vulgate version: *Tu es Petrus, et super hanc petram aedificabo Ecclesiam meam.*[98]

In interpreting Matthew 16:18, Luther the Augustinian friar conflicted with contemporary Dominican and Franciscan friars such as the Dominican Cardinal Cajetan and the two Franciscans, Alveldt and Murner, and also with the theologian and humanist Jerome Emser (1477–1527) at the court of Duke George of Saxony. Emser objected to Luther's translations in the *September Testament*, as it soon became known that Luther was its translator.[99] According to Emser,

[95] WA 10^3:210.11 - 211.18.

[96] *Wider das Papstum zu Rom, vom Teufel gestiftet* (1545), WA 54:206-299, here 248 and 253. Luther saw this verse directed against the papacy as he knew it: *das Bapstum zu grund stoertze und zu nicht machet,* WA 54:231.10; at this point Luther was reminded of the Leipzig Disputation "against the D[octor] Sow Eck," *wider D. Saw Eken* (line 11).

[97] *Matth. 16 ... Quod autem Petrus aut papa non possint esse fundamentum aut petra ista ecclesiae, probatur multis modis....* WA Br 3:209,12-21 (no. 697); LW 49:61-62.

[98] WA DB 5:500. 41 - 501.1.

[99] *Aus was Grund und Ursach Luthers Dolmetschung über das Neue Testament dem gemeinen Mann billig verboten worden sei.* Critical edition by Adolf Laube and Ulman Weiss (eds.), *Flugschriften gegen die Reformation (1518–1524)* (Berlin: Akademie Verlag, 1997), 509-29.

Luther perverted the texts and added false glosses and prefaces, all "to his own advantage".[100] Apparently, Emser was of the opinion that translations may not be liberal (*ad sensum*), but have to be literal (*ad verbum*). Emser, however, had nothing to say about Matthew 16:18, perhaps because Luther's version of it was not controversial to him at all.

We may recapitulate: Luther's contemporary Dominican and Franciscan opponents appear to have taken from the history of the interpretation of Matthew 16:18 and from the history of the effect *(Wirkungsgeschichte)* of this verse only those elements that support the equation, rock=Peter the person, disregarding Augustine's own revision in his *Reconsiderations (Retractationes)*, and also disregarding all the other scholars and canon lawyers who argued with 1 Corinthians 10:4 (*petra autem erat Christus*) that *petra* in Matthew 16:18 most of all means Christ. Luther drew out the ancient line that the rock is Christ; everything else is derived and dependent upon Christ. In a table talk of the 1530s Luther declared that those who take Matthew 16:18 to mean the political primacy of the papacy are on the wrong track *(Holzweg)*, because this text is concerned with the "keys" and with the "forgiveness of sins".[101]

In the context of these polemics and controversies, Friar Caspar Amman made his own distinct contribution to the issue of interpreting Matthew 16:18. Generally, Amman sided with his confrère Luther against the authors from the other two religious orders and against other secular priests. In addition, however, Amman simultaneously criticized Luther for the inconsistency he displayed in his translation of Matthew 16:18 in the *September Testament*, where he had offered the reading quoted above: *du bist Petrus, vnnd auff disen felss will ich bawen meyne gemeyne* (You are Peter and on this rock I will build my community). Amman appears to have been at odds with Luther because Luther did not pay attention to the original meaning of the name "Peter" as "recognizer" as, for example, Bede and Hrabanus had pointed out. This neglect appears to be the main reason for Amman to write his letter to Luther on 26 October 1522. Before I

[100] *Auff seyn vorteyl*; In: *Annotationes des hochgelerten vnd Christlichen doctors Hieronymi Emßers seligen / ueber Luthers new Testament...* (1524), 215, as quoted in Gardt 99, note 54.

[101] *Holzweg: Als da der Papst diesen Spruch Matth. am sechzehenden auf sein Primat zeucht: [16:18], da doch der Text redet von Schlüsseln und Vergebung der Sünden; so bringet der Papst seinen Dieterich, weltliche Kaiserthume und Königreiche einzunehmen und zu besitzen.* WA Tr 1:223,2-5 (no. 4322).

present its first English translation, a biographical sketch of this humanistic friar from Lauingen is in order.[102]

III. Caspar Amman and his Understanding of Matthew 16:18

Amman was born about 1450 at Hasselt in Belgium; thus, he was about 33 years older than Luther. Amman became an Augustinian friar at Lauingen (on the Danube) in southwestern Germany. In 1477 he was sent to Italy (perhaps to Siena, Bologna, and Ferrara?) in order to study theology and canon law. He returned with the double major, *Doctor sacrae paginae et pontificiorum canonum*. He became prior of his friary in 1485, provincial of the Augustinian province of Swabia and the Upper Rhine region from 1500 to 1503, and again from 1514 to 1518. For five years, from 1505 to 1510, according to Amman's preface in his German translation of the Hebrew Psalter which is dedicated to his professor of Hebrew, Johannes Boeschenstein (or Joannes Boschenstain, 1472–1540), he—now advanced in age—studied Hebrew under the much younger instructor at the University of Ingolstadt.[103] Boeschenstein was the author of several books.[104]

Among Amman's fellow students taught by Boeschenstein were the humanist Johann Eck (or Eckius, *orator et doctor theologiae,* later on one of Luther's most outspoken opponents), Sebastianus Sperantius (or Sprentz, later Bishop of Brixen, c. 1480–1525),[105] and Eberhardus Caesare de Forchaim (or Caeser, Keiser of Forchheim) with his son Bartholomaeus who in January 1519 was a candidate for the Hebrew teaching position at the University of Wittenberg.[106] They were listed

[102] See Wagner, 42-64 (see n. 2 above); Clemen, 162-67; Adalbero Kunzelmann, *Geschichte der deutschen Augustiner-Eremiten* (7 vols., Würzburg, 1969-), 2:160 with n. 566; Posset, entry "Amman" in *Biographisch-Bibliographisches Kirchenlexikon* 16:49-52.

[103] ... *Als nun du aller liebster johann [Boeschenstein] mein erster schuolmaister biss in das fünfft jar der hebraischen zungen jnn meinem hohen alter gewesst bist...* Amman, preface in *Psalter des kuniglichen prophetten Davids geteutscht nach wahrhafftigem text der hebraischen zungen* (Augsburg: Sigmund Grimm, 1523), quoted after Wagner 53; see also Kunzelmann, 2:161, n. 566.

[104] *Elementale introductorium in hebreas literas teutonice et hebraice legendas,* 1514; *Hebraicae Grammaticae,* 1518; *Rudimenta Hebraica Mosche Kimhi,* 1520; and *Septem Psalmi Poenitentiales,* 1520.

[105] See the biographical sketch in Conradin Bonorand, *Joachim Vadian und der Humanismus im Bereich des Erzbistums Salzburg* (St. Gallen, Switzerland: Verlag der Fehr'schen Buchhandlung AG, 1980), 204-06.

[106] See WA Br 1:297 with n. 1. Bartholomaeus is the author of the *Elementale hebraicum* (Leipzig: Melchior Lotther, 1516). However, Matthaeus Aurogallus (1490-1543), author of the *Compendium Hebreae grammatices* (1523) was apparently hired for Wittenberg.

as Boeschenstein's students *(auditores)* in the preface to his book on learning Hebrew, *Elementale introductorium in hebreas literas teutonice et hebraice legendas*, dedicated to Johann Reuchlin, dated 2 June 1514, and published at Augsburg.[107] Amman was listed as *theologiae doctor, provincialis ordinis divi Augustini*. He became one of the most known humanists of his time and an expert of the three sacred languages. An inscription on a wall of his friary at Lauingen celebrated the Hebrew language as the font of all the others:

Hebraei fontem	The Hebrews drink from the source,
Graeci rivulos	the Greeks from the small creeks,
Latini paludem bibunt.[108]	the Latins from the swamp.

The images of "creeks" (rivulets) and their "source" (spring) may have originated from Saint Jerome in his search of the "Hebrew truth".[109] Amman was fluent in Latin as were most of the scholars of that time. He knew Greek as we may derive from the fact that he used a Greek dictionary.[110] Most of all, he was an expert in Hebrew,

[107] The preface was edited by Ludwig Geiger, *Johann Reuchlins Briefwechsel gesammelt und herausgegeben* (Stuttgart: Fues, 1875; reprint Hildesheim, 1962), 216; the other Hebraists who are mentioned by Boeschenstein are: Henricus de Sax (St Peter church at Basel, and canon of Constance), Joannes Schlupf (doctor of theology), Wolfgangus Schwarzenstainer (doctor of civil and ecclesiastical law), Udalricus Jung (doctor of medicine), Joannes Faltermair (doctor of civil and ecclesiastical law), Georgius Oberhofer (philosopher), Joannes Vischer of Dietfurt (philosopher), the nobleman Guilhermus Troenberk, Joannes Voegelin (philosopher), Joannes Pinicianus (priest at Augsburg, *presbiter Augustensis*), and Henricus Vitellius.

[108] Hedwig Vonschott, *Geistiges Leben im Augustinerorden am Ende des Mittelalters und zu Beginn der Neuzeit* (Berlin, 1915; reprint: Vaduz: Kraus Reprint Ltd., 1965), 103; Wagner, 46; see Luther's version of this adage below with n. 144.

[109] *Sicut autem in nouo testamento, si quando apud Latinos quaestio exoritur et est inter exemplaria uarietas, recurrimus ad fontem Graeci sermonis, quo nouum scriptum est instrumentum, ita et in ueteri testamento, si quando inter Graecos Latinosque diuersitas est, ad Hebraicam confugimus ueritatem, ut, quicquid de fonte proficiscitur, hoc quaeramus in riuulis, Epistola* 106,2, CSEL 55:249.3-9. See also Ep 20,2 *(ad Damasum): omissis opinionum rivulis ad ipsum fontem, unde ab evangelistis sumptum est, recurramus,* CSEL 54:104.14f.

[110] The dictionary is mentioned in his correspondence of 18 August 1521 with the Benedictine humanist, Veit Bild (1481–1529) of Augsburg; see Alfred Schroeder, "Der Humanist Veit Bild, Moench bei St. Ulrich," *Zeitschrift des Historischen Vereins für Schwaben und Neuburg* 20 (1893): 173-227, here 207 (nos. 171 and 176); Vonschott, 103-5. The degree of Amman's knowledge of Greek is not known. He must have been one of the few who wanted to learn this language at around 1500 in Germany when only a few scholars knew Greek. See Louis Kukenheim, *Contributions a l'histoire de la grammaire grecque, latine, et hébraique a l'époque de la Renaissance* (Leiden: E. J. Brill, 1951), 7; on p. 139 Caspar Ammonius [sic] is listed as the author of an unedited Hebrew textbook.

unlike Erasmus who early on had given up on mastering this language.[111] As one of the first scholars ever, Amman translated the entire Psalter directly from the Hebrew into the vernacular and edited it with a dedication to Boeschenstein, affirming that he translated "into German from the Hebrew truth" *(in teutsch auss hebraischer warhait)*, or as the title itself says: "The Psalter of the royal Prophet David translated into German from the true text of the Hebrew tongue."[112] By this he meant being truthful to the Hebrew original text in following the humanistic principle of observing the *Hebraica veritas*. However, his translation had the great disadvantage of not being understood very well in other parts of the empire where other dialects were spoken. Therefore, his translation efforts did not make history in the way Luther's did, who translated into the Saxon chancery language that was understood universally.[113] This Saxon chancery version was also very close to the official language used at the international court of Emperor Maximilian (1459–1519), as it represented a felicitous compromise between the various dialects of Northern and Southern Germany.

Amman also considered himself a student of the German Christian Hebraist Johann Reuchlin (1455–1522) and of the Spanish Christian Hebraist Matthaeus Adrianus (died 1521?). The latter was the author of an introduction to Hebrew *(Introductio utilissima,* 1513). Amman was so very familiar with Hebrew that he was able to read and write letters in Hebrew.[114] Amman's (and Luther's) religious superior in Rome, Prior General Egidio da Viterbo, later a cardinal, asked Amman on 15 December 1513 to send him a list of Hebrew books, and since he knew that Amman knew Reuchlin, Egidio wanted in particular the list of books of Reuchlin's library.[115] In contrast to

[111] See Roland H. Bainton, *Erasmus of Christendom* (New York: Crossroad, 1982), 227.

[112] Amman, *Psalter des küniglichen prophetten Dauids geteutscht nach wahrhafftigem text der hebraischen zungen* (1523), quoted after Wagner 52.

[113] Luther: *Ich rede nach der sächsischen Canzeley* : "I speak the language of the Saxon chancery, which all the German princes and kings in Germany are using; all imperial cities and princely courts write in the way of the Saxon and our prince's chancery; therefore it is the most commonly used German language." WA Tr 1:524.42-525.1; see also WA Tr 2:639.17 and 30 (no. 2758a and b). See on this Heinrich Bornkamm, *Luther in Mid-Career 1521–1530* (Philadelphia: Fortress, 1983), 49.

[114] The letter of Adrianus is extant at the university library in Munich; see Hans Striedl, ed., *Verzeichnis der orientalischen Handschriften in Deutschland. Vol. 6,2: Hebräische Handschriften, Teil 2* (Wiesbaden: Franz Steiner Verlag, 1965), 305 (no. 489). Amman's letter to Reuchlin of 23 September 1515 in Hebrew characters is edited by Eric Zimmer, "Hebrew Letters of Two Sixteenth Century German Humanists," *Revue des études juives* 141 (1982) 379-86, here 385.

[115] The Latin text excerpt is found in Geiger, *Johann Reuchlins Briefwechsel,*

the Dominicans in Rome, the Augustinian Egidio was convinced that Reuchlin was serving the Church well with his defense of Hebrew books including the Talmud.[116] Later, Reuchlin himself sent Egidio his book *de arte cabbalistica*, for which Egidio thanked him on 24 May 1517.[117] To Amman the Prior General wrote (in a note attached to his letter of 15 December 1513): "You would give us the greatest treasures, riches, and kingdoms, if you would procure codices for us. We will be eternally grateful for them."[118] Egidio's scholarly hunger for Hebrew was so great that since 1509 he had hired the Jewish humanist Elia(s) Levita (c. 1460–1549), also known as Elia Bahur, son of Asher the German,[119] to teach him Hebrew at home.

Amman had contacts also with the Augustinian Friar Felix Pratensis (= Felix de Prato, or Felice da Prato, died 1539 in Rome), a rabbi who converted to Christianity, was baptized in 1513, and joined the Augustinian order. In 1515 he published a fresh translation of the Psalter from Hebrew into Latin.[120] He became a master of theology, teacher of Hebrew, and editor of Hebrew books in Venice where he was the director of Daniel Bomberg's printing press/bookstore. This Christian Hebraist (who was also called *Israelita*) informed Amman on 4 October 1514 that he was unable to procure the Hebrew Bible which Amman had requested,[121] as this first rabbinical Bible was not available until 1517/1518, then edited by him (Felice) with a dedication to Pope Leo X, a patron to the Jews and humanists alike. This Bible was published by Bomberg in Venice.[122]

Furthermore, Amman had friendly relations with the language scholar, cartographer, and Franciscan Friar Sebastian Münster (1488/89–1552/53)[123] who was born at Ingelheim on the Rhine; he became

260, n. 1: ... *Gratissimam nobis rem feceris, si ad nos quam primum mittas indicem librorum omnium, quos ille idem praeceptor* [Reuchlin] *habet tuus...*

[116] See David Werner Amram, *The Makers of Hebrew Books in Italy* (Philadelphia: Julius H. Greenstone, 1909; reprint: London: Holland Press, 1963), 167 and 239.

[117] See Geiger, *Johann Reuchlins Briefwechsel,* 276.

[118] As quoted by Wagner, 50, n. 1. This portion of Egidio's letter of 15 December 1513 to Amman in not reprinted in Geiger's edition, but mentioned by Francis X. Martin, *Friar, Reformer, and Renaissance Scholar: Life and Work of Giles of Viterbo 1469–1532* (Villanova: Augustinian Press, 1992), 163.

[119] He was called "the German" because he was born in Ipsheim near Nuremberg.

[120] *Psalterium ex Hebraeo ad verbum fere translatum* (printed by Herman Liechtenstein in 1515). On the production of Hebrew books in Venice at that time, see Amram, 146-224; on Felice da Prato's year of baptism, see 152. See also WA DB 10^2,2:158, n. 4 and 185, n. 3.

[121] See Wagner, 50f; Vonschott, 104f.

[122] See Amram, 156.

[123] See Wagner, 49.

of follower of Luther in the 1520s; later he married the widow of a printer in Basel; his step-son Heinrich Petri became his printer. Münster was the editor of the Bible in Hebrew with Latin translation *(Hebraica Biblia)* which was completed in 1534/35. His Hebrew text is derived from Felice da Prato's edition of 1524/25.[124] In his preface Münster acknowledged that he utilized Hebrew exegetes in order to arrive at the "Hebrew truth".[125]

Amman also knew the linguist Georg Simler (ca. 1475–1535),[126] a friend of Reuchlin and Philipp Melanchthon's professor of Greek and Latin at Pforzheim and Tübingen.[127] Amman was so well connected and known that the humanist Wolfgang Fabritius Capito (1478–1541), a student of Adrianus, sought his advice on linguistic matters as he was editing his Hebrew grammar in Basel, which was printed by Froben in 1518. In it Capito called Amman an extraordinary learned man in this sacred language,[128] and he considered himself his student, as did Johann Oecolampadius (1482–1531).[129] The seventeenth century Christian Hebraist, Theodorus Ebertus, ranked Amman about as high as the most famous of the German Hebraists, Johann Reuchlin.[130]

Friar Amman's connections to the leading Hebrew scholars of his time and their great respect for his scholarship demonstrate him as one of the most significant biblical humanists who specialized in the Hebrew language. Amman and the two other members of the Augustinian order, Egidio da Viterbo and Felice da Prato (Israelita),

[124] Jaroslav Pelikan, *The Reformation of the Bible. The Bible of the Reformation* (New Haven and London: Yale University Press, 1996), 106. A copy of the *Hebraica Biblia* is today at the Newberry Library in Chicago. In 1528 Pagninus edited a new Latin translation of the Bible. Leo Juda of Zurich published his in 1545, and Tremellius his in 1579; apparently, a more accurate Latin version was desired as long as Latin remained the language of the learned.

[125] *Hebraica Biblia*; see Frank Rosenthal, "The Rise of Christian Hebraism in the Sixteenth Century," *Historia Judaica* 7 (1945): 167-91, here 186f.

[126] See Wagner, 49.

[127] See Reinhard Pohlke, "Melanchthon und sein Griechischlehrer Georg Simler—zwei Vermittler des Griechischen in Deutschland," in Stefan Rhein, Armin Schlechter, and Udo Wennemuth, eds, *Philipp Melanchthon in Südwestdeutschland: Bildungsstationen eines Reformators* (Karlsruhe: Badische Landesbibliothek, 1997), 39-61. Simler's other famous student was Franciscus Irenicus (1497–1554), author of *Exegeseos Germaniae* (Hagenau and Nuremberg: Thomas Anshelm, 1518) which is a description of the land and its people in twelve volumes (500 pages).

[128] *Sanctaequae linguae haud vulgariter doctus*, Capito, *Hebraicarum institutionum libri duo* (Basel: Froben, 1518), as quoted in Wagner 48, n. 4.

[129] See Wagner, 49.

[130] *Reuchlino aequalis fere fuit Caspar Ammonius … patronus harum literarum et cultor,* Theodorus Ebertus, *Elogia Ictorum, qui Ebraicam linguam promoverant, 8*, as found in Wagner, 48, n. 4; Vonschott, 104.

represent the three outstanding Christian Hebraists within the religious order to which Luther belonged.[131]

It is probably safe to say that Luther was as eager a student of Hebrew as Amman, since both were determined to learn from Reuchlin's expertise.[132] However, out of his concern as a curate (*Seelsorger*) Luther at that time was concerned primarily with translating the Bible into communicable German, not emphasizing from where it was translated, that is, from the original biblical languages, while Amman concentrated on the original texts (*ad verbum*, "literally," as Amman pointed out in the 1515 edition of his Psalter translation from Hebrew into Latin); he was less concerned about the good communicability of his translation. Luther in his *September Testament* only indicated that it was written in "German" (*Das Newe Testament Deutzsch*). Melanchthon had to proof-read it because Luther's knowledge of Greek was inadequate. Luther was unable to read, for example, what his confrère and confidant Johann Lang of the friary at Erfurt, wrote to him on 18 December 1519 because Lang had written the letter in Greek.[133] Luther himself never claimed to have translated exclusively from the Greek original. Out of his concern for pastoral care, all he wanted was to give the Germans a vernacular version which they were able to understand.[134] In a table talk of the 1530s Luther supposedly said: "I do not know Greek or Hebrew."[135] This was an understatement, since he had made great efforts to take the original languages into consideration, such as in

[131] See David Gutierrez, *The Augustinians from the Protestant Reformation to the Peace of Westphalia 1518–1648* (2 vols., Villanova: Augustinian Historical Institute, 1979) 2:143.

[132] As to Luther, see his letter to Reuchlin of 14 December 1518, WA Br 1:269.

[133] *Non satis intellexi quid velles, cum scriberes Graece,* WA Br 1:597.25.

[134] See Hermann Dippelt, "Hatte Luthers Verdeutschung des Neuen Testaments den griechischen Text zur Grundlage?," ARG 38 (1941): 300-30; Rudolf Riedlinger, "Welchen Grundtext übersetzte Martin Luther für seine Deutsche Bibel?," *Jahrbuch der österreichischen Byzantinistik* 42 (1992): 325-30; idem, "Nach welcher Vorlage übersetzte Martin Luther den Hebräerbrief für das Septembertestament von 1522?," *Römische Historische Mitteilungen* 30 (1988): 93-112. Riedlinger came to the same conclusions as Dippelt; see also Franz Posset, "What Bible Version Did Luther Use in his Academic Work?" which is Chapter 2 in *Luther's Catholic Christology According to his Johannine Lectures of 1527* (Milwaukee: Northwestern Publishing House, 1988), 66-89. Heinz Bluhm euphemistically wrote of *Martin Luther—Creative Translator* (St Louis: Concordia, 1965).

[135] WA TR 1:524 (1532). *Ut nec Graeca nec Hebraica nec Latina possum (intelligo),* WA TR 4:608.13f (comparing himself to the Christian Hebraist, Dr Johann Forstemius [or Forster, 1496–1556], who was a member of the team of Bible translators up to 1535 at Wittenberg).

his *Operationes in Psalmos* of 1519–1521.[136] Luther possessed a Hebrew textbook which he had received from Lang.[137] Luther also appears to have used Reuchlin's Hebrew textbook.[138] In the preface Reuchlin indicated that he was interested in the "Hebrew truth".[139] The same concern guided Luther in the 1520s when he worked on the revision of the Latin Bible (Vulgate) "according to the Hebrew truth," as he wrote in a letter dated 21 March 1527, in which he also asked prayers for him and his project.[140] However, Luther strongly felt his linguistic inadequacies as he admitted in a table talk in the 1530s.[141] He includes a reference to the same adage on the three languages that was found on the wall in Amman's friary at Lauingen. This popular imagery of spring-creek-swamp (or puddles) was also shared by Cardinal Ximenes de Cisneros in his "Prologue to the Books

[136] Luther frankly admitted that his translation is not *ad verbum* (literal), but *ad sensum* (liberal, to catch the sense, meaning of the original). Luther: *nostra translatio ad verbum nihil est, ad sensum autem propriissima;* WA 5:73 (*Operationes*); see on this Andreas Gardt, "Die Übersetzungstheorie Martin Luthers," *Zeitschrift für deutsche Philologie* 3 (1992): 87-111. Luther's theory of translating is reader-orientated; see the digest in English of Gardt's article, in *Luther Digest* 3 (1995): 27-29.

[137] See WA 9:115; Bornkamm, *Luther in Mid-Career 1521–1530,* 86.

[138] See WA Br 2:547.2ff. Luther corresponded with Reuchlin on 14 December 1518; Luther quoted from Reuchlin's *De Arte Cabalistica* in his letter to Spalatin of 29 June 1518; an English translation of Reuchlin's book is provided by Martin Goodman, *On the Art of the Kabbalah* (University of Nebraska Press, 1993). See also Spalatin's letter to Luther of 1514: WA Br 1:23 (no. 7).

[139] See Geiger, *Johann Reuchlins Briefwechsel,* 96.

[140] *Sum in opere Biblia corrigendi ad veritatem Ebraicam, ora pro nobis,* WA Br 4:177.23f (no. 1089).

[141] "If I were younger I would want to learn this tongue [Hebrew] because without it one can never rightly understand the Sacred Scriptures. The New Testament, though written in Greek, is full of Hebraisms and of Hebraic expressions. Therefore they have said corrrectly: The Hebrews drink from the [original] spring, the Greeks from the small creeks which issue from the spring, the Latins, however, drink from the puddle.

I am no Hebraist, as regards grammar and rules, for I let myself not be bound but pass freely through [them]. Though a man knows and understands a language he cannot properly translate one tongue into another. Translating is a special grace and gift of God. … Indeed St. Jerome's version and method ought to be preferred.… Lyra has been the best Hebraist above all others and a busy interpreter of the Old Testament. If, however, I would study Hebrew, I should take as guides the purest and best grammarians such as David Kimhi and Moses Kimhi who are the purest." *Wenn ich jünger wäre.… Die Ebräer trinken aus der Bornquelle; die Griechen aber aus den Wässerlin, die aus der Quelle fließen; die Lateinischen aber aus der Pfützen …,* WA TR 1:525.15-39 (no. 1040). On this, see Rosenthal 167-91, who, however, did not mention Amman as one of the most prominent Christian Hebraists of that time.

of the Old and New Testaments Printed in Their Various Languages."[142] This saying must have been common knowledge,[143] based on Jerome as mentioned. Already in a letter of December 1519 Luther had written to Jerome Dungersheim (1465–1540) that he preferred to follow the creeks up to the spring, something which Saint Bernard, too, had taken pride in doing.[144] Evidently, Luther shared with contemporary humanists the conviction that one has to turn away from the puddles and return to the clear waters of the original spring.

At the time when church and state tried to enforce the Edict of Worms against Luther, Amman stayed at a priest-friend's house at Dillingen (near Augsburg) during the months of May and June, 1522. His friend was Kaspar Haslach who had held the preacher position at Dillingen since 1519 and who had wanted Amman to tutor him in Hebrew. As the Luther affair was in full swing, they must have conversed about it. Kaspar Haslach unequivocally sided publicly with Luther and therefore was cited to his bishop's court at Augsburg on 8 July 1522. He retracted and thus avoided further trouble.[145] Amman, too, was convinced of Luther's cause. To his friend Kaspar (or Gaspar) he dedicated the pamphlet which he felt compelled to write on the issues related to the proper understanding of Matthew 16:18. His booklet has the long explanatory title:

> Master Gaspar Amman's true exposition of the words of Christ, "You are peter [sic] and on this rock I will build my Church," "You will be called cephas that is translated as "Peter" "and I will give you the keys of the kingdom of heaven" against the false interpretation of Doctor Thomas Murner; ladled from the Hebrew

[142] John C. Olin, *Catholic Reform from Cardinal Ximenes to the Council of Trent 1495–1563: An Essay with Illustrative Documents and a Brief Study of St. Ignatius Loyola* (New York: Fordham University Press, 1990), 63.

[143] Kaspar Schatzgeyer used it in 1501, according to Theo Bell, *Divus Bernhardus: Bernhard von Clairvaux in Martin Luthers Schriften* (Mainz: Philipp von Zabern, 1993), 167, n. 213.

[144] *Rivulos ad fontem usque sequi, quod et Bernhardus se facere gloriatur.* WA Br 1:602. 44-46 (no. 235). In 1539 Luther repeated that with Bernard he too prefers to drink from the spring rather than from the brooks, WA 50:525.23-30 (*Von den Konziliis und Kirchen*); see Franz Posset, *Pater Bernhardus: Martin Luther and Bernard of Clairvaux* (Kalamazoo: Cistercian Publications, 1999), 143f, 159.

[145] Haslach, however, did not give up his sympathies for Luther. In one of the books which he possessed he entered the note that he was grateful to God that he lived in a time when Martin Luther spread the gospel truth. In 1544 his book ended up in the "Preacher's Library" of the Lutheran Nikolai Church in Isny (southwestern Germany). See Immanuel Kammerer and Ulrich Weible, *Bibliothek der Nikolaikirche Isny* (Munich and Zurich: Verlag Schnell & Steiner, 1976).

font. Friar Gaspar Amman, Augustinian, [with] best wishes to Gaspar Haslach, priest and theologian.[146]

Amman wanted to refute false interpretations on the basis of the "Hebrew font" (*ex fonte Hebreo*). In the title of this pamphlet he mentioned by name only the Franciscan Thomas Murner as his target, but he also had in mind his confrère Martin Luther whom he mentioned in the text itself several times in both favorable and unfavorable terms.

Why had Murner become his target? At the end of 1520 Murner had written on the papacy as the highest authority of the Christian faith and in this context he had used Matthew 16:18 and John 1:42 for his argumentation.[147] Amman was incensed by Murner's pseudo-scholarly use of the Scriptures. He decided to go public against this false interpretation (*contra falsam expositionem*). In his preface he scolded Murner for his foolishness and called him just an inexperienced child when it comes to the knowledge of Hebrew. One should flee from the work by this Franciscan, he recommended, and instead one should read what "our Augustinian, Luther" had to say in his "most Christian exposition of the Epistle of Paul to the Galatians." In it one may find the best information which Luther "drew from the true interpretation of the Hebrew words."[148] Amman proclaimed his fellow Augustinian to be "the new prophet and sharpest defender of the evangelical truth."[149] Amman asserted that he did not want to write against the power of the Roman pope, but only against the false interpretation of Christ's words, as he developed his position from the "true font of the Hebrews".[150] He was convinced that Jesus spoke to his disciples in Hebrew, not in Latin or Greek. For support Amman quoted Bede's interlinear gloss on Matthew 4:5 (on "Peter") where "Peter" is interpreted as "recognizer".[151] Amman then presented his reconstruction of Christ's word to Peter in Matthew 16:18 in He-

[146] Edited by Otto Clemen, "Eine Abhandlung Kaspar Ammans" ARG 4 (1906): 162-83 with text on 167-80.

[147] Murner, *Uon dem babystenthum, Deutsche Schriften*, vol. 7:17f. Luther referred to Murner's interpretation in his response to both Emser and Murner, *Auf das überchristlich, übergeistlich und überkünstlich Buch Bocks Emsers zu Leipzig Antwort. Darin auch Murnarrs seines Gesellen gedacht wird* (1521), WA 7:614-688, here 685,35-687,14. The Church is built invisibly on the rock Christ: *unsichtlich auff den felß Christum gepawen stett*, WA 7:686,35f. Luther ridiculed the attempt to make "Peter" out of "petra": *machenn auß petra Petrum*, WA 7:687,3.

[148] *Et illic inuenies quam dulcissimos christiane informationis sensus, ex vera hebraicarum dictionum interpretatione suxit,* Clemen, 168.

[149] *Euangelice veritatis propugnator,* Clemen, 169.

[150] *Expositiones ex vero hebreorum fonte,* Clemen, 169.

[151] *Beda: pethrus agnoscens,* Clemen, 170.

brew characters, and in his Latin translation: "And I tell you: You are the recognizer and on this heavenly recognition I will build my Church."[152] Amman showed further proof from Scripture arguing with a passage from the story of Joseph in Genesis 40:8 in which the Hebrew word *pithron* (cognition) is used which is derived from the Hebrew root word *pother* (to which he connected "Peter"). As Joseph revealed the heavenly interpretation of a dream, so Peter had the heavenly insight that Christ is the Son of God. Amman interpreted this Hebrew word in the same way as Reuchlin did.[153] Therefore, the original truth of Christ's word to Simon is this:

> You are Peter, and on this *pethram* I will build my Church, which in translation reads: You are the recognizer, and on this heavenly recognition I will build my Church.[154]

At this point in the pamphlet Amman inserted his criticism of Luther's (and "several others'") understanding that failed to read this text with the Hebrew original in mind. However, he was glad to see that Luther had explained the "Hebrew truth" in a spiritual way in his commentary on the Psalms *(Operationes in Psalmos)*:

> O Martin Luther, servant of Christ, why I ask have you given so little attention, along with several others, to this most true sentence [Matthew 16:18]? Why did you sleep here, while often elsewhere you have explained the Hebrew truth *(Hebraicam veritatem)* in a spiritual way, as you evidently had done in your most noble exposition of the Psalms?[155]

Amman deplored that Luther did not consult any of the Hebrew specialists such as Matthaeus Adrianus who recently had been hired for the University of Wittenberg where Luther himself was teach-

[152] Clemen has *himlische erkantnuß* here (171), while the WA editor of Amman's letter has *haimliche Bekanntnuß* (WA Br 2:608.47). Apparently, both expressions were understood as synonyms in German; see below with n. 174.

[153] *Rudimenta hebraica* (1506), 443: *pathar solvit aenigmata et coniectavit somnia, exposuit arcana, Gen. 40 … Inde pithron coniectatio, interpretatio, eiusdem 40*, as quoted in WA Br 2:610, n. 14.

[154] *Videamus nunc veritatem principalem verborum christi d[omini]. Et ego dico tibi, quia tu es Petrus, et super hanc pethram ecclesiam meam vnnd ich sag dir, du bist der erkenner, vnd auff dise himlische erkantnuß will ich bawen mein kirchenn.* Clemen, 171. As to the translation of "Peter" into German *erkenner* (recognizer, confessor), Amman is in agreement (whether he knows it or not) also with the medieval preacher, the so-called *St. Georgener Prediger*, who declared that "Peter" means *erkenner*: *'Peter' daz ist also vil gesprochen alz ain erkenner*; see Jacob Grimm und Wilhelm Grimm, *Deutsches Wörterbuch* (Stuttgart and Leipzig: Hirzel, 1996), s. v. "Erkenner," vol. 8:1863f.

[155] *O Martine Luthere, …* , Clemen, 172.

ing.[156] Amman nevertheless liked Luther very much, and because of his *amor* for him he felt compelled to write on this issue according to the original meaning of the text. While Luther at least had made an effort to do his work on the basis of the original texts, as much as he was able to, even though he was not learned enough in them, Murner failed completely to take the original languages into consideration. Amman therefore challenged Murner to reveal the sources from which he understood the verse. Apparently Murner was unable to say anything based on the "Greek small creeks" and only false things based on the "Hebrew font":

> But I tell you, that your interpretation ... which takes *petra* to mean the Apostle Peter is utterly false, erroneous, and very detrimental. But the [translation] of the words of Christ which I proposed from the Hebrew font, is most true, Catholic, and of the greatest use.[157]

Amman found himself in agreement with Erasmus: "O Murfool *[murnar]*, listen, therefore, to the most learned and pure man, Erasmus of Rotterdam," and his bilingual edition of the New Testament with annotations. Amman quoted from Erasmus' 1516 edition: "And on this rock, that is this solid profession of faith, I will build my Church." From the 1519 edition he quoted Erasmus' reaction that this verse had been twisted to fit the Roman pontiff while it was meant for all Christians according to the "elegant" homily of Origen. Amman continued that this interpretation is in agreement with Augustine, Aegidius Romanus, Albertus Magnus, Hugo Cardinalis, and *Lira* (Lyra).[158]

During his pastoral work Amman is said to have refused to read from his pulpit the emperor's edict and the pope's bull of excommunication against Luther. He even may have preached openly against both bull and edict. No wonder that he was arrested by the local territorial lord, Ottheinrich, who delivered him to the Bishop of Augsburg who imprisoned him in 1523. Apparently Amman was free again in summer of 1524, when he died in peace with the

[156] Apparently, Amman knew that Adrianus had become professor of Hebrew at Wittenberg in 1520/1521. On teaching Hebrew at Wittenberg, see Hans-Jürgen Zobel, "Die Hebraisten an der Universität Wittenberg (1502–1817) in Julia Männchen and Ernst-Joachim Waschke, eds, *Altes Testament—Literatursammlung und Heilige Schrift* (Berlin: Walter de Gruyter, 1993), 201-28, here 209.

[157] Clemen, 172.

[158] Clemen, 172f. Amman's booklet cannot be dealt with in full length here. It contains numerous other ideas worthy of further investigation.

Church.[159] The famous reformer Urbanus Rhegius (1489–1441) at Augsburg ranked Amman first among all of the Hebrew scholars.[160]

That in those days the interpretation of Matthew 16:18 was hotly debated may be seen (in addition to what has been said already) from several pamphlets of the early 1520s. At the beginning of 1522, Erasmus' third edition of the New Testament in Greek and Latin appeared. In March 1522, his *Paraphrases* became available. Based on either his 1516 edition or his 1522 edition of the New Testament, a pamphlet with the German version of his remarks on Matthew 16:18 was published at Augsburg.[161] Also in 1522 an anonymous pamphlet was circulating in German on *The Rock of the Christian Church*.[162] The train of its argumentation is the same as in Amman's Latin booklet against Murner and in his letter to Luther of 26 October 1522, so that one may safely assume that Amman was also the author/translator of this third text. The main points are presented in the identical sequence in both the Latin and German pamphlets. However, any hints or references to Luther were deleted in the vernacular version.

Amman's private letter was meant as some sort of scholarly, fraternal correction. The letter is dated 26 October 1522, that is, one month after the publication of the *September Testament* which Amman evidently and immediately had recognized as Luther's work. Amman was displeased with Luther's treatment of Matthew 16:18 in it. He deplored that Luther was not thoroughly linguistic enough on this point, and he bluntly told him that his interpretation was not much better than Murner's. Amman had no problem with Luther's translation of "community" instead of "Church". This issue did not even

[159] See Wagner, 61; Vonschott, 105, Kunzelmann, vol. 2:161 (n. 566); Adolar Zumkeller, entry "Amman" in *Lexikon für Theologie und Kirche* 1 (1957): 439.

[160] Regius' letter of 22 July 1524 to Wolfgang Rychardus, physician at Ulm; edited in Theodor Kolde, *Analecta Lutherana* (Gotha 1883), 45, as in Wagner, 51.

[161] See Bigane, 28.

[162] *Der felß der Christenlichen Kirchen. Außlegung dyser nachfolgenden wort Christi. Du byst Petrus oder ein felß, vnd auff den felßen wird ich bawen mein kirchenn. Du wirdst gehaissen ein haubt dz das außgelegt wirt ein felß Und dir wird ich geben die schlüßel des reichs der hymel* (Coburg: Aegidius Fellenfuerst, 1522), edited by Otto Clemen, 180-83, on the basis of the original that he had found in the Royal Library in Berlin (Cu 7437). This original edition from Coburg was destroyed during war. Fortunately, another print of the same text is extant at the Bavarian State Library in Munich. This print was produced by Georg Erlinger at Bamberg in 1522. Research has shown that Georg Erlinger and Aegidius Fellenfuerst are one and the same person; see Karl Schottenloher, "Aegidius Fellenfuerst in Coburg und Georg Erliner in Bamberg," *Zentralblatt für Bibliothekswesen* 28 (1911): 57-64. I am grateful to Karla Faust from the Staatbibliothek in Berlin for pointing this out to me.

come up. Amman was upset that Luther did not take into consideration that Christ may have spoken with his apostles in Hebrew, "not in Greek nor Syriac," and that Luther did not make any efforts to find the original meaning of Christ's words. Unfortunately, it is not known whether Luther received this letter, and if so, whether he responded to it. In any case, Amman's linguistic hints concerning "Peter" had no lasting effect on Luther, as Luther in his comments of 1531/1535 on Galatians 2:14 ignored the issue of *Cephe* completely. He instead focused exclusively on the great importance of the distinction of Law and Gospel.[163]

Letter from Caspar Amman to Martin Luther

In the following I present an English translation, for the first time, of Amman's multi-lingual letter. His Hebrew characters will be underlined in the English translation, his German words will be in italics; the Greek words were interspersed by Amman in Latin transliteration, as all this was dealt with in Latin.[164]

[163] See WA 40-I:206-14; LW 26:115-20.

[164] The letter is extant in two copies, one is today in St. Gallen, Switzerland, Kantonsbibliothek (Vadiana), Vadianische Sammlung, Ms. 31 Brief 107, with the heading: *Ad doct. Mart. Luth.*; the other at the Zentralbibliothek Zurich, Handschriftenabteilung, Thesaurus Hottingerianus (Hottinger Collection), Ms F 43.34r-v with the heading: *Caspar Amman S. D. Mart. Luthero*; the letter is edited in WA Br 2:607-10 (no. 543). There are some obscurities in the edited text which compel me to translate rather freely at times. I am grateful to Dr. Gottfried Krodel of Valparaiso for reviewing and improving my translation, and to Dr. John Beck of Concordia University Wisconsin for reviewing my translation of the Hebrew.

Caspar Amman to Mart. Luther

Life and peace, joy and happiness to you and to all who love you and who are loved by you

Reverend Father! Recently your most sweet labor came into my hands, that is, the New Testament, translated by you into the language of our people. I greatly rejoiced, especially because on the basis of many of your [previous] works[165] I had understood you to be a thalmidem,[166] a student of the language of the sanctuary, [and] I was confident to find what I desired so long. My hopes were disappointed, however, and I feel pain! For I have often read your boiling hot writings, including [your] interpretation which is also that of Erasmus of Rotterdam,[167] of Christ's words in Matthew 16[:18], "You are petrus," [sic] etc. I accepted his [interpretation] as the original and most true one, although he does not carefully derive his interpretation from Christ's words, [as his is] a forced [twisted, interpretation]; I am saying [this] to you, as you are a Father who is always ready to appease,[168] and [please] accept [now my interpretation] (so that you may have one which is clearer, which at a first glance looks [so] simple). Recently this reckless Tho[mas] Murnar [Murner] has written some booklets against you; one of them dealt with

[165] Amman may have thought of Luther's *Commentary on Galatians*, his *Operationes in Psalmos*, and/or his *Seven Penitential Psalms*, which show Luther working with the original biblical texts.

[166] Hebrew for "pupil" as in 1 Chronicles 25:8.

[167] Erasmus: Petrus in Greek means stone, *petros*, which is *cephas* in Syriac, as Jerome testifies, with the meaning solidity. Christ calls him a stone that he be solid [like a stone] in his confession of faith; see Latin text in n. 5 to the edition of this letter: *Petrus autem Graecis saxum significat, pétros, quemadmodum et Cephas Syro sermone, ut testis est Hieronymus, soliditatem sonat. Saxum enim illum appellat, quod solidus sit in confessione fidei.*

[168] The Latin *pientissime* which is used here is not to be confused with *piissime*!

Ad doct. Mart. Luth.

Page one of the copy of the letter by Caspar Amman to Martin Luther, of 26 October 1522. Today in St. Gallen, Switzerland, Kantonsbibliothek (Vadiana), Vadianische Sammlung, Ms, 31 Brief 107, with the heading: *Ad doct. Mart. Luth.*

the power of the pope[169] in which among other things he interprets the words of Christ quoted above as follows: "You are petrus," etc.: *You are the rock and on this rock I will build my Church, and nobody can take this meaning away from me because it is clearer than the sun.*

A similar case[170] is John [1:42]: "You will be called cephas," etc.: *"You will be called a head, which is interpreted "a rock,"* whereby he [Murner] understands these words, pethrus and cephas, to be Greek and not Hebrew words. You, too, [like Murner] interpret these words in this way, or rather as Syriac as you do in your annotation on Matthew 16.[171] I am not happy at all about the erroneous position of Murner because I have known the man well and in person, and [I know] he is [only] a boy when it comes to the more rare languages. But I often wondered, feeling shame [for you], and having my heart tremble, when in several of your writings you proposed the same improper meaning of these words (inadvertently, I believe), especially in the case of the first word, petrus, while you leave the second word untranslated and you [simply] write cephas. I myself am driven first of all by the argument that Christ is a born Hebrew who spoke Hebrew with his Hebrew disciples, not Greek or Syriac. Secondly, even if these two mentioned words could be Syriac words, as you and other rather learned men assume, such an assumption for the phrase in question does not wash with the original sense of Christ's original words, a sense which Erasmus and you [too] obtain by force. Here, therefore, are the original Hebrew characters of the Hebrew words: <u>pother</u> <u>coephe</u>, in Latin [transliteration]: pöther [sic] coephe which according

[169] *Uon dem babstenthum das ist von der hochsten oberkeit Christlichs glauben wyder doctor Martinum Luther,* printed by Johann Grieninger at Strasbourg on 13 December 1520; *Deutsche Schriften* vol. 7:17f; see n. 69 above.

[170] The editor has a question mark here, indicating uncertainty about the handwriting.

[171] *(Petrus) Cepha Syrisch, Petros kriechisch heyst auff deutsch eyn fels vnd alle Christen sind petri vmb der bekentnis willen, die hie Petrus thut, wilche ist der felss, darauff Petrus vnd alle petri bawet sind, gemyn ist die bekentnis also auch der name* (marginal note), WA DB 6:76 (1522). Luther followed Erasmus who argued that Jesus spoke Syriac as his mother tongue; see Clemen, 162. Amman insisted that Jesus spoke Hebrew.

to the Latin declension are pethrus, cephas. If originally you only had been inclined to deal with them, you would have translated them better and more agreeable to the mind of Christ. What I say about the first word, pethrus, is clearly stated in the Glo[ssa] Ord[inaria], that is Bede's, where one reads on Matthew 4[:5] that pethrus means recognizer;[172] and in the same place in the Glo[ssa] Interlinear[ris] there is the same Hebrew interpretation which again is Bede's, or rather S[aint] Jero[me]'s, who proposes it in his interpretations of Luke. About this Hebrew word pother, see also Dr. Joh[ann] Reuch[lin]'s dictionary[173] on pathar from which is derived pithron, that is, cognition; when it is put into Latin characters it is pethra as is plenty apparent to those who understand the language of the Hebrews and of the Latins. If therefore Christ spoke this phrase principally and intentionally about [Peter's] knowledge of himself [Christ], his response to Simon was this [in the Hebrew original]: And I tell you that you are the interpreter of heavenly things, and on this hidden interpretation I will build my assembly, [or translated into] the vernacular: *And I tell you that you are the confessor of heavenly things, and on this hidden* [or, *divine*] *confession I will build my Church.*[174] These Hebrew words which Christ uttered indicate and prove in a stronger and clearer way

[172] *Petrus, agnoscens*; see above.

[173] *Rudimenta hebraica* (1506), 443.

[174] Amman uses two different German adjectives, *himmlisch* and *haimlich*, to qualify Simon's words; *haimlich* here may have the connotation "divine, occult, figurative," see Jacob and Wilhelm Grimm, *Deutsches Wörterbuch* vol. 4-2: 878 (Leipzig: Hirzel, 1877). *Bekenner* is translated here with "confessor," and *Bekanntnuß* with "confession"; the German word *Bekenner* is closely related to *Erkenner* which Amman uses further below, and which designates a person who understands something that is hidden, who has insight. The editor Clemen (171) has *himlische erkantnuß* here, while the WA editor of Amman's letter has *haimliche Bekanntnuß* (WA Br 2:608.47). Evidently, *haimliche Bekanntnuß* is identical with *himlische erkantnuß*, and also with *hymlische erkennung,* because in the German pamphlet *Der felß der Christenlichen Kirchen* (Clemen, 181, attributed to Amman) not only are the adjectives "heavenly" and "hidden" exchanged, but also the nouns *erkenner* and *bekenner*, as we read there: *Vnnd ich sag dir, dw byst ein erkenner haymlicher ding, vnd auff dyse hymlische erkennung wird ich bawenn mein kirchenn.*

this original meaning of Christ's words, and without any coercion, than if they were understood as Syriac words and thus interpreted extraneously. See the "apostoli"[175] about these Hebrew words, pethrus and pethra, in Genesis 40[:8], where the two downcast eunuchs who were imprisoned with Joseph said to him in Hebrew: We have had dreams, but there is no one to interpret them for us. Joseph responded to them (further below [that is Genesis 40:12]): This is what it means, see pother/interpreter, pithron/interpretation, that is pethrus, pethra, where Joseph himself was made a pother/interpreter, that is, a pether, or a "person who recognizes arcane things". All the more so one has to expound pethros in this way in our passage.

On the second key expression, cephas, in Hebrew, coephe, S[aint] Jero[me] says [in his commentary][176] on Galatians 2 that in Hebrew and Syriac it is the same word and means pethrus. However, we leave this aside as less significant because it does not contribute anything to [the interpretation of our] text, and we should accept what is of major significance, namely the Hebrew. Then [however] he [Jerome] said something very worthwhile concerning our text, something ... that is truly meaningful, as also Dr. Joh[ann] Reuch[lin] explains in his dictionary on cepha,[177] that is, bishop, superintendent, which is an expression which helps us with our text; [it is his reference to] Ezechiel 3[:17]: Son of man, I have appointed you a watchman for the house of Israel, that is, son of man, I have given you as a watchman etc. And so literally Christ said to Simon most fittingly: You are to be called a watchman, which means, a recognizer, or in the vernacular: "*You are to be called a watchman which means a recognizer.*" Would Christ have spoken here in Greek or Syriac? No way! Here Christ wanted to give Simon two additional names different from the other apostles, namely that he be called pethra because of his divine knowledge and cephas because of his pas-

[175] The editor has a question mark behind *apostoli.*

[176] *Commentariorum in epistolam ad Galatas lib. 1 cap. 2* (PL 26:341); see above n. 11.

[177] *Rudimenta hebraica*, 456: coephe *speculator, contemplator Ezechielis 3 (V.17); Speculatorem dedi de domui Israel, i. e. episcopum*, as quoted in WA Br 2:610, n. 17.

toral commission and watchful attention. In this way he determined: the Church as the Bride of Christ is to be built on him [Christ] who was recognized and confessed by pethro, so that her gardeners would be the watchmen, that is, bishops, seers, that is, those who recognize and see; not blind people and sleepyheads, as it was said of certain false teachers and prophets in the house of the Lord [according to] Isaiah 56[:10]: My watchmen are blind.

You, therefore, Reverend Father and Christian brother, whom I enjoy in the Lord, may you agree with me after you have read all this and reasonably chewed on it, [and may] you declare yourself in a better way some day in the future. Or if I err, may you correct the erring [brother] fraternally while you consult well my works, and while you pray for me, an old fool and decrepit … [and for my] salvation by the Messiah. And the Lord will guard you from all evil for ever.[178]

From Lauingen, on October 26, in the year of Christ, 1522.
Your Confrère Caspar Amman, Augustinian.

[178] Psalm 121:7.

A SEARCH FOR THE AUTHENTIC LUTHER: KENNETH HAGEN'S APPROACH TO LUTHER STUDIES

JOAN SKOCIR

> After working on Luther and hermeneutics, sometimes together, more often separately, for over twenty-five years, I have come to see Luther as part of his medieval, Roman Catholic, Augustinian-Benedictine traditions ... his conclusions are there for all who wish to ground their contemporary theology in Scripture.[1]

For Kenneth Hagen, the major key to Luther's biblical theology is Scripture itself in what Ulrich Asendorf calls "Holy Scripture as programmatic entry."[2] This is not a study of Luther and Scripture using our contemporary exegetical methods[3] nor is Luther perceived as having achieved a hermeneutical breakthrough in anticipation of the Reformation or the Enlightenment. Instead, Hagen points to Luther's wholistic immersion in Scripture that drew from and reinforced the traditional monastic approach as the discipline of *sacra pagina*, the sacred page. The sacred page is the totality of Scripture spread out before the mind's eye as the one Word in the unity of the one Spirit who authors and empowers it.

In this essay I will attempt to show that in Hagen's estimation, the richness—the depth, breadth, height, and width[4]—of Scripture forms the substance of Luther's biblical theology, which not only reflects upon Scripture but more importantly draws it forth for all to experience as the deepest well of life-giving water. The essay will be presented in two interrelated parts. The first will study Hagen's ap-

[1] Kenneth Hagen, "*Omnis homo mendax*: Luther on Psalm 116" in *Biblical Interpretation in the Era of the Reformation: Essays Presented to David C. Steinmetz in Honor of His Sixtieth Birthday* (Grand Rapids: William B. Eerdmans Publishing Co., 1996), 102. See also his "Changes in the Understanding of Luther: The Development of the Young Luther" in *Theological Studies* 29:3 (September 1968), 472-496.

[2] Ulrich Asendorf, "Holy Scripture and Holy Spirit" in this book, 1.

[3] See Hagen's "Does Method Drive Biblical Study?" in *Logia* X, vol. 1 (Epiphany, 2001), 37-40. Writes Hagen: "It never occurred to them [historical authors] that method drives interpretation, especially since method did not exist. For historical authors, biblical study drives biblical study" (40).

[4] The thirteenth-century Franciscan Bonaventure, whose approach to Scripture is in the monastic tradition, described Scripture in these terms. See the preface to his *Breviloquium*, translated by Edwin E. Nemmers (St. Louis: B. Herder, 1946).

proach to Luther on Scripture as grounded in the sacred page. The second will focus on Hagen's reflections on Luther's biblical theology, especially the theology of testament, to illustrate the richness of Luther's thought and of Hagen's approach.

The essay will confirm that in his quest for the authentic Luther, Hagen attempts to place Luther's thought in the context of Luther's own time and to retrieve it from later imaging or editing that filtered it through presuppositions and concepts unknown to Luther. It will suggest that in his study of Luther, Hagen approaches Luther's biblical theology in a similar way in which Luther's *enarrationes* approach Scripture, to comprehensively draw forth its fullness and power.

Sacra Pagina

Luther's approach to Scripture in the sixteenth century, characterized by phrases such as "Scripture interprets itself" or "Scripture is its own authority," expressed a thousand years of monastic biblical tradition. For example, in the fifth century Augustine set this interpretative tone in his *De doctrina Christiana* in which he maintained that the seemingly difficult passages in Scripture can be made clear by searching for other, more literal passages for explanation.[5] In his thirteenth-century lectures on the six days of creation, the Franciscan Bonaventure emphasized this tradition:

> The whole of Scripture is like a single zither, and the lesser string does not produce harmony by itself, but only in combination with the others. Likewise, any single passage of Scripture depends upon some other, or rather, any single passage is related to a thousand others.[6]

In the monasteries and friaries, Scripture was not only the focus of study but a wellspring for daily life that centered on the sacred page. Regarding the discipline of the sacred page, Franz Posset points to "the well-known monastic scheme: *lectio, oratio, meditatio,*

[5] Augustine, *De doctrina Christiana* in Corpus Christianorum XXXII (Turnholti : Typographi Brepols Editores Pontificiti, 1952) II 9 :14, 40-41.

[6] Bonaventure, *Collations on the Six Days* in The Works of Bonaventure, Vol. 5, translated by José de Vinck (Paterson: St. Anthony Guild Press, 1970), XIX 7:288. Luther respected Bonaventure: "Bonaventura ist der beste unter den Schultheologen und Kirchenscribenten." Martin Luthers sämmtliche Schriften, vol. 22 (St. Louis: Concordia Publishing House, 1887), 1390.3. See also WA 43:581.11f.

contemplatio"[7] from which Luther may have drawn his equally well-known threefold rule for Scripture study—that *oratio, meditatio,* and *tentatio* make the theologian. Hagen has written:

> The monastery became the place and the monks' daily liturgy was the context for the practice of theology. Holy Writ was the sacred page, the canon of Scripture was the rule of faith. The goal of life for the medieval pilgrim (*viator*), as well as the final goal of theology, was to go home, home to God, home to the Trinity (in Augustine's words).
>
> The sacred page was seen as coming directly from God, about God, and for the pilgrim's journey to God. Theology, whether expressed in doctrine, liturgy, or catechesis, was the discipline of the sacred page.[8]

Hagen suggests, however, that in the rise of the schools from about the twelfth century onward, the relationship of Scripture and theology began to take on a new discipline, that of *sacra doctrina*, sacred doctrine, whose goal was faith seeking understanding. The universities trained theologians through academic methods such as dialectic and *quaestio* that were used for theological deliberation and demonstration. Scripture remained the major focus of theology; Thomas Aquinas maintained that Holy Scripture and sacred doctrine are one sacred science, which "proceeds from principles made known by the light of a higher science, namely, the science of God and the blessed"[9] revealed in Scripture. But a perceptible change in the relationship occurred. Reminiscent of Aquinas's opinion that doctrinal demonstrations must be based on the literal sense,[10] *sacra doctrina* focused on the Aristotelian thing-in-itself more than on the Platonic thing-signified-by-the-thing that was usually considered the spiritual interpretation. Yet "literal" did not have the same meaning for

[7] Franz Posset, "The *Sacra Pagina* Approach to Scripture" in his *Pater Bernhardus: Martin Luther and Bernard of Clairvaux* (Kalamazoo: Cistercian Publications, 1999), 134. In this chapter, Posset offers further insights into the threefold rule, which he believes is summed up in the orational for Luther, that is, prayer in humility and the fear of God, 133-50.

[8] Kenneth Hagen, "Martin Luther" in *Historical Handbook of Major Biblical Interpreters*, edited by Donald K. McKim (Downers Grove, Illinois, and Leicester, England: InterVarsity Press, 1998), 214.

[9] Thomas Aquinas, ST I.1.2 Although he is probably more remembered for his *Summa Theologiae* and philosophical works, Aquinas also lectured on Scripture continuously throughout his entire teaching career. The lectures, which in recent years have begun to be translated to English or to French for a wider audience, include much of the Old Testament and all of the New Testament except for Revelation.

[10] See Aquinas, ST I.1.10.

the medieval mind that it does for our empirical age. In his even-handed treatment of *sacra doctrina* that acknowledges the "sacred" as well as the "doctrine",[11] Hagen recalls that the thing-signified-by-the-thing could be the actual literal meaning. For example, "God's right arm" signifies God's power, the true literal meaning since the thing-in-itself is a metaphor that points beyond itself.

In the fourteenth century, the Franciscan Nicholas of Lyra proposed further distinctions between literal meanings with his double-literal senses—the historic-literal and the prophetic-literal. In this distinction, Solomon could literally be considered a king of Israel or literally a prophetic figure of Christ. Or both. Hagen holds that the traditional fourfold senses (historical-literal, allegorical, tropological, anagogical) continued to be used. But the wide acceptance of the double-literal sense in the later Middle Ages resulted in "an increasing attention to the texts."[12]

Influenced by the new publishing possibilities of the printing press and an increased interest in early manuscripts and classical texts, humanism became a third major development in Scripture study prior to and throughout the Reformation. In the discipline of *sacra littera*, Scripture as sacred literature, Hagen suggests that the goal of study shifted to an absorption with original languages, philology, and moral concerns. Especially as promoted by Erasmus of Rotterdam, the goal was "the reform of Church and society through education for the purpose of piety and knowledge."[13]

Along with these major trends, Hagen also acknowledges other biblical currents that remained active in the later medieval period—piety (especially that of *devotio moderna*), the continued use of various senses of scripture, biblical commentaries, and German mysticism. More importantly, he does not take the view that Luther rejected much of the intellectual and spiritual world that preceded and surrounded him.[14] On the contrary, he fleshes out Luther as a resourceful, creative man of his time, who used whatever tools he considered valuable in humanism as well as in scholasticism, in German mysticism and *devotio moderna*, and in traditional exegesis, includ-

[11] Kenneth Hagen, "The History of Scripture in the Church" in *The Bible in the Churches: How Various Christians Interpret the Scriptures* (Milwaukee: Marquette University Press, third edition, 1998), especially 5-9. *The Bible in the Churches*, edited by Hagen, has become widely used as a textbook.

[12] Ibid., 7. See also James Kiecker, "Comparative Hermeneutics: The *Glossa ordinaria*, Nicholas of Lyra, and Martin Luther on the Song of Songs" in this book, especially 112-22.

[13] *Bible in the Churches*, 12.

[14] Ibid., 17.

ing allegory and references to the Fathers of the Church. Notwithstanding Luther's criticism of excesses he saw in scholasticism, elements of all of these appear in his work from time to time when they can be used to promote the message of Christ. Hagen places Luther's approach to Scripture into the context of historical exegesis by showing that he shared exegetical particulars with others and that especially "The *Glossa ordinaria* provided him with a wealth of resources, as did Faber Stapulensis."[15]

But Luther is also distinct in his approach to Scripture for several reasons. Hagen maintains that Luther is unique and original among exegetes in his thoroughgoing emphasis on sharp contrasts. For Luther, the sacred page is filled with paradoxes. In Psalm 116 (115), for example, "focus on the lie casts the truth into the clearest light. In the truth of Christ, my lie ceases to be."[16] Hagen also explores Psalm 116 (115) to show that for Luther, as for Paul, Scripture echoes itself. He maintains that Luther follows Paul's echo and completion in Romans 3:4 of the Psalm's phrase *omnis homo mendax* (everyone is a liar): *autem Deus verax omnis autem homo mendax* (but God must be true, though everyone is a liar). "Together with Luther's paradoxical theology and the unity of Scripture, one could say, therefore, that Romans 3:4 is actually on the *sacra pagina* of Psalm 116:11."[17] It is not necessary for Scripture to repeat itself even though some physical distance exists between a passage and its echo or paradox.

Moreover, Hagen writes: "Luther's distinction is his construction of Scripture as containing a single testament (will, promise) of Christ."[18] While he acknowledges that Luther made use of humanist and scholastic studies when he considered them useful, Hagen shows that Luther's theology is unfailingly centered on the sacred page, an approach in which the experience of the Word is soteriologically essential. Scripture—the message of Christ, *was Christum treibt*, what promotes Christ—is not primarily a book for silent study but for *enarratio*, that is, for bringing out the message of Christ loudly and clearly to the world. The Word is the very thing that gives life for death, that must be brought out boldly to ears that will hear and hearts that will burn within as did those of the disciples on the road

[15] "*Omnis homo mendax*," 93. Hagen also here compares Luther on Psalm 116 with Jerome, Augustine, Arnobius the Younger, Gerhoh of Reichersberg, Peter Lombard, and Rusch's Strasbourg Bible, among others.

[16] Ibid., 99.

[17] *Omnis homo mendax*, 87.

[18] *Bible in the Churches*, 17. Testament will be explored more fully in part two of this essay.

to Emmaus at Jesus' testimony. "For Luther, theology meant confession of faith, proclamation, profession in public, 'the testimony of my faith in Christ'."[19]

As Timothy Maschke has rightly shown,[20] Luther merged Scripture and present life. For example, Hagen has said that one does not look at Adam so much as a person who originated sin but rather that "I am Adam," experiencing his temptations and failure in the here and now. This approach erases the passage of time in favor of human relationship to God that is true for any and all time. God is always God. Humans are always human. Sin is always sin. And salvation is revealed in Abraham as well as in any person of faith who clings to God's promises manifested in Christ as Word made flesh.

For Luther as for Paul, Scripture reflects this inclusiveness and immediacy. As Søren Kierkegaard's memorable phrase maintains, there are no disciples at second hand. All stand at the foot of the cross. The grammar of faith is not dependent on time and space, just as the message and words of Scripture have a unity that transcends the historical moment. Thus Luther could connect the testimony of Paul to the testimony of others in Scripture as though they were spoken from the same mouth. Or he could contrast them in a paradoxical way as though they purposefully recognized the other as paradoxical.

In his "It Is All in the *Et Cetera*," Hagen shows that the elliptical reference, noted as "etc" or "ec" in medieval manuscripts and folios, is not used merely to save space. On the contrary, in the unity of Scripture and the discipline of the sacred page in which much of Scripture is put to memory, the *et cetera* is a gateway to the full meaning of a reference. This is not only true of the context immediately surrounding the citation; the *et cetera* ultimately opens the mind to the totality of Scripture and to all the other places that are appropriately contextual to the immediate reference. Hagen refers to monastic Bible interpreters as "walking concordances"[21] for whom the unity of Scripture was a given. "For Luther, it was absolutely necessary that God's Word be consistent in its grammar, rhetoric, and theology."[22] In Luther's perspective, Paul and Isaiah and the other

[19] Kenneth Hagen, "Luther on Atonement—Reconfigured" in *Concordia Theological Quarterly* 61 (1997): 256.

[20] See Timothy Maschke, "Contemporaneity: A Hermeneutical Perspective in Martin Luther's Work," 165-82 of this book.

[21] "Martin Luther" in *Historical Handbook*, 219.

[22] Kenneth Hagen, "It Is All in the Et Cetera: Luther and the Elliptical Reference," *Luther-Bulletin: Tijdschrift vor interconfessioneel Lutheronderzoek* 31 (November 1994): 65. See also Hagen's "Did Peter Err? The Text is the Best Judge: Luther

biblical writers worked on the same page, the sacred page full of echo and self-interpretation.

As Gordon Isaac has also pointed out,[23] Hagen considers Luther not a commentator on Scripture in the manner of modern exegesis but one who uses the tradition of *enarratio* "to narrate, to exit the text [that is, to bring it out], and apply the message in public."[24] Luther did not use quotation marks when he cited Scripture in his commentaries because he followed the medieval practice of weaving Scripture into the flow of the *enarratio*. "As far as Luther was concerned, he did not add anything to Scripture, certainly not interpretation. Interpretation was to be avoided."[25] Hagen cautions that Luther did not claim his texts to be the Word of God, but he knew the performance power of the words. "What he was seeking to drive (*was Christum treibt*) was not his own point of view but the same that Paul was seeking to promote, namely Jesus Christ."[26]

From Hagen's extensive work with original Luther prints, he has written knowledgeable critiques of modern editing of Luther's works, especially in the *Weimarer Ausgabe*, that impose editorial practices on Luther's texts as though he were a nineteenth-century exegete. Divisions by verses in Scripture were not generally used until Robert Stephanus's 1551 New Testament in which he devised verse divisions that are still used today. Before that, the continuity of the texts was not interrupted by verse numbers.[27] Yet the addition of quotation marks for Bible citations and "[t]he entire effort by the WA to add chapter-and-verse references to the margins change both the format and the argument of the original."[27] As though it were footnotes, ancient references, or proof texts, Scripture is set apart and separated from Luther's texts. Hagen maintains that to limit a reference to chapter and verse is to limit the reality of Luther's approach in which the whole of Scripture is his field of vision:

on Gal. 2.11" in *Augustine, the Harvest, and Theology* (1300-1650). Essays Dedicated to Heiko Augustinus Oberman in Honor of his Sixtieth Birthday, edited by Kenneth Hagen (Leiden: E. J. Brill, 1990), 110-26 . This article shows the textual issue echoed in the later "It Is All in the *Et Cetera*."

[23] See Gordon L. Isaac, "The Changing Image of Luther as Biblical Expositor," 67-85 of this book.

[24] "It Is All in the Et Cetera," 58.

[25] Ibid., 58.

[26] Ibid., 60.

[27] See *Bible in the Churches*, 24. Chapter divisions were not specified until Stephen Langton proposed them in the early thirteenth century; his divisions are still used today with only small modifications.

AD GALATAS. FOLIO.XII.

hodie,ſimili prudētia,& docerētur,& ſeruarentur. Nunc vero ita reg
nant,vt in ijs ſalus cōſtituta putetur,& fides ꝓpe ſit extincta. PAV
LVS fidē facit dominā liberrimā oīm legum humanarū. Nos leges
humanas facimus tyrannos fidei. Nec ipſas tñ,ꝓceres & magnates
pili faciunt,non ſine ſcandalorū vaſtiſſimo gurgite eccleſiā vorātes,
& ſolos ſubditos,tot oneribus importabilibus opprimentes, aut libertatem eorum Chriſtianam,per hos pecuniarū laqueos captiuam,
denuo fœdiſſime vendētes,diſpenſantes,indulgentes.

CAPITVLVM SECVNDVM.

DEinde poſt annos quatuordecim,iterum
aſcendi Hieroſolymā, cum Barnaba, aſ-
ſumpto & Tito. Aſcendi aūt,ſcd'm reue-
lationem,& contuli cum illis Euangeliū,quod præ
dico in gentibus. Seorſum aūt ijs,q videbantur aliquid eſſe,ne forte in uacuū currerē,aut cucurriſſem.

POSTQVAM ſatis probauit,nullius hoīs Magiſterio,ſe Apl'm
factū,ſed diuina reuelatione nunc ꝓbat ſe eandē reuelationē,tam cer
tā firmamq; habuiſſe,vt nullos prorſus hoīes,etiā Apl'os,ſit verit⁹
habere iudices,tū nullorū quoq; importunitati ceſſerit. PRIMVM
(inqt)poſt annos q̄tuordecim: quib⁹,ſi annos tres,q̄s ſupra memora
uit,adiūxeris iam decē & ſeptē, aut decē & octo annos, cum p̄dicaſ
ſe inueniēs,anq̄ cōferre voluerit ita,vt impoſſibile videatur,qd' tot
locis,tot populis p̄dicarat,potuiſſe reuocari. Ideoq; nō ſua cauſa aſcen
dit,q̄ſi timuerit(vt Hiero,ſentit)ne falſum per decē & ſeptē annos p̄-
dicaſſet ſed vt oſtenderet alijs,non inuacuū ſeſe cucurriſſe,approbātib⁹
& cæteris Apl'is,ſuū curſum. Si enī dubitaſſet,verū ne an falſum do-
ceret,inſignis & inauditæ temeritatis ac impietatis fuerat,diſlata neceſſaria collatōe: tot pp'los ludere incerta doctrina. SECVNDO nō
aſcēdiſſet vnq̄,niſi reulatōe dei monitus,nō aliorū importunitate cō
motus. tm̄ abeſt,vt de doctrinæ certitudine diffiſus, cōtulerit nulla
habēs prorſus neceſſitatē aſcendēdi in hanc cauſam. TERTIO,ad
ipſam Hieroſolymā: vbi erant principes tam ſynagogæ, q̄ eccleſiæ:
paratus cū oībus conferre nec multitudinē iudeorū,nec legis acerrīos
æmulatores formidans. QVARTO,nō ſolus,ſed cū Barnaba &
Tito,diuerſo gñe,aptiſſimos teſtes ne aliud egiſſe pñs,aliud abſens,
agere crederet. vt ſi qd ꝓ iudeis nimiū faceret, Titus gentilis ꝓderet.
Si rurſus nimis ꝓ gētibus,Barnabas iudeus obſiſteret. Quare, fiducia eius vide hos duos ſecū duxit,& vtrūq; teſtē habuit. Deniq; cum
vtroq; ſeſe offerēs,manifeſtū facturus,qd' cū Tito gentilē,cū Barna
ba iudeū eſſe licuerit. Et ſic euāgelij libertatē i vtroq; ꝓbaret, qd' cir
cūcidi licz,& tñ circūcidi nō ſit neceſſariū,ita & de tota lege ſentiēdū.

D ij

NOTA

Quot annos Paulus prædicauerit, pri⁹ q̄ cū alijs conferre voluerit.

Original print: Luther (1519) on Paul's Letter to the Galatians, chapter 2. See also page 81 for another view. Hagen based much of his *Luther's Approach to Scripture as seen in his "Commentaries" on Galatians, 1519-1538* upon the 1519 print.

> To correct Luther's text as the WA does is to correct his theology, and that is the argument presented here. Luther did not see Scripture as sacred literature in need of exegesis. He saw it as sacred page in need of public defense.[29]

Hagen also suggests that it is inappropriate to use nineteenth- and twentieth-century terminology for sixteenth-century scriptural approaches because terms such as hermeneutics or historical-critical were not used in Luther's time. Thus to speak of "Luther's hermeneutics" brings with it the baggage of modern philosophical presuppositions that are foreign to the sixteenth century, which had only "rules" for exposition.[30] Furthermore, he criticizes later editors for adding headings and titles to Luther's works that were not present in the original prints. In his "Luther's So-Called *Judenschriften*," Hagen maintains that this practice can take the form of editorial comment on what the editors perceive as the meaning of a work—in this case, *Judenschriften* perceived as Luther writing against the Jews, when valid arguments can be made from the texts for other possibilities in the literary context of the sixteenth century.[31]

Hagen's point is that the above-mentioned editorial practices tend to place Luther into a modern framework rather than his own scriptural world, which reflected the more wholistic medieval approach and the discipline of the sacred page.

[28] Ibid., 58. For a more extensive critique, see also Hagen's *Luther's Approach to Scripture as seen in his 'Commentaries' on Galatians,* 1519-1538 (Tübingen: J. C. B. Mohr [Paul Siebeck], 1993), especially Chapter 1.

[29] *Luther's Approach to Scripture*, 34. See also "The First Translation of Luther's *Lectures on Hebrews*: A Review Article" in *Church History* (June 1965): 204-213, which shows Hagen's early concern regarding the WA and accuracy in portraying Luther's work.

[30] Kenneth Hagen, "Niels Hemmingson's *De Methodis* (1555)" in *The Bible in the Sixteenth Century* (Durham and London: Duke University Press, 1990), 181. Hagen refers here to Flacius, who held that "to use a philosophy (such as is entailed in hermeneutics) is to bring with it a whole host of presuppositions."

[31] See Kenneth Hagen, "Luther's So-Called *Judenschriften*: A Genre Approach," *Archiv für Reformationsgeschichte* 90 (1999) 130-158. In another critique, Hagen explores the idea that Luther taught a two-kingdom division between secular and religious authority, in which one was not to interfere with the other. He concludes that Luther actually taught a number of variations on "kingdoms," or regimes or hierarchies, rather than solidifying only two that could be considered his final answer. See "Luther's Doctrine of the Two Kingdoms." In *God and Caesar Revisited,* edited by John R. Stephenson. Luther Academy Conference Papers No. 1." (Shorewood, Minn.: Luther Academy [USA], 1995), 15-29.

A Theology of Testament

From the totality of the sacred page[32] and Luther's use of *enarratio*, Hagen points to Luther's theology as expressing God's marvelous deeds from the fullness of scriptural revelation. For reasons of space, this essay will focus on what Hagen considers a soteriological centerpiece of Luther's theology, that is, Luther's theology of testament, especially as it relates to atonement and its soteriological implications.

In his "Luther on Atonement—Reconfigured," Hagen faults Gustav Aulén's influential *Christus Victor* (1953) for its attempt to place Luther on atonement into a theoretical mode. While Hagen acknowledges that there is some value in organizing Luther's thoughts in this way, he maintains that a theology of atonement is never a theory for Luther, but a public witness of what God has actually done—the final *fecit* (what happened) rather than speculations about the preliminary *potuit* (what is possible for God) or *decuit* (what is fitting for God), a sequence often used in medieval doctrinal deliberation.[33] For similar reasons, Luther criticized scholastic theology for its speculative tendencies that appeared to him to be a theology of glory, an emphasis on what might be rather than what is. Instead, he emphasized the struggle between life and death, not an academic or theoretical exercise but the critical battle between the Gospel of Christ and the devil. Because the stakes are so high and the enemy so insidious, the struggle calls for strong testimony and vigilance.

> It means to defend the faith against the pseudo-prophets and pseudo-apostles, the false teachers who both Paul and Luther were convinced return all too quickly to the very centers of faith.[34]

Rather than silencing the demons, defending the faith brings them forth in eschatological conflict, a theme that Hagen reiterates in his Luther on Galatians: "The conviction of Scripture is that God and the Devil are active, very active in the affairs of people. ... They are engaged in cosmic battle."[35] He forcefully describes the uncompro-

[32] Or "whole biblical theology," as Ulrich Asendorf puts it; see his "Martin Luthers Theologie gesamtbiblischer Erneuerung. Eine Skizze über die Bedeutung seiner Genesis-Vorlesung (1535-1545)" in *Kerygma und Dogma*43, no. 3 (July/September 1997): 186-201, abridged in *Luther Digest* Vol. 8 (St. Louis: The Luther Academy, 2000) as "Martin Luther's Theology of Whole Biblical Renewal. An Overview of the Significance of his Genesis Lectures 1535-1545," 18-23.

[33] "Atonement—Reconfigured," 256.

[34] Ibid., 255.

[35] *Luther's Approach to Scripture,* 24.

mising consequences of this struggle that impelled Luther to bear such urgent witness to Christ:

> Life and death are the options of life here and now. The way of righteousness leads to length of days. The way of the wicked brings self-destruction; sin carries with it a built-in destructive mechanism; to do evil is to kill the self. Eternal life and death are the long-term results of what happens in the here and now. The wages of sin are death. The free gift of God is eternal life.[36]

For Luther, "the doctrine of Christian righteousness is too great to describe or understand"[37] in limited ways or by use of reason. Aulén translated Luther's *Versöhnung* as atonement and accompanied it with related theoretical conclusions, but Hagen shows that *Versöhnung* also means reconciliation (Matt. 5:24). He refers to the American Edition of Luther's works that often translates Luther's German *Bezahlung* (payment), *Opfer* (sacrifice), and *gnug thun* (be sufficient) and Latin *placare* (appease), *propiciatio* (propitiation), *satisfactio* (satisfaction), and *reconciliatio* (reconciliation) as atonement. Hagen adds that any theory of atonement explains away one of the mysteries of the faith. Atonement is not open to theorizing but to praise and thanks to God. His further point is that atonement embraces "many pieces" for Luther—"*enarratio*, joyous exchange, theology of testament, theology of the cross, theology of the worm and the devil, and sacrament and example."[38]

Of these, Hagen demonstrates that testament "was the means for theologizing about the Christian faith for Luther,"[39] the message as well as the medium (*per modum testamenti*). Luther said: "That little word 'testament' is a short summary of all God's wonders and grace fulfilled in Christ."[40] The "whole Gospel" is summarized in the testament of Christ, which encompasses at least five elements.[41] "Testament embraces the will of God, the person of God, the death of God, the resurrection of God, and the gift of God."[42] The point here is that every element of testament comes from God; the elements may also be expressed as the promise, theology of the Word, theology of the cross, the gift of grace, and faith.

[36] Ibid., 25.

[37] "Atonement—Reconfigured," 255.

[38] Ibid., 253.

[39] Ibid., 258.

[40] Martin Luther, *Ein Sermon von dem neuen Testament* (1520), WA 6:357.25-27, quoted in "Atonement—Reconfigured," 259.

[41] See "Atonement—Reconfigured," 259. WA 6:374.3-9.

[42] *Luther's Approach to Scripture*, 93.

A. The Promise

In the unity of the sacred page, there is one Word, one promise, one testament of Christ. Testament as such is primarily discussed in Galatians, Romans, and Hebrews, but the promise is found in all the books of the Bible. The testament *is* the promise. Hagen shows that testament is "a rhetorical device to drive home a very hard point about the divine mystery."[43] God initiated the promise from the beginning without human entreaty because in their sinfulness humans are blind to the need for reconciliation. Since God himself promises and bequeaths, the promise is the foundation and rock of testament. The testament *is* the promise and it is found in all books of the Bible since it is a reality present from the beginning to the end of time. Hagen quotes Luther: "All the fathers in the Old Testament together with all the holy prophets have the same faith and Gospel as we have. It is all one truth of the promise."[44] From his *Luther's Approach to Scripture*, Hagen emphasizes that:

> The testament of God is eternal; the promise is constant and continuous; God is consistent and faithful throughout the Old and New Testament era, throughout the past, present, and future church.[45]

B. Theology of the Word

As the second element in testament, Luther's theology of the Word emphasizes that "the Word is the living eternal promise of the testament of Christ,"[46] the new testament that is to be preached to all the world. From promise through inheritance, God's redemptive will proclaimed in Scripture is a reality from the beginning to the end of time. Hagen calls the Word "the dynamic manifestation of the person of God,"[47] accomplishing everything from making the promise to creating the response of faith to bringing about the inheritance by dying on the cross:

> Christ is the eternal Word of God, present in Old Testament times in the form of promise, present in New Testament times in the

[43] Ibid.

[44] "Atonement—Reconfigured," 260. Hagen here quotes Luther's *Das Magnificat* (1521), WA 7:600.1-9; LW 7:354.

[45] *Luther's Approach to Scripture*, 94.

[46] "Atonement—Reconfigured," 260.

[47] *Luther's Approach to Scripture*, 94.

> person of Jesus, and present in the Church through Word and sacrament. In all cases, Christ the Word is the effective means of grace. Christ is at the core of God's plan of salvation. God promises through prophets; God delivers in person. All of Scripture leads to Christ, and Christ leads to salvation.[48]

For Luther, old and new are not necessarily descriptions of Hebrew and Christian Scriptures but frequently of the law as the old way of receiving God's testament and the Spirit or Gospel as the new way. "With reference to God, there is one testament; with reference to men, there are two"[49] and the soteriological possibilities are both dialectical and antithetical. Both old and new ways conflict with each other in each person just as they exist antithetically and dialogically in the whole of Scripture. Hagen writes: Luther "felt that the Old Testament is more christological than the New,"[50] which he believes might explain Luther's preoccupation with the Old Testament. For Luther, testament is contained in all the laws of Moses. "The New Testament is contained and expressed in the Old to him who sees by faith both gospel and promise in the law."[51] The key is grace and faith; without them, the law is seen not as promise but as condemning because it is impossible to fulfill God's commands. Yet the law is God's Word as well as is the Gospel. Law and Gospel interact in the work of salvation, each with its necessary function. There is only one Word, one promise, one testament. The senses of Scripture are not of primary importance to Luther compared to its soteriological Word of testament. The exegetical role, therefore, is not so much trying to understand or analyze God's salvific actions as it is bearing witness to them for all to hear.

[48] Kenneth Hagen, "Biblical Interpretation in the Middle Ages and the Reformation," paper given at Bethany College, October 26, 2000, to be published.

[49] Kenneth Hagen, *A Theology of Testament in the Young Luther: The Lectures on Hebrews* (Leiden: E. J. Brill, 1974), 69. Luther's theology of testament has absorbed Hagen throughout his career. *A Theology of Testament* (1974) follows his masterful 1968 Harvard dissertation *Luther's Lectures on Hebrews in the Light of Medieval Commentaries on Hebrews* (Cambridge, Mass.: Harvard University, 1968), 851 pages, and in turn is followed by *Hebrews Commenting from Erasmus to Bèze* 1516-1598 in "Beiträge zur Geschichte der biblischen Exegese," vol. 23 (Tübingen: J. C. B. Mohr [Paul Siebeck], 1981). See also "The First Translation of Luther's *Lectures on Hebrews*," previously cited, and "The Problem of Testament in Luther's *Lectures on Hebrews*" in *Harvard Theological Review* 63 (1970): 61-90.

[50] Ibid., 61.

[51] Ibid., 63. Here, Hagen quotes WA 3:167.28-34.

C. Theology of the Cross

The third element in testament is the theology of the cross. Hagen writes: "Luther does not conceive of salvation in terms of progressive transformation as did Augustine but in terms of the ever-present Word of God, faith, and inheritance, all grounded in the death of Christ."[52] For Luther, old and new refer to contrasting responses to the Word, not to time elements or progression, because "The full force of God's testament is present at every point in time."[53] For some, Luther's entire theology is a theology of the cross. Hagen also sees the cross as an essential element in theology of testament—the need for the testator to die in order that the inheritance be given to the heirs. For Luther, "*theologia crucis* means *theologica testamenti*—the cross is assumed and not argued."[54]

In the humiliation of the cross, God totally identified with the human situation to redeem it. In contrast to a theology of glory that speculates what is fitting for God or what God could have done, the cross presents the reality of what God actually did and "makes credible and effective God's eternal promises."[55] The cross contradicts reason. It is fitting for a criminal, a great sinner, but not for God as reason conceives of God. Can God die? "God could not die unless he became man, thus, the incarnation and the death of Christ are comprehended most concisely in this one word 'testament'."[56] Christ on the cross becomes sinner and sin for us ... for me. "The cross is final proof that the testament of God in Christ is valid."[57]

D. The Gift of Grace

Hagen continually emphasizes that all aspects of testament are God's unilateral doing. The fourth element in testament is grace freely given. He writes: For Luther, "grace is God's self-authenticating Word that accomplishes its purpose without any action on our part."[58] God's testament is unilateral, not covenantal in the usual sense of reciprocal actions. The heirs have done absolutely nothing to deserve the

[52] "Atonement—Reconfigured," 263.
[53] Ibid.
[54] *Theology of Testament*, 118.
[55] *Luther's Approach to Scripture*, 95.
[56] Martin Luther, *De captivitate Babylonica*, WA 6:514.6-10, quoted in "Atonement—Reconfigured," 261.
[57] "Atonement—Reconfigured," 262.
[58] Ibid.

inheritance, nor has the testator deserved to die. But God's unilateral promise of forgiveness and eternal life invests God's actions with surety. God does not lie nor is God's Word untrustworthy. The promise and all it entails are God's entirely gratuitous gift. Hagen shows that the grace of the unilateral testament is the cross and resurrection, with the cross as final proof that the testament is valid and with the resurrection completing God's action.

E. Faith

The fifth element in the theology of testament is faith. Through the Holy Spirit working in the Word, grace gives the gift of faith—of confidence in the promise and inheritance. Since God's testament is unilateral, there is no need to depend on one's own reason or works to facilitate or consummate it. Hagen asserts that for Luther "the Christian has an absolute ground for the certainty of his salvation because his salvation is in Christ—Christ for us and for me."[59] We live by faith, but we are suspended between earth and heaven, so to speak, until the final consummation on the last day because we are simultaneously justified by grace and faith and yet we remain sinners. Luther speaks of the justified as a new creation in the sense of *ex nihilo*, that is, not transformed from the former self but newly created. The old person remains; the struggle continues within between old and new—the old ways and person with the new. Scripture itself contains the antithetical and dialectical struggle between old and new. The eschatological struggle between flesh and Spirit, between devil and celestial forces, continues to the end of time. But for people of faith the victory has been won on the cross. In this life they exist in exile under the contradiction of the cross, standing confidently in its shadow and sign of Christ's victory over death. Hagen has eloquently written:

> In such an exile they are protected and made new only by the 'staff' of God, the power of his Word. By their faith, these people are captivated by Christ, their priest without example, and are in the present related to him through conformity to him. Their faith rests in his testament to them—the promise of forgiveness of sins. Their confidence is made certain because of the *sacramentum* and *exemplum* of Christ's passion and resurrection.[60]

[59] Ibid.
[60] *A Theology of Testament*, 116.

CONCLUSIONS

From the very beginning of his career, Kenneth Hagen has emphasized Luther's theology of testament, which Luther himself considered a summary of the whole Gospel. The harmony between this and the discipline of the sacred page is obvious, for both Scripture and soteriology are unlocked in a wholistic way—with "one Word, one promise, one testament" the key. For Hagen, Luther is never one-dimensional, not limited to only one particular emphasis such as justification by faith or theology of the cross. In the theology of testament, all the elements are essential, just as Scripture reveals the saving works of God that are too profound for only one or another theological characterization or explanation. Without grace there is no faith; without the cross there is no justification; without the Word authenticating it, there is no promise to cling to; without the promise, all is lost. From the very beginning of his career, Hagen has written of the richness of Luther's theology of testament. Through his search for the real Luther, Hagen attempts to present Luther's work as authentically as possible to our age. In so doing, he carries on Luther's work, not primarily as an academic exercise but from conviction and soteriological purpose.

From his studies of original prints, Hagen is rightly concerned over the distortions that later editing introduced to Luther's works, which makes Hagen's quest for the authentic Luther all the more urgent.[61] In seeking the authentic Luther, Hagen situates him in the monastic scriptural context of his own time while carefully distinguishing the things that made Luther's approach unique. Space has not permitted here the extensive comparisons that Hagen makes between Luther and exegetes that preceded him. Suffice it to say that most exegetes had unique emphases. The idea that all of Scripture centered on Christ was also quite commonly held throughout the Middle Ages.[62] However, few exegetes approached Scripture with Luther's passion to get the message of Christ out to a world sorely in need of salvation.

[61] See also Ulrich Asendorf, *Die unvollendete Reformation oder: Die theologische Verantwortung der Freiheit*, Ratzeburger Hefte, vol. 2 (Erlangen: Martin-Luther-Verlag, 1983) which begins by listing numerous ways that each era appropriated Luther to conform him to its own perspective.

[62] See *De doctrina Christiana*, in which Augustine presents seven rules for Scripture study, from Tyconius the Donatist. The first rule is that Scripture is about Christ and his body the Church.

Hagen writes in a style that often emulates Luther and Luther's approach to Scripture. One might say that Hagen applies *enarratio* to Luther and Paul in a similar way to Luther's *enarratio*, not only to explain or analyze but more importantly to draw out the soteriological message. In that urgency, Luther and Hagen are as one.

LUTHER AND STAUPITZ: THE UNRESOLVED PROBLEM OF THE FORERUNNER

David C. Steinmetz

When I was first asked to say something about Johann von Staupitz at the International Medieval Institute in Kalamazoo in 1998, I was reluctant to accept.[1] After all, I had written two books about Staupitz, some miscellaneous articles and reviews, and even a concluding postscript to his life and thought in the *Oxford Encyclopedia of the Reformation*.[2] What possible use could it be, I wondered, to rehearse views that had been laid before the scholarly world in their first form as long ago as 1968 and summarized in their mature form as recently as 1996? Whatever I know about Staupitz, whatever I think about his significance, is for the most part already in print. Aside from a brief comment on a few small points or a slight alteration of still others, I have almost nothing to add to that written record.

However, it occurred to me on further reflection that Staupitz had represented for me from the very beginning a series of troubling methodological problems. I had tried to resolve many of these problems but had never been completely satisfied with my solutions. Perhaps it might be useful for me to lay out some of the issues that had concerned me as I was writing my two books on Staupitz and to offer, if not a resolution of all worrying methodological problems, at

[1] The first form of this essay was a brief informal talk at Kalamazoo on May 9, 1998, as part of a panel on the problem of the forerunner. I revised this essay for publication in this Festschrift while a resident Member of the Center for Theological Inquiry in Princeton, NJ, during the fall semester, 1999.

[2] The observations in this essay are based on previous essays and books, in which the evidence that lies at the foundation of my remarks is detailed. Readers are advised to consult those works for more specific information on the theology of Staupitz and his relationship to Luther. Especially important are *Misericordia Dei: The Theology of Johannes von Staupitz in its Late Medieval Setting*, Studies in Medieval and Reformation Thought 4 (Leiden: E. J. Brill, 1968); *Luther and Staupitz: An Essay In the Origins of the Protestant Reformation*, Duke Monographs in Medieval and Renaissance Studies 4 (Durham, N. C., 1980); and "Staupitz, Johann von" in the *Oxford Encyclopedia of the Reformation* IV (New York and Oxford: Oxford University Press, 1996), 109-11.

least a fair warning of their existence. Some of these problems were created for me by analytical categories I had inherited; others by the fuzziness and ambiguity of the evidence with which I had to work.

Johann von Staupitz was a middle rank ecclesiastical functionary in the Order of the Hermits of St. Augustine and a professor at the newly-founded University of Wittenberg. He knew young Luther personally and acted from time to time as his confessor and patron. At the height of his career, he was the Provincial of Saxony for his order and the Vicar General of the Observant Augustinian cloisters throughout Germany. He died in 1524, while serving as the abbot of St. Peter's Benedictine cloister in Salzburg.

There are at least three reasons why he is or should be interesting to historians. The first reason is, of course, fairly obvious: namely, his proximity to the young Luther, especially during the years 1505 to 1512 for which we have very little direct evidence about Luther's early theological development. Like John of Paltz, who wrote an influential theological manual for pastors, Staupitz was one of a very few of Luther's contemporaries in the Augustinian Order in Germany to leave a substantial literary deposit, consisting in his case of letters, sermons, devotional tracts, and theological treatises. Unfortunately we have none of Staupitz's university lectures from Tübingen or Wittenberg and can only guess at their content and method. Still we do have enough evidence to recreate to some extent the theological world of Johann von Staupitz before his first encounter with Luther as well as during the early years of Luther's career as a lecturer on the Bible.

Johann von Staupitz
from a painting at the Benedictine
Arch abbey St. Peter in Salzburg, Austria

The second reason why historians should have an interest in Staupitz is because he is genuinely interesting in his own right. We have learned, sometimes by bitter experience, that it is dangerous to measure the knowledge of the early Church Fathers in the sixteenth century by comparing the knowledge of, say, Erasmus or Melanchthon with the information available in modern critical editions. In order to assess the quality of patristic learning in late medieval Europe we have to determine which texts were known at that time and in what editions or anthologies. We also need to know how they were commonly understood. In this respect Staupitz is an important witness for the understanding of the theology of St. Augustine in the Augustinian Order on the eve of the Reformation. His early sermons on Job are thick with citations from Augustine and his later treatise on predestination, while not offering much in the way of direct citation, nevertheless gives a strongly Augustinian reading of Paul.

Staupitz also made some forays into scholastic theology. Anyone who hopes, as I once did, to find very much in the way of technical theology in Staupitz is doomed to disappointment. However, scarcity of reference to the technical vocabulary of late scholasticism is not the same thing as a complete absence of any reference at all. Particularly interesting in this connection is Staupitz's redefinition of sanctifying (or, as Protestants would prefer to say, justifying) grace. Traditional scholastic theology had defined *gratia gratum faciens* (the grace that makes pleasing) as the grace that makes sinners pleasing to God. Such a definition was impossible for Staupitz since he was convinced that it was the logically prior act of divine predestination and not the subsequent infusion of divine love that made sinners pleasing to God. *Gratia gratum faciens* could therefore only be defined by him as the grace that made God pleasing to sinners, a sort of *gratia deum peccatoribus gratum faciens*. Needless to say, this was an untraditional reading of the term that broke sharply with common usage.

The third reason for interest in Staupitz is closely related to the first. Luther claimed that Staupitz had exercised an extremely important influence on him, going so far as to claim that Staupitz was the father of the new Protestant theology. He had, as Luther put it, "begun the doctrine." If this claim is extravagant (as I think it is) or true only in an indirect, even Pickwickian, sense (as I am willing to concede), it nevertheless has fascinated historians for more than a century. Carl Ullmann in a famous book published in 1842 labeled Staupitz a reformer before the Reformation and the label has stuck in some modified form or other to the present day.[3] It was certainly in the framework of Staupitz's relationship to and influence on Luther that I first engaged him, indirectly in *Misericordia Dei*, where I focused on Staupitz's late medieval context, and more explicitly in *Luther*

[3] Carl Ullmann, *Reformers before the Reformation*, translated by Robert Menzies (Edinburgh: T. & T. Clark, 1855).

and Staupitz, where I examined the relationship itself. Did the surviving evidence, I wondered, allow me to describe that relationship more precisely? Could a credible case be presented that might survive rigorous cross-examination by unsympathetic critics?

It was exactly at this point that difficulties began to surface. The first difficulty for me was largely a question of proper periodization. Was it appropriate to speak of Staupitz as a forerunner? The concept of "forerunner" has traditionally been embedded in an older Protestant narrative of the sixteenth century that regards medieval theology and practice as thoroughly wrongheaded if not simply heretical. In this view the Reformation is a necessary, perhaps even inevitable, and certainly commendable correction of an inadequate Christian worldview and its replacement with a superior Christian theology and practice, whether Lutheran, Reformed, Anglican, or Anabaptist. A popular variation of this narrative, which makes the Enlightenment its ultimate if not its proximate goal, extols Protestants over Catholics and Erasmian humanists over both. In such narratives Protestantism is described as simultaneously an original and refreshing break with the Church's medieval past and as an historical phenomenon that in all its newness and originality is not completely unprecedented. Protestants in their attempt to find historical antecedents appealed to an informal tradition created by a small group of medieval theologians who had dissented from the majority viewpoint of their own time in ways that foreshadowed the views of the later reformers. For the most part these prereformers were figures outside the orthodox establishment, prominent dissenters like John Wyclif and Jan Hus or relatively more obscure figures like the cathedral preacher John Ruchrath of Wesel, the chaplain John Pupper of Goch,[4] or the former Parisian theologian Wessel Gansfort of Groningen.

The late Sir Herbert Butterfield called this sort of evolutionary narrative a Whig interpretation of history and it is with a kind of intellectual Whiggery that the concept of forerunner has usually been encumbered. Ironically, such a reading of the Christian past differs from the early Protestant self-understanding by focusing on minority voices in the late medieval Church, figures who were out of step with the dominant views of their times on one issue or another. But leaders of the new movement like Melanchthon and Calvin thought they were in step with the great Christian mainstream, supported by

[4] For a brief introduction to John Pupper of Goch, see my "*Libertas Christiana*: Studies in the Theology of John Pupper of Goch (d. 1475)," *Harvard Theological Review* 65 (1972): 191-230.

a broad consensus of ancient Fathers as well as what Calvin called the sounder schoolmen. They spent a good deal of their time demonstrating just how mainstream they thought they were and how aberrational they considered the views of their opponents to be. They were happy to confess that they were out of step with the late medieval Church, a Church that never seemed to tire of innovations and amendments to ancient theology and practice. They wanted to be, in the happy phrase of the poet Peter Viereck, unadjusted to the age but adjusted to the ages. For them it was far more important to be governed by what they regarded as the plain sense of Scripture and the golden tradition of the undivided Christian Church.

When Cardinal Sadoleto complained to the city of Geneva that the early Protestants had broken with ancient tradition and embraced theological innovation, Calvin turned the charge on its head.[5] The so-called ancient tradition Sadoleto cherished and recommended to others was not ancient at all, but a relatively recent mixture of medieval innovations introduced over time through theological laxity and inattention. Evangelicals like Calvin and Melanchthon intended to sweep such innovations away and reintroduce the Church to its own authentic past. What Sadoleto called heresy and schism was in reality the evangelical recalling of the Church from the heresy and schism into which it had inadvertently fallen (and which Sadoleto mislabeled Catholic tradition) and toward the full recovery of its oldest and best traditions (which he improperly derided as innovation).

In his influential collection of late medieval texts published in 1966 and called *Forerunners of the Reformation*, Heiko Oberman attempted to rescue the concept of forerunner by redefining it.[6] At a time, now more than thirty years ago, when many historians were inclined, for whatever reasons, to emphasize the discontinuity between the Middle Ages and the Reformation and to find on every hand nothing but differences, Oberman pressed the case for continuity and reinterpreted the so-called forerunners as important symbols of the strong and continuous bonds that existed between the sixteenth century and the age immediately preceding it. Forerunners were in his view participants in an ongoing conversation, "not necessarily" always "friendly," that continued into the sixteenth century.

[5] John Calvin, OS I: 437-89. Sadoleto's text is printed in his *Opera quae extant omnia*, Vol. 4 (Verona, 1737–1738).

[6] Heiko A. Oberman, ed., *Forerunners of the Reformation: The Shape of Late Medieval Thought Illustrated by Key Documents*, translated by Paul L. Nyhus (New York: Holt, Rinehart, and Winston, 1966).

I could not agree more with Oberman's emphasis on continuity between the later Middle Ages and the Reformation. My own work in the history of biblical interpretation has deepened my sense of how pervasive and influential those ties were and how dangerous it is to overlook or ignore them. In biblical interpretation the continuities extend not only to the identification of central theological themes and important exegetical problems in the biblical text but even to the smaller details of exegetical lore. However, the history of biblical interpretation can also make us wary about the category of forerunner, even when it is detached from the older Protestant narrative and given a careful and sophisticated redefinition.

Who, for example, is the forerunner of Calvin's exegesis of Romans 4?[7] As a general rule Calvin does not tell us whom he has read or when he has read them, though he confesses a partiality for Augustine's theology (though not his exegesis) and Chrysostom's exegesis (though not his theology). We can only get some sense of the originality or lack of originality of Calvin's exegesis by comparing it, not with the exegesis of a list of possible forerunners, but with the interpretation of the eighty or so authors, ancient and modern, whose commentaries on Paul were readily available in print in the sixteenth century. Moreover, we cannot specify in advance whose exegesis may prove more important for Calvin or whose less. When Calvin appeals in his explication of Romans 4 to the example of Phineas, who murdered a Midianite woman and her Israelite lover out of zeal for God, in order to deal with the suggestion of Psalm 106:31 that Phineas had been justified by his works, Calvin was, of course, repeating a point made by his Strasbourg friend and associate, Martin Bucer, in his *Metaphrases et Enarrationes* on Romans. However, it is a point also made by Brenz, Hemmingsen, Hyperius, Cornerus, Alesius, Selnecker, Vermigli, Salmeron, and the antecedent exegetical tradition. While we can rule out most of Calvin's contemporaries except Bucer as a possible channel for the transmission of this exegetical detail to Calvin, it is clear that Bucer was repeating a medieval exegetical commonplace that Calvin could have learned elsewhere. No special explanation is required to account for its appearance in Calvin's exegesis and none should be given.

Similarly, when Calvin identifies the speaker in Romans 7 as a Christian under grace rather than a Jew under the law, he sides with the exegesis of the older Augustine against the exegesis of the younger.[8]

[7] David C. Steinmetz, *Calvin in Context* (New York and Oxford: Oxford University Press, 1995), 64-78.

[8] Ibid., 110-21.

By doing so, he identifies with the exegesis of Bucer and Melanchthon and breaks with the medieval tradition of Peter Lombard, Nicholas of Lyra, and Denis the Carthusian (though not of Thomas Aquinas). Yet the very same exegetical point is made in Calvin's own day by such Catholic authors as Thomas de Vio Cardinal Cajetan, O.P., Girolamo Cardinal Seripando, O.E.S.A., Ambrosius Catharinus Politus, O.P., and Domingo de Soto, O.P. Indeed, of Calvin's contemporaries who wrote on Romans, only Jacopo Cardinal Sadoleto, the antitrinitarian Fausto Sozzini, and the former Capuchin preacher turned radical Protestant, Bernardino Ochino, had much enthusiasm for affirming that Romans 7 describes a human being under the law. When Calvin identifies the "I" of Romans 7 as a Christian under grace, he is uttering what had become in his own day an exegetical commonplace. His exegesis was formed, not by a chain of dissident forerunners, but by the dominant exegetical tradition of the sixteenth century. As an interpreter of Paul, Calvin is clearly taking part in a conversation that began in the distant ecclesiastical past and that will continue long after his death into the indeterminate future. But it is a conversation for which the analytical category of forerunner is not of much practical help.

In the end I am not certain whether the concept of forerunner can be separated entirely from the older Protestant narrative, though I applaud every effort to try to do so. After all, the word "forerunner" like the word "typology" suggests that something is coming which is more important than what is here already and that what is here already derives its full meaning and significance from what is still future. It does not, I am afraid, strike me with the force of self-evident truth that the sixteenth century is marked by greater zeal for the reform of the Church or more calamitous failures to maintain Christian unity than the preceding century.

Talk of forerunners can obscure the fact of how remarkable the period from the Great Schism to the Fifth Lateran Council really was. During that century three popes were deposed and a scandalous division in Latin Christianity was resolved. The Hussites pressed their own dissident reform program through bitter religious wars to an uneasy accommodation with Catholic Christendom. The breach with Orthodox Christians in the East was temporarily if unsatisfactorily and only partially resolved (a breach that involved far more Christians than were represented by the Protestant Reformation in the next century). The fall of Constantinople to the Turks isolated the Russians from the Greeks, from whom they were already alienated by the attempt of Constantinople to reach a last minute accommodation with Western Christians on (as the Russians judged) largely Western terms. All of which led to the independence of the Russian Church from the Greeks and the attempt by Russian Christians to create in Moscow a Third Rome to replace two that had fallen. The fifteenth century is the century of Jean Gerson and Pierre d'Ailly, of Denis the Carthusian and Nicholas of Cusa, of Julian of Norwich and Margery Kempe, of Jan Hus and Wessel Gansfort, of Catherine of Genoa and Gabriel Biel, of Sir John Oldcastle and Thomas Netter, of Lorenzo Valla and Francesco Zabarella. It is a century of reforms attempted and reforms averted, of crusading Church councils and reluctant popes, of old quarrels concluded and new schisms entrenched, of luminous successes and miserable failures. We have to be very careful not to allow the concept of forerunner to obscure any of that rich diversity and to remember that every age is equidistant from God.

And then there are the problems with the evidence concerning Staupitz himself. On this subject I can be relatively brief. Almost all of the direct evidence we have about his relationship with Luther comes from Luther himself. We have almost no corroborating evidence from Staupitz, from whom we do have protestations of affection and high regard. Since many of the conversations Luther had that were important to him took place during the sacrament of confession, it is not astonishing that we know nothing about them from Staupitz. To have left any written record about them would have broken the seal of the confessional, even if it were clear, as it is not, that these conversations were as memorable to Staupitz as they were to the young and impressionable Luther.

The oldest piece of direct evidence we have from Luther dates from 1518 and is found in the dedication to Luther's *Resolutiones*.[9] There is a striking similarity in language between this early dedication and the preface to the 1545 Latin edition of his works. In 1545 Luther confesses to have been troubled as a young man by the word *iustitia*. In 1518 he claims that the word that really troubled him at the time was *penitentia*, a word that is not unrelated to *iustitia* but is also not the same. According to this early testimony Luther was struck during one of Staupitz's colloquies with the friars at Erfurt by the observation that penitence begins with the love of God, whereas Luther had thought until then that love belonged to the final stage of repentance. What did Luther mean by this observation? He provided no explanation at the time. We have to move therefore from direct to indirect evidence.

[9] WA 1:525.

The problem which this quotation poses for historians is to construct a credible picture of the theology of each man during the critical years 1505 to 1512 and to build a plausible explanation of the meaning of Luther's remark on the basis of such a reconstruction. In 1505 Luther entered the Augustinian cloister; in 1512 he was installed as a theological professor in Wittenberg. The likelihood that Luther had his most important conversations with Staupitz during this period is very high. The difficulty is that we have very little from either man during these crucial years. From Luther we have at least one sermon, and some annotations on Augustine and on the Sentences of Peter Lombard; from Staupitz we have nothing at all. The reconstruction of Staupitz's theology depends therefore on sermons he preached at Tübingen in 1497/98 (which Luther did not hear and which were never published during his lifetime) and a series of sermons he preached at Nuremberg in 1516 (which were reworked and published in Latin and German as a treatise on predestination and its execution in time). Aside from these two sources we have one short legal treatise from 1500, a revision of the Augustinian constitutions from 1504, several collections of sermons in manuscript, and a few treatises on issues of spirituality, including a posthumous treatise on faith. The German sermons and spiritual writings date from 1512 or later.

Unfortunately, the works we have from both are not readily comparable. The main documents we have from Luther are university lectures on the Psalms, Romans and Hebrews. Luther provides a running gloss and lengthier scholia that comment verse by verse on the entire text of each book. Although the pages of his lectures crackle with fresh ideas, the form is traditional and modeled on standard late medieval exegetical lectures. While Staupitz comments verse by verse on the opening sections of Job (alas, not the Psalms), he organizes the text topically for preaching in the modern style rather than following the older patristic model adopted by earlier preachers. Although his little book on predestination is more or less Pauline, it does not offer a verse by verse commentary on Paul but is marked rather by an allusive intertextuality.

In addition to the difficulties I experienced with the direct and indirect evidence from Staupitz and Luther, I found problems in the historical literature as well. The secondary literature on Staupitz and Luther was both helpful in its content and troubling in its methodology. Reading this literature I became deeply skeptical of the methods commonly used by historians to demonstrate influence. Generally speaking, historians have often appealed to similarities in thought with little or no supporting documentary evidence and with few safeguards against *post hoc propter hoc* reasoning. I discussed these issues fully in *Luther and Staupitz* and there is no time to repeat the arguments of that book here. I only want to repeat the two methodological principles I suggested there and to add, by way of conclusion to this brief essay, a third principle. The first two principles were both negative: (1) that an historian has not demonstrated influence when he or she has proven similarities in thought; and (2) that influence is not a synonym for agreement.

To those two negative principles may be added a third positive axiom: (3) that the best way to demonstrate influence is to establish first the larger context. Historians frequently have gone in the opposite direction, neglecting the larger context and fixating on questions of influence. How often have historians painfully traced in the dim half-light of the past an idea as it was transmitted from one thinker to another only to turn on the lights and discover that the idea they had traced with such effort and in such meticulous detail was in fact a commonplace idea held by almost everyone! Indeed, it would have been far more astonishing if thinker A had not held the position so carefully traced than that he might have learned it first from thinker B. As the old adage points out, when everyone is somebody then no one is anybody. Questions of influence are of no great importance when the ideas involved are commonplaces. At the same time the discovery that an important idea was a commonplace is itself a discovery of considerable historical importance.

I suppose it was issues like this that shifted questions of influence to the back burner of my mind and reoriented me toward questions of context. By examining all the commentators who wrote commentaries on John and whose writings were readily available in the sixteenth century in printed editions (sometimes in multiple editions), we can establish a cloud of forerunners (as opposed to direct influences) for any theologian who comments on John. Like a soil scientist who takes a core sample from the earth to examine its various levels, historians who examine the whole history of the interpretation of John 6 (or at least a very representative sampling of that history) will establish the boundaries set by the tradition of interpretation in the Christian Churches. Such a procedure sets a necessary framework within which to assess the originality of later commentators and even to trace lines of influence. In historical work as in navigation a straight line is not necessarily the shortest distance between two points.

In the end I think we can only keep the idea of forerunners of the Reformation if like Oberman we redefine it. My suggestion would be to redefine it even more broadly than Oberman did thirty-three years ago and extend it to embrace everyone who took part in the long conversations in the Church, not always friendly, about issues that really mattered and who left written records that were accessible in the sixteenth century. It is the full debate and not merely pieces of it that set the framework for the wrenching arguments of the sixteenth century. Such a redefinition shifts the accent from forerunner as influence to forerunner as context. It may be objected, I think wrongly, that such a redefinition of forerunner would define the category out of existence. I do not myself think so. But even if it did, the gain would be worth it.

MEDIEVAL PIETY IN LUTHER'S *COMMENTARY ON THE MAGNIFICAT*

George H. Tavard

Martin Luther's *Commentary on the Magnificat* was composed, apparently with many interruptions, in 1520 and 1521, at the same time as several of his basic reformatory pamphlets. It was written for the edification of seventeen-year old John Frederick of Saxony (1503–1554), the nephew of Frederick the Wise who would succeed his uncle and become Elector of Saxony in 1532. This was early enough in Luther's career to show traces of his intellectual and religious background in the Middle Ages. Neither the liturgical ritual nor the course of studies at the University of Wittenberg had yet been radically altered. Allusions to standard medieval practices and ideas are therefore not rare in the commentary. More surprising perhaps to modern readers is the evidence of Luther's Marian piety.[1]

Marian Liturgy

In the medieval context Mary's canticle is not only biblical; it is also a liturgical hymn that is used in daily prayer. As Luther notes in dedicating the work to John Frederick, it "is sung in all the churches at vespers, and to a particular and appropriate setting that distinguishes it from the other chants" (125[2]). The universality and official

[1] The ecumenical dialogues that have examined the Mariology of the Reformation have considered the doctrines rather than the piety of the Reformers. Thus: H. George Anderson, J. Francis Stafford, Joseph A. Burgess, eds., *Lutherans and Catholics in Dialogue, VII: The One Mediator, the Saints, and Mary*, nn. 6-19 (Minneapolis: Augsburg, 1992), 23-26; Groupe des Dombes, *Marie dans le dessein de Dieu et la communion des saints, I: Dans l'histoire et l'écriture*, nn. 55-64 (Paris: Bayard-Editions, 1997), 39-43.

[2] The quotations are taken from the English translation by A. T. W. Steinhaeuser, in *Works of Martin Luther*, vol.III (Philadelphia: Muhlenberg Press, 1943); the numbers in parentheses refer to the page of this edition, one reference applying to all quotes until another number is given. This translation, slightly revised, is also found in Jaroslav Pelikan, ed., *Luther's Works*, vol. 21 (St. Louis: Concordia Publishing House, 1956), 295-358.

character of the chant are underlined with some irony since they stand in sharp contrast with a real neglect of what the hymn means: "The whole world is nowadays filled with praise and service of God, with singing and preaching, with organs and trumpets, and the *Magnificat* is magnificently sung" (138). Such pomp emphasizes the hypocrisy of the times. Solemnity is ambiguous in that it can be the work of "two kinds of false spirits."

Some will not sing unless they evidently enjoy God's manifest favors: "We sing only when it fares well with us; as soon as it fares ill, we have done with singing and no longer esteem God highly, but suppose He can or will do nothing for us. Then the *Magnificat* also must languish." Others take personal pride in the good gifts of God, and then "they magnify themselves." Praise and singing can be merely exterior, done indeed with pomp and circumstance to the accompaniment of trumpet and organ. It should, however, be interior, when one truly imitates the Virgin, who "leaves herself out, and ascribes everything to God alone, from whom she received it." Meanwhile, there are those who so extol her that she seems to eclipse God. In a way they then apply to her the liturgical practice of Passiontide, when, beginning on the fifth Sunday in Lent, crucifixes and statues are veiled by purple cloth that is removed after the Good Friday liturgy. They thus "hide the Virgin's comfortable picture. ... For they deprive us of her example from which we might take comfort" (157).

Luther obviously takes it for granted, not only that young John Frederick is familiar with these practices, but also that, as the well-educated, theologically aware, and pious ruler that he ought to become, he will have frequent occasions to reflect on the Holy Virgin's hymn. Since Luther has no plan as yet to abandon the Roman ritual, the choice of Mary's song as an instrument of education and edification is a good one. The Elector of Saxony and his retinue often attend solemn vespers, in which the singing of the *Magnificat* is a high point. In fact, Mary's *Magnificat* is still featured in the Catholic liturgy of vespers after Vatican Council II and the reforms of Paul VI. In his time and place, however, Luther is very much aware of deviations of piety, and not only in relation to the sale of indulgences that has provoked him into the challenge of the Ninety-Five Theses. "Alas!", he exclaims, today the service of God is likely to evoke, not the divine works, but

> the ringing of bells, the wood and stones of churches, the incense-pot, the flicker of candles, the mumbling in the churches, the gold, silver, and precious stones in the vestments of choir-boys and cel-

> ebrants, of chalices and monstrances, of organs and images, processions and church going, and most of all the babbling of lips and the rattling of rosaries ... (191).

External adjuncts of faith in liturgical celebrations do not constitute the true worship of God. "Of such service," Luther goes on, "God knows nothing at all, while we know nothing but this. We chant the *Magnificat* daily, to a special tone and with gorgeous pomp, and yet the oftener we sing it the more we silence its true music and meaning." Attention should be exclusively turned to what God does.

The Praise of Mary

A similar note of fidelity to the customary liturgy is struck by the titles that Luther applies to Mary. She is primarily the Mother of God, *Mater Dei* or *Dei genitrix*, Θεοτόχος, in keeping with the theological tradition that was endorsed at the Council of Ephesus. As such, she is "the tender Mother of God," "the Holy Mother" (137), "the Most Blessed Mother of God" (161). These last two titles extol what God has done for her, while the first describes her maternal tenderness toward her son, which is itself a witness to the reality of the Incarnation: the Word incarnate truly gave himself a fully human mother. Still in relation to the divine motherhood, Mary is called "the stem and root," the "rod and flower" being Christ (130). She is likened to "the generation of David or Jesse" that was frequently represented in the decoration of medieval churches. That she belonged to the lineage of David evokes at the same time the royal dignity of a king chosen by God, and the sorry state in which the dynasty had fallen at the time of the Incarnation of the divine Word. The royal line of David and Solomon was far from its former glory. It had become "so impoverished and despised that it was like unto a dead stem," the priests of the Old Testament having usurped all honor and power. It was, however, to a "poor and lonely maiden" (131) of the Davidic line, and not to a daughter of Annas or Caiaphas, that the Word of God was born.

Next in importance to her being the Mother of God, Mary is the Holy Virgin. Although it seemed indeed "unlikely that Mary the Virgin should become the mother of such a child" (130), she "became a mother in a supernatural manner and without violation of her virginity." This formulation of the mystery covers what medieval theology called virginity *ante partum* and virginity *in partu*. Mary conceived her child from the Holy Spirit; and his birth did not break her hymen, thus leaving her physical virginity intact. This is of course, as Luther remarks, "above nature." Mary, however, took no pride in it: "It is no less a miracle that she refrained from pride and arrogance than that she received the gifts she did" (139). As this shows, Mary's virginity was of the spirit and of the soul no less than of the body.

The Visitation.
Albrecht Dürer, woodcut (1503).

At this point Luther accepts the medieval division of the soul, which was said to have a superior and an inferior part. Spirit (*spiritus*) is "the highest, deepest, and noblest part," that is "enabled to lay hold on things incomprehensible, invisible, and eternal. It is in brief the dwelling place of faith and the Word of God" (132). At its summit this higher part of the soul coincides with what the scholastics in the Augustinian tradition had called *synderesis*. Soul, or its lower part (*anima*), is the same faculty as spirit, but seen as it informs and uses the body. Because it is ruled by reason rather than by grace or faith, this lower level is prone to error: "Unless the spirit, which is lighted with the brighter light of faith, controls this light of reason, it cannot but be in error" (133).

As Mother of God and Holy Virgin, Mary is "the foremost example of the grace of God" (157). In her song of thanksgiving, however, she brings attention to God, not to herself. It is then in the horizon of contemplative prayer that Luther evokes John Frederick "regarding her," seeing her lowliness, her humility, and realizing that God "regards, embraces, and blesses so poor and despised a mortal" (156). At such a spectacle he will find himself "moved to love and praise God for His grace," and his heart will be "strengthened in faith and love and hope." He will be inspired to fulfill Mary's wish, for it is her desire that one should come "through her to God" (156), an expression that Luther uses twice in four lines.

Artists, however, should not depict Mary in glory, for this would set her so far above common humanity that it would make us "timid and afraid" before her. Setting her "above all examples," they would deprive us of her example. What they ought to show is Mary's humble stance before God. For it was in her low estate and her unworthiness that she was graced by God. In her, God joined "his exceeding riches with her utter poverty, the divine glory with her shame, the divine greatness with her smallness, the divine goodness with her lack of merit, the divine grace with her unworthiness" (157).

The divine riches that were given to Mary have made this humble virgin "the Queen of Heaven." Luther was of course familiar with depictions of the coronation of the *Dei genitrix* as Queen of Heaven that could be seen in medieval churches. It is not, however, to pictures or windows but to hymnody that he draws attention at this point (162), specifically to the hymn, *Regina coeli*, which, in the Roman liturgy of the hours, was the final antiphon of each day from Easter Sunday to the Friday in the octave of Pentecost. The hymn, however, suggests an objection to what Luther has said about Mary's lowliness, for it mentions her worth and merit. Did she merit the Incarnation? Not any more, Luther explains, than the "holy Cross" did. Although it was "a thing of wood and incapable of merit," similar language was commonly used of it. God's choice of the Virgin was, like the choice of the Cross, "pure grace and not a reward, that we might not take away from God's grace, worship, and honor by ascribing too great things to her. It is better to take away too much from her than from the grace of God." Queen of Heaven she is indeed. This "is a true enough name and yet does not make her a goddess." Luther even imagines Mary in heaven on the model of what he takes to have been her life on earth, when she was "tending the cattle and doing the housework"(130), performing the many tasks of a German peasant housewife. More elaborately Luther repeats:

> She seeks not any glory, but goes about her wonted household duties, milking the cows, cooking the meals, washing pots and kettles, sweeping out the rooms, and performing the works of a maid-servant or housemother in lowly and despised tasks (164).

It is of course most unlikely that in Nazareth Joseph and Mary had any cattle to tend. The point, however, lies in the contrast between what Mary herself does and what God does in her. Her Queenship comes from God. In placing her in this privileged position God indeed willed to act for her sake, but not for her alone. God so acted for the sake of all the saints, and this should be acknowledged in prayer: "We ought to call upon her, that for her sake God may grant and do what we request. Thus also all other saints are to be invoked, so that the work may be every way God's alone" (164).

In these passages Luther did not ignore that the Mother of God occupied a distinguished place in German piety. Her Queenship was at the center of a well-known writing by the Dominican Friar Henry Suso (c. 1295–1366), one of the great mystics of the Rhineland. In the *Little Book of Eternal Wisdom* (ch.16), Suso ascribed the Queenship of Mary directly to God's loving choice of her and indirectly to human sin. Certainly many of his formulations would have been alien to Luther's language of praise, as when he prayed: "O Lady of heaven and earth, arise and be a mediatrix."[3] Nonetheless, Suso praised Mary in words that Luther could recognize: "O Beloved, charming bride of God!" He also associated Eve to Mary in the work of redemption: "Blessed be Eve for bringing us the sweet fruit of heaven."[4] In context, the sweet fruit of heaven is not Mary herself, but her child the Infant Jesus.

DUAL PATTERNS

An interesting aspect of Luther's commentary on the *Magnificat* emerges from consideration of its structure, or rather of its interlocking structures. A first structure, superficial, is naturally given by the *Magnificat* itself as Luther successively reflects on its ten verses. Necessary as this sequence is to the logic of the biblical canticle, it does not itself reveal Luther's profound intention and meaning.

A deeper structure runs through the text as the commentator's considerations run back and forth between what God alone does in Mary and, beyond her, in all creation, and the sinful self-sufficiency of human creatures who stubbornly cling to their own works. This is a duality, in that the Creator is not the creature and vice versa. It cannot, however, be called bipolar, since bipolarity implies an interdependence, and therefore a certain equality, of the two poles. In this instance, however, there can be no equality between God and the

[3] Henry Suso *The Exemplar, with Two German Sermons* in *Classics of Western Spirituality* (New York: Paulist Press, 1989), 258.

[4] Ibid., 257.

Virgin. The Creator evidently dominates. At the same time this is not a dualism, for dualism suggests an opposition of the two. The dual structure, however, opens the possibility of human arrogance and of revolt against God. A fine line runs between the dual, the bipolar, and the dualistic. It leads to the paradox that the condition of human happiness and holiness does not lie in personal achievement, but in renunciation to every human effort and in self-abandonment to God.

This is the point where Luther locates the contrast between Mary and the rest of humanity. Acting on our own, "we cannot leave his tender gifts undefiled nor keep an even mind, but let our spirits rise and fall according as he gives or takes away his gifts" (139). On the contrary, "Mary's heart remains at all times the same; she lets God have his way with her and draws from it all only a good comfort, joy, and trust in God" (139). "She leaves herself out and ascribes everything to God alone, from whom she received it" (138). Mary follows what Luther had called the theology of the Cross in article 21 of the *Heidelberg Disputation*. Her attitude also reflects article 27: "The work of Christ shall rightly be called an active work, and ours that which is worked, so the one which is worked is well-pleasing to God thanks to the active work."

Another duality appears in what may be named the parable of the water and the well. As he explains Mary's humility Luther remarks that some people pretend to be humble in order to be admired and exalted, which is what they earnestly desire in their false humility. They are like men who "carry water to the well" (146), a foolish exercise indeed! The well in question is evidently the well of honor and dignity. The hypocrites try to fill it up first so that others will draw the water and praise them highly. In contrast, the truly humble "never aspire to the heights" (147). They do not carry water to the well. On the contrary, "here the water flows from the well."[5] If honor comes to them it appears unexpectedly. "True humility never knows that it is humble; for if it knew this, it would turn proud from contemplation of so fine a virtue." The Virgin was truly humble. Her humility may serve to illustrate what Luther designates as the "contrary works of God" (180).

[5] In St. Teresa's *Autobiography*, terminated before 1568, four ways of watering a garden (drawing it from a well, getting it from a water-wheel or aqueduct, or from a river overflow, or from rain) illustrate four ways of prayer: *The Book of Her Life*, ch.II, n.7 [Kieran Kavanaugh and Otilio Rodriguez, editors. *The Collected Works of St. Teresa of Avila*, vol. 1 (Washington, D.C.: ICS Publication, 1976), 81].

The Contrary Works of God

A modern reader, aware of the Shoah, may feel uncomfortable before an unexpected aspect of the *Commentary on the Magnificat*, that is itself tied to another duality. Luther reflects on the "second work" of God that is the topic of verse 6: "He has shown the strength of his arm; he has scattered the proud in the imagination of their hearts." The arm is the power of God, that is understood only by faith (177). God works either through the creatures, visibly, or by himself, in secret. These secret deeds are done "only among the two divisions of mankind, the godly and the wicked" (178). In the perspective of the theology of the Cross, God acts powerfully through the weakness of the just: "Where man's strength ends God's strength begins, provided faith be present and wait on Him." This was manifest at the Cross itself and, later, in the death of the Christian martyrs. Reversely, God interiorly weakens the powerful wicked, and one has only to wait long enough to see them collapse.

In light of these contrary works of God, Luther admires the "mastery" with which Mary "here hit the perverse hypocrites" (181). She refers in particular to the "enemies of divine truth, such as the Jews in their opposition to Christ, and the men of today" (182). Luther describes the men of today with irony. They "have good hearts and mean well, they call upon God and pity the poor Jesus, who was so unrighteous and proud, and not so pious as they." They are, however, "the most venomous and pernicious folk on earth, their hearts abysses of Satanic pride." While they are not named, it is not difficult to see the pope and his supporters being assimilated to the reprobate Jews.

Luther at this point does not dwell on the Jewish question as this was posed by the very context of medieval society. He does not fall into the popular anti-semitism that had existed at least since the Crusades. Writing for a young man who was expected eventually to rule over an important duchy, Martin Luther felt a certain responsibility to teach him what was the theological status of Jews in a Christian society. As he reflected on Judaism within the horizon of Mary's *Magnificat* he did not pursue the usual line of the numerous *Adversus Judaeos* that had been composed in the Middle Ages by monastic or scholastic theologians. The Jews' guilt for their continuing opposition to Christ and to divine truth had been a commonplace of such literature. Nor did Luther follow the lead of another teacher of the nobility, Thomas Aquinas, who, in an opusculum, *De regimine*

Judaeorum,[6] had answered questions from the duchess of Brabant regarding legal justice in the treatment of the Jews who lived in her territories. Rather than examine laws and customs on taxation, questions of ethics concerning the nature of usury, or the wearing of specific garments that had been decreed in 1215 by the IV Lateran Council,[7] Luther went straight to the theological point, the mystery of Israel, which he believed was the topic of verses 9 and 10 of the *Magnificat*: "He has holpen his Servant Israel in remembrance of his mercy,/ As he spoke to our Fathers, to Abraham and to his seed for ever."

Luther's understanding of these verses is centered on "the very greatest of all God's works, the Incarnation of the Son of God" (191). As the Virgin acknowledged in her song, it was for the sake of Israel, and not just for herself, that the Word became flesh. But—and here again Luther relies on a dual mode of thinking—"she divides Israel into two parts, and refers only to that part that is God's Servant." God's servants can only be those who acknowledge the divine works.

> Unless we learn and experience these works of God, there will be no service of God, no Israel, no grace, no mercy, no God, though we kill ourselves with singing and ringing in the churches, and drag into them all the goods in all the world.

It follows that "the Israel that is God's servant" is no other than "his own beloved people, for whose sake He also became man to redeem them from the power of the devil, of sin, death and hell, and to lead them to righteousness, eternal life, and salvation." The vocation of Israel is correlative to a divine promise. God, however, waited a very long time to fulfill this promise, "until it seemed as though He had forgotten—even," Luther boldly remarks, "as all His works seem as though He was forgetting us ... ." (192).

The identity of Israel raises the basic problem that stands between Christians and Jews, between those who recognize the Messiah, and those who do not. Luther admits that "the word Israel means the Jews alone, and not us Gentiles." However, "because they [the Jews] would not have Him," God has now made Israel "purely spiritual." This is illustrated by the new name that was given to Jacob after his wrestling through the night with the angel (Gen. 28:10-22).

[6] Pierre Mandonnet, editor, *Scti Thomae Aquinatis Opuscula Omnia,* vol. I, (Paris: Lethielleux, 1927), 488-94.

[7] *Constitutio 68: Ut Judaei discernantur a christianis in habitu* in *Conciliorum Oecumenicorum Decreta* (Basel: Herder, 1962), 242; other constitutions that relate to Jews are 67 (the "usury of Jews"), 69 (that Jews must not hold public office), 70 (that converts from Judaism must not continue to practice Jewish rites).

He was named "Israel, as a patriarch who was not only Jacob, the father of fleshly children, but Israel, the father of spiritual children." Luther sees an analogy between Jacob's wrestling and the union of Christian believers with God. The Christian Church is "joined to God as a bride to a bridegroom, so that the bride has a right to and power over her Bridegroom's body and all His possessions" (193). This union with the heavenly Spouse "comes to pass through faith," an acceptance of God's word and will that opens an entirely new reciprocity between God and the faithful: "By faith man does what God wills; God in turn does what man wills." There "would be much more to say on this subject," Luther concludes, "for Israel is a strange and profound mystery."

THE MYSTERY OF ISRAEL

As he reads the last verse of the *Magnificat*, Luther returns to his reflection on Israel and the Jews. He rehearses the story of sin and redemption. With Mary he ascribes "this work of the Incarnation solely to the undeserved promise of divine grace that was made to Abraham." Apart from Christ, who is the true Seed of Abraham, all humans remain under the curse and no one, whether Jew or Gentile, can be saved. Furthermore, it was the curse that made the virginity of the Mother of Christ necessary. For "the Seed itself must first be blessed and neither touched nor tainted by that curse, but be pure blessing, full of grace and truth" (194-195). The Jews, however, "always confidently expected" that the Seed would come from the sons of Abraham, that is, from one of them, while It was born "of this one daughter of his, Mary, alone" (195). The Jewishness of Jesus owed nothing to male power. It came entirely through a girl, in whom the God of Israel finally fulfilled his promise. The Christocentric reading of the Old Testament that Luther follows here had itself been at the source of typology in medieval exegesis. As Luther says, "the whole Bible hangs on this oath of God, for in the Bible everything has to do with Christ" (196). One cannot argue from the Law against this centering of the Bible in Christ, since the Law that was given to Moses did not invalidate the promise previously made to Abraham. A literal reading of the Law even led to forget Abraham, so that the prophets of Israel were put to death by "the Jews" (197).

Turning to the Jews of his time, Luther notes, with Mary, that they remain "His seed forever." The promised grace "is to continue to Abraham's seed [that is, to the Jews] from that time forth, throughout all time, down to the last day" (197). On the one hand, most

Jews "are hardened." On the other, "there are always some, however few, that are converted to Christ and believe in Him." God's promise does not lie. It was made to Abraham and to his seed "not for one year or for a thousand years, but *in saecula*, that is, from one generation to another, without end." Further, "they alone, and not we Gentiles, have this promise ... ."

How then should one behave toward Jews? In view of the reputation of gross anti-semitism that has been attached to Luther's name because of the violent pamphlets he wrote in his last years, it is striking that his recurring term at this point, as he describes the proper behavior of Christians towards Jews, is kindness. We ought not, he says, to "treat the Jews with so unkindly a spirit." The motivation for such kindness, however, is not quite satisfactory to the contemporary mind: "For there may be future Christians among them!" With his predecessors in the medieval Church Luther sees the Jews in the perspective of their conversion. This at least testifies to his conviction that the ties between the Old Testament and the New are very close.[8] In any case, the conversion of Jews, Luther insists, must be free. They should be set a good example and be attracted to the Messiah by our own fidelity: "If we lived Christian lives, and led them with kindness to Christ, there would be the proper response. ... Tell them the truth in all kindness ... ." And "if they will not receive it, let them go." Unbelieving Jews (which was the sense of the liturgical expression used in the supplications of Good Friday, *pro perfidis Judaeis*) should not be treated more harshly than the "many Christians who despise Christ, do not hear his word, and are worse than Jews or heathen! Yet we leave them in peace ... ." The Christian cause, as Luther also says, "rests upon pure grace," and therefore, one should conclude, not upon coercion.

Did John Frederick remember this advice when, in 1535, he outlawed Jewish settlements in Saxony? There were of course precedents for John Frederick's decision, notably the expulsion of Jews from Castile and Aragon in 1492 by Isabel and Ferdinand. And in 1535 Luther approved of the duke's decision. In Spain the decision seems to have been prompted by the failure of the two-year long Disputation of Tortosa (1413–1414) to convince the Sephardic rabbis that Jesus was indeed the Messiah.[9] Even apart from any reference

[8] Only Nicholas of Cusa (1400/01–1464) among theologians had advocated another point of view as he envisaged the reconciliation of the three Religions of the Book, notably in *De concordantia catholica* and *De pace fidei*.

[9] Antonio Pacios Lopez, *La Disputa de Tortosa*, 2 vol. (Madrid: Instituto Arias Montano, 1957).

to Tortosa, Luther's attitude in 1535 reflected a conviction that stood in the background of the medieval writings *Adversus Judaeos*: On the basis of the Old Testament the Jewish people are so close to Christianity that once the true doctrine has been properly explained, as Luther was convinced he had done, the continuing rejection of Jesus seems completely incomprehensible and therefore reprehensible!

THREEFOLD AND SIXFOLD PATTERNS

In addition to the binary structure of thought that serves as a backdrop to Luther's view of Jews, trinitarian structures emerge from time to time in the *Commentary on the Magnificat.*

A reference to the three dimensions of the human being has already been noted in connection with Mary's words, "My soul doth magnify the Lord." There is a threefoldness in human nature, which is made of "three parts: spirit, soul, and body" (132). Each part, and even "the whole man," can again be divided in two, since the human person is "spirit and flesh" and shares the qualities of each, thus being both good and evil. The ensuing sixfold division of the soul was fairly common in medieval mysticism. In 1259 it provided the structure of Bonaventure's *Itinerarium mentis in Deum*. For the Seraphic Doctor the division was entirely positive: six stages of the ascent to God are paired as the soul penetrates "in" and "through" the traces, the image, and the Names of God which are Being and Goodness. Luther has not altered the basic schema: body is the realm of God's traces (*vestigium*), soul is the image (*imago*), and spirit, the level of the human being that is aware of the Names of God, corresponds to the *similitudo* of the Vulgate in Gen. 1:26.

The sixfold division recurs when Luther analyses the "six works" of God[10] (169) that the Virgin described in her song. The Creator's gifts to the creatures belong in three categories inasmuch as they can be classified as belonging to "wisdom, might, and riches" (168). Under wisdom, God places "all spiritual possessions and gifts by which a man will gain popularity, fame, and a good report." Under might, God "includes all authority, nobility, friends, high station, and honor." Under riches, one finds "good health, beauty, pleasure, strength, and every external good that may befall the body" (168-169). God, how-

[10] The editors of the English translation refer only to "the first work of God, which is mercy" (169) in verse 5, "the second: breaking spiritual pride" (177) in verse 6, and "the third: putting down the mighty" (182) in verse 7. There are nonetheless six works of God in Luther's *Commentary*.

ever, is not found in such worldly goods, but rather in three goods of the spiritual order, "loving-kindness, judgment, and righteousness" (168), that are given to "the poor in spirit, the oppressed, and they that lack the necessaries of life" (169). Hence the six works of God that the Virgin celebrates: mercy (169-177), breaking spiritual pride (177-182), putting down the mighty (182-184), exalting the lowly (185), feeding the hungry, and sending the rich empty away, these last two works of God being treated together (185-190).

In this structure the threefold Greek division of the human being does not contradict the twofold Latin distinction of *anima* and *corpus*. The two systems are in fact meshed together to form a sixfold pattern, a structure that was undoubtedly facilitated by its analogy with the differentiations between σῶμα or σάρξ, ψῦχή, and νοῦς or πνεῦμα that are found in the New Testament[11] and other early Christian writings. Luther, however, was not doing mere exegesis as he commented on the *Magnificat*. He made himself the bearer of a tradition he had inherited, which had a literary and a spiritual dimension. The literary dimension carried forward the medieval fondness for interweaving strands, as when two directions combined with three points of view bring about six considerations, that may be followed, as in Bonaventure's *Itinerarium*, by a concluding seventh, so that the writing can, however remotely, evoke the sevenfold sacramental system and the seven gifts of the Holy Spirit. Likewise, in *Le Miroir des âmes simples et anéanties*, Marguerite Porete (c.1250–1310), the great mystic, probably a béguine,[12] who was burnt in Paris by the Inquisition although she was undoubtedly orthodox,[13] described six states

[11] 1 Thess. 5:23: "spirit, soul, and body."

[12] The bégards and béguines, who were often confused with the Brethren of the Free Spirit, were condemned at the Council of Vienne (1312–1313): decrees 16 and 28, *Conciliorum Oecumenicorum Decreta* (Basel: Herder, 1962), 350, 359-61. Despite these decrees *Le Miroir* was translated in Latin around 1310, in English, Italian, and two other Latin versions in the mid-fourteenth century and later. Emilie Zum Brunn and Georgette Epiney-Burgard, *Women Mystics of the Middle Ages* (St. Paul, Minn.: Paragon House, 1989), 212 n. 7.

[13] Her book carried the endorsement of three theologians, notably Godefroid de Fontaines (d.c.1306), former regent of the Faculty of Theology at the University of Paris (Zum Brunn, *Women Mystics*, 209 n. 2). After spending eighteenth months in prison she was declared a relapsed heretic on 30 May 1310 on the basis of her refusal to swear to tell the truth. Being turned over to the secular arm she died by fire on 1 June, along with a copy of *Le Miroir*. The bishops who condemned her were also involved in the trial of the Knights Templar during their persecution by King Philippe le Bel.

of the soul, to be followed by a seventh "of which we will have no understanding till our soul has left our body."[14]

The sixfold pattern of ascent derives ultimately from the Dionysian hierarchies, though Denys's three levels are commonly divided (or multiplied) by two rather than by three, as they are in his writings. Luther's use of such a literary device was facilitated by his perception of a structural analogy between the human person and the three courts of "the tabernacle fashioned by Moses" (133) that are described in Exodus 26. In the depths of the tabernacle the Holy of Holies was God's dwelling place; it remained in obscurity, enfolded in the unfathomable darkness of the divine Being. In front of it the holy was lit by the sevenfold candlestick. And the outer court lay "under the open sky and in full light of the sun." Luther's reflection on the biblical outline is reminiscent of the mystical ascent:

> In this tabernacle we have a figure of the Christian man. His spirit is the Holy of Holies, where God dwells in the darkness of faith, where no light is, for he believes that which he neither sees nor comprehends. His soul is the holy place with its seven lamps, that is, all manner of reason, discrimination, knowledge, and understanding of visible and bodily things. His body is the forecourt, open to all, so that men may see his works and manner of life.

NEGATIVE THEOLOGY

If it is seen in reverse, the order given by Luther again evokes a medieval conception of the ascent to God. The pilgrim along the spiritual way passes from bodily or material needs to reason and intellectual knowledge, and thence to the darkness of faith. At the first or material level one finds the point of departure of the spiritual way, since in order to enter and make progress it is necessary to be freed from whatever remains merely material in oneself. This is the active and passive asceticism of purgation, or purgative way. At the second level one catches insights that were previously unknown. Reason has to be used, though one should be aware of its inadequacies when it is contrasted with the intimations of the higher world of spirit. This is illumination, or the illuminative way. Many good people linger at

[14] Although I have used the French edition, *Le Miroir des âmes simples et anéanties*, I will cite the English translation, by Ellen Bobinsky, *The Mirror of Simple Souls* in *Classics of Western Spirituality* (New York: Paulist Press, 1993), ch. 61:138-39; ch. 118:189-94 (citation, 194); in chs. 123-29:202-15, she develops seven points of meditation leading the soul to will the will of God.

this second level. The third level is, to the human reason, total darkness, for it coincides with the realm of faith, where God is manifested beyond merely human comprehension. This is union, or the unitive way. However, rather than explain the third stage by reference to higher graces that are given to the saints in their spiritual progress, as medieval authors would have done, Luther identifies it squarely with "faith pure and simple, for the spirit has nothing to do with things comprehensible" (133).

That God is a night to the intellect, and thereby to the soul, had been commonplace among medieval authors. Marguerite Porete had written, not only that the soul enamored of God "is saved by faith without works,"[15] but also that the soul necessarily enters a state of both unknowing and unwilling, *non-savoir* and *non-vouloir.*[16] Even if Luther had not read her book he was acquainted with a similar doctrine among the mystics of the Rhineland. Meister Eckhart (c.1260–c.1327) had explained that, when applied to God, human language attributes human qualities to the Divinity, an attribution that cannot be literally true. Therefore, Eckhart concluded, "distinctions are lost in God,"[17] and one cannot speak of God at all in any way that would be remotely adequate. The real God is infinitely beyond the spoken God. In the same vein Johannes Tauler (1300–1361) had referred to the Divinity that is above all Names, "above mode, above being, above goodness," and therefore unspeakable by human mouth, unthinkable by human mind. Before God the proper attitude is *Gelassenheit*, abandonment.[18] In *The Little Book of Truth*, Henry Suso also had written of God: "... one could call him an eternal Nothing,"[19] since no name taken from human experience can be applied strictly to the divine. Negative theology had been strongly underlined at the Renaissance, when Nicholas of Cusa (1400–1464) made it one of the meanings of the *docta ignorantia* that he identified as a condition and a fruit of the experiential knowledge of God. In the less sophisticated *De imitatione Christi* (15th c.) it took the form of the principle that practice is better than knowledge. And the author

[15] *The Mirror*, ch. 11: 89

[16] *The Mirror*, ch. 12:92; ch. 57:134 (To those who are lost, "*demoiselle Connaissance, illuminée par la grâce divine,...enseigne le droit chemin royal par le pays du rien-vouloir*"); ch. 84:159; ch. 133:216.

[17] This is the title of Sermon 23: Raymond Blackney, editor, *Meister Eckhart,* (New York: Harper, 1957), 203.

[18] Alois Maria Haas, "Schools of Late Medieval Mysticism," in *Christian Spirituality. High Middle Ages and Reformation*, Jill Raitt, editor (New York: Crossroad, 1987), 152.

[19] Henry Suso, 309.

of *Theologia germanica* had written: "To God as Godhead we can ascribed neither will nor knowing nor manifest revelation nor any particular thing that can be named, spoken, or conceived by thought."[20] Already in this book the ineffable knowledge of God, equivalently, unknowing God, was closely related to justification by faith.

Evidently, these authors, who were trained in medieval theology, were familiar with the scholastic theories of analogical predication. Most of them were not writing, however, primarily for theologians, concerned about orthodoxy of thought and accuracy of language, but for spirituals, eager for a true experience of God. They also knew that one of the first Christian presentations of both the triple way and the apophatic approach to God was found in the works of Denys, who was believed to be the Areopagite. That this was evidence of a Neoplatonist connection would have been of little concern to them.

Martin Luther was thus acquainted with the radically negative theology of the Catholic mystics. He often referred to the inadequacy of human thought in theology, and he pointed to the hiddenness of God, *Deus absconditus*, who cannot be truly known outside of the revelation given by Christ. It was therefore in keeping with the traditional understanding of the mystical night that at this point in the commentary Luther remarked: The "holiness of the spirit is the scene of the sorest conflict and the source of the greatest danger," because of the temptation to rely on one's own works and one's own thoughts rather than walk "solely by faith, that is, a firm confidence in the unseen grace of God that is promised us" (134).

LEGENDARY ILLUSTRATIONS

An apophatic approach to God is often hidden by recourse to allegorical illustrations. Thus it is that, further on in his commentary, Luther draws on medieval folklore as he alludes to what must have been the legendary report of a vision seen "once upon a time" by "a godly woman" (141). In the vision as it is narrated here three virgins were seated in a church or chapel near the altar. A boy who remains unidentified "leapt from the altar" and went to each of them in turn. The first he caressed tenderly; he lifted the veil of the second and smiled at her; he hit the third and tore her hair before vanishing back into the altar. The third alone, Luther explains, and this must

[20] Bengt Hägglund, ed., *The Theologia Germanica of Martin Luther* in *Classics of Western Spirituality* (New York: Paulist Press, 1980), ch. 29:101.

have been part of the story, is "the true bride of Christ," the first being "a figure of the impure and self-seeking spirits," and the second a figure of those who "make a beginning of serving God" but are "not willing to be free from all self-seeking and enjoyment." In other words, the reality is often the opposite of what it seems to human eyes.

There would be little point in debating whether Luther believed that such a vision had truly been seen. The medieval mind tended to be credulous about heavenly visitations. Even for those who were more critical, however, visions belonged to the hagiographic genre. Whether historical or not their content had an educational purpose. They could be invented and attributed to holy people. Luther's mind ran along similar lines. He was not loath to borrow convenient examples or arguments from folklore and legend, when these seemed to confirm his major theological convictions.

Such was the case with the unexpected introduction of a popular image of the European folklore. The third virgin of the vision is highly favored by God although she seems despicable to human eyes. Luther designates her as "that poor Cinderella." In the classical fairy-tale Cinderella is the servant-girl who is entrusted only with the most menial tasks of the kitchen. She looks after the ashes of the fire. Historically the legend of Cinderella seems to have come from Egypt. It was first reported by the Greek geographer Strabo (64bc–24ad), who cited historical or legendary stories to illustrate the countries he described. It was included in the *Varia historia*[21] of the Sophist philosopher Claudius Aelianus (c.170–235[22]), who transmitted it to the Latin world and hence to the Middle Ages, where it was subjected to several modifications. The heroin was no longer Rhodopis (a Greek feminine name that was also used in Rome), but Cinderella, the "ash-girl," a despised servant rather than a beautiful courtesan. Her shoe was lost at a ball rather than stolen by an eagle who then dropped it in the lap of the king of Memphis. In Egypt the story may eventually have been read allegorically, Rhodopis being taken as a symbol of light, that is bound to triumph in the long run even if it is obscured from time to time. For Aelianus the Sophist it rather illustrated the absurdity of human life and of existence in general.

[21] *Varia historia* is in *Loeb Classical Library*, n. 486 (1997), Bk. 13 n. 33.

[22] *Oxford Companion to Classical Literature*, 2nd ed., (Oxford University Press, 1989); *Lempiris's Classical Dictionary of Proper Names*, 3rd edition (London/New York: Routledge and Keagan Paul), gives different dates: Aelianus would have died in 140 at 60 years of age.

As he brought in this legendary figure to underline a theological point, however, Luther radically changed the meaning of the story. While the German expression he used, *das arme asschen prodlin*,[23] better conveys a connotation of dire misery than the anglicized Latin, "poor Cinderella," Luther turned it into an image of true spirit, the highest level of soul, in keeping with Christ's assurance that it is the meek who will inherit the earth and the poor who are rich in God. In the eyes of the world the poor ash-servant is despicable. She, however, praises God constantly in her poverty, and in this she becomes a model for the disciples of Jesus:

> For her there is naught but want and misery: she seeks to enjoy nothing, and is content to know that God is good, even though she should never once experience it, though that is impossible. She keeps an even mind in both estates; she loves and praises God's goodness just as much when she does not feel it as when she does. She neither falls upon the good things when they are given, nor falls away when they are removed. That is the true bride of Christ, who says to Him; I seek not Thine but Thee (141).

David in the Old Testament, king though he was, exemplifies the spirit of Cinderella. In the New Testament it is present in the Virgin Mary, who was of course in Nazareth much closer than king David to the destitute condition of the ash-girl: "Such a spirit is manifested here by Mary the Mother of God" (142). She "exults only in faith" and rejoices "only in God, whom she did not feel, and who is her salvation, known by her in faith alone." Mary "clings only to God's goodness, that she neither sees nor feels." This is the meaning of the words, "My spirit rejoices in God my Savior." On the basis of her faith Luther then affirms:

> ... The wondrous pure spirit of Mary is worthy of the greater praise, because, having such overwhelming honors heaped upon her head, she does not suffer that to make her stumble, but acts as though she did not see it ... .

Since the life of faith is bound to pass through severe testing and to undergo much suffering, the Mother of God is for all believers a model and an inspiration: "Such are the truly lowly, naked, hungry, and God-fearing spirits."

The lesson of Cinderella is supported by another tale, which, Luther says, dates back to the time of the Council of Constance (1414–

[23] *WA* 7:557; *LW* 21:310. In modern German Cinderella is called *Aschenbrödel*.

1418). Two cardinals, going on horseback, "beheld a shepherd standing in a field and weeping" (154). One of them, "being a good soul," went over to comfort the shepherd. This man was crying because, seeing a toad, he had reflected that he had never given thanks to God for not being "hideous like this reptile." When he heard this the cardinal also was struck in his heart, and he "trembled so violently that he fell from his mount." He had to be carried home. The scholar that he was reflected on what St. Augustine had written in the *Confessions*: "The unlearned start up and take heaven by violence, and we with all our learning, see how we wallow in flesh and blood" (154).

The ignorance of the learned and the knowledge of the ignorant present further facets of the theme of unknowing. The exaltation of poverty was especially dear to the Franciscan school on account of the paradigmatic example of St. Francis. As applied to the intellect it had become the unknowing of the common mystical tradition, Luther therefore belonged in a long spiritual tradition when he commented:

> Now I trow this shepherd was neither rich nor comely nor powerful; nevertheless he had so clear an insight into God's good gifts and pondered them so deeply that he found therein more than he could comprehend.

This spiritual tradition is that of monastic theology. The binary and trinary structure of Luther's presentation had direct antecedents in the contemplative writings of the Victorines and, as we have seen, it had been very much alive in the works of Bonaventure. Largely because the theology of the schools was focused on the *quaestio*, which itself was remotely modelled on Peter Abelard's *Sic et non*, this type of structure tended to be relegated, in the heyday of scholasticism, along with the allegorical senses of the Bible, to formal sermons and spiritual writings. In his last work, however, Bonaventure had clearly affirmed the superiority of monastic over scholastic thought:

> There is a twofold discipline, the scholastic and the monastic, which relates to mores, and the scholastic discipline without the monastic is not sufficient to acquire wisdom, for it is not only by listening, but by practicing, that one becomes wise.[24]

Luther's recourse to pre-scholastic patterns in his commentary on Mary's *Magnificat* places this work squarely in the tradition of

[24] *Collationes in Hexaëmeron*, II, 3; these lectures were given in Paris in 1273 as Bonaventure's contribution to the struggle against the Averroists in the Faculty of Arts of the University.

monastic theology. The apophatic emphasis that he shared with late medieval mystics leads to a similar conclusion.

DEVOTION TO MARY

That Martin Luther in 1520–21 practiced and recommended a certain devotion to the Mother of God is clear. This devotion was not focused on the angelic greeting, *Ave Maria*, but on Mary's hymn, *Magnificat*. It entailed meditating on her words and hence on Mary herself, on her life, her relation to Christ, the conditions of true discipleship, and the primacy of faith. It implied giving the Mother of God "the honor and devotion that are her due" (155), namely, praise, imitation, and above all giving thanks to God for choosing her as the Mother of the Word made flesh. Such a devotion was squarely founded in Scripture, in the early christological and trinitarian dogmas, and in the nature of faith as God's gift and not a human achievement. As Luther told John Frederick, "This sacred hymn ... ought indeed to be learned and kept in mind by all who would rule well and be helpful lords ... . It is a fine custom that this canticle is sung in all the churches daily at vespers ... ." (125). To a future ruler as to every good Christian Mary's hymn was a model of total reliance on God and suspicion of human judgments and motivations:

> I beseech and exhort your Grace in all your life to fear nothing on earth, nay, not even hell itself, so much as that which the Mother of God calls, *mens cordis sui* [verse 6]. That is the greatest, closest, mightiest, and most destructive foe of all mankind, and especially of rulers. Its name is reason, good sense, and opinion ... (199).

Opposite to this perverse *ratio*, the Virgin Mary and her song of thanksgiving stand as models of true *pietas*, a word which, in its original sense, that was still operative at the end of the Middle Ages, designated the mutual affection between parents and children. The praise of Mary is part of the Christian joy.

Contrasted with the Marian devotion that was manifest in the sermons of Ulrich Zwingli,[25] Luther's piety was better grounded in the experience and doctrine of justification. A former chaplain of the pilgrimage of Einsiedeln, the Swiss reformer took it for granted that all good Christians frequently recite *Ave Maria* as a personal prayer.

[25] Tavard, *The Thousand Faces of the Virgin Mary* (Collegeville: The Liturgical Press, 1998): Zwingli, 104-9; Luther, 109-17; Calvin,117-26.

Luther, however, listed the recitation of rosaries among the meaningless practices of the hypocrites. His attitude to Mary was also in sharp contrast with the minimalism of Calvin, who both praised God's gifts to the Virgin and professed little admiration for her. As he read the account of the Annunciation he saw little more than an obedient little girl, submissive to the angel as she was to her parents, who however happened to be "agreeable"[26] to God. Joseph, a powerful man who restrained himself in marriage, was, from a human point of view, more admirable![27]

On the whole, Martin Luther showed a deeper understanding of the heartfelt popular devotion that had been inherited from medieval times, even when he was critical of abuses. And as he meditated on *Magnificat* he looked at Mary with the eyes of faith and he saw the mercy of God at work.

[26] Ibid., 119. Rather than *Ave gratia plena*, Calvin rendered the angelic greeting as *Ave gratiam consequuta*; in French, however, he used a more delicate expression, "*Réjouis-toi, agréable ... .*"

[27] Ibid., 118.

DR. KENNETH GEORGE HAGEN

PROFESSOR OF THEOLOGY
MARQUETTE UNIVERSITY

Education:

1958-1961 Harvard Divinity School, Cambridge, Mass.
1961-1965 Harvard Divinity School, Cambridge, Mass.
1964-1965 Universität, Bonn Germany

Degrees:

BA 1958 Augsburg College, Minneapolis, Minn.
STB 1961 Harvard Divinity School
ThD 1967 Harvard University

Academic Experience:

1963-1965 Teaching Fellow, Harvard Divinity School
1965-1967 Asst. Professor, Religion, Concordia-Moorhead
1967-1968 Visiting Professor, Theology, Marquette University
1968-1971 Assistant Professor, Theology, Marquette University
1971-Sum. Visiting Professor, University of San Francisco
1971-1983 Associate Professor, Theology, Marquette University
1979-1980 Fulbright Professor, Universitetet i Oslo
1983-2000 Professor, Theology, Marquette University

I. PUBLICATIONS:

A. Books:

1968 *Luther's Lectures on Hebrews in the Light of Medieval Commentaries on Hebrews.* Cambridge, Mass.: Harvard University, 1968. 851 pages.

1974 *A Theology of Testament in the Young Luther: "The Lectures on Hebrews."* "Studies in Medieval and Reformation Thought," vol. 12. Leiden: E. J. Brill, 1974. 139 pages.

1974 *Foundations of Theology in the Continental Reformation: Questions of Authority.* Milwaukee: Central Press, 1974. 247 pages. Revised 1999.

1981 *Hebrews Commenting from Erasmus to Bèze* 1516-1598. "Beiträge zur Geschichte der biblischen Exegese," vol. 23. Tübingen: J. C. B. Mohr (Paul Siebeck), 1981. 132 pages.

1987ff. *Introduction to Theology 001.* Milwaukee: Econoprint, 1987, 1988; Marquette University, 1989, 1990. 160 pages.

1993 *Luther's Approach to Scripture as seen in his "Commentaries" on Galatians,* 1519-1538. Tübingen: J. C. B. Mohr (Paul Siebeck), 1993. xiii, 194 pages.

Edited Books:

1977 *Annotated Bibliography of Luther Studies,* 1967-1976. "Sixteenth Century Bibliography," vol. 9. St. Louis: Center for Reformation Research, 1977; with Jack Bigane. 84 pages.

1985 *Annotated Bibliography of Luther Studies,* 1977-1983. "Sixteenth Century Bibliography," vol. 24. St. Louis: Center for Reformation Research, 1985; with Franz Posset. 99 pages.

1985 *The Bible in the Churches.* New York: Paulist Press, 1985; with Harrington, et al. 151 pages.

1990 *Augustine, The Harvest, and Theology* (1300-1650). Essays Dedicated to Heiko Augustinus Oberman in Honor of his Sixtieth Birthday, edited with Introduction. Leiden: E. J. Brill, 1990. 383 pages.

1991 *Annotated Bibliography of Luther Studies,* 1984-1989. "Sixteenth Century Bibliography," vol. 29. St. Louis: Center for Reformation Research, 1991; with Franz Posset and Terry Thomas. 150 pages.

1993 *Luther Digest.* An Annual Abridgment of Luther Studies, edited with Foreword, vol. 1. Fort Wayne, Ind.: The Luther Academy, 1993. ix, 140 pages.

1994 *The Quadrilog: Tradition and the Future of Ecumenism.* Essays in Honor of George H. Tavard, edited with Introduction. Collegeville, Minn.: The Liturgical Press, 1994. 421 pages.

1994 *Luther Digest.* An Annual Abridgment of Luther Studies, edited with Foreword, vol. 2. Shorewood, Minn.: The Luther Academy, 1994. x, 153 pages.

1994 *The Bible in the Churches.* How Various Christians Interpret the Scriptures. 2d ed. Milwaukee: Marquette University Press, 1994. vi, 185 pages.

1994 *Reformation Texts With Translation (1350-1650).* General Editor. Volume 1 (vol. 1: Biblical Studies). Girolamo Savonarola, O.P. *Prison Meditations on Psalms 51 and 31.* Introduced, translated, and edited by John Patrick Donnelly, S.J. Milwaukee: Marquette University Press, 1994. 142 pages.

1995 *Luther Digest.* An Annual Abridgment of Luther Studies, edited with Foreword, vol. 3. Shorewood, Minn.: The Luther Academy, 1995. xi, 175 pages.

1995 *Reformation Texts With Translation (1350-1650).* General Editor. Volume 2 (vol. 2: Biblical Studies). Philipp Melanchthon, *Annotations on the First Epistle to the Corinthians.* Introduced, translated, and edited by John Patrick Donnelly, S.J. Milwaukee: Marquette University Press, 1995. 178 pages.

1996 *Luther Digest.* An Annual Abridgment of Luther Studies, edited with Foreword, vol. 4. Crestwood, Mo.: The Luther Academy, 1996. x, 242 pages.

1997 *Luther Digest.* An Annual Abridgment of Luther Studies, edited with Foreword, vol. 5. Crestwood, Mo.: The Luther Academy, 1997. x, 209 pages.

1998 *Reformation Texts With Translation (1350-1650).* General Editor. Volume 3 (vol. 1: Women of the Reformation). *Convents Confront the Reformation: Catholic and Protestant Nuns in Germany.* Introduced and edited by Merry Wiesner-Hanks. Translated by Joan Skocir and Merry Wiesner-Hanks. Milwaukee: Marquette University Press, 1996; second ed., 1998. 110 pages.

1998 *The Bible in the Churches.* How Various Christians Interpret the Scriptures. 3rd ed. Milwaukee: Marquette University Press, 1998. vi, 218 pages.

1998 *Reformation Texts With Translation (1350-1650).* General Editor. Volume 4 (vol. 3: Biblical Studies). Nicholas of Lyra. *The Postilla of Nicholas of Lyra on the Song of Songs.* Introduced, translated, and edited by James George Kiecker. Milwaukee: Marquette University Press, 1998. 128 pages.

1998 *Luther Digest.* An Annual Abridgment of Luther Studies, edited with Introduction, vol. 6. Crestwood, Mo.: The Luther Academy, 1998. x, 230 pages.

1999 *Luther Digest.* An Annual Abridgment of Luther Studies, edited with Introduction, vol. 7. Crestwood, Mo.: The Luther Academy, 1999. x, 190 pages.

2000 *Reformation Texts With Translation (1350-1650).* General Editor. Volume 5 (vol. 2: Women of the Reformation). *This Tight Embrace: Luisa de Carvajal y Mendoza (1566-1614).* Edited and translated by Elizabeth Rhodes. Milwaukee: Marquette University Press, 2000.

2000 *Luther Digest.* An Annual Abridgment of Luther Studies, edited with Introduction, vol. 8. St. Louis, Mo.: The Luther Academy, 2000. x, 232 pages.

2001 *Reformation Texts With Translation (1350-1650).* General Editor. Volume 6 (vol. 3: Women of the Reformation). *"Elisabeth's Manly Courage": Testimonials and Songs of Martyred Anabaptist Women in the Low Countries,* Edited and translated by Hermina Joldersma and Louis Grijp. Milwaukee: Marquette University Press, 2001.

B. Chapters in Books:

1985ff. "The History of Scripture in the Church." In *The Bible in the Churches,* edited by Kenneth Hagen, 3-34. New York: Paulist Press, 1985; revised for the 2d ed., 1-27. Milwaukee: Marquette University Press, 1994; revised for the 3rd ed., 1-28. Milwaukee: Marquette University Press, 1998.

1987 "Luthers Korsteologi." In *Theologi på tidens torg: Festskrift til Peter Wilhelm Bøckman,* edited by Peder Borgen, et al. "Publikasjoner utgitt av Religionsvitenskapelig institutt Universitetet i Trondheim," vol. 23, 71-81. Trondheim: Tapir, 1987.

1990 "Did Peter Err? The Text is the Best Judge. Luther on Gal. 2.11." In *Augustine, the Harvest, and Theology* (1300-1650). Essays Dedicated to Heiko Augustinus Oberman in Honor of his Sixtieth Birthday, edited by Kenneth Hagen, 110-126. Leiden: E. J. Brill, 1990.

1990 "What did the term *Commentarius* mean to sixteenth-century theologians?" In *Théorie et pratique de l'exégèse.* Actes du troisième colloque international sur l'histoire de l'exégèse biblique au XVIe siècle (Genève, 31 août - 2 septembre 1988), edited by Irena Backus and Francis Higman. "Etudes de Philologie et d'Histoire," vol. 43, 13-38. Geneva: Libraire Droz, 1990.

1990 "'*De Exegetica Methodo*,' Niels Hemmingsen's *De Methodis* (1555)." In *The Bible in the Sixteenth Century*, edited by David Steinmetz. "Duke Monographs in Medieval and Renaissance Studies," vol. 11, 181-196, 252-255. Durham, N.C.: Duke University Press, 1990.

1995 "Luther's Doctrine of the Two Kingdoms." In *God and Caesar Revisited*, edited by John R. Stephenson, 15-29. "Luther Academy Conference Papers No. 1." Shorewood, Minn.: Luther Academy [USA], 1995.

1996 "*Omnis homo mendax:* Luther on Psalm 116." In *Biblical Interpretation in the Era of the Reformation.* Essays Presented to David C. Steinmetz in Honor of His Sixtieth Birthday, edited by Richard A. Muller and John L. Thompson, 85-102. Grand Rapids, Mich.: William B. Eerdmans Publishing Company, 1996.

1998 "Luther, Martin (1483-1546)." In *Historical Handbook of Major Biblical Interpreters*, edited by Donald K. McKim, 212-220. Downers Grove, Ill.: InterVarsity Press, 1998.

C. Articles:

1965 "The First Translation of Luther's Lectures on Hebrews: A Review Article," *Church History* 34 (June 1965) 204-214.

1966 "What is the True Church: A History of Heresy from Donatism to Pietism," *Discourse 10* (Spring 1967) 157-174.

1968 "Who is Martin Luther? - a 450-year-old Question," *Discourse* 11 (Summer 1968) 348-352.

1968 "Changes in the Understanding of Luther. The Development of the Young Luther," *Theological Studies* 29 (September 1968) 472-496.

1969 "An Addition to the Letters of John Lang: Introduction and Translation," *Archiv für Reformationsgeschichte* 60/1 (1969) 27-32.

1970 "The Problem of Testament in Luther's Lectures on Hebrews," *Harvard Theological Review* 63 (January 1970) 61-90.

1971 "Roman Catholicism and Lutheranism Today," *Metanoia* 3 (March 1971) 4-6.

1971 "Hus's 'Donatism,'" *Augustinianum* 11 (December 1971) 541-547.

1972 "From Testament to Covenant in the Early Sixteenth Century," *The Sixteenth Century Journal* 3 (April 1972) 1-24.

1975 "Religious Toleration: Apathy or Commitment," *Contact* 8 (Winter 1975) 13-19.

1977 "A Conciliar Hermeneutic of Trent on Tradition," *Annuarium Historiae Conciliorum. Internationale Zeitschrift für Konziliengeschichtsforschung* 9 (1977/2) 401-411.

1979 "En Metemarks Testament," *Norsk teologisk tidsskrifit* 80/4 (1979) 239-251.

1981 "Av og om Luther på norsk," *Norsk teologisk tidsskrift* 82/2 (1981) 79-101.

1982 "The Testament of a Worm: Luther on Testament and Covenant," *Consensus. A Canadian Lutheran Journal of Theology* 8/1 (January 1982) 12-20.

1983 "Gjennomslag for Luther i Norge?" *Kirke og kultur* 88/9-10 (1983) 601-612.

1986 "Luther in Norway," *Lutherjahrbuch* 53 (1986) 31-54.

1986 "Mary and the Saints: Article 21 and the Roman Response," *Dialog. A Journal of Theology* 25 (1986) 212-214.

1987 "The Historical Context of the Smalcald Articles," *Concordia Theological Quarterly* 51 (October 1987) 245-253.

1994 "IT IS ALL IN THE ET CETERA: Luther and the Elliptical Reference," *Luther-Bulletin: Tidschrift voor interconfessioneel Lutheronderzoek* 3 (November 1994) 57-67.

1997 "Luther on Atonement—Reconfigured," *Concordia Theological Quarterly* 61 (1997) 251-276.

1999 "Luther's So-Called *Judenschriften*: A Genre Approach," *Archiv für Reformationsgeschichte* 90 (1999) 130-158.

D. Book Reviews:

1968 Review of *Oecumenica 1967: An Annual Symposium of Ecumenical Research,* ed. Kantzenbach and Vajta for *Book News Letter of Augsburg Publishing House* (February 1968).

1968 Review of H. J. McSorley, *Luthers Lehre vom unfreien Willen* for *Church History* 37 (December 1968) 458-459. *Luther: Right or Wrong?* for *Church History 39* (June 1970) 250.

1969 Review of Joseph Lortz, *The Reformation in Germany* for *Theological Studies* 30 (December 1969) 717-719.

1970 Review of Jared Wicks, *Man Yearning for Grace: Luther's Early Spiritual Teaching* for *Theological Studies* 31 (March 1970) 190-192.

1972 Review of W. P. Stephens, *The Holy Spirit in the Theology of Martin Bucer* for *Anglican Theological Review* 54 (January 1972) 44-45.

1972 Review of Carl S. Meyer, ed., *Sixteenth-Century Essays and Studies I* for *Church History* 41 (June 1972) 264-265.

1974 Review of *Modern Eucharistic Agreement,* Foreword by Alan C. Clark and an Introduction by H. R. McAdoo for *Journal of Ecumenical Studies* 11 (Summer 1974) 540-541.

1975 Review of *Luther and the Dawn of the Modern Era: Papers for the Fourth International Congress for Luther Research,* ed. Heiko A. Oberman for *Theological Studies* 36 (December 1975) 800-802.

1975 Review of Hans Holfelder, *Tentatio et Consolatio: Studien zu Bugenhagens "Interpretatio in Librum Psalmorum"* for *Church History* 44 (December 1975) 533.

1977 Review of John Loeschen, *Wrestling with Luther. An Introduction to His Thought* for *The Journal of Religion* 57 (July 1977) 320-321.

1980 Review of *Martin Luther verker i utva lg,* volumes 1 and 2, ed. Lønning and Rasmussen for *Church History* 49 (December 1980) 486.

1981 Review of *Histoire de l'exégèse au XVIe siècle: Textes du colloque international tenu a Genève en 1976,* ed. Fatio and Fraenkel for *Church History* 50 (September 1981) 369.

1982 Review of Walter Kaiser, *Toward an Exegetical Theology* for *Theology Today* 39 (April 1982) 82-83.

1985 Review of Heiko A. Oberman, *The Roots of Anti-Semitism in the Age of the Renaissance and Reformation* for *Word and World* (Summer 1985) 331-332.

1986 Review of Alister McGrath, *Luther's Theology of the Cross: Martin Luther's Theological Breakthrough* for *The Journal of Religion* 66 (October 1986) 440-441.

1990 Review of John L. Farthing, *Thomas Aquinas and Gabriel Biel. Interpretations of St. Thomas Aquinas in German Nominalism on the Eve of the Reformation* for *Renaissance Quarterly* 43 (Winter 1990) 851-852.

1995 Review of Stefan Streiff, *"Novis linguis loqui." Martin Luthers Disputation über Joh 1, 14. "verbum caro factum est" aus dem Jahr 1539,* Forschungen zur systematischen und ökumenischen Theologie, 70 for *The Sixteenth Century Journal 26* (Winter 1995) 1068-69.

1997 Review of Scott H. Hendrix, *Tradition and Authority in the Reformation,* Collected Studies Series, CS 535 for *The Catholic Historical Review* 83 (October 1997) 798-800.

1998 Review of *Ioannis Calvini Opera Exegetica, Commentarius in Epistolam ad Hebraeos,* vol. XIX, ed. T. H. L. Parker. Genève: Librairie Droz S.A., 1996 for *Bibliothèque d'Humanisme et Renaissance* 60 (1998) 554-558.

2000 Review of Ulrich Asendorf, *Lectura in Biblia: Luthers Genesisvorlesung (1535-1545),* Forschungen zur systematischen und ökumenischen Theologie, 87 for *The Sixteenth Century Journal* 31 (spring 2000) 299-302.

E. Other Publications:

1965 Translation of G.W. Locher, "Die Wandlung des Zwingli-Bildes in der neueren Forschung," *Zwingliana* 11 (1963) for *Church History* 34 (March 1965) 3-24.

1967 Summary of dissertation, "Luther's Lectures on Hebrews in the Light of Medieval Commentaries on Hebrews," *Harvard Theological Review* 60 (October 1967) 488-489.

1967 Four Abstracts from *Ökumenische Rundschau* 15 (1957) for *Journal of Ecumenical Studies* 4 (Spring 1967) 333.

1969 "Lutherans and Catholics: How Close?" *Marquette University Magazine* (Spring 1969).

1985 "Der Dean," *The Marquette Free Press* 4 (October 1985) 7.

1997 "Martin Luther: 'On Christian Freedom'," *Introduction to Theology*. Marquette Department of Theology: Book of Readings, 1997.

2001 "Does Method Drive Biblical Study" for *Logia, A Journal of Lutheran Theology,* vol. X, 1 (Epiphany 2001): 37-40.

F. Research in Progress:

Medieval Manuscripts on the Psalter

Luther on Vocation, Wingren Revisited

Critical Edition of Calvin on the Canonical Epistles

Volume of Collected Articles, Revised and Expanded

G. Other Scholarly Activities:

1986 Miller Memorial Lectures, Valparaiso University

1981-1992 U.S. Lutheran/Roman Catholic Theological Dialogue

1982-1985 Council for the International Exchange of Scholars

1986-1989 Medieval Philosophical Texts in Translation

1992ff. Organizer and editor of serial (journal) *Luther Digest,* published by the Luther Academy (USA)

1994ff. Organizer and editor-in-chief of series, REFORMATION TEXTS WITH TRANSLATION, published by Marquette University Press

II. PARTICIPATION IN PROFESSIONAL MEETINGS AND/OR PAPERS PRESENTED:

1968 Paper at American Society of Church History annual meeting in New York, December 1968, entitled "The Problem of Testament in Luther's Lectures on Hebrews."

1969 Paper at Barth Symposium, Marquette University, December 1969, entitled "Barth and Nineteenth Century Protestantism."

1970 Paper at American Academy of Religion annual meeting in New York, October 1970, entitled "From Testament to Covenant in the Early Sixteenth Century."

1970 Paper at Sixteenth Century Studies Conference annual meeting in St. Louis, October 1970, entitled "From Testament to Covenant in the Early Sixteenth Century."

1971 Chair of "The Reformation," Sixth Conference on Medieval Studies, The Medieval Institute, Kalamazoo, May 1971.

1971 Participant, Fourth International Congress for Luther Research, St. Louis, August 1971.

1974 Paper at Ninth Conference on Medieval Studies, Kalamazoo, May 1974, entitled "Medieval Exegesis of Hebrews and St. Augustine: The Relationship between the Two Testaments."

1975 Paper at Joint Session of American Society for Reformation Research and American Catholic Historical Association annual meeting in Atlanta, December 1975, entitled "A Conciliar Hermeneutic of Trent on Tradition" (and organizer of session).

1976 Paper at Sixteenth Century Studies Conference annual meeting in St. Louis, October 1976, entitled "The Testament of a Worm. Luther on Testament and Covenant to 1525."

1977 Participant, Fifth International Congress for Luther Research, Lund, Sweden, August 1977.

1977 Paper at Joint Session of the American Academy of Religion and the American Society for Reformation Research annual meeting in San Francisco, December 1977, entitled "Early Sixteenth Century Commentaries on Hebrews as Source for the History of Christian Thought."

1979ff. Chair, Group, American Academy of Religion, 16th century exegetica, 1979-1984.

1980 Foredrag, Norsk kirkehistorisk samfunn, spring meeting, Oslo, May 1980, entitled "Luther in Norway."

1981 Participant, Colloquium on The Reformation: Old and New, with Hans Küng, School for Ministry, Detroit, October 1981.

1981 Respondent to Prof. Helmar Junghans, Leipzig, annual Sixteenth Century Studies Conference, Iowa City, October 1981.

1982 Paper at Second International Colloquy on the History of Biblical Exegesis in the Sixteenth Century, Duke University, September 1982, entitled "'De exegetica methodo': Niels Hemmingsen's *De Methodis* (1555)."

1983 Paper at University of Oslo, May 1983, entitled "Luthers Bibelsyn."

1983 Participant, Sixth International Congress for Luther Research, Erfurt, Germany, August 1983.

1983 Paper at University of Oslo, August 1983, entitled "Luthers gjennomslag i Norge."

1983 Chair, Luther and the Middle Ages, the 500th Anniversary, at Marquette University, September 1983.

1984 Paper at College Theology Society annual convention in Milwaukee, June 1984, entitled "Welcome to Scholasticism: Pannenberg on the Church."

1985 Commentator at American Society of Church History annual meeting in New York, December 1985, session entitled "Late Medieval Thomism and the Reformation."

1986 Paper at conference to introduce *Lutheran Quarterly,* New Series, Schaumburg, August 1986, entitled "The Biblical Pulpit" (and member, editorial board).

1986 Paper at American Academy of Religion annual meeting in Atlanta, November 1986, entitled "Catholic Theology in American Higher Education."

1987 Papers at the Tenth Annual Symposium on the Lutheran Confessions at Concordia Theological Seminary in Fort Wayne, January 1987, entitled "Historical Context of the Smalcald Articles" and "The Catholicity and Ecumenicity of the Smalcald Articles."

1988 Participant, Seventh International Congress for Luther Research, Oslo, Norway, 14-21 August 1988.

1988 Opening plenary lecture at Third International Colloquy on the History of Biblical Exegesis in the Sixteenth Century, University of Geneva, 31 August 1988, entitled "What did the term *Commentarius* mean to 16th century theologians?"

1989 Chair, Reformation in Switzerland, Sixteenth Century Studies Conference annual meeting in Minneapolis, October 1989.

1989 Council Meeting, American Society of Church History. San Francisco, CA, 27-30 December 1989.

1989 Discussant, U.S. Lutheran/Catholic Theological Dialogue. New Orleans, LA, 20-24 September 1989.

1990 Discussant, U.S. Lutheran/Catholic Theological Dialogue. Lantana, FL, 14-18 February 1990.

1990 Chair, Theology of the Reformation, The Reformation in Germany in Europe: Interpretations and Issues (international conference), Washington D.C., 25-30 September 1990.

1990 Respondent, "The Reformation of the Refugees," American Society of Church History, New York, 27-30 December 1990.

1990 Discussant, U.S. Lutheran/Catholic Theological Dialogue. Erlanger, KY, 19-23 September 1990.

1991 Discussant, U.S. Lutheran/Catholic Theological Dialogue. Lantana, FL, 6-10 March 1991.

1992 Discussant, U.S. Lutheran/Catholic Theological Dialogue. Delray Beach, FL, 12-16 February 1992.

1992 Respondent, "Lifting the Veil of Carlstadt," Sixteenth Century Studies Conference annual meeting in Atlanta, October 1992.

1992 Paper at Sixteenth Century Studies Conference annual meeting in Atlanta, October 1992, entitled "'It's all in the etc.' Luther and the Elliptical Reference."

1992 Commentator at American Society of Church History annual meeting in Washington, D.C., December 1992, session entitled "The Bible in the Sixteenth Century."

1994 Paper at National Free Conference #5: The Association of Confessional Lutherans and the Luther Academy Lecture Series 1, April 1994, entitled "Luther's Doctrine of the Two Kingdoms."

1996 Paper at the 1996 Symposia Series on the Lutheran Confessions at Concordia Theological Seminary in Fort Wayne, January 1996, entitled "Luther on Atonement—Reconfigured."

1998 Paper at National Free Conference #9: The Association of Confessional Lutherans and the Luther Academy Lecture Series 5, April 1998, entitled "The Doctrines of Vocation and Ethics and Martin Luther."

1999 Paper at National Free Conference #10: The Association of Confessional Lutherans and the Luther Academy Lecture Series 6, April 1999, entitled "Dr. Robert D. Preus: Confessional Systematician and Teacher of the Confessions."

1999 Paper at The Sixth Annual Symposium on Catechesis, Concordia Catechetical Academy, June 1999, entitled "Luther on Vocation: a Response to Wingren & American Evangelicalism."

III. MEMBERSHIP IN PROFESSIONAL SOCIETIES:

American Society of Church History (Nominating Committee/ Council, 1986-89)

American Society for Reformation Research

Luther-Gesellschaft

Editorial Board, *Lutheran Quarterly*

Editorial Board, *Logia*

Fulbright Alumni Association

Sixteenth Century Studies Conference

Board, Luther Academy (USA)

IV. HONORS, GRANTS:

A. Honors:

Norwegian Academy of Science and Letters, 1986-

Distinguished Alumnus Citation for 1982, Augsburg College

B. Grants:

1958 Harvard Divinity School Grants

1963-65 Rockefeller Doctoral Fellowships in Religion

1966 Lutheran World Federation Grant, International Luther Research Congress, Finland (August)

1968-70 Research Grants from Marquette University

1970 Summer Faculty Fellowship, Marquette

1970 Newberry Library Grant (summer)

1974 Summer Faculty Fellowship, Marquette

1975-77 Research Grants from Marquette

1976 Newberry Library Fellowship (summer)

1977	American Philosophical Society Grant (summer)
1979-80	Senior Fulbright-Hays Fellowship to Oslo, Norway
1982	Wolfenbüttel Library Grant (3 months), Germany
1982-84	Marshall Fund, Norway-America Association, Oslo, Norway
1982-85	Norway's Council for Scientific Research, NAVF (3 months each year)
1985	Guest of the Library, Wolfenbüttel, Germany (5 months) Summer Faculty Fellowship, Marquette
1991	Bradley Institute for Democracy (2 months)
1993	Research Grant, Marquette
1994	Resident Scholar at the Institute for Ecumenical and Cultural Research, September 1994 to June 1995 (Collegeville, Minn.)

V. LISTED IN:

Directory of American Scholars, 8th ed.

Directory of International Biography, 10th, 12th, 13th ed.

International Scholars Directory, 1st ed.

Who's Who in Religion, 4th ed.

Who's Who in America, 48th ed.

VI. PH.D. DISSERTATIONS DIRECTED AND PUBLISHED

Martin Luther Commentator on the Sentences of Peter Lombard: Theological Methods and Selected Theological Problems.
Lawrence Murphy, S.J., 1971.

The Image of Israel in Christian Theology in German-Speaking Countries since 1945.
Eva Fleischer, 1971.

Luther's Theology as a Theology of Testament, 1513-1520.
Frank Nieman, 1973.

The Doctrine of God in the Writings of Dietrich Bonhoeffer.
Edward Theisen, 1973.

A Notion of Covenant in the Thought of William Tyndale, John Bale, John Bradford, and John Hooper.
Judith Moberly Mayotte, 1976.

Lutheran Hymnody, The Germanization of Medieval Latin Hymns by Martin Luther.
Waldemar Heidkte, 1978.

The Hermeneutical Principles and Exegetical Methods of Nicholas of Lyra, O.F.M. (Ca. 1270-1349).
James Kiecker, 1978.

"Tu est petrus, et super hanc petram aedificabo ecclesiam meam": The Rock in Sixteenth-Century Roman Catholic Exegesis.
John Bigane, III, 1979.

"Bona Opera," The Study of the Development of the Doctrine in Philip Melanchthon.
Carl Maxcey, 1979.

Luther's Catholic Christology According to His Johannine Lectures of 1527.
Franz Posset, 1984.

The Paul-Luther Relationship in Terms of Their Interpretation of Scripture.
Terry Thomas, 1985.

Martin Luther and the Jews.
Olaf Roynesdal, 1986.

Anselm and Luther on the Atonement: Was it "Necessary"?
Burnell Eckardt, 1991.

The Understanding and Use of Allegory in the Lectures on the Epistle of Saint Paul to the Galatians by Doctor Martin Luther.
Timothy Maschke, 1993.

Catholic Magisterial Appreciation of Luther.
Gregory Sobolewski, 1993.

The Doctrine of the Trinity in the Hymns of Martin Luther.
Paul Grime, 1994.

Wendelin Steinbach's Lectures on the Letter to the Galatians: A Late Medieval Approach to Pauline Authority and Teaching.
Daniel Metzger, 1994.

In Public Defense of the Ministry of Moses: Luther's Enarratio on Psalm 90, 1534-35.
Gordon Isaac, 1996.

Rhyme and Reason in Erasmus' 1516 Greek Text of Revelation 22:16-21.
Edward F. Maniscalco, 1996.

Towards a Moral Theology of Christian Humanism: An Inquiry into the Writings of Saint Thomas More.
William Hansen, 1997.

The Place of John Wyclif's Eucharistic Theology within the Catholic Tradition: Logica Scripturae and Sensus Catholicus.
Ian C. Levy, 1997.

Luther and Theosis: Deification in the Theology of Martin Luther.
Paul Lehninger, 1999.

PH.D. DISSERTATIONS IN PROGRESS

"*Ad Romanos* Expounded by the Wittenberg Theologians, Melanchthon and Bugenhagen. Applying Scripture or Aristotle."
Michael Zamzow.

"*Ecclesia nondum perfecta sit*: John Calvin's Use of St. Paul in His Polemic Against the Anabaptists and Catholics."
Anthony DiStefano.

"Martin Luther's Incarnational Theology: Intentions and Consequences of Luther's Christology in his Late Disputations."
Melvin G. Vance.

"Nicholas of Lyra's Use of St. Thomas Aquinas' Biblical Commentaries in his Postilla on Job and Psalms."
Troy Pflibsen

"Cajetan's Psalter Translation and *Enarrationes*. Link to the Past? Transition to the Future?"
Joan Skocir

INDEX OF NAMES

A

B

N

O

P

Q

R

S

T

INDEX OF SCRIPTURE CITATIONS

INDEX OF SUBJECTS

D

E

F

G